COMMERCIAL ARBITRATION: CASES AND PROBLEMS

COMMERCIAL ARBITRATION: CASES AND PROBLEMS

DOCUMENTARY SUPPLEMENT

Third Edition

Christopher R. Drahozal
John M. Rounds Professor of Law
University of Kansas School of Law

ISBN: 978–0–7698–5–9866 (print)
ISBN: 978–0–3271–9462–0 (eBook)

> ### NOTE TO USERS
> To ensure that you are using the latest materials available in this area, please be sure to periodically check the LexisNexis Law School web site for downloadable updates and supplements at www.lexisnexis.com/lawschool.

Editorial Offices
121 Chanlon Rd., New Providence, NJ 07974 (908) 464-6800
201 Mission St., San Francisco, CA 94105-1831 (415) 908-3200
www.lexisnexis.com

MATTHEW◆BENDER

Table of Contents

Table of Contents

CONVENTION ON THE RECOGNITION AND ENFORCEMENT OF FOREIGN ARBITRAL AWARDS

Article I

1. This Convention shall apply to the recognition and enforcement of arbitral awards made in the territory of a State other than the State where the recognition and enforcement of such awards are sought, and arising out of differences between persons, whether physical or legal. It shall also apply to arbitral awards not considered as domestic awards in the State where their recognition and enforcement are sought.

2. The term "arbitral awards" shall include not only awards made by arbitrators appointed for each case but also those made by permanent arbitral bodies to which the parties have submitted.

3. When signing, ratifying or acceding to this Convention, or notifying extension under article X hereof, any State may on the basis of reciprocity declare that it will apply the Convention to the recognition and enforcement of awards made only in the territory of another Contracting State. It may also declare that it will apply the Convention only to differences arising out of legal relationships, whether contractual or not, which are considered as commercial under the national law of the State making such declaration.

Article II

1. Each Contracting State shall recognize an agreement in writing under which the parties undertake to submit to arbitration all or any differences which have arisen or which may arise between them in respect of a defined legal relationship, whether contractual or not, concerning a subject matter capable of settlement by arbitration.

2. The term "agreement in writing" shall include an arbitral clause in a contract or an arbitration agreement, signed by the parties or contained in an exchange of letters or telegrams.

3. The court of a Contracting State, when seized of an action in a matter in respect of which the parties have made an agreement within the meaning of this article, shall, at the request of one of the parties, refer the parties to arbitration, unless it finds that the said agreement is null and void, inoperative or incapable of being performed.

Article III

Each Contracting State shall recognize arbitral awards as binding and enforce them in accordance with the rules of procedure of the territory where the award is relied upon, under the conditions laid down in the following articles. There shall not be imposed substantially more onerous conditions or higher fees or charges on the recognition or enforcement of arbitral awards to which this Convention applies than are imposed on the recognition or enforcement of domestic arbitral awards.

Article IV

1. To obtain the recognition and enforcement mentioned in the preceding article, the party applying for recognition and enforcement shall, at the time of the application, supply:

    (a)   The duly authenticated original award or a duly certified copy thereof;

    (b)   The original agreement referred to in article II or a duly certified copy thereof.

2. If the said award or agreement is not made in an official language of the country in which the award is relied upon, the party applying for recognition and enforcement of the award shall produce a translation of these documents into such language. The translation shall be certified by an official or sworn translator or by a diplomatic or consular agent.

Article V

1. Recognition and enforcement of the award may be refused, at the request of the party against whom it is invoked, only if that party furnishes to the competent authority where the recognition and enforcement is sought, proof that:

    (a)   The parties to the agreement referred to in article II were, under the law applicable to them, under some incapacity, or the said agreement is not valid under the law to which the parties have subjected it or, failing any indication thereon, under the law of the country where the award was made; or

    (b)   The party against whom the award is invoked was not given proper notice of the appointment of the arbitrator or of the arbitration proceedings or was otherwise unable to present his case; or

    (c)   The award deals with a difference not contemplated by or not falling within the terms of the submission to arbitration, or it contains decisions on matters beyond the scope of the submission to arbitration, provided that, if the decisions on matters submitted to arbitration can be separated from those not so submitted, that part of the award which contains decisions on matters submitted to arbitration may be recognized and enforced; or

    (d)   The composition of the arbitral authority or the arbitral procedure was not in accordance with the agreement of the parties, or, failing such agreement, was not in accordance with the law of the country where the arbitration took place; or

    (e)   The award has not yet become binding on the parties, or has been set aside or suspended by a competent authority of the country in which, or under the law of which, that award was made.

2. Recognition and enforcement of an arbitral award may also be refused if the competent authority in the country where recognition and enforcement is sought finds that:

    (a)   The subject matter of the difference is not capable of settlement by arbitration under the law of that country; or

(b) The recognition or enforcement of the award would be contrary to the public policy of that country.

Article VI

If an application for the setting aside or suspension of the award has been made to a competent authority referred to in article V(1)(e), the authority before which the award is sought to be relied upon may, if it considers it proper, adjourn the decision on the enforcement of the award and may also, on the application of the party claiming enforcement of the award, order the other party to give suitable security.

Article VII

1. The provisions of the present Convention shall not affect the validity of multilateral or bilateral agreements concerning the recognition and enforcement of arbitral awards entered into by the Contracting States nor deprive any interested party of any right he may have to avail himself of an arbitral award in the manner and to the extent allowed by the law or the treaties of the county where such award is sought to be relied upon.

2. The Geneva Protocol on Arbitration Clauses of 1923 and the Geneva Convention on the Execution of Foreign Arbitral Awards of 1927 shall cease to have effect between Contracting States on their becoming bound and to the extent that they become bound, by this Convention.

Article VIII

1. This Convention shall be open until 31 December 1958 for signature on behalf of any Member of the United Nations and also on behalf of any other State which is or hereafter becomes a member of any specialized agency of the United Nations, or which is or hereafter becomes a party to the Statute of the International Court of Justice, or any other State to which an invitation has been addressed by the General Assembly of the United Nations.

2. This Convention shall be ratified and the instrument of ratification shall be deposited with the Secretary-General of the United Nations.

Article IX

1. This Convention shall be open for accession to all States referred to in article VIII.

2. Accession shall be effected by the deposit of an instrument of accession with the Secretary-General of the United Nations.

Article X

1. Any State may, at the time of signature, ratification or accession, declare that this Convention shall extend to all or any of the territories for the international relations of which it is responsible. Such a declaration shall take effect when the Convention enters into force for the State concerned.

2. At any time thereafter any such extension shall be made by notification

addressed to the Secretary-General of the United Nations and shall take effect as from the ninetieth day after the day of receipt by the Secretary-General of the United Nations of this notification, or as from the date of entry into force of the Convention for the State concerned, whichever is the later.

3. With respect to those territories to which this Convention is not extended at the time of signature, ratification or accession, each State concerned shall consider the possibility of taking the necessary steps in order to extend the application of this Convention to such territories subject, where necessary for constitutional reasons, to the consent of the Governments of such territories.

Article XI

In the case of a federal or non-unitary State, the following provisions shall apply:

(a) With respect to those articles of this Convention that come within the legislative jurisdiction of the federal authority, the obligations of the Federal Government shall to this extent be the same as those of Contracting States which are not federal States;

(b) With respect to those articles of this Convention that come within the legislative jurisdiction of constituent states or provinces which are not, under the constitutional system of the federation, bound to take legislative action, the federal Government shall bring such articles with a favourable recommendation to the notice of the appropriate authorities of constituent states or provinces at the earliest possible moment;

(c) A federal State Party to this Convention shall, at the request of any other Contracting State transmitted through the Secretary-General of the United Nations, supply a statement of the law and practice of the federation and its constituent units in regard to any particular provision of this Convention, showing the extent to which effect has been given to that provision by legislative or other action.

Article XII

1. This Convention shall come into force on the ninetieth day following the date of deposit of the third instrument of ratification or accession.

2. For each State ratifying or acceding to this Convention after the deposit of the third instrument of ratification or accession, this Convention shall enter into force on the ninetieth day after deposit by such State of its instrument of ratification or accession.

Article XIII

1. Any Contracting State may denounce this Convention by a written notification to the Secretary-General of the United Nations. Denunciation shall take effect one year after the date of receipt of the notification by the Secretary-General.

2. Any State which has made a declaration or notification under article X may, at any time thereafter, by notification to the Secretary-General of the United Nations, declare that this Convention shall cease to extend to the territory concerned one year after the date of the receipt of the notification by the Secretary-General.

3. This Convention shall continue to be applicable to arbitral awards in respect of which recognition or enforcement proceedings have been instituted before the denunciation takes effect.

Article XIV

A Contracting State shall not be entitled to avail itself of the present Convention against other Contracting States except to the extent that it is itself bound to apply the Convention.

Article XV

The Secretary-General of the United Nations shall notify the States contemplated in article VIII of the following:

(a) Signatures and ratifications in accordance with article VIII;

(b) Accessions in accordance with article IX;

(c) Declarations and notifications under articles I, X and XI;

(d) The date upon which this Convention enters into force in accordance with article XII;

(e) Denunciations and notifications in accordance with article XIII.

Article XVI

1. This Convention, of which the Chinese, English, French, Russian and Spanish texts shall be equally authentic, shall be deposited in the archives of the United Nations.

2. The Secretary-General of the United Nations shall transmit a certified copy of this Convention to the States contemplated in article VIII.

Done at New York June 10, 1958: entered into force for the United States December 29, 1970, subject to declarations.

States which are parties (June 1, 2012):

Afghanistan, Albania, Algeria, Antigua and Barbuda, Argentina, Armenia, Australia, Austria, Azerbaijan, Bahamas, Bahrain, Bangladesh, Barbados, Belarus, Belgium, Benin, Bolivia, Bosnia and Herzegovina, Botswana, Brazil, Brunei Darussalam, Bulgaria, Burkina Faso, Cambodia, Cameroon, Canada, Central African Republic, Chile, China, Colombia, Cook Islands, Costa Rica, Cote d'Ivoire, Croatia, Cuba, Cyprus, Czech Republic, Denmark, Djibouti, Dominica, Dominican Republic, Ecuador, Egypt, El Salvador, Estonia, Fiji, Finland, France, Gabon, Georgia, Germany, Ghana, Greece, Guatemala, Guinea, Haiti, Holy See, Honduras, Hungary, Iceland, India, Indonesia, Ireland, Islamic Republic of Iran, Israel, Italy, Jamaica, Japan, Jordan, Kazakhstan, Kenya, Kuwait, Kyrgyzstan, Lao People's Democratic Republic, Latvia, Lebanon, Lesotho, Liberia, Liechtenstein, Lithuania, Luxembourg, Madagascar, Malaysia, Mali, Malta, Marshall Islands, Mauritania, Mauritius, Mexico, Monaco, Mongolia, Montenegro, Morocco, Mozambique, Nepal, Netherlands, New Zealand, Nicaragua, Niger, Nigeria, Norway, Oman, Pakistan, Panama, Paraguay, Peru, Philippines, Poland, Portugal, Qatar, Republic of Korea,

Republic of Moldova, Romania, Russian Federation, Rwanda, Saint Vincent and the Grenadines, San Marino, Saudi Arabia, Senegal, Serbia, Singapore, Slovakia, Slovenia, South Africa, Spain, Sri Lanka, Sweden, Switzerland, Syrian Arab Republic, Tajikistan, Thailand, the former Yugoslav Republic of Macedonia, Trinidad and Tobago, Tunisia, Turkey, Uganda, Ukraine, United Arab Emirates, United Kingdom, United Republic of Tanzania, United States, Uruguay, Uzbekistan, Venezuela, Viet Nam, Zambia, Zimbabwe

United States reservations:

The United States of America will apply the Convention, on the basis of reciprocity, to the recognition and enforcement of only those awards made in the territory of another Contracting State.

The United States of America will apply the Convention only to differences arising out of legal relationships, whether contractual or not, which are considered as commercial under the national law of the United States.

The Convention applies to all of the territories for the international relations of which the United States of America is responsible.

RECOMMENDATION REGARDING THE INTERPRETATION OF ARTICLE II, PARAGRAPH 2, AND ARTICLE VII, PARAGRAPH 1, OF THE NEW YORK CONVENTION

Adopted by UNCITRAL on 7 July 2006

The United Nations Commission on International Trade Law,

Recalling General Assembly resolution 2205 (XXI) of 17 December 1966, which established the United Nations Commission on International Trade Law with the object of promoting the progressive harmonization and unification of the law of international trade by, inter alia, promoting ways and means of ensuring a uniform interpretation and application of international conventions and uniform laws in the field of the law of international trade,

Conscious of the fact that the different legal, social and economic systems of the world, together with different levels of development, are represented in the Commission,

Recalling successive resolutions of the General Assembly reaffirming the mandate of the Commission as the core legal body within the United Nations system in the field of international trade law to coordinate legal activities in this field,

Convinced that the wide adoption of the Convention on the Recognition and Enforcement of Foreign Arbitral Awards, done in New York on 10 June 1958, has been a significant achievement in the promotion of the rule of law, particularly in the field of international trade,

Recalling that the Conference of Plenipotentiaries which prepared and opened the Convention for signature adopted a resolution, which states, inter alia, that the Conference "considers that greater uniformity of national laws on arbitration would further the effectiveness of arbitration in the settlement of private law disputes,"

Bearing in mind differing interpretations of the form requirements under the Convention that result in part from differences of expression as between the five equally authentic texts of the Convention,

Taking into account article VII, paragraph 1, of the Convention, a purpose of which is to enable the enforcement of foreign arbitral awards to the greatest extent, in particular by recognizing the right of any interested party to avail itself of law or treaties of the country where the award is sought to be relied upon, including where such law or treaties offer a regime more favourable than the Convention,

Considering the wide use of electronic commerce,

Taking into account international legal instruments, such as the 1985 UNCITRAL Model Law on International Commercial Arbitration, as subsequently revised, particularly with respect to article 7, the UNCITRAL Model Law on Electronic Commerce, the UNCITRAL Model Law on Electronic Signatures and the United Nations Convention on the Use of Electronic Communications in International Contracts,

Taking into account also enactments of domestic legislation, as well as case law, more favourable than the Convention in respect of form requirement governing

7

arbitration agreements, arbitration proceedings and the enforcement of arbitral awards,

Considering that, in interpreting the Convention, regard is to be had to the need to promote recognition and enforcement of arbitral awards,

1. *Recommends* that article II, paragraph 2, of the Convention on the Recognition and Enforcement of Foreign Arbitral Awards, done in New York, 10 June 1958, be applied recognizing that the circumstances described therein are not exhaustive;

2. *Recommends also* that article VII, paragraph 1, of the Convention on the Recognition and Enforcement of Foreign Arbitral Awards, done in New York, 10 June 1958, should be applied to allow any interested party to avail itself of rights it may have, under the law or treaties of the country where an arbitration agreement is sought to be relied upon, to seek recognition of the validity of such an arbitration agreement.

INTER-AMERICAN CONVENTION ON INTERNATIONAL COMMERCIAL ARBITRATION

The Governments of the Member States of the Organization of American States, desirous of concluding a convention on international commercial arbitration, have agreed as follows:

Article 1

An agreement in which the parties undertake to submit to arbitral decision any differences that may arise or have arisen between them with respect to a commercial transaction is valid. The agreement shall be set forth in an instrument signed by the parties, or in the form of an exchange of letters, telegrams, or telex communications.

Article 2

Arbitrators shall be appointed in the manner agreed upon by the parties. Their appointment may be delegated to a third party, whether a natural or juridical person. Arbitrators may be nationals or foreigners.

Article 3

In the absence of an express agreement between the parties, the arbitration shall be conducted in accordance with the rules of procedure of the Inter-American Commercial Arbitration Commission.

Article 4

An arbitral decision or award that is not appealable under the applicable law or procedural rules shall have the force of a final judicial judgment. Its execution or recognition may be ordered in the same manner as that of decisions handed down by national or foreign ordinary courts, in accordance with the procedural laws of the country where it is to be executed and the provisions of international treaties.

Article 5

1. The recognition and execution of the decision may be refused, at the request of the party against which it is made, only if such party is able to prove to the competent authority of the State in which recognition and execution are requested:

(a) That the parties to the agreement were subject to some incapacity under the applicable law or that the agreement is not valid under the law to which the parties have submitted it, or, if such law is not specified, under the law of the State in which the decision was made; or

(b) That the party against which the arbitral decision has been made was not duly notified of the appointment of the arbitrator or of the arbitration procedure to be followed, or was unable, for any other reason, to present his defense; or

(c)   That the decision concerns a dispute not envisaged in the agreement between the parties to submit to arbitration; nevertheless, if the provisions of the decision that refer to issues submitted to arbitration can be separated from those not submitted to arbitration, the former may be recognized and executed; or

(d)   That the constitution of the arbitral tribunal or the arbitration procedure has not been carried out in accordance with the terms of the agreement signed by the parties or, in the absence of such agreement, that the constitution of the arbitral tribunal or the arbitration procedure has not been carried out in accordance with the law of the State where the arbitration took place; or

(e)   That the decision is not yet binding on the parties or has been annulled or suspended by a competent authority of the State in which, or according to the law of which, the decision has been made.

2. The recognition and execution of an arbitral decision may also be refused if the competent authority of the State in which the recognition and execution is requested finds:

(a)   That the subject of the dispute cannot be settled by arbitration under the law of that State; or

(b)   That the recognition or execution of the decision would be contrary to the public policy ("order public") of that State.

Article 6

If the competent authority mentioned in Article 5.1(e) has been requested to annul or suspend the arbitral decision, the authority before which such decision is invoked may, if it deems it appropriate, postpone a decision on the execution of the arbitral decision and, at the request of the party requesting execution, may also instruct the other party to provide appropriate guaranties.

Article 7

This Convention shall be open for signature by the Member States of the Organization of American States.

Article 8

This Convention is subject to ratification. The instruments of ratification shall be deposited with the General Secretariat of the Organization of American States.

Article 9

This Convention shall remain open for accession by any other State. The instruments of accession shall be deposited with the General Secretariat of the Organization of American States.

Article 10

This Convention shall enter into force on the 30th day following the date of deposit of the second instrument of ratification. For each State ratifying or acceding to the Convention after the deposit of the second instrument of ratification, the Convention shall enter into force on the 30th day after deposit by such State of its instrument of ratification or accession.

Article 11

If a State Party has two or more territorial units in which different systems of law apply in relation to the matters dealt with in this Convention, it may, at the time of signature, ratification or accession, declare that this Convention shall extend to all its territorial units or only to one or more of them.

Such declaration may be modified by subsequent declarations, which shall expressly indicate the territorial unit or units to which the Convention applies. Such subsequent declarations shall be transmitted to the General Secretariat of the Organization of American States, and shall become effective 30 days after the date of their receipt.

Article 12

This Convention shall remain in force indefinitely, but any of the States Parties may denounce it. The instrument of denunciation shall be deposited with the General Secretariat of the Organization of American States. After one year from the date of deposit of the instrument of denunciation, the Convention shall no longer be in effect for the denouncing State, but shall remain in effect for the other States Parties.

Article 13

The original instrument of this Convention, the English, French, Portuguese and Spanish texts of which are equally authentic, shall be deposited with the General Secretariat of the Organization of American States. The Secretariat shall notify the Member States of the Organization of American States and the States that have acceded to the Convention of the signatures, deposits of instruments of ratification, accession, and denunciation as well as of reservations, if any. It shall also transmit the declarations referred to in Article 11 of this Convention.

IN WITNESS WHEREOF the undersigned Plenipotentiaries, being duly authorized thereto by their respective Governments, have signed this Convention.

DONE AT PANAMA CITY, Republic of Panama, this thirtieth day of January one thousand nine hundred and seventy-five.

States which are parties (as of June 1, 2012): Argentina, Bolivia, Brazil, Chile, Colombia, Costa Rica, Dominican Republic, Ecuador, El Salvador, Guatemala, Honduras, Mexico, Nicaragua, Panama, Paraguay, Peru, United States, Uruguay, Venezuela

United States reservations:

1. Unless there is an express agreement among the parties to an arbitration agreement to the contrary, where the requirements for application of both the Inter-American Convention on International Commercial Arbitration and the Convention on the Recognition and Enforcement of Foreign Arbitral Awards are

met, if a majority of such parties are citizens of a state or states that have ratified or acceded to the Inter-American Convention and are member states of the Organization of American States, the Inter- American Convention shall apply. In all other cases, the Convention on the Recognition and Enforcement of Foreign Arbitral Awards shall apply.

2. The United States of America will apply the rules of procedure of the Inter-American Commercial Arbitration Commission which are in effect on the date that the United States of America deposits its instrument of ratification, unless the United States of America makes a later official determination to adopt and apply subsequent amendments to such rules.

3. The United States of America will apply the Convention, on the basis of reciprocity, to the recognition and enforcement of only those awards made in the territory of another Contracting State.

FEDERAL ARBITRATION ACT

9 U.S.C. § 1.   "Maritime transactions" and "commerce" defined; exceptions to operation of title

"Maritime transactions," as herein defined, means charter parties, bills of lading of water carriers, agreements relating to wharfage, supplies furnished vessels or repairs to vessels, collisions, or any other matters in foreign commerce which, if the subject of controversy, would be embraced within admiralty jurisdiction; "commerce," as herein defined, means commerce among the several States or with foreign nations, or in any Territory of the United States or in the District of Columbia, or between any such Territory and another, or between any such Territory and any State or foreign nation, or between the District of Columbia and any State or Territory or foreign nation, but nothing herein contained shall apply to contracts of employment of seamen, railroad employees, or any other class of workers engaged in foreign or interstate commerce.

9 U.S.C. § 2.   Validity, irrevocability and enforcement of agreements to arbitrate

A written provision in any maritime transaction or a contract evidencing a transaction involving commerce to settle by arbitration a controversy thereafter arising out of such contract or transaction, or the refusal to perform the whole or any part thereof, or an agreement in writing to submit to arbitration an existing controversy arising out of such a contract, transaction, or refusal, shall be valid, irrevocable, and enforceable, save upon such grounds as exist at law or in equity for the revocation of any contract.

9 U.S.C. § 3.   Stay of proceedings where issue therein referable to arbitration

If any suit or proceeding be brought in any of the courts of the United States upon any issue referable to arbitration under an agreement in writing for such arbitration, the court in which such suit is pending, upon being satisfied that the issue involved in such suit or proceeding is referable to arbitration under such an agreement, shall on application of one of the parties stay the trial of the action until such arbitration has been had in accordance with the terms of the agreement, providing the applicant for the stay is not in default in proceeding with such arbitration.

9 U.S.C. § 4.   Failure to arbitrate under agreement; petition to United States court having jurisdiction for order to compel arbitration; notice and service thereof; hearing and determination

A party aggrieved by the alleged failure, neglect, or refusal of another to arbitrate under a written agreement for arbitration may petition any United States district court which, save for such agreement, would have jurisdiction under title 28, in a civil action or in admiralty of the subject matter of a suit arising out of the controversy between the parties, for an order directing that such arbitration proceed in the manner provided for in such agreement. Five days' notice in writing of such application shall be served upon the party in default. Service thereof shall be made in the manner provided by the Federal Rules of Civil Procedure. The court shall hear the parties, and upon being satisfied that the making of the agreement for arbitration or the failure to comply therewith is not in issue, the court shall make an order directing the parties to proceed to arbitration in accordance with the terms of the agreement. The hearing and proceedings, under such agreement, shall be within the district in which the petition for an order directing such arbitration is filed. If the making of the arbitration agreement or the failure, neglect, or refusal to perform the same be in issue, the court shall proceed summarily to the trial thereof. If no jury trial be demanded by the party alleged to be in default, or if the matter in dispute is within admiralty jurisdiction, the court shall hear and determine such issue. Where such an issue is raised, the party alleged to be in default may, except in cases of admiralty, on or before the return day of the notice of application, demand a jury trial of such issue, and upon such demand the court shall make an order referring the issue or issues to a jury in the manner provided by the Federal Rules of Civil Procedure, or may specially call a jury for that purpose. If the jury find that no agreement in writing for arbitration was made or that there is no default in proceeding thereunder, the proceeding shall be dismissed. If the jury find that an agreement for arbitration was made in writing and that there is a default in proceeding thereunder, the court shall make an order summarily directing the parties to proceed with the arbitration in accordance with the terms thereof.

9 U.S.C. § 5.   Appointment of arbitrators or umpire

If in the agreement provision be made for a method of naming or appointing an arbitrator or arbitrators or an umpire, such method shall be followed; but if no method be provided therein, or if a method be provided and any party thereto shall fail to avail himself of such method, or if for any other reason there shall be a lapse in the naming of an arbitrator or arbitrators or umpire, or in filling a vacancy, then upon the application of either party to the controversy the court shall designate and appoint an arbitrator or arbitrators or umpire, as the case may require, who shall act under the said agreement with the same force and effect as if he or they had been specifically named therein; and unless otherwise provided in the agreement the arbitration shall be by a single arbitrator.

9 U.S.C. § 6.   Application heard as motion

Any application to the court hereunder shall be made and heard in the manner provided by law for the making and hearing of motions, except as otherwise herein expressly provided.

9 U.S.C. § 7.   Witnesses before arbitrators; fees; compelling attendance

The arbitrators selected either as prescribed in this title or otherwise, or a majority of them, may summon in writing any person to attend before them or any of them as a witness and in a proper case to bring with him or them any book, record, document, or paper which may be deemed material as evidence in the case. The fees for such attendance shall be the same as the fees of witnesses before masters of the United States courts. Said summons shall issue in the name of the arbitrator or arbitrators, or a majority of them, and shall be signed by the arbitrators, or a majority of them, and shall be directed to the said person and shall be served in the same manner as subpoenas to appear and testify before the court; if any person or persons so summoned to testify shall refuse or neglect to obey said summons, upon petition the United States district court for the district in which such arbitrators, or a majority of them, are sitting may compel the attendance of such person or persons before said arbitrator or arbitrators, or punish said person or persons for contempt in the same manner provided by law for securing the attendance of witnesses or their punishment for neglect or refusal to attend in the courts of the United States.

9 U.S.C. § 8.   Proceedings begun by libel in admiralty and seizure of vessel or property

If the basis of jurisdiction be a cause of action otherwise justiciable in admiralty, then, notwithstanding anything herein to the contrary, the party claiming to be aggrieved may begin his proceeding hereunder by libel and seizure of the vessel or other property of the other party according to the usual course of admiralty proceedings, and the court shall then have jurisdiction to direct the parties to proceed with the arbitration and shall retain jurisdiction to enter its decree upon the award.

9 U.S.C. § 9.   Award of arbitrators; confirmation; jurisdiction; procedure

If the parties in their agreement have agreed that a judgment of the court shall be entered upon the award made pursuant to the arbitration, and shall specify the court, then at any time within one year after the award is made any party to the arbitration may apply to the court so specified for an order confirming the award, and thereupon the court must grant such an order unless the award is vacated, modified, or corrected as prescribed in sections 10 and 11 of this title. If no court is specified in the agreement of the parties, then such application may be made to the United States court in and for the district within which such award was made. Notice of the application shall be served upon the adverse party, and thereupon the court shall have jurisdiction of such party as though he had appeared generally in the proceeding. If the adverse party is a resident of the district within which the award was made, such service shall be made upon the adverse party or his attorney as prescribed by law for service of notice of motion in an action in the same court. If the adverse party shall be a nonresident, then the notice of the application shall be served by the marshal of any district within which the adverse party may be found in like manner as other process of the court.

9 U.S.C. § 10.   Same; vacation; grounds; rehearing

(a) In any of the following cases the United States court in and for the district wherein the award was made may make an order vacating the award upon the application of any party to the arbitration—

(1) where the award was procured by corruption, fraud, or undue means;

(2) where there was evident partiality or corruption in the arbitrators, or either of them;

(3) where the arbitrators were guilty of misconduct in refusing to postpone the hearing, upon sufficient cause shown, or in refusing to hear evidence pertinent and material to the controversy; or of any other misbehavior by which the rights of any party have been prejudiced; or

(4) where the arbitrators exceeded their powers, or so imperfectly executed them that a mutual, final, and definite award upon the subject matter submitted was not made.

(b) If an award is vacated and the time within which the agreement required the award to be made has not expired, the court may, in its discretion, direct a rehearing by the arbitrators.

(c) The United States district court for the district wherein an award was made that was issued pursuant to section 580 of title 5 may make an order vacating the award upon the application of a person, other than a party to the arbitration, who is adversely affected or aggrieved by the award, if the use of arbitration or the award is clearly inconsistent with the factors set forth in section 572 of title 5.

9 U.S.C. § 11. Same; modification or correction; grounds; order

In either of the following cases the United States court in and for the district wherein the award was made may make an order modifying or correcting the award upon the application of any party to the arbitration—

(a) Where there was an evident material miscalculation of figures or an evident material mistake in the description of any person, thing, or property referred to in the award.

(b) Where the arbitrators have awarded upon a matter not submitted to them, unless it is a matter not affecting the merits of the decision upon the matter submitted.

(c) Where the award is imperfect in matter of form not affecting the merits of the controversy.

The order may modify and correct the award, so as to effect the intent thereof and promote justice between the parties.

9 U.S.C. § 12. Notice of motions to vacate or modify; service; stay of proceedings

Notice of a motion to vacate, modify, or correct an award must be served upon the adverse party or his attorney within three months after the award is filed or delivered. If the adverse party is a resident of the district within which the award was made, such service shall be made upon the adverse party or his attorney as prescribed by law for service of notice of motion in an action in the same court. If the adverse party shall be a nonresident then the notice of the application shall be served by the marshal of any district within which the adverse party may be found in like manner as other process of the court. For the purposes of the motion any judge who might make an order to stay the proceedings in an action brought in the same court may make an order, to be served with the notice of motion, staying the proceedings of the adverse party to enforce the award.

9 U.S.C. § 13. Papers filed with order on motions; judgment; docketing; force and effect; enforcement

The party moving for an order confirming, modifying, or correcting an award shall, at the time such order is filed with the clerk for the entry of judgment thereon, also file the following papers with the clerk:

(a) The agreement; the selection or appointment, if any, of an additional arbitrator or umpire; and each written extension of the time, if any, within which to make the award.

(b) The award.

(c) Each notice, affidavit, or other paper used upon an application to confirm, modify, or correct the award, and a copy of each order of the court upon such an application.

The judgment shall be docketed as if it was rendered in an action.

The judgment so entered shall have the same force and effect, in all respects, as, and be subject to all the provisions of law relating to, a judgment in an action; and it may be enforced as if it had been rendered in an action in the court in which it is entered.

9 U.S.C. § 14.   Contracts not affected

This title shall not apply to contracts made prior to January 1, 1926.

9 U.S.C. § 15.   Inapplicability of the Act of State doctrine

Enforcement of arbitral agreements, confirmation of arbitral awards, and execution upon judgments based on orders confirming such awards shall not be refused on the basis of the Act of State doctrine.

9 U.S.C. § 16.   Appeals

(a) An appeal may be taken from—

(1) an order—

(A) refusing a stay of any action under section 3 of this title,

(B) denying a petition under section 4 of this title to order arbitration to proceed,

(C) denying an application under section 206 of this title to compel arbitration,

(D) confirming or denying confirmation of an award or partial award, or

(E) modifying, correcting, or vacating an award;

(2) an interlocutory order granting, continuing, or modifying an injunction against an arbitration that is subject to this title; or

(3) a final decision with respect to an arbitration that is subject to this title.

(b) Except as otherwise provided in section 1292(b) of title 28, an appeal may not be taken from an interlocutory order—

(1) granting a stay of any action under section 3 of this title;

(2) directing arbitration to proceed under section 4 of this title;

(3) compelling arbitration under section 206 of this title; or

(4) refusing to enjoin an arbitration that is subject to this title.

CHAPTER 2 — CONVENTION ON THE RECOGNITION AND ENFORCEMENT OF FOREIGN ARBITRAL AWARDS

9 U.S.C. § 201. Enforcement of Convention

The Convention on the Recognition and Enforcement of Foreign Arbitral Awards of June 10, 1958, shall be enforced in United States courts in accordance with this chapter.

9 U.S.C. § 202. Agreement or award falling under the Convention

An arbitration agreement or arbitral award arising out of a legal relationship, whether contractual or not, which is considered as commercial, including a transaction, contract, or agreement described in section 2 of this title, falls under the Convention. An agreement or award arising out of such a relationship which is entirely between citizens of the United States shall be deemed not to fall under the Convention unless that relationship involves property located abroad, envisages performance or enforcement abroad, or has some other reasonable relation with one or more foreign states. For the purpose of this section a corporation is a citizen of the United States if it is incorporated or has its principal place of business in the United States.

9 U.S.C. § 203. Jurisdiction; amount in controversy

An action or proceeding falling under the Convention shall be deemed to arise under the laws and treaties of the United States. The district courts of the United States (including the courts enumerated in section 460 of title 28) shall have original jurisdiction over such an action or proceeding, regardless of the amount in controversy.

9 U.S.C. § 204. Venue

An action or proceeding over which the district courts have jurisdiction pursuant to section 203 of this title may be brought in any such court in which save for the arbitration agreement an action or proceeding with respect to the controversy between the parties could be brought, or in such court for the district and division which embraces the place designated in the agreement as the place of arbitration if such place is within the United States.

9 U.S.C. § 205. Removal of cases from State courts

Where the subject matter of an action or proceeding pending in a State court relates to an arbitration agreement or award falling under the Convention, the defendant or the defendants may, at any time before the trial thereof, remove such action or proceeding to the district court of the United States for the district and division embracing the place where the action or proceeding is pending. The procedure for removal of causes otherwise provided by law shall apply, except that the ground for removal provided in this section need not appear on the face of the complaint but may be shown in the petition for removal. For the purposes of Chapter 1 of this title any action or proceeding removed under this section shall be deemed to have been brought in the district court to which it is removed.

9 U.S.C. § 206.   Order to compel arbitration; appointment of arbitrators

A court having jurisdiction under this chapter may direct that arbitration be held in accordance with the agreement at any place therein provided for, whether that place is within or without the United States. Such court may also appoint arbitrators in accordance with the provisions of the agreement.

9 U.S.C. § 207.   Award of arbitrators; confirmation; jurisdiction; proceeding

Within three years after an arbitral award falling under the Convention is made, any party to the arbitration may apply to any court having jurisdiction under this chapter for an order confirming the award as against any other party to the arbitration. The court shall confirm the award unless it finds one of the grounds for refusal or deferral of recognition or enforcement of the award specified in the said Convention.

9 U.S.C. § 208.   Chapter 1; residual application

Chapter 1 applies to actions and proceedings brought under this chapter to the extent that that chapter is not in conflict with this chapter or the Convention as ratified by the United States.

CHAPTER 3 — INTER-AMERICAN CONVENTION ON INTERNATIONAL COMMERCIAL ARBITRATION

9 U.S.C. § 301.   Enforcement of Convention

The Inter-American Convention on International Commercial Arbitration of January 30, 1975, shall be enforced in United States courts in accordance with this chapter.

9 U.S.C. § 302.   Incorporation by reference

Sections 202, 203, 204, 205, and 207 of this title shall apply to this chapter as if specifically set forth herein, except that for the purposes of this chapter "the Convention" shall mean the Inter-American Convention.

9 U.S.C. § 303.   Order to compel arbitration; appointment of arbitrators; locale

(a) A court having jurisdiction under this chapter may direct that arbitration be held in accordance with the agreement at any place therein provided for, whether that place is within or without the United States. The court may also appoint arbitrators in accordance with the provisions of the agreement.

(b) In the event the agreement does not make provision for the place of arbitration or the appointment of arbitrators, the court shall direct that the arbitration shall be held and the arbitrators be appointed in accordance with Article 3 of the Inter-American Convention.

9 U.S.C. § 304.   Recognition and enforcement of foreign arbitral decisions and awards; reciprocity

Arbitral decisions or awards made in the territory of a foreign State shall, on the basis of reciprocity, be recognized and enforced under this chapter only if that State has ratified or acceded to the Inter-American Convention.

9 U.S.C. § 305. Relationship between the Inter-American Convention and the Convention on the Recognition and Enforcement of Foreign Arbitral Awards of June 10, 1958

When the requirements for application of both the Inter-American Convention and the Convention on the Recognition and Enforcement of Foreign Arbitral Awards of June 10, 1958, are met, determination as to which Convention applies shall, unless otherwise expressly agreed, be made as follows:

(1) If a majority of the parties to the arbitration agreement are citizens of a State or States that have ratified or acceded to the Inter-American Convention and are member States of the Organization of American States, the Inter-American Convention shall apply.

(2) In all other cases the Convention on the Recognition and Enforcement of Foreign Arbitral Awards of June 10, 1958, shall apply.

9 U.S.C. § 306. Applicable rules of Inter-American Commercial Arbitration Commission

(a) For the purposes of this chapter the rules of procedure of the Inter-American Commercial Arbitration Commission referred to in Article 3 of the Inter-American Convention shall, subject to subsection (b) of this section, be those rules as promulgated by the Commission on July 1, 1988.

(b) In the event the rules of procedure of the Inter-American Commercial Arbitration Commission are modified or amended in accordance with the procedures for amendment of the rules of that Commission, the Secretary of State, by regulation in accordance with section 553 of title 5, consistent with the aims and purposes of this Convention, may prescribe that such modifications or amendments shall be effective for purposes of this chapter.

9 U.S.C. § 307. Chapter 1; residual application

Chapter 1 applies to actions and proceedings brought under this chapter to the extent chapter 1 is not in conflict with this chapter or the Inter-American Convention as ratified by the United States.

§ 294. Voluntary arbitration

(a) A contract involving a patent or any right under a patent may contain a provision requiring arbitration of any dispute relating to patent validity or infringement arising under the contract. In the absence of such a provision, the parties to an existing patent validity or infringement dispute may agree in writing to settle such dispute by arbitration. Any such provision or agreement shall be valid, irrevocable, and enforceable, except for any grounds that exist at law or in equity for revocation of a contract.

(b) Arbitration of such disputes, awards by arbitrators and confirmation of awards shall be governed by title 9, to the extent such title is not inconsistent with this section. In any such arbitration proceeding, the defenses provided for under section 282 [35 USC § 282] shall be considered by the arbitrator if raised by any party to the proceeding.

(c) An award by an arbitrator shall be final and binding between the parties to the arbitration but shall have no force or effect on any other person. The parties to an arbitration may agree that in the event a patent which is the subject matter of an award is subsequently determined to be invalid or unenforceable in a judgment rendered by a court of competent jurisdiction from which no appeal can or has been taken, such award may be modified by any court of competent jurisdiction upon application by any party to the arbitration. Any such modification shall govern the rights and obligations between such parties from the date of such modification.

(d) When an award is made by an arbitrator, the patentee, his assignee or licensee shall give notice thereof in writing to the Director. There shall be a separate notice prepared for each patent involved in such proceeding. Such notice shall set forth the names and addresses of the parties, the name of the inventor, and the name of the patent owner, shall designate the number of the patent, and shall contain a copy of the award. If an award is modified by a court, the party requesting such modification shall give notice of such modification to the Director. The Director shall, upon receipt of either notice, enter the same in the record of the prosecution of such patent. If the required notice is not filed with the Director, any party to the proceeding may provide such notice to the Director.

(e) The award shall be unenforceable until the notice required by subsection (d) is received by the Director.

MOTOR VEHICLE FRANCHISE CONTRACT ARBITRATION FAIRNESS ACT

15 U.S.C. § 1226.   Motor vehicle franchise contract dispute resolution process

(a) —Election of arbitration.

(1) —Definitions. For purposes of this subsection—

(A) —the term "motor vehicle" has the meaning given such term in section 30102(6) of title 49 of the United States Code; and

(B) —the term "motor vehicle franchise contract" means a contract under which a motor vehicle manufacturer, importer, or distributor sells motor vehicles to any other person for resale to an ultimate purchaser and authorizes such other person to repair and service the manufacturer's motor vehicles.

(2) —Consent required. Notwithstanding any other provision of law, whenever a motor vehicle franchise contract provides for the use of arbitration to resolve a controversy arising out of or relating to such contract, arbitration may be used to settle such controversy only if after such controversy arises all parties to such controversy consent in writing to use arbitration to settle such controversy.

(3) —Explanation required. Notwithstanding any other provision of law, whenever arbitration is elected to settle a dispute under a motor vehicle franchise contract, the arbitrator shall provide the parties to such contract with a written explanation of the factual and legal basis for the award.

(b) —Application. Subsection (a) shall apply to contracts entered into, amended, altered, modified, renewed, or extended after the date of the enactment of this Act.

(As enacted, Nov. 2, 2002, Pub. L. 107-273, 116 Stat. 1835)

MILITARY LENDING ACT

10 USC § 987. Terms of consumer credit extended to members and dependents: limitations

(e) Limitations. It shall be unlawful for any creditor to extend consumer credit to a covered member or a dependent of such a member with respect to which—

. . .

(3) the creditor requires the borrower to submit to arbitration or imposes onerous legal notice provisions in the case of a dispute;

. . .

(f) Penalties and remedies.

(1) Misdemeanor. A creditor who knowingly violates this section shall be fined as provided in title 18, or imprisoned for not more than one year, or both.

(2) Preservation of other remedies. The remedies and rights provided under this section are in addition to and do not preclude any remedy otherwise available under law to the person claiming relief under this section, including any award for consequential and punitive damages.

(3) Contract void. Any credit agreement, promissory note, or other contract prohibited under this section is void from the inception of such contract.

(4) Arbitration. Notwithstanding section 2 of title 9, or any other Federal or State law, rule, or regulation, no agreement to arbitrate any dispute involving the extension of consumer credit shall be enforceable against any covered member or dependent of such a member, or any person who was a covered member or dependent of that member when the agreement was made.

. . .

(i) Definitions. In this section:

(1) Covered member. The term "covered member" means a member of the armed forces who is—

(A) on active duty under a call or order that does not specify a period of 30 days or less; or

(B) on active Guard and Reserve Duty.

(2) Dependent. The term "dependent", with respect to a covered member, means—

(A) the member's spouse;

(B) the member's child (as defined in section 101(4) of title 38); or

(C) an individual for whom the member provided more than one-half of the individual's support for 180 days immediately preceding an extension of consumer credit covered by this section.

. . .

(5) Creditor. The term "creditor" means a person—

(A) who—

(i) is engaged in the business of extending consumer credit; and

(ii) meets such additional criteria as are specified for such purpose in regulations prescribed under this section; or

(B) who is an assignee of a person described in subparagraph (A) with respect to any consumer credit extended.

(6) Consumer credit. The term "consumer credit" has the meaning provided for such term in regulations prescribed under this section, except that such term does not include (A) a residential mortgage, or (B) a loan procured in the course of purchasing a car or other personal property, when that loan is offered for the express purpose of financing the purchase and is secured by the car or personal property procured.

7 USC § 197c

§ 197c. Arbitration

(a) In general. Any livestock or poultry contract that contains a provision requiring the use of arbitration to resolve any controversy that may arise under the contract shall contain a provision that allows a producer or grower, prior to entering the contract, to decline to be bound by the arbitration provision.

(b) Disclosure. Any livestock or poultry contract that contains a provision requiring the use of arbitration shall contain terms that conspicuously disclose the right of the contract producer or grower, prior to entering the contract, to decline the requirement to use arbitration to resolve any controversy that may arise under the livestock or poultry contract.

(c) Dispute resolution. Any contract producer or grower that declines a requirement of arbitration pursuant to subsection (b) has the right, to nonetheless seek to resolve any controversy that may arise under the livestock or poultry contract, if, after the controversy arises, both parties consent in writing to use arbitration to settle the controversy.

(d) Application. Subsections (a) (b) and (c) shall apply to any contract entered into, amended, altered, modified, renewed, or extended after the date of the enactment of the Food, Conservation, and Energy Act of 2008 [enacted June 18, 2008].

(e) Unlawful practice. Any action by or on behalf of a packer, swine contractor, or live poultry dealer that violates this section (including any action that has the intent or effect of limiting the ability of a producer or grower to freely make a choice described in subsection (b)) is an unlawful practice under this Act.

(f) Regulations. The Secretary shall promulgate regulations to—

(1) carry out this section; and

(2) establish criteria that the Secretary will consider in determining whether the arbitration process provided in a contract provides a meaningful opportunity for the grower or producer to participate fully in the arbitration process.

DEPARTMENT OF DEFENSE APPROPRIATIONS ACT, 2010

Pub. L. No. 111-118 (2009)

Sec. 8116.

(a) None of the funds appropriated or otherwise made available by this Act may be expended for any Federal contract for an amount in excess of $1,000,000 that is awarded more than 60 days after the effective date of this Act, unless the contractor agrees not to:

(1) enter into any agreement with any of its employees or independent contractors that requires, as a condition of employment, that the employee or independent contractor agree to resolve through arbitration any claim under title VII of the Civil Rights Act of 1964 or any tort related to or arising out of sexual assault or harassment, including assault and battery, intentional infliction of emotional distress, false imprisonment, or negligent hiring, supervision, or retention; or

(2) take any action to enforce any provision of an existing agreement with an employee or independent contractor that mandates that the employee or independent contractor resolve through arbitration any claim under title VII of the Civil Rights Act of 1964 or any tort related to or arising out of sexual assault or harassment, including assault and battery, intentional infliction of emotional distress, false imprisonment, or negligent hiring, supervision, or retention.

(b) None of the funds appropriated or otherwise made available by this Act may be expended for any Federal contract awarded more than 180 days after the effective date of this Act unless the contractor certifies that it requires each covered subcontractor to agree not to enter into, and not to take any action to enforce any provision of, any agreement as described in paragraphs (1) and (2) of subsection (a), with respect to any employee or independent contractor performing work related to such subcontract. For purposes of this subsection, a 'covered subcontractor' is an entity that has a subcontract in excess of $1,000,000 on a contract subject to subsection (a).

(c) The prohibitions in this section do not apply with respect to a contractor's or subcontractor's agreements with employees or independent contractors that may not be enforced in a court of the United States.

(d) The Secretary of Defense may waive the application of subsection (a) or (b) to a particular contractor or subcontractor for the purposes of a particular contract or subcontract if the Secretary or the Deputy Secretary personally determines that the waiver is necessary to avoid harm to national security interests of the United States, and that the term of the contract or subcontract is not longer than necessary to avoid such harm. The determination shall set forth with specificity the grounds for the waiver and for the contract or subcontract term selected, and shall state any alternatives considered in lieu of a waiver and the reasons each such alternative would not avoid harm to national security interests of the United States. The Secretary of Defense shall transmit to Congress, and simultaneously make public, any determination under this subsection not less than 15 business days before the contract or subcontract addressed in the determination may be awarded.

SELECTED PROVISIONS OF 48 C.F.R.

Subpart 222.74—Restrictions on the Use of Mandatory Arbitration Agreements

222.7400 Scope of subpart.

This subpart implements section 8116 of the Defense Appropriations Act for Fiscal Year 2010 (Pub. L. 111–118) and similar sections in subsequent DoD appropriations acts.

222.7401 Definition.

Covered subcontractor, as used in this subpart, is defined in the clause at 252.222–7006, Restrictions on the Use of Mandatory Arbitration Agreements.

222.7402 Policy.

(a) Departments and agencies are prohibited from using funds appropriated or otherwise made available by the Fiscal Year 2010 Defense Appropriations Act (Pub. L. 111–118) or subsequent DoD appropriations acts for any contract (including task or delivery orders and bilateral modifications adding new work) in excess of $1 million, unless the contractor agrees not to—

(1) Enter into any agreement with any of its employees or independent contractors that requires, as a condition of employment, that the employee or independent contractor agree to resolve through arbitration—

(i) Any claim under title VII of the Civil Rights Act of 1964; or

(ii) Any tort related to or arising out of sexual assault or harassment, including assault and battery, intentional infliction of emotional distress, false imprisonment, or negligent hiring, supervision, or retention; or

(2) Take any action to enforce any provision of an existing agreement with an employee or independent contractor that mandates that the employee or independent contractor resolve through arbitration—

(i) Any claim under title VII of the Civil Rights Act of 1964; or

(ii) Any tort related to or arising out of sexual assault or harassment, including assault and battery, intentional infliction of emotional distress, false imprisonment, or negligent hiring, supervision, or retention.

(b) No funds appropriated or otherwise made available by the Fiscal Year 2010 Defense Appropriations Act (Pub. L. 111–118) or subsequent DoD appropriations acts may be expended unless the contractor certifies that it requires each covered subcontractor to agree not to enter into, and not to take any action to enforce, any provision of any agreement, as described in paragraph (a) of this section, with respect to any employee or independent contractor performing work related to such subcontract.

222.7403 Applicability.

This requirement does not apply to the acquisition of commercial items (including commercially available off-the-shelf items).

222.7404   Waiver.

(a) The Secretary of Defense may waive, in accordance with paragraphs (b) through (d) of this section, the applicability of paragraphs (a) or (b) of 222.7402 to a particular contract or subcontract, if the Secretary or the Deputy Secretary personally determines that the waiver is necessary to avoid harm to national security interests of the United States, and that the term of the contract or subcontract is not longer than necessary to avoid such harm.

(b) The waiver determination shall set forth the grounds for the waiver with specificity, stating any alternatives considered, and explain why each of the alternatives would not avoid harm to national security interests.

(c) The contracting officer shall submit requests for waivers in accordance with agency procedures.

(d) The Secretary of Defense will transmit the determination to Congress and simultaneously publish it in the Federal Register, not less than 15 business days before the contract or subcontract addressed in the determination may be awarded.

222.7405   Contract clause.

Use the clause at 252.222–7006, Restrictions on the Use of Mandatory Arbitration Agreements, in all solicitations and contracts (including task or delivery orders and bilateral modifications adding new work) valued in excess of $1 million utilizing funds appropriated or otherwise made available by the Defense Appropriations Act for Fiscal Year 2010 (Pub. L. 111–118) or subsequent DoD appropriations acts, except in contracts for the acquisition of commercial items, including commercially available off-the-shelf items.

252.222-7006   Restrictions on the Use of Mandatory Arbitration Agreements.

As prescribed in 222.7405, use the following clause:

RESTRICTIONS ON THE USE OF MANDATORY ARBITRATION AGREE-MENTS (DEC 2010)

(a)   Definitions. As used in this clause—

"Covered subcontractor" means any entity that has a subcontract valued in excess of $1 million, except a subcontract for the acquisition of commercial items, including commercially available off-the-shelf items.

"Subcontract" means any contract, as defined in Federal Acquisition Regulation subpart 2.1, to furnish supplies or services for performance of this contract or a higher-tier subcontract thereunder.

(b)   The Contractor—

(1)   Agrees not to—

(i) Enter into any agreement with any of its employees or independent contractors that requires, as a condition of employment, that the employee or independent contractor agree to resolve through arbitration—

(A) Any claim under title VII of the Civil Rights Act of 1964; or

(B) Any tort related to or arising out of sexual assault or harassment, including assault and battery, intentional infliction of emotional distress, false imprisonment, or negligent hiring, supervision, or retention; or

(ii) Take any action to enforce any provision of an existing agreement with an employee or independent contractor that mandates that the employee or independent contractor resolve through arbitration—

(A) Any claim under title VII of the Civil Rights Act of 1964; or

(B) Any tort related to or arising out of sexual assault or harassment, including assault and battery, intentional infliction of emotional distress, false imprisonment, or negligent hiring, supervision, or retention; and

(2) Certifies, by signature of the contract, that it requires each covered subcontractor to agree not to enter into, and not to take any action to enforce, any provision of any existing agreements, as described in paragraph (b)(1) of this clause, with respect to any employee or independent contractor performing work related to such subcontract.

(c) The prohibitions of this clause do not apply with respect to a contractor's or subcontractor's agreements with employees or independent contractors that may not be enforced in a court of the United States.

(d) The Secretary of Defense may waive the applicability of the restrictions of paragraph (b) of this clause in accordance with Defense Federal Acquisition Regulation Supplement 222.7404.

(End of clause)

DODD-FRANK WALL STREET REFORM AND CONSUMER PROTECTION ACT

Pub. L. No. 111-203 (2010) (excerpts)

SEC. 531. REGULATION OF CREDIT FOR REINSURANCE AND REINSURANCE AGREEMENTS.

. . .

(b) ADDITIONAL PREEMPTION OF EXTRATERRITORIAL APPLICATION OF STATE LAW.—In addition to the application of subsection (a), all laws, regulations, provisions, or other actions of a State that is not the domiciliary State of the ceding insurer, except those with respect to taxes and assessments on insurance companies or insurance income, are preempted to the extent that they—

(1) restrict or eliminate the rights of the ceding insurer or the assuming insurer to resolve disputes pursuant to contractual arbitration to the extent such contractual provision is not inconsistent with the provisions of title 9, United States Code;

. . .

SEC. 748. COMMODITY WHISTLEBLOWER INCENTIVES AND PROTECTION.

The Commodity Exchange Act (7 U.S.C. 1 et seq.) is amended by adding at the end the following:

"SEC. 23. COMMODITY WHISTLEBLOWER INCENTIVES AND PROTECTION.

. . .

(n) NONENFORCEABILITY OF CERTAIN PROVISIONS WAIVING RIGHTS AND REMEDIES OR REQUIRING ARBITRATION OF DISPUTES.—

(1) WAIVER OF RIGHTS AND REMEDIES. —The rights and remedies provided for in this section may not be waived by any agreement, policy form, or condition of employment including by a predispute arbitration agreement.

(2) PREDISPUTE ARBITRATION AGREEMENTS. —No predispute arbitration agreement shall be valid or enforceable, if the agreement requires arbitration of a dispute arising under this section."

. . .

SEC. 919B. STUDY ON IMPROVED INVESTOR ACCESS TO INFORMATION ON INVESTMENT ADVISERS AND BROKER-DEALERS.

(a) STUDY.—

(1) IN GENERAL.— Not later than 6 months after the date of enactment of this Act, the Commission shall complete a study, including recommendations, of ways to improve the access of investors to registration information (including

disciplinary actions, regulatory, judicial, and arbitration proceedings, and other information) about registered and previously registered investment advisers, associated persons of investment advisers, brokers and dealers and their associated persons on the existing Central Registration Depository and Investment Adviser Registration Depository systems, as well as identify additional information that should be made publicly available.

. . .

SEC. 921. AUTHORITY TO RESTRICT MANDATORY PRE-DISPUTE ARBITRATION.

(a) AMENDMENT TO SECURITIES EXCHANGE ACT OF 1934.— Section 15 of the Securities Exchange Act of 1934 (15 U.S.C. 78o), as amended by this title, is further amended by adding at the end the following new subsection:

"(o) AUTHORITY TO RESTRICT MANDATORY PREDISPUTE ARBITRATION.— The Commission, by rule, may prohibit, or impose conditions or limitations on the use of, agreements that require customers or clients of any broker, dealer, or municipal securities dealer to arbitrate any future dispute between them arising under the Federal securities laws, the rules and regulations thereunder, or the rules of a self-regulatory organization if it finds that such prohibition, imposition of conditions, or limitations are in the public interest and for the protection of investors."

(b) AMENDMENT TO INVESTMENT ADVISERS ACT OF 1940.— Section 205 of the Investment Advisers Act of 1940 (15 U.S.C. 80b–5) is amended by adding at the end the following new subsection:

"(f) AUTHORITY TO RESTRICT MANDATORY PREDISPUTE ARBITRATION.— The Commission, by rule, may prohibit, or impose conditions or limitations on the use of, agreements that require customers or clients of any investment adviser to arbitrate any future dispute between them arising under the Federal securities laws, the rules and regulations thereunder, or the rules of a self-regulatory organization if it finds that such prohibition, imposition of conditions, or limitations are in the public interest and for the protection of investors."

. . .

SEC. 922. WHISTLEBLOWER PROTECTION.

. . .

(c) SECTION 1514A OF TITLE 18, UNITED STATES CODE.—

. . .

(2) PRIVATE SECURITIES LITIGATION WITNESSES; NONENFORCEABILITY; INFORMATION.— Section 1514A of title 18, United States Code, is amended by adding at the end the following:

. . .

"(e) NONENFORCEABILITY OF CERTAIN PROVISIONS WAIVING RIGHTS AND REMEDIES OR REQUIRING ARBITRATION OF DISPUTES.—

(1)   WAIVER OF RIGHTS AND REMEDIES.— The rights and remedies provided for in this section may not be waived by any agreement, policy form, or condition of employment, including by a predispute arbitration agreement.

(2)   PREDISPUTE ARBITRATION AGREEMENTS.— No predispute arbitration agreement shall be valid or enforceable, if the agreement requires arbitration of a dispute arising under this section."

. . .

SEC. 964.   REPORT ON OVERSIGHT OF NATIONAL SECURITIES ASSOCIATIONS.

(a)   REPORT REQUIRED.— Not later than 2 years after the date of enactment of this Act, and every 3 years thereafter, the Comptroller General of the United States shall submit to the Committee on Banking, Housing, and Urban Affairs of the Senate and the Committee on Financial Services of the House of Representatives a report that includes an evaluation of the oversight by the Commission of national securities associations registered under section 15A of the Securities Exchange Act of 1934 (15 U.S.C. 78o–3) with respect to—

. . .

(4) the arbitration services provided by the national securities associations;

. . .

SEC. 1028.   AUTHORITY TO RESTRICT MANDATORY PRE-DISPUTE ARBITRATION.

(a)   STUDY AND REPORT.— The Bureau shall conduct a study of, and shall provide a report to Congress concerning, the use of agreements providing for arbitration of any future dispute between covered persons and consumers in connection with the offering or providing of consumer financial products or services.

(b)   FURTHER AUTHORITY.— The Bureau, by regulation, may prohibit or impose conditions or limitations on the use of an agreement between a covered person and a consumer for a consumer financial product or service providing for arbitration of any future dispute between the parties, if the Bureau finds that such a prohibition or imposition of conditions or limitations is in the public interest and for the protection of consumers. The findings in such rule shall be consistent with the study conducted under subsection (a).

(c)   LIMITATION.— The authority described in subsection (b) may not be construed to prohibit or restrict a consumer from entering into a voluntary arbitration agreement with a covered person after a dispute has arisen.

. . .

SEC. 1057.   EMPLOYEE PROTECTION.

. . .

(d)   UNENFORCEABILITY OF CERTAIN AGREEMENTS.—

(1)   NO WAIVER OF RIGHTS AND REMEDIES.— Except as provided

under paragraph (3), and notwithstanding any other provision of law, the rights and remedies provided for in this section may not be waived by any agreement, policy, form, or condition of employment, including by any predispute arbitration agreement.

(2) NO PREDISPUTE ARBITRATION AGREEMENTS.— Except as provided under paragraph (3), and notwithstanding any other provision of law, no predispute arbitration agreement shall be valid or enforceable to the extent that it requires arbitration of a dispute arising under this section.

(3) EXCEPTION.— Notwithstanding paragraphs (1) and (2), an arbitration provision in a collective bargaining agreement shall be enforceable as to disputes arising under subsection (a)(4), unless the Bureau determines, by rule, that such provision is inconsistent with the purposes of this title.

SEC. 1414. ADDITIONAL STANDARDS AND REQUIREMENTS.

(a) IN GENERAL.— Section 129C of the Truth in Lending Act is amended by inserting after subsection (b) (as added by this title) the following new subsections:

. . .

"(e) ARBITRATION.—

(1) IN GENERAL.— No residential mortgage loan and no extension of credit under an open end consumer credit plan secured by the principal dwelling of the consumer may include terms which require arbitration or any other nonjudicial procedure as the method for resolving any controversy or settling any claims arising out of the transaction.

(2) POST-CONTROVERSY AGREEMENTS.— Subject to paragraph (3), paragraph (1) shall not be construed as limiting the right of the consumer and the creditor or any assignee to agree to arbitration or any other nonjudicial procedure as the method for resolving any controversy at any time after a dispute or claim under the transaction arises.

(3) NO WAIVER OF STATUTORY CAUSE OF ACTION.— No provision of any residential mortgage loan or of any extension of credit under an open end consumer credit plan secured by the principal dwelling of the consumer, and no other agreement between the consumer and the creditor relating to the residential mortgage loan or extension of credit referred to in paragraph (1), shall be applied or interpreted so as to bar a consumer from bringing an action in an appropriate district court of the United States, or any other court of competent jurisdiction, pursuant to section 130 or any other provision of law, for damages or other relief in connection with any alleged violation of this section, any other provision of this title, or any other Federal law."

ARBITRATION FAIRNESS ACT OF 2011

H.R. 1873

To amend title 9 of the United States Code with respect to arbitration

IN THE HOUSE OF REPRESENTATIVES

May 12, 2011

Mr. Johnson of Georgia . . . introduced the following bill; which was referred to the Committee on the Judiciary

A BILL

To amend title 9 of the United States Code with respect to arbitration.

Be it enacted by the Senate and House of Representatives of the United States of America in Congress assembled,

SECTION 1. SHORT TITLE.

This Act may be cited as the 'Arbitration Fairness Act of 2011.'

SEC. 2. FINDINGS.

The Congress finds the following:

(1) The Federal Arbitration Act (now enacted as chapter 1 of title 9 of the United States Code) was intended to apply to disputes between commercial entities of generally similar sophistication and bargaining power.

(2) A series of decisions by the Supreme Court of the United States have changed the meaning of the Act so that it now extends to consumer disputes and employment disputes.

(3) Most consumers and employees have little or no meaningful choice whether to submit their claims to arbitration. Often, consumers and employees are not even aware that they have given up their rights.

(4) Mandatory arbitration undermines the development of public law because there is inadequate transparency and inadequate judicial review of arbitrators' decisions.

(5) Arbitration can be an acceptable alternative when consent to the arbitration is truly voluntary, and occurs after the dispute arises.

SEC. 3. ARBITRATION OF EMPLOYMENT, CONSUMER, AND CIVIL RIGHTS DISPUTES.

(a) In General—Title 9 of the United States Code is amended by adding at the end the following:

'CHAPTER 4—ARBITRATION OF EMPLOYMENT, CONSUMER, AND CIVIL RIGHTS DISPUTES

'Sec.

'401. Definitions.

'402. Validity and enforceability.

'Sec. 401. Definitions

'In this chapter—

'(1) the term 'civil rights dispute' means a dispute—

'(A) arising under—

'(i) the Constitution of the United States or the constitution of a State; or

'(ii) a Federal or State statute that prohibits discrimination on the basis of race, sex, disability, religion, national origin, or any invidious basis in education, employment, credit, housing, public accommodations and facilities, voting, or program funded or conducted by the Federal Government or State government, including any statute enforced by the Civil Rights Division of the Department of Justice and any statute enumerated in section 62(e) of the Internal Revenue Code of 1986 (relating to unlawful discrimination); and

'(B) in which at least 1 party alleging a violation of the Constitution of the United States, a State constitution, or a statute prohibiting discrimination is an individual;

'(2) the term 'consumer dispute' means a dispute between an individual who seeks or acquires real or personal property, services (including services relating to securities and other investments), money, or credit for personal, family, or household purposes and the seller or provider of such property, services, money, or credit;

'(3) the term 'employment dispute' means a dispute between an employer and employee arising out of the relationship of employer and employee as defined in section 3 of the Fair Labor Standards Act of 1938 (29 U.S.C. 203); and

'(4) the term 'predispute arbitration agreement' means any agreement to arbitrate a dispute that had not yet arisen at the time of the making of the agreement.

'Sec. 402. Validity and enforceability

'(a) In General— Notwithstanding any other provision of this title, no predispute arbitration agreement shall be valid or enforceable if it requires arbitration of an employment dispute, consumer dispute, or civil rights dispute.

'(b) Applicability—

'(1) IN GENERAL— An issue as to whether this chapter applies to an arbitration agreement shall be determined under Federal law. The applicability of this chapter to an agreement to arbitrate and the validity and enforceability of an agreement to which this chapter applies shall be determined by the court, rather than an arbitrator, irrespective of whether the party resisting arbitration challenges the arbitration agreement specifically or in conjunction with other terms of the contract containing such agreement.

'(2)   COLLECTIVE BARGAINING AGREEMENTS— Nothing in this chapter shall apply to any arbitration provision in a contract between an employer and a labor organization or between labor organizations, except that no such arbitration provision shall have the effect of waiving the right of an employee to seek judicial enforcement of a right arising under a provision of the Constitution of the United States, a State constitution, or a Federal or State statute, or public policy arising therefrom.'.

(b) Technical and Conforming Amendments—

(1)   IN GENERAL— Title 9 of the United States Code is amended—

(A) in section 1, by striking 'of seamen,' and all that follows through 'interstate commerce';

(B) in section 2, by inserting 'or as otherwise provided in chapter 4' before the period at the end;

(C) in section 208—

(i) in the section heading, by striking 'Chapter 1; residual application' and inserting 'Application'; and

(ii) by adding at the end the following: 'This chapter applies to the extent that this chapter is not in conflict with chapter 4.'; and

(D) in section 307—

(i) in the section heading, by striking 'Chapter 1; residual application' and inserting 'Application'; and

(ii) by adding at the end the following: 'This chapter applies to the extent that this chapter is not in conflict with chapter 4.'.

(2)   TABLE OF SECTIONS—

(A)   CHAPTER 2— The table of sections for chapter 2 of title 9, United States Code, is amended by striking the item relating to section 208 and inserting the following:

'208. Application.'.

(B)   CHAPTER 3— The table of sections for chapter 3 of title 9, United States Code, is amended by striking the item relating to section 307 and inserting the following:

'307. Application.'

(3)   TABLE OF CHAPTERS— The table of chapters for title 9, United States Code, is amended by adding at the end the following:

'4. Arbitration of employment, consumer, and civil rights disputes.

SEC. 4. EFFECTIVE DATE.

This Act, and the amendments made by this Act, shall take effect on the date of enactment of this Act and shall apply with respect to any dispute or claim that arises on or after such date.

SELECTED PROVISIONS OF 28 U.S.C.

28 U.S.C. § 1331. Federal question

The district courts shall have original jurisdiction of all civil actions arising under the Constitution, laws, or treaties of the United States.

28 U.S.C. § 1332. Diversity of citizenship; amount in controversy; costs

(a) The district courts shall have original jurisdiction of all civil actions where the matter in controversy exceeds the sum or value of $75,000, exclusive of interest and costs, and is between—

(1) citizens of different States;

(2) citizens of a State and citizens or subjects of a foreign state, except that the district court shall not have original jurisdiction under this subsection of an action between citizens of a State and citizens or subjects of a foreign state who are lawfully admitted for permanent residence in the United States and are domiciled in the same State;

(3) citizens of different States and in which citizens or subjects of a foreign state are additional parties; and

(4) a foreign state, defined in section 1603(a) of this title, as plaintiff and citizens of a State or of different States.

. . .

(c) For purposes of this section and section 1441 of this title—

(1) a corporation shall be deemed to be a citizen of every State and foreign state by which it has been incorporated and of the State or foreign state where it has its principal place of business . . . .

28 U.S.C. § 1391. Venue generally

(a) Applicability of section. Except as otherwise provided by law—

(1) this section shall govern the venue of all civil actions brought in district courts of the United States; and

(2) the proper venue for a civil action shall be determined without regard to whether the action is local or transitory in nature.

(b) Venue in general. A civil action may be brought in—

(1) a judicial district in which any defendant resides, if all defendants are residents of the State in which the district is located;

(2) a judicial district in which a substantial part of the events or omissions giving rise to the claim occurred, or a substantial part of property that is the subject of the action is situated; or

(3) if there is no district in which an action may otherwise be brought as provided in this section, any judicial district in which any defendant is subject to the court's personal jurisdiction with respect to such action.

(c)   Residency. For all venue purposes—

(1) a natural person, including an alien lawfully admitted for permanent residence in the United States, shall be deemed to reside in the judicial district in which that person is domiciled;

(2) an entity with the capacity to sue and be sued in its common name under applicable law, whether or not incorporated, shall be deemed to reside, if a defendant, in any judicial district in which such defendant is subject to the court's personal jurisdiction with respect to the civil action in question and, if a plaintiff, only in the judicial district in which it maintains its principal place of business; and

(3) a defendant not resident in the United States may be sued in any judicial district, and the joinder of such a defendant shall be disregarded in determining where the action may be brought with respect to other defendants.

(d)   Residency of corporations in States with multiple districts.— For purposes of venue under this chapter, in a State which has more than one judicial district and in which a defendant that is a corporation is subject to personal jurisdiction at the time an action is commenced, such corporation shall be deemed to reside in any district in that State within which its contacts would be sufficient to subject it to personal jurisdiction if that district were a separate State, and, if there is no such district, the corporation shall be deemed to reside in the district within which it has the most significant contacts.

. . .

28 U.S.C. § 1441.   Actions removable generally

(a) Except as otherwise expressly provided by Act of Congress, any civil action brought in a State court of which the district courts of the United States have original jurisdiction, may be removed by the defendant or the defendants, to the district court of the United States for the district and division embracing the place where such action is pending.

(b) Removal based on diversity of citizenship.

(1) In determining whether a civil action is removable on the basis of the jurisdiction under section 1332(a) of this title, the citizenship of defendants sued under fictitious names shall be disregarded.

(2) A civil action otherwise removable solely on the basis of the jurisdiction under section 1332(a) of this title may not be removed if any of the parties in interest properly joined and served as defendants is a citizen of the State in which such action is brought.

. . .

28 U.S.C. § 1782.   Assistance to foreign and international tribunals and to litigants before such tribunals

(a) The district court of the district in which a person resides or is found may order him to give his testimony or statement or to produce a document or other thing for use in a proceeding in a foreign or international tribunal, including criminal investigations conducted before formal accusation. The order may be made pursuant to a letter rogatory issued, or request made, by a foreign or international tribunal or upon the application of any interested person and may direct that the testimony or statement be given, or the document or other thing be produced, before a person appointed by the court. By virtue of his appointment, the person appointed has power to administer any necessary oath and take the testimony or statement. The order may prescribe the practice and procedure, which may be in whole or part the practice and procedure of the foreign country or the international tribunal, for taking the testimony or statement or producing the document or other thing. To the extent that the order does not prescribe otherwise, the testimony or statement shall be taken, and the document or other thing produced, in accordance with the Federal Rules of Civil Procedure.

A person may not be compelled to give his testimony or statement or to produce a document or other thing in violation of any legally applicable privilege.

(b) This chapter does not preclude a person within the United States from voluntarily giving his testimony or statement, or producing a document or other thing, for use in a proceeding in a foreign or international tribunal before any person and in any manner acceptable to him.

28 U.S.C. § 2201.   Creation of remedy

(a) In the case of an actual controversy within its jurisdiction, . . . any court of the United States, upon the filing of an appropriate pleading, may declare the rights and other legal relations of any interested party seeking such declaration, whether or not further relief is or could be sought. Any such declaration shall have the force and effect of a final judgment or decree and shall be reviewable as such.

. . .

28 U.S.C. § 2283.   Stay of State court proceedings

A court of the United States may not grant an injunction to stay proceedings in a State court except as expressly authorized by Act of Congress, or where necessary in aid of its jurisdiction, or to protect or effectuate its judgments.

UNIFORM ARBITRATION ACT*

§ 1. Validity of Arbitration Agreement.

A written agreement to submit any existing controversy to arbitration or a provision in a written contract to submit to arbitration any controversy thereafter arising between the parties is valid, enforceable and irrevocable, save upon such grounds as exist at law or in equity for the revocation of any contract. This act also applies to arbitration agreements between employers and employees or between their respective representatives [unless otherwise provided in the agreement].

§ 2. Proceedings to Compel or Stay Arbitration.

(a) On application of a party showing an agreement described in Section 1, and the opposing party's refusal to arbitrate, the Court shall order the parties to proceed with arbitration, but if the opposing party denies the existence of the agreement to arbitrate, the Court shall proceed summarily to the determination of the issue so raised and shall order arbitration if found for the moving party, otherwise, the application shall be denied.

(b) On application, the court may stay an arbitration proceeding commenced or threatened on a showing that there is no agreement to arbitrate. Such an issue, when in substantial and bona fide dispute, shall be forthwith and summarily tried and the stay ordered if found for the moving party. If found for the opposing party, the court shall order the parties to proceed to arbitration.

(c) If an issue referable to arbitration under the alleged agreement is involved in an action or proceeding pending in a court having jurisdiction to hear applications under subdivision (a) of this Section, the application shall be made therein. Otherwise and subject to Section 18, the application may be made in any court of competent jurisdiction.

(d) Any action or proceeding involving an issue subject to arbitration shall be stayed if an order for arbitration or an application therefor has been made under this section or, if the issue is severable, the stay may be with respect thereto only. When the application is made in such action or proceeding, the order for arbitration shall include such stay.

(e) An order for arbitration shall not be refused on the ground that the claim in issue lacks merit or bona fides or because any fault or grounds for the claim sought to be arbitrated have not been shown.

§ 3. Appointment of Arbitrators by Court.

If the arbitration agreement provides a method of appointment of arbitrators, this method shall be followed. In the absence thereof, or if the agreed method fails or for any reason cannot be followed, or when an arbitrator appointed fails or is unable to act and his successor has not been duly appointed, the court on application of a party shall appoint one or more arbitrators. An arbitrator so appointed has all the powers of one specifically named in the agreement.

---

§ 4. Majority Action by Arbitrators.

The powers of the arbitrators may be exercised by a majority unless otherwise provided by the agreement or by this act.

§ 5. Hearing.

Unless otherwise provided by the agreement:

(a) The arbitrators shall appoint a time and place for the hearing and cause notification to the parties to be served personally or by registered mail not less than five days before the hearing. Appearance at the hearing waives such notice. The arbitrators may adjourn the hearing from time to time as necessary and, on request of a party and for good cause, or upon their own motion may postpone the hearing to a time not later than the date fixed by the agreement for making the award unless the parties consent to a later date. The arbitrators may hear and determine the controversy upon the evidence produced notwithstanding the failure of a party duly notified to appear. The court on application may direct the arbitrators to proceed promptly with the hearing and determination of the controversy.

(b) The parties are entitled to be heard, to present evidence material to the controversy and to cross-examine witnesses appearing at the hearing.

(c) The hearing shall be conducted by all the arbitrators but a majority may determine any question and render a final award. If, during the course of the hearing, an arbitrator for any reason ceases to act, the remaining arbitrator or arbitrators appointed to act as neutrals may continue with the hearing and determination of the controversy.

§ 6. Representation by Attorney.

A party has the right to be represented by an attorney at any proceeding or hearing under this act. A waiver thereof prior to the proceeding or hearing is ineffective.

§ 7. Witnesses, Subpoenas, Depositions.

(a) The arbitrators may issue (cause to be issued) subpoenas for the attendance of witnesses and for the production of books, records, documents and other evidence, and shall have the power to administer oaths. Subpoenas so issued shall be served, and upon application to the Court by a party or the arbitrators, enforced, in the manner provided by law for the service and enforcement of subpoenas in a civil action.

(b) On application of a party and for use as evidence, the arbitrators may permit a deposition to be taken, in the manner and upon the terms designated by the arbitrators, of a witness who cannot be subpoenaed or is unable to attend the hearing.

(c) All provisions of law compelling a person under subpoena to testify are applicable.

(d) Fees for attendance as a witness shall be the same as for a witness in the Court.

§ 8.   Award.

(a) The award shall be in writing and signed by the arbitrators joining in the award. The arbitrators shall deliver a copy to each party personally or by registered mail, or as provided in the agreement.

(b) An award shall be made within the time fixed therefor by the agreement or, if not so fixed, within such time as the court orders on application of a party. The parties may extend the time in writing either before or after the expiration thereof. A party waives the objection that an award was not made within the time required unless he notifies the arbitrators of his objection prior to the delivery of the award to him.

§ 9.   Change of Award by Arbitrators.

On application of a party or, if an application to the court is pending under Sections 11, 12 or 13, on submission to the arbitrators by the court under such conditions as the court may order, the arbitrators may modify or correct the award upon the grounds stated in paragraphs (1) and (3) of subdivision (a) of Section 13, or for the purpose of clarifying the award. The application shall be made within twenty days after delivery of the award to the applicant. Written notice thereof shall be given forthwith to the opposing party, stating he must serve his objections thereto, if any, within ten days from the notice. The award so modified or corrected is subject to the provisions of Sections 11, 12 and 13.

§ 10.   Fees and Expenses of Arbitration.

Unless otherwise provided in the agreement to arbitrate, the arbitrators' expenses and fees, together with other expenses, not including counsel fees, incurred in the conduct of the arbitration, shall be paid as provided in the award.

§ 11.   Confirmation of an Award.

Upon application of a party, the Court shall confirm an award, unless within the time limits hereinafter imposed grounds are urged for vacating or modifying or correcting the award, in which case the court shall proceed as provided in Sections 12 and 13.

§ 12.   Vacating an Award.

(a) Upon application of a party, the court shall vacate an award where:

(1) The award was procured by corruption, fraud or other undue means;

(2) There was evident partiality by an arbitrator appointed as a neutral or corruption in any of the arbitrators or misconduct prejudicing the rights of any party;

(3) The arbitrators exceeded their powers;

(4) The arbitrators refused to postpone the hearing upon sufficient cause being shown therefor or refused to hear evidence material to the controversy or otherwise so conducted the hearing, contrary to the provisions of Section 5, as to prejudice substantially the rights of a party; or

(5) There was no arbitration agreement and the issue was not adversely determined in proceedings under Section 2 and the party did not participate in the arbitration hearing without raising the objection; but the fact that the relief was such that it could not or would not be granted by a court of law or equity is not ground for vacating or refusing to confirm the award.

(b) An application under this Section shall be made within ninety days after delivery of a copy of the award to the applicant, except that, if predicated upon corruption, fraud or other undue means, it shall be made within ninety days after such grounds are known or should have been known.

(c) In vacating the award on grounds other than stated in clause (5) of Subsection (a) the court may order a rehearing before new arbitrators chosen as provided in the agreement, or in the absence thereof, by the court in accordance with Section 3, or if the award is vacated on grounds set forth in clauses (3) and (4) of Subsection (a) the court may order a rehearing before the arbitrators who made the award or their successors appointed in accordance with Section 3. The time within which the agreement requires the award to be made is applicable to the rehearing and commences from the date of the order.

(d) If the application to vacate is denied and no motion to modify or correct the award is pending, the court shall confirm the award. As amended Aug. 1956.

§ 13. Modification or Correction of Award.

(a) Upon application made within ninety days after delivery of a copy of the award to the applicant, the court shall modify or correct the award where:

(1) There was an evident miscalculation of figures or an evident mistake in the description of any person, thing or property referred to in the award;

(2) The arbitrators have awarded upon a matter not submitted to them and the award may be corrected without affecting the merits of the decision upon the issues submitted; or

(3) The award is imperfect in a matter of form, not affecting the merits of the controversy.

(b) If the application is granted, the court shall modify and correct the award so as to effect its intent and shall confirm the award as so modified and corrected. Otherwise, the court shall confirm the award as made.

(c) An application to modify or correct an award may be joined in the alternative with an application to vacate the award.

§ 14. Judgment or Decree on Award.

Upon the granting of an order confirming, modifying or correcting an award, judgment or decree shall be entered in conformity therewith and be enforced as any other judgment or decree. Costs of the application and of the proceedings subsequent thereto, and disbursements may be awarded by the court.

§ 15. Judgment Roll, Docketing.

(a) On entry of judgment or decree, the clerk shall prepare the judgment roll consisting, to the extent filed, of the following:

    (1) The agreement and each written extension of the time within which to make the award;

    (2) The award;

    (3) A copy of the order confirming, modifying or correcting the award; and

    (4) A copy of the judgment or decree.

  (b) The judgment or decree may be docketed as if rendered in an action.

§ 16. Applications to Court.

Except as otherwise provided, an application to the court under this act shall be by motion and shall be heard in the manner and upon the notice provided by law or rule of court for the making and hearing of motions. Unless the parties have agreed otherwise, notice of an initial application for an order shall be served in the manner provided by law for the service of a summons in an action.

§ 17. Court, Jurisdiction.

The term "court" means any court of competent jurisdiction of this State. The making of an agreement described in Section 1 providing for arbitration in this State confers jurisdiction on the court to enforce the agreement under this Act and to enter judgment on an award thereunder.

§ 18. Venue.

An initial application shall be made to the court of the [county] in which the agreement provides the arbitration hearing shall be held or, if the hearing has been held, in the county in which it was held. Otherwise the application shall be made in the [county] where the adverse party resides or has a place of business or, if he has no residence or place of business in this State, to the court of any [county]. All subsequent applications shall be made to the court hearing the initial application unless the court otherwise directs.

§ 19. Appeals.

  (a) An appeal may be taken from:

    (1) An order denying an application to compel arbitration made under Section 2;

    (2) An order granting an application to stay arbitration made under Section 2(b);

    (3) An order confirming or denying confirmation of an award;

    (4) An order modifying or correcting an award;

    (5) An order vacating an award without directing a rehearing; or

    (6) A judgment or decree entered pursuant to the provisions of this act.

  (b) The appeal shall be taken in the manner and to the same extent as from orders or judgments in a civil action.

§ 20.   Act Not Retroactive.

This act applies only to agreements made subsequent to the taking effect of this act.

§ 21.   Uniformity of Interpretation.

This act shall be so construed as to effectuate its general purpose to make uniform the law of those states which enact it.

§ 22.   Constitutionality.

If any provision of this act or the application thereof to any person or circumstance is held invalid, the invalidity shall not affect other provisions or applications of the act which can be given effect without the invalid provision or application, and to this end the provisions of this act are severable.

§ 23.   Short Title.

This act may be cited as the Uniform Arbitration Act.

§ 24.   Repeal.

All acts or parts of acts which are inconsistent with the provisions of this act are hereby repealed.

§ 25.   Time of Taking Effect.

This act shall take effect . . .

UNIFORM ARBITRATION ACT (2000)*

SECTION 1. DEFINITIONS.

In this [Act]:

(1) "Arbitration organization" means an association, agency, board, commission, or other entity that is neutral and initiates, sponsors, or administers an arbitration proceeding or is involved in the appointment of an arbitrator.

(2) "Arbitrator" means an individual appointed to render an award, alone or with others, in a controversy that is subject to an agreement to arbitrate.

(3) "Court" means [a court of competent jurisdiction in this State].

(4) "Knowledge" means actual knowledge.

(5) "Person" means an individual, corporation, business trust, estate, trust, partnership, limited liability company, association, joint venture, government; governmental subdivision, agency, or instrumentality; public corporation; or any other legal or commercial entity.

(6) "Record" means information that is inscribed on a tangible medium or that is stored in an electronic or other medium and is retrievable in perceivable form.

SECTION 2. NOTICE.

(a) Except as otherwise provided in this [Act], a person gives notice to another person by taking action that is reasonably necessary to inform the other person in ordinary course, whether or not the other person acquires knowledge of the notice.

(b) A person has notice if the person has knowledge of the notice or has received notice.

(c) A person receives notice when it comes to the person's attention or the notice is delivered at the person's place of residence or place of business, or at another location held out by the person as a place of delivery of such communications.

SECTION 3.   WHEN [ACT] APPLIES.

(a) This [Act] governs an agreement to arbitrate made on or after [the effective date of this [Act]].

(b) This [Act] governs an agreement to arbitrate made before [the effective date of this [Act]] if all the parties to the agreement or to the arbitration proceeding so agree in a record.

(c) On or after [a delayed date], this [Act] governs an agreement to arbitrate whenever made.

SECTION 4.   EFFECT OF AGREEMENT TO ARBITRATE; NONWAIVABLE PROVISIONS.

(a) Except as otherwise provided in subsections (b) and (c), a party to an agreement to arbitrate or to an arbitration proceeding may waive or, the parties may vary the effect of, the requirements of this [Act] to the extent permitted by law.

(b) Before a controversy arises that is subject to an agreement to arbitrate, a party to the agreement may not:

(1) waive or agree to vary the effect of the requirements of Section 5(a), 6(a), 8, 17(a), 17(b), 26, or 28;

(2) agree to unreasonably restrict the right under Section 9 to notice of the initiation of an arbitration proceeding;

(3) agree to unreasonably restrict the right under Section 12 to disclosure of any facts by a neutral arbitrator; or

(4) waive the right under Section 16 of a party to an agreement to arbitrate to be represented by a lawyer at any proceeding or hearing under this [Act], but an employer and a labor organization may waive the right to representation by a lawyer in a labor arbitration.

(c) A party to an agreement to arbitrate or arbitration proceeding may not waive, or the parties may not vary the effect of, the requirements of this section or Section 3(a) or (c), 7, 14, 18, 20(d) or (e), 22, 23, 24, 25(a) or (b), 29, 30, 31, or 32.

SECTION 5.   [APPLICATION] FOR JUDICIAL RELIEF.

(a) Except as otherwise provided in Section 28, an [application] for judicial relief under this [Act] must be made by [motion] to the court and heard in the manner provided by law or rule of court for making and hearing [motions].

(b) Unless a civil action involving the agreement to arbitrate is pending, notice of an initial [motion] to the court under this [Act] must be served in the manner provided by law for the service of a summons in a civil action. Otherwise, notice of the motion must be given in the manner provided by law or rule of court for serving [motions] in pending cases.

SECTION 6.   VALIDITY OF AGREEMENT TO ARBITRATE.

(a) An agreement contained in a record to submit to arbitration any existing or subsequent controversy arising between the parties to the agreement is valid, enforceable, and irrevocable except upon a ground that exists at law or in equity for the revocation of a contract.

(b) The court shall decide whether an agreement to arbitrate exists or a controversy is subject to an agreement to arbitrate.

(c) An arbitrator shall decide whether a condition precedent to arbitrability has been fulfilled and whether a contract containing a valid agreement to arbitrate is enforceable.

(d) If a party to a judicial proceeding challenges the existence of, or claims that a controversy is not subject to, an agreement to arbitrate, the arbitration proceeding may continue pending final resolution of the issue by the court, unless the court otherwise orders.

SECTION 7.   [MOTION] TO COMPEL OR STAY ARBITRATION.

(a) On [motion] of a person showing an agreement to arbitrate and alleging another person's refusal to arbitrate pursuant to the agreement:

(1) if the refusing party does not appear or does not oppose the [motion], the court shall order the parties to arbitrate; and

(2) if the refusing party opposes the [motion], the court shall proceed summarily to decide the issue and order the parties to arbitrate unless it finds that there is no enforceable agreement to arbitrate.

(b) On [motion] of a person alleging that an arbitration proceeding has been initiated or threatened but that there is no agreement to arbitrate, the court shall proceed summarily to decide the issue. If the court finds that there is an enforceable agreement to arbitrate, it shall order the parties to arbitrate.

(c) If the court finds that there is no enforceable agreement, it may not pursuant to subsection (a) or (b) order the parties to arbitrate.

(d) The court may not refuse to order arbitration because the claim subject to arbitration lacks merit or grounds for the claim have not been established.

(e) If a proceeding involving a claim referable to arbitration under an alleged agreement to arbitrate is pending in court, a [motion] under this section must be made in that court. Otherwise a [motion] under this section may be made in any court as provided in Section 27.

(f) If a party makes a [motion] to the court to order arbitration, the court on just terms shall stay any judicial proceeding that involves a claim alleged to be subject to the arbitration until the court renders a final decision under this section.

(g) If the court orders arbitration, the court on just terms shall stay any judicial proceeding that involves a claim subject to the arbitration. If a claim subject to the arbitration is severable, the court may limit the stay to that claim.

SECTION 8.   PROVISIONAL REMEDIES.

(a) Before an arbitrator is appointed and is authorized and able to act, the court, upon [motion] of a party to an arbitration proceeding and for good cause shown, may enter an order for provisional remedies to protect the effectiveness of the arbitration proceeding to the same extent and under the same conditions as if the controversy were the subject of a civil action.

(b) After an arbitrator is appointed and is authorized and able to act:

(1) the arbitrator may issue such orders for provisional remedies, including interim awards, as the arbitrator finds necessary to protect the effectiveness of the arbitration proceeding and to promote the fair and expeditious resolution of the controversy, to the same extent and under the same conditions as if the controversy were the subject of a civil action and

(2) a party to an arbitration proceeding may move the court for a provisional remedy only if the matter is urgent and the arbitrator is not able to act timely or the arbitrator cannot provide an adequate remedy.

(c) A party does not waive a right of arbitration by making a [motion] under subsection (a) or (b).

SECTION 9. INITIATION OF ARBITRATION.

(a) A person initiates an arbitration proceeding by giving notice in a record to the other parties to the agreement to arbitrate in the agreed manner between the parties or, in the absence of agreement, by certified or registered mail, return receipt requested and obtained, or by service as authorized for the commencement of a civil action. The notice must describe the nature of the controversy and the remedy sought.

(b) Unless a person objects for lack or insufficiency of notice under Section 15(c) not later than the beginning of the arbitration hearing, the person by appearing at the hearing waives any objection to lack of or insufficiency of notice.

SECTION 10. CONSOLIDATION OF SEPARATE ARBITRATION PROCEEDINGS.

(a) Except as otherwise provided in subsection (c), upon [motion] of a party to an agreement to arbitrate or to an arbitration proceeding, the court may order consolidation of separate arbitration proceedings as to all or some of the claims if:

(1) there are separate agreements to arbitrate or separate arbitration proceedings between the same persons or one of them is a party to a separate agreement to arbitrate or a separate arbitration proceeding with a third person;

(2) the claims subject to the agreements to arbitrate arise in substantial part from the same transaction or series of related transactions;

(3) the existence of a common issue of law or fact creates the possibility of conflicting decisions in the separate arbitration proceedings; and

(4) prejudice resulting from a failure to consolidate is not outweighed by the risk of undue delay or prejudice to the rights of or hardship to parties opposing consolidation.

(b) The court may order consolidation of separate arbitration proceedings as to some claims and allow other claims to be resolved in separate arbitration proceedings.

(c) The court may not order consolidation of the claims of a party to an agreement to arbitrate if the agreement prohibits consolidation.

SECTION 11. APPOINTMENT OF ARBITRATOR; SERVICE AS A NEUTRAL ARBITRATOR.

(a) If the parties to an agreement to arbitrate agree on a method for appointing an arbitrator, that method must be followed, unless the method fails. If the parties have not agreed on a method, the agreed method fails, or an arbitrator appointed fails or is unable to act and a successor has not been appointed, the court, on [motion] of a party to the arbitration proceeding, shall appoint the arbitrator. An arbitrator so appointed has all the powers of an arbitrator designated in the agreement to arbitrate or appointed pursuant to the agreed method.

(b) An individual who has a known, direct, and material interest in the outcome of the arbitration proceeding or a known, existing, and substantial relationship with a party may not serve as an arbitrator required by an agreement to be neutral.

SECTION 12.   DISCLOSURE BY ARBITRATOR.

(a) Before accepting appointment, an individual who is requested to serve as an arbitrator, after making a reasonable inquiry, shall disclose to all parties to the agreement to arbitrate and arbitration proceeding and to any other arbitrators any known facts that a reasonable person would consider likely to affect the impartiality of the arbitrator in the arbitration proceeding, including:

(1) a financial or personal interest in the outcome of the arbitration proceeding; and

(2) an existing or past relationship with any of the parties to the agreement to arbitrate or the arbitration proceeding, their counsel or representatives, a witness, or another arbitrator.

(b) An arbitrator has a continuing obligation to disclose to all parties to the agreement to arbitrate and arbitration proceeding and to any other arbitrators any facts that the arbitrator learns after accepting appointment which a reasonable person would consider likely to affect the impartiality of the arbitrator.

(c) If an arbitrator discloses a fact required by subsection (a) or (b) to be disclosed and a party timely objects to the appointment or continued service of the arbitrator based upon the fact disclosed, the objection may be a ground under Section 23(a)(2) for vacating an award made by the arbitrator.

(d) If the arbitrator did not disclose a fact as required by subsection (a) or (b), upon timely objection by a party, the court under Section 23(a)(2) may vacate an award.

(e) An arbitrator appointed as a neutral arbitrator who does not disclose a known, direct, and material interest in the outcome of the arbitration proceeding or a known, existing, and substantial relationship with a party is presumed to act with evident partiality under Section 23(a)(2).

(f) If the parties to an arbitration proceeding agree to the procedures of an arbitration organization or any other procedures for challenges to arbitrators before an award is made, substantial compliance with those procedures is a condition precedent to a [motion] to vacate an award on that ground under Section 23(a)(2).

SECTION 13.   ACTION BY MAJORITY.

If there is more than one arbitrator, the powers of an arbitrator must be exercised by a majority of the arbitrators, but all of them shall conduct the hearing under Section 15(c).

SECTION 14.   IMMUNITY OF ARBITRATOR; COMPETENCY TO TESTIFY; ATTORNEY'S FEES AND COSTS.

(a) An arbitrator or an arbitration organization acting in that capacity is immune from civil liability to the same extent as a judge of a court of this State acting in a judicial capacity.

(b) The immunity afforded by this section supplements any immunity under other law.

(c) The failure of an arbitrator to make a disclosure required by Section 12 does not cause any loss of immunity under this section.

(d) In a judicial, administrative, or similar proceeding, an arbitrator or representative of an arbitration organization is not competent to testify, and may not be required to produce records as to any statement, conduct, decision, or ruling occurring during the arbitration proceeding, to the same extent as a judge of a court of this State acting in a judicial capacity. This subsection does not apply:

(1) to the extent necessary to determine the claim of an arbitrator, arbitration organization, or representative of the arbitration organization against a party to the arbitration proceeding; or

(2) to a hearing on a [motion] to vacate an award under Section 23(a)(1) or (2) if the [movant] establishes prima facie that a ground for vacating the award exists.

(e) If a person commences a civil action against an arbitrator, arbitration organization, or representative of an arbitration organization arising from the services of the arbitrator, organization, or representative or if a person seeks to compel an arbitrator or a representative of an arbitration organization to testify or produce records in violation of subsection (d), and the court decides that the arbitrator, arbitration organization, or representative of an arbitration organization is immune from civil liability or that the arbitrator or representative of the organization is not competent to testify, the court shall award to the arbitrator, organization, or representative reasonable attorney's fees and other reasonable expenses of litigation.

SECTION 15.   ARBITRATION PROCESS.

(a) An arbitrator may conduct an arbitration in such manner as the arbitrator considers appropriate for a fair and expeditious disposition of the proceeding. The authority conferred upon the arbitrator includes the power to hold conferences with the parties to the arbitration proceeding before the hearing and, among other matters, determine the admissibility, relevance, materiality and weight of any evidence.

(b) An arbitrator may decide a request for summary disposition of a claim or particular issue:

(1) if all interested parties agree; or

(2) upon request of one party to the arbitration proceeding if that party gives notice to all other parties to the proceeding, and the other parties have a

reasonable opportunity to respond.

(c) If an arbitrator orders a hearing, the arbitrator shall set a time and place and give notice of the hearing not less than five days before the hearing begins. Unless a party to the arbitration proceeding makes an objection to lack or insufficiency of notice not later than the beginning of the hearing, the party's appearance at the hearing waives the objection. Upon request of a party to the arbitration proceeding and for good cause shown, or upon the arbitrator's own initiative, the arbitrator may adjourn the hearing from time to time as necessary but may not postpone the hearing to a time later than that fixed by the agreement to arbitrate for making the award unless the parties to the arbitration proceeding consent to a later date. The arbitrator may hear and decide the controversy upon the evidence produced although a party who was duly notified of the arbitration proceeding did not appear. The court, on request, may direct the arbitrator to conduct the hearing promptly and render a timely decision.

(d) At a hearing under subsection (c), a party to the arbitration proceeding has a right to be heard, to present evidence material to the controversy, and to cross-examine witnesses appearing at the hearing.

(e) If an arbitrator ceases or is unable to act during the arbitration proceeding, a replacement arbitrator must be appointed in accordance with Section 11 to continue the proceeding and to resolve the controversy.

SECTION 16. REPRESENTATION BY LAWYER.

A party to an arbitration proceeding may be represented by a lawyer.

SECTION 17. WITNESSES; SUBPOENAS; DEPOSITIONS; DISCOVERY.

(a) An arbitrator may issue a subpoena for the attendance of a witness and for the production of records and other evidence at any hearing and may administer oaths. A subpoena must be served in the manner for service of subpoenas in a civil action and, upon [motion] to the court by a party to the arbitration proceeding or the arbitrator, enforced in the manner for enforcement of subpoenas in a civil action.

(b) In order to make the proceedings fair, expeditious, and cost effective, upon request of a party to or a witness in an arbitration proceeding, an arbitrator may permit a deposition of any witness to be taken for use as evidence at the hearing, including a witness who cannot be subpoenaed for or is unable to attend a hearing. The arbitrator shall determine the conditions under which the deposition is taken.

(c) An arbitrator may permit such discovery as the arbitrator decides is appropriate in the circumstances, taking into account the needs of the parties to the arbitration proceeding and other affected persons and the desirability of making the proceeding fair, expeditious, and cost effective.

(d) If an arbitrator permits discovery under subsection (c), the arbitrator may order a party to the arbitration proceeding to comply with the arbitrator's discovery-related orders, issue subpoenas for the attendance of a witness and for the production of records and other evidence at a discovery proceeding, and take action against a noncomplying party to the extent a court could if the controversy were the subject of a civil action in this State.

(e) An arbitrator may issue a protective order to prevent the disclosure of privileged information, confidential information, trade secrets, and other information protected from disclosure to the extent a court could if the controversy were the subject of a civil action in this State.

(f) All laws compelling a person under subpoena to testify and all fees for attending a judicial proceeding, a deposition, or a discovery proceeding as a witness apply to an arbitration proceeding as if the controversy were the subject of a civil action in this State.

(g) The court may enforce a subpoena or discovery-related order for the attendance of a witness within this State and for the production of records and other evidence issued by an arbitrator in connection with an arbitration proceeding in another State upon conditions determined by the court so as to make the arbitration proceeding fair, expeditious, and cost effective. A subpoena or discovery-related order issued by an arbitrator in another State must be served in the manner provided by law for service of subpoenas in a civil action in this State and, upon [motion] to the court by a party to the arbitration proceeding or the arbitrator, enforced in the manner provided by law for enforcement of subpoenas in a civil action in this State.

SECTION 18. JUDICIAL ENFORCEMENT OF PREAWARD RULING BY ARBITRATOR.

If an arbitrator makes a preaward ruling in favor of a party to the arbitration proceeding, the party may request the arbitrator to incorporate the ruling into an award under Section 19. A prevailing party may make a [motion] to the court for an expedited order to confirm the award under Section 22, in which case the court shall summarily decide the [motion]. The court shall issue an order to confirm the award unless the court vacates, modifies, or corrects the award under Section 23 or 24.

SECTION 19. AWARD.

(a) An arbitrator shall make a record of an award. The record must be signed or otherwise authenticated by any arbitrator who concurs with the award. The arbitrator or the arbitration organization shall give notice of the award, including a copy of the award, to each party to the arbitration proceeding.

(b) An award must be made within the time specified by the agreement to arbitrate or, if not specified therein, within the time ordered by the court. The court may extend or the parties to the arbitration proceeding may agree in a record to extend the time. The court or the parties may do so within or after the time specified or ordered. A party waives any objection that an award was not timely made unless the party gives notice of the objection to the arbitrator before receiving notice of the award.

SECTION 20. CHANGE OF AWARD BY ARBITRATOR.

(a) On [motion] to an arbitrator by a party to an arbitration proceeding, the arbitrator may modify or correct an award:

(1) upon a ground stated in Section 24(a)(1) or (3);

(2) because the arbitrator has not made a final and definite award upon a claim submitted by the parties to the arbitration proceeding; or

(3) to clarify the award.

(b) A [motion] under subsection (a) must be made and notice given to all parties within 20 days after the movant receives notice of the award.

(c) A party to the arbitration proceeding must give notice of any objection to the [motion] within 10 days after receipt of the notice.

(d) If a [motion] to the court is pending under Section 22, 23, or 24, the court may submit the claim to the arbitrator to consider whether to modify or correct the award:

(1) upon a ground stated in Section 24(a)(1) or (3);

(2) because the arbitrator has not made a final and definite award upon a claim submitted by the parties to the arbitration proceeding; or

(3) to clarify the award.

(e) An award modified or corrected pursuant to this section is subject to Sections 19(a), 22, 23, and 24.

SECTION 21.   REMEDIES; FEES AND EXPENSES OF ARBITRATION PROCEEDING.

(a) An arbitrator may award punitive damages or other exemplary relief if such an award is authorized by law in a civil action involving the same claim and the evidence produced at the hearing justifies the award under the legal standards otherwise applicable to the claim.

(b) An arbitrator may award reasonable attorney's fees and other reasonable expenses of arbitration if such an award is authorized by law in a civil action involving the same claim or by the agreement of the parties to the arbitration proceeding.

(c) As to all remedies other than those authorized by subsections (a) and (b), an arbitrator may order such remedies as the arbitrator considers just and appropriate under the circumstances of the arbitration proceeding. The fact that such a remedy could not or would not be granted by the court is not a ground for refusing to confirm an award under Section 22 or for vacating an award under Section 23.

(d) An arbitrator's expenses and fees, together with other expenses, must be paid as provided in the award.

(e) If an arbitrator awards punitive damages or other exemplary relief under subsection (a), the arbitrator shall specify in the award the basis in fact justifying and the basis in law authorizing the award and state separately the amount of the punitive damages or other exemplary relief.

SECTION 22.   CONFIRMATION OF AWARD.

After a party to an arbitration proceeding receives notice of an award, the party may make a [motion] to the court for an order confirming the award at which time the court shall issue a confirming order unless the award is modified or corrected pursuant to Section 20 or 24 or is vacated pursuant to Section 23.

SECTION 23. VACATING AWARD.

(a) Upon [motion] to the court by a party to an arbitration proceeding, the court shall vacate an award made in the arbitration proceeding if:

(1) the award was procured by corruption, fraud, or other undue means;

(2) there was:

(A) evident partiality by an arbitrator appointed as a neutral arbitrator;

(B) corruption by an arbitrator; or

(C) misconduct by an arbitrator prejudicing the rights of a party to the arbitration proceeding;

(3) an arbitrator refused to postpone the hearing upon showing of sufficient cause for postponement, refused to consider evidence material to the controversy, or otherwise conducted the hearing contrary to Section 15, so as to prejudice substantially the rights of a party to the arbitration proceeding;

(4) an arbitrator exceeded the arbitrator's powers;

(5) there was no agreement to arbitrate, unless the person participated in the arbitration proceeding without raising the objection under Section 15(c) not later than the beginning of the arbitration hearing; or

(6) the arbitration was conducted without proper notice of the initiation of an arbitration as required in Section 9 so as to prejudice substantially the rights of a party to the arbitration proceeding.

(b) A [motion] under this section must be filed within 90 days after the [movant] receives notice of the award pursuant to Section 19 or within 90 days after the [movant] receives notice of a modified or corrected award pursuant to Section 20, unless the [movant] alleges that the award was procured by corruption, fraud, or other undue means, in which case the [motion] must be made within 90 days after the ground is known or by the exercise of reasonable care would have been known by the [movant].

(c) If the court vacates an award on a ground other than that set forth in subsection (a)(5), it may order a rehearing. If the award is vacated on a ground stated in subsection (a)(1) or (2), the rehearing must be before a new arbitrator. If the award is vacated on a ground stated in subsection (a)(3), (4), or (6), the rehearing may be before the arbitrator who made the award or the arbitrator's successor. The arbitrator must render the decision in the rehearing within the same time as that provided in Section 19(b) for an award.

(d) If the court denies a [motion] to vacate an award, it shall confirm the award unless a [motion] to modify or correct the award is pending.

SECTION 24. MODIFICATION OR CORRECTION OF AWARD.

(a) Upon [motion] made within 90 days after the [movant] receives notice of the award pursuant to Section 19 or within 90 days after the [movant] receives notice of a modified or corrected award pursuant to Section 20, the court shall modify or correct the award if:

(1) there was an evident mathematical miscalculation or an evident mistake in the description of a person, thing, or property referred to in the award;

(2) the arbitrator has made an award on a claim not submitted to the arbitrator and the award may be corrected without affecting the merits of the decision upon the claims submitted; or

(3) the award is imperfect in a matter of form not affecting the merits of the decision on the claims submitted.

(b) If a [motion] made under subsection (a) is granted, the court shall modify or correct and confirm the award as modified or corrected. Otherwise, unless a motion to vacate is pending, the court shall confirm the award.

(c) A [motion] to modify or correct an award pursuant to this section may be joined with a [motion] to vacate the award.

SECTION 25.   JUDGMENT ON AWARD; ATTORNEY'S FEES AND LITIGATION EXPENSES.

(a) Upon granting an order confirming, vacating without directing a rehearing, modifying, or correcting an award, the court shall enter a judgment in conformity therewith. The judgment may be recorded, docketed, and enforced as any other judgment in a civil action.

(b) A court may allow reasonable costs of the [motion] and subsequent judicial proceedings.

(c) On [application] of a prevailing party to a contested judicial proceeding under Section 22, 23, or 24, the court may add reasonable attorney's fees and other reasonable expenses of litigation incurred in a judicial proceeding after the award is made to a judgment confirming, vacating without directing a rehearing, modifying, or correcting an award.

SECTION 26.   JURISDICTION.

(a) A court of this State having jurisdiction over the controversy and the parties may enforce an agreement to arbitrate.

(b) An agreement to arbitrate providing for arbitration in this State confers exclusive jurisdiction on the court to enter judgment on an award under this [Act].

SECTION 27.   VENUE.

A [motion] pursuant to Section 5 must be made in the court of the [county] in which the agreement to arbitrate specifies the arbitration hearing is to be held or, if the hearing has been held, in the court of the [county] in which it was held. Otherwise, the [motion] may be made in the court of any [county] in which an adverse party resides or has a place of business or, if no adverse party has a residence or place of business in this State, in the court of any [county] in this State.

All subsequent [motions] must be made in the court hearing the initial [motion] unless the court otherwise directs.

SECTION 28. APPEALS.

(a) An appeal may be taken from:

(1) an order denying a [motion] to compel arbitration;

(2) an order granting a [motion] to stay arbitration;

(3) an order confirming or denying confirmation of an award;

(4) an order modifying or correcting an award;

(5) an order vacating an award without directing a rehearing; or

(6) a final judgment entered pursuant to this [Act].

(b) An appeal under this section must be taken as from an order or a judgment in a civil action.

SECTION 29. UNIFORMITY OF APPLICATION AND CONSTRUCTION.

In applying and construing this uniform act, consideration must be given to the need to promote uniformity of the law with respect to its subject matter among States that enact it.

SECTION 30. RELATIONSHIP TO ELECTRONIC SIGNATURES IN GLOBAL AND NATIONAL COMMERCE ACT.

The provisions of this Act governing the legal effect, validity, or enforceability of electronic records or electronic signatures, and of contracts performed with the use of such records or signatures conform to the requirements of Section 102 of the Electronic Signatures in Global and National Commerce Act.

SECTION 31. EFFECTIVE DATE.

This [Act] takes effect on [effective date].

SECTION 32. REPEAL.

Effective on [delayed date should be the same as that in Section 3(c)], the [Uniform Arbitration Act] is repealed.

SECTION 33. SAVINGS CLAUSE.

This [Act] does not affect an action or proceeding commenced or right accrued before this [Act] takes effect. Subject to Section 3 of this [Act], an arbitration agreement made before the effective date of this [Act] is governed by the [Uniform Arbitration Act].

SELECTED PROVISIONS OF THE CALIFORNIA CODE OF CIVIL PROCEDURE

§ 1281.85. Ethics standards

(a) Beginning July 1, 2002, a person serving as a neutral arbitrator pursuant to an arbitration agreement shall comply with the ethics standards for arbitrators adopted by the Judicial Council pursuant to this section. The Judicial Council shall adopt ethical standards for all neutral arbitrators effective July 1, 2002. These standards shall be consistent with the standards established for arbitrators in the judicial arbitration program and may expand but may not limit the disclosure and disqualification requirements established by this chapter. The standards shall address the disclosure of interests, relationships, or affiliations that may constitute conflicts of interest, including prior service as an arbitrator or other dispute resolution neutral entity, disqualifications, acceptance of gifts, and establishment of future professional relationships.

(b) Subdivision (a) does not apply to an arbitration conducted pursuant to the terms of a public or private sector collective bargaining agreement.

(c) The ethics requirements and standards of this chapter are nonnegotiable and shall not be waived.

§ 1281.9. Disclosure required of proposed nominee; Disqualification as neutral arbitrator

(a) In any arbitration pursuant to an arbitration agreement, when a person is to serve as a neutral arbitrator, the proposed neutral arbitrator shall disclose all matters that could cause a person aware of the facts to reasonably entertain a doubt that the proposed neutral arbitrator would be able to be impartial, including all of the following:

(1) The existence of any ground specified in Section 170.1 for disqualification of a judge. For purposes of paragraph (8) of subdivision (a) of Section 170.1, the proposed neutral arbitrator shall disclose whether or not he or she has a current arrangement concerning prospective employment or other compensated service as a dispute resolution neutral or is participating in, or, within the last two years, has participated in, discussions regarding such prospective employment or service with a party to the proceeding.

(2) Any matters required to be disclosed by the ethics standards for neutral arbitrators adopted by the Judicial Council pursuant to this chapter.

(3) The names of the parties to all prior or pending noncollective bargaining cases in which the proposed neutral arbitrator served or is serving as a party arbitrator for any party to the arbitration proceeding or for a lawyer for a party and the results of each case arbitrated to conclusion, including the date of the arbitration award, identification of the prevailing party, the names of the parties' attorneys and the amount of monetary damages awarded, if any. In order to preserve confidentiality, it shall be sufficient to give the name of any party who is not a party to the pending arbitration as "claimant" or "respondent" if the party is an individual and not a business or corporate entity.

(4) The names of the parties to all prior or pending noncollective bargaining cases involving any party to the arbitration or lawyer for a party for which the proposed neutral arbitrator served or is serving as neutral arbitrator, and the results of each case arbitrated to conclusion, including the date of the arbitration award, identification of the prevailing party, the names of the parties' attorneys and the amount of monetary damages awarded, if any. In order to preserve confidentiality, it shall be sufficient to give the name of any party not a party to the pending arbitration as "claimant" or "respondent" if the party is an individual and not a business or corporate entity.

(5) Any attorney-client relationship the proposed neutral arbitrator has or had with any party or lawyer for a party to the arbitration proceeding.

(6) Any professional or significant personal relationship the proposed neutral arbitrator or his or her spouse or minor child living in the household has or has had with any party to the arbitration proceeding or lawyer for a party.

(b) Subject only to the disclosure requirements of law, the proposed neutral arbitrator shall disclose all matters required to be disclosed pursuant to this section to all parties in writing within 10 calendar days of service of notice of the proposed nomination or appointment.

(c) For purposes of this section, "lawyer for a party" includes any lawyer or law firm currently associated in the practice of law with the lawyer hired to represent a party.

(d) For purposes of this section, "prior cases" means noncollective bargaining cases in which an arbitration award was rendered within five years prior to the date of the proposed nomination or appointment.

(e) For purposes of this section, "any arbitration" does not include an arbitration conducted pursuant to the terms of a public or private sector collective bargaining agreement.

§ 1281.92. Prohibited activities by private arbitration company

(a) No private arbitration company may administer a consumer arbitration, or provide any other services related to a consumer arbitration, if the company has, or within the preceding year has had, a financial interest, as defined in Section 170.5, in any party or attorney for a party.

(b) No private arbitration company may administer a consumer arbitration, or provide any other services related to a consumer arbitration, if any party or attorney for a party has, or within the preceding year has had, any type of financial interest in the private arbitration company.

(c) This section shall operate only prospectively so as not to prohibit the administration of consumer arbitrations on the basis of financial interests held prior to January 1, 2003.

(d) This section applies to all consumer arbitration agreements subject to this article, and to all consumer arbitration proceedings conducted in California.

(e) This section shall become operative on January 1, 2003.

§ 1281.96. Publication of consumer arbitration information by private arbitration company

(a) Except as provided in paragraph (2) of subdivision (b), any private arbitration company that administers or is otherwise involved in, a consumer arbitration, shall collect, publish at least quarterly, and make available to the public in a computer-searchable format, which shall be accessible at the Internet Web site of the private arbitration company, if any, and on paper upon request, all of the following information regarding each consumer arbitration within the preceding five years:

(1) The name of the nonconsumer party, if the nonconsumer party is a corporation or other business entity.

(2) The type of dispute involved, including goods, banking, insurance, health care, employment, and, if it involves employment, the amount of the employee's annual wage divided into the following ranges: less than one hundred thousand dollars ($100,000), one hundred thousand dollars ($100,000) to two hundred fifty thousand dollars ($250,000), inclusive, and over two hundred fifty thousand dollars ($250,000).

(3) Whether the consumer or nonconsumer party was the prevailing party.

(4) On how many occasions, if any, the nonconsumer party has previously been a party in an arbitration or mediation administered by the private arbitration company.

(5) Whether the consumer party was represented by an attorney.

(6) The date the private arbitration company received the demand for arbitration, the date the arbitrator was appointed, and the date of disposition by the arbitrator or private arbitration company.

(7) The type of disposition of the dispute, if known, including withdrawal, abandonment, settlement, award after hearing, award without hearing, default, or dismissal without hearing.

(8) The amount of the claim, the amount of the award, and any other relief granted, if any.

(9) The name of the arbitrator, his or her total fee for the case, and the percentage of the arbitrator's fee allocated to each party.

(b) (1) If the information required by subdivision (a) is provided by the private arbitration company in a computer-searchable format at the company's Internet Web site and may be downloaded without any fee, the company may charge the actual cost of copying to any person who requests the information on paper. If the information required by subdivision (a) is not accessible by the Internet, the company shall provide that information without charge to any person who requests the information on paper.

(2) Notwithstanding paragraph (1), a private arbitration company that receives funding pursuant to Chapter 8 (commencing with Section 465) of Division 1 of the Business and Professions Code, and that administers or conducts fewer than 50 consumer arbitrations per year may collect and publish the information required

by subdivision (a) semiannually, provide the information only on paper, and charge the actual cost of copying.

(c) This section shall apply to any consumer arbitration commenced on or after January 1, 2003.

(d) No private arbitration company shall have any liability for collecting, publishing, or distributing the information required by this section.

§ 1284.3.   Fees and costs charged to consumer by private arbitration company

(a) No neutral arbitrator or private arbitration company shall administer a consumer arbitration under any agreement or rule requiring that a consumer who is a party to the arbitration pay the fees and costs incurred by an opposing party if the consumer does not prevail in the arbitration, including, but not limited to, the fees and costs of the arbitrator, provider organization, attorney, or witnesses.

(b) (1) All fees and costs charged to or assessed upon a consumer party by a private arbitration company in a consumer arbitration, exclusive of arbitrator fees, shall be waived for an indigent consumer. For the purposes of this section, "indigent consumer" means a person having a gross monthly income that is less than 300 percent of the federal poverty guidelines. Nothing in this section shall affect the ability of a private arbitration company to shift fees that would otherwise be charged or assessed upon a consumer party to a nonconsumer party.

(2) Prior to requesting or obtaining any fee, a private arbitration company shall provide written notice of the right to obtain a waiver of fees to a consumer or prospective consumer in a manner calculated to bring the matter to the attention of a reasonable consumer, including, but not limited to, prominently placing a notice in its first written communication to the consumer and in any invoice, bill, submission form, fee schedule, rules, or code of procedure.

(3) Any consumer requesting a waiver of fees or costs may establish his or her eligibility by making a declaration under oath on a form provided to the consumer by the private arbitration company for signature stating his or her monthly income and the number of persons living in his or her household. No private arbitration company may require a consumer to provide any further statement or evidence of indigence.

(4) Any information obtained by a private arbitration company about a consumer's identity, financial condition, income, wealth, or fee waiver request shall be kept confidential and may not be disclosed to any adverse party or any nonparty to the arbitration, except a private arbitration company may not keep confidential the number of waiver requests received or granted, or the total amount of fees waived.

(c) This section applies to all consumer arbitration agreements subject to this article, and to all consumer arbitration proceedings conducted in California.

§ 1286.2.   Grounds to vacate award; Petition to vacate award

(a) Subject to Section 1286.4, the court shall vacate the award if the court determines any of the following:

(1) The award was procured by corruption, fraud or other undue means.

(2) There was corruption in any of the arbitrators.

(3) The rights of the party were substantially prejudiced by misconduct of a neutral arbitrator.

(4) The arbitrators exceeded their powers and the award cannot be corrected without affecting the merits of the decision upon the controversy submitted.

(5) The rights of the party were substantially prejudiced by the refusal of the arbitrators to postpone the hearing upon sufficient cause being shown therefor or by the refusal of the arbitrators to hear evidence material to the controversy or by other conduct of the arbitrators contrary to the provisions of this title.

(6) An arbitrator making the award either:

(A) failed to disclose within the time required for disclosure a ground for disqualification of which the arbitrator was then aware; or

(B) was subject to disqualification upon grounds specified in Section 1281.91 but failed upon receipt of timely demand to disqualify himself or herself as required by that provision. However, this subdivision does not apply to arbitration proceedings conducted under a collective bargaining agreement between employers and employees or between their respective representatives.

. . .

§ 170.1.   Grounds for disqualification

(a) A judge shall be disqualified if any one or more of the following are true:

(1) (A) The judge has personal knowledge of disputed evidentiary facts concerning the proceeding.

(B) A judge shall be deemed to have personal knowledge within the meaning of this paragraph if the judge, or the spouse of the judge, or a person within the third degree of relationship to either of them, or the spouse of such a person is to the judge's knowledge likely to be a material witness in the proceeding.

(2) (A) The judge served as a lawyer in the proceeding, or in any other proceeding involving the same issues he or she served as a lawyer for a party in the present proceeding or gave advice to a party in the present proceeding upon a matter involved in the action or proceeding.

(B) A judge shall be deemed to have served as a lawyer in the proceeding if within the past two years:

(i) A party to the proceeding, or an officer, director, or trustee of a party, was a client of the judge when the judge was in the private practice of law or a client of a lawyer with whom the judge was associated in the private practice of law.

(ii) A lawyer in the proceeding was associated in the private practice of law with the judge.

(C) A judge who served as a lawyer for, or officer of, a public agency that is a party to the proceeding shall be deemed to have served as a lawyer in the proceeding if he or she personally advised or in any way represented the public agency concerning the factual or legal issues in the proceeding.

(3) (A) The judge has a financial interest in the subject matter in a proceeding or in a party to the proceeding.

(B) A judge shall be deemed to have a financial interest within the meaning of this paragraph if:

(i) A spouse or minor child living in the household has a financial interest.

(ii) The judge or the spouse of the judge is a fiduciary who has a financial interest.

(C) A judge has a duty to make reasonable efforts to inform himself or herself about his or her personal and fiduciary interests and those of his or her spouse and the personal financial interests of children living in the household.

(4) The judge, or the spouse of the judge, or a person within the third degree of relationship to either of them, or the spouse of such a person is a party to the proceeding or an officer, director, or trustee of a party.

(5) A lawyer or a spouse of a lawyer in the proceeding is the spouse, former spouse, child, sibling, or parent of the judge or the judge's spouse or if such a person is associated in the private practice of law with a lawyer in the proceeding.

(6) (A) For any reason:

(i) The judge believes his or her recusal would further the interests of justice.

(ii) The judge believes there is a substantial doubt as to his or her capacity to be impartial.

(iii) A person aware of the facts might reasonably entertain a doubt that the judge would be able to be impartial.

(B) Bias or prejudice toward a lawyer in the proceeding may be grounds for disqualification.

(7) By reason of permanent or temporary physical impairment, the judge is unable to properly perceive the evidence or is unable to properly conduct the proceeding.

(8) (A) The judge has a current arrangement concerning prospective employment or other compensated service as a dispute resolution neutral or is participating in, or, within the last two years has participated in, discussions regarding prospective employment or service as a dispute resolution neutral, or has been engaged in that employment or service, and any of the following applies:

(i) The arrangement is, or the prior employment or discussion was, with a party to the proceeding.

(ii) The matter before the judge includes issues relating to the enforcement of either an agreement to submit a dispute to an alternative dispute resolution process or an award or other final decision by a dispute resolution neutral.

(iii) The judge directs the parties to participate in an alternative dispute resolution process in which the dispute resolution neutral will be an individual or entity with whom the judge has the arrangement, has previously been employed or served, or is discussing or has discussed the employment or service.

(iv) The judge will select a dispute resolution neutral or entity to conduct an alternative dispute resolution process in the matter before the judge, and among those available for selection is an individual or entity with whom the judge has the arrangement, with whom the judge has previously been employed or served, or with whom the judge is discussing or has discussed the employment or service.

(B) For the purposes of this paragraph, all of the following apply:

(i) "Participating in discussions" or "has participated in discussion" means that the judge solicited or otherwise indicated an interest in accepting or negotiating possible employment or service as an alternative dispute resolution neutral, or responded to an unsolicited statement regarding, or an offer of, that employment or service by expressing an interest in that employment or service, making an inquiry regarding the employment or service, or encouraging the person making the statement or offer to provide additional information about that possible employment or service. If a judge's response to an unsolicited statement regarding, a question about, or offer of, prospective employment or other compensated service as a dispute resolution neutral is limited to responding negatively, declining the offer, or declining to discuss that employment or service, that response does not constitute participating in discussions.

(ii) "Party" includes the parent, subsidiary, or other legal affiliate of any entity that is a party and is involved in the transaction, contract, or facts that gave rise to the issues subject to the proceeding.

(iii) "Dispute resolution neutral" means an arbitrator, mediator, temporary judge appointed under Section 21 of Article VI of the California Constitution, referee appointed under Section 638 or 639, special master, neutral evaluator, settlement officer, or settlement facilitator.

(9) (A) The judge has received a contribution in excess of one thousand five hundred dollars ($1500) from a party or lawyer in the proceeding, and either of the following applies:

(i) The contribution was received in support of the judge's last election, if the last election was within the last six years.

(ii) The contribution was received in anticipation of an upcoming election.

(B) Notwithstanding subparagraph (A), the judge shall be disqualified based on a contribution of a lesser amount if subparagraph (A) of paragraph (6) applies.

(C) The judge shall disclose any contribution from a party or lawyer in a matter that is before the court that is required to be reported under subdivision (f) of Section 84211 of the Government Code, even if the amount would not require disqualification under this paragraph. The manner of disclosure shall be the same as that provided in Canon 3E of the Code of Judicial Ethics.

(D) Notwithstanding paragraph (1) of subdivision (b) of Section 170.3, the disqualification required under this paragraph may be waived by the party that did not make the contribution unless there are other circumstances that would prohibit a waiver pursuant to paragraph (2) of subdivision (b) of Section 170.3.

(b) A judge before whom a proceeding was tried or heard shall be disqualified from participating in any appellate review of that proceeding.

(c) At the request of a party or on its own motion an appellate court shall consider whether in the interests of justice it should direct that further proceedings be heard before a trial judge other than the judge whose judgment or order was reviewed by the appellate court.

JUDICIAL COUNCIL OF CALIFORNIA, ETHICS STANDARDS FOR NEUTRAL ARBITRATORS IN CONTRACTUAL ARBITRATION

Effective January 1, 2003

Standard 1. Purpose, intent, and construction

(a) These standards are adopted under the authority of Code of Civil Procedure section 1281.85 and establish the minimum standards of conduct for neutral arbitrators who are subject to these standards. They are intended to guide the conduct of arbitrators, to inform and protect participants in arbitration, and to promote public confidence in the arbitration process.

(b) For arbitration to be effective there must be broad public confidence in the integrity and fairness of the process. Arbitrators are responsible to the parties, the other participants, and the public for conducting themselves in accordance with these standards so as to merit that confidence.

(c) These standards are to be construed and applied to further the purpose and intent expressed in subdivisions (a) and (b) and in conformance with all applicable law.

(d) These standards are not intended to affect any existing civil cause of action or create any new civil cause of action.

Comment to Standard 1

Code of Civil Procedure section 1281.85 provides that, beginning July 1, 2002, a person serving as a neutral arbitrator pursuant to an arbitration agreement shall comply with the ethics standards for arbitrators adopted by the Judicial Council pursuant to that section.

While the grounds for vacating an arbitration award are established by statute, not these standards, an arbitrator's violation of these standards may, under some circumstances, fall within one of those statutory grounds. (See Code Civ. Proc., § 1286.2.) A failure to disclose within the time required for disclosure a ground for disqualification of which the arbitrator was then aware is a ground for vacatur of the arbitrator's award. (See Code Civ. Proc., § 1286.2(a)(6)(A).) Violations of other obligations under these standards may also constitute grounds for vacating an arbitration award under section 1286.2(a)(3) if "the rights of the party were substantially prejudiced" by the violation.

While vacatur may be an available remedy for violation of these standards, these standards are not intended to affect any civil cause of action that may currently exist nor to create any new civil cause of action. These standards are also not intended to establish a ceiling on what is considered good practice in arbitration or to discourage efforts to educate arbitrators about best practices.

Standard 2. Definitions

As used in these standards:

(a) **Arbitrator and neutral arbitrator**

(1) "Arbitrator" and "neutral arbitrator" mean any arbitrator who is subject to these standards and who is to serve impartially, whether selected or appointed:

(A) Jointly by the parties or by the arbitrators selected by the parties;

(B) By the court, when the parties or the arbitrators selected by the parties fail to select an arbitrator who was to be selected jointly by them; or

(C) By a dispute resolution provider organization, under an agreement of the parties.

(2) Where the context includes events or acts occurring before an appointment is final, "arbitrator" and "neutral arbitrator" include a person who has been served with notice of a proposed nomination or appointment.

(b) "Applicable law" means constitutional provisions, statutes, decisional law, California Rules of Court, and other statewide rules or regulations that apply to arbitrators who are subject to these standards.

(c) "Conclusion of the arbitration" means the following:

(1) When the arbitrator is disqualified or withdraws or the case is settled or dismissed before the arbitrator makes an award, the date on which the arbitrator's appointment is terminated;

(2) When the arbitrator makes an award and no party makes a timely application to the arbitrator to correct the award, the final date for making an application to the arbitrator for correction; or

(3) When a party makes a timely application to the arbitrator to correct the award, the date on which the arbitrator serves a corrected award or a denial on each party, or the date on which denial occurs by operation of law.

(d) "Consumer arbitration" means an arbitration conducted under a predispute arbitration provision contained in a contract that meets the criteria listed in paragraphs (1) through (3) below. "Consumer arbitration" excludes arbitration proceedings conducted under or arising out of public or private sector labor-relations laws, regulations, charter provisions, ordinances, statutes, or agreements.

(1) The contract is with a consumer party, as defined in these standards;

(2) The contract was drafted by or on behalf of the nonconsumer party; and

(3) The consumer party was required to accept the arbitration provision in the contract.

(e) "Consumer party" is a party to an arbitration agreement who, in the context of that arbitration agreement, is any of the following:

(1) An individual who seeks or acquires, including by lease, any goods or services primarily for personal, family, or household purposes including, but not limited to, financial services, insurance, and other goods and services as defined in section 1761 of the Civil Code;

(2) An individual who is an enrollee, a subscriber, or insured in a health-care service plan within the meaning of section 1345 of the Health and Safety Code or health-care insurance plan within the meaning of section 106 of the Insurance Code;

(3) An individual with a medical malpractice claim that is subject to the arbitration agreement; or

(4) An employee or an applicant for employment in a dispute arising out of or relating to the employee's employment or the applicant's prospective employment that is subject to the arbitration agreement.

(f) "Dispute resolution neutral" means a temporary judge appointed under article VI, section 21 of the California Constitution, a referee appointed under Code of Civil Procedure section 638 or 639, an arbitrator, a neutral evaluator, a special master, a mediator, a settlement officer, or a settlement facilitator.

(g) "Dispute resolution provider organization" and "provider organization" mean any nongovernmental entity that, or individual who, coordinates, administers, or provides the services of two or more dispute resolution neutrals.

(h) "Domestic partner" means a domestic partner as defined in Family Code section 297.

(i) "Financial interest" means a financial interest within the meaning of Code of Civil Procedure section 170.5.

(j) "Gift" means a gift as defined in Code of Civil Procedure section 170.9(l).

(k) "Honoraria" means honoraria as defined in Code of Civil Procedure section 170.9(h) and (i).

(l) "Lawyer in the arbitration" means the lawyer hired to represent a party in the arbitration.

(m) "Lawyer for a party" means the lawyer hired to represent a party in the arbitration and any lawyer or law firm currently associated in the practice of law with the lawyer hired to represent a party in the arbitration.

(n) "Member of the arbitrator's immediate family" means the arbitrator's spouse or domestic partner and any minor child living in the arbitrator's household.

(o) "Member of the arbitrator's extended family" means the parents, grandparents, great-grandparents, children, grandchildren, great-grandchildren, siblings, uncles, aunts, nephews, and nieces of the arbitrator or the arbitrator's spouse or domestic partner or the spouse of such person.

(p)   Party

(1) "Party" means a party to the arbitration agreement:

(A) Who seeks to arbitrate a controversy pursuant to the agreement;

(B) Against whom such arbitration is sought; or

(C) Who is made a party to such arbitration by order of a court or the arbitrator upon such party's application, upon the application of any other party to the arbitration, or upon the arbitrator's own determination.

(2) "Party" includes the representative of a party, unless the context requires a different meaning.

(q) "Party-arbitrator" means an arbitrator selected unilaterally by a party.

(r) "Private practice of law" means private practice of law as defined in Code of Civil Procedure section 170.5.

(s) "Significant personal relationship" includes a close personal friendship.

Comment to Standard 2

Subdivision (a). The definition of "arbitrator" and "neutral arbitrator" in this standard is intended to include all arbitrators who are to serve in a neutral and impartial manner and to exclude unilaterally selected arbitrators.

Subdivisions (l) and (m). Arbitrators should take special care to note that there are two different terms used in these standards to refer to lawyers who represent parties in the arbitration. In particular, arbitrators should note that the term "lawyer for a party" includes any lawyer or law firm currently associated in the practice of law with the lawyer hired to represent a party in the arbitration.

Subdivision (p)(2). While this provision generally permits an arbitrator to provide required information or notices to a party's attorney as that party's representative, a party's attorney should not be treated as a "party" for purposes of identifying matters that an arbitrator must disclose under standards 7 or 8, as those standards contain separate, specific requirements concerning the disclosure of relationships with a party's attorney.

Other terms that may be pertinent to these standards are defined in Code of Civil Procedure section 1280.

Standard 3. Application and effective date

(a) Except as otherwise provided in this standard and standard 8, these standards apply to all persons who are appointed to serve as neutral arbitrators on or after July 1, 2002, in any arbitration under an arbitration agreement, if:

(1) The arbitration agreement is subject to the provisions of title 9 of part III of the Code of Civil Procedure (commencing with section 1280); or

(2) The arbitration hearing is to be conducted in California.

(b) These standards do not apply to:

(1) Party arbitrators, as defined in these standards; or

(2) Any arbitrator serving in:

(A) An international arbitration proceeding subject to the provisions of title 9.3 of part III of the Code of Civil Procedure;

(B) A judicial arbitration proceeding subject to the provisions of chapter 2.5 of title 3 of part III of the Code of Civil Procedure;

(C) An attorney-client fee arbitration proceeding subject to the provisions of article 13 of chapter 4 of division 3 of the Business and Professions Code;

(D) An automobile warranty dispute resolution process certified under California Code of Regulations title 16, division 33.1;

(E) An arbitration of a workers' compensation dispute under Labor Code sections 5270 through 5277;

(F) An arbitration conducted by the Workers' Compensation Appeals Board under Labor Code section 5308;

(G) An arbitration of a complaint filed against a contractor with the Contractors State License Board under Business and Professions Code sections 7085 through 7085.7; or

(H) An arbitration conducted under or arising out of public or private sector labor-relations laws, regulations, charter provisions, ordinances, statutes, or agreements.

(c) Persons who are serving in arbitrations in which they were appointed to serve as arbitrators before July 1, 2002, are not subject to these standards in those arbitrations. Persons who are serving in arbitrations in which they were appointed to serve as arbitrators before January 1, 2003, are not subject to standard 8 in those arbitrations.

Comment to Standard 3

With the exception of standard 8, these standards apply to all neutral arbitrators appointed on or after July 1, 2002, who meet the criteria of subdivision (a). Arbitration provider organizations, although not themselves subject to these standards, should be aware of them when performing administrative functions that involve arbitrators who are subject to these standards. A provider organization's policies and actions should facilitate, not impede, compliance with the standards by arbitrators who are affiliated with the provider organization.

Standard 4. Duration of duty

(a) Except as otherwise provided in these standards, an arbitrator must comply with these ethics standards from acceptance of appointment until the conclusion of the arbitration.

(b) If, after the conclusion of the arbitration, a case is referred back to the arbitrator for reconsideration or rehearing, the arbitrator must comply with these ethics standards from the date the case is referred back to the arbitrator until the arbitration is again concluded.

Standard 5. General duty

An arbitrator must act in a manner that upholds the integrity and fairness of the arbitration process. He or she must maintain impartiality toward all participants in the arbitration at all times.

Comment to Standard 5

This standard establishes the overarching ethical duty of arbitrators. The remaining standards should be construed as establishing specific requirements that implement this overarching duty in particular situations.

Maintaining impartiality toward all participants during all stages of the arbitration is central to upholding the integrity and fairness of the arbitration. An arbitrator must perform his or her duties impartially, without bias or prejudice, and must not, in performing these duties, by words or conduct manifest partiality, bias, or prejudice, including but not limited to partiality, bias, or prejudice based upon race, sex, religion, national origin, disability, age, sexual orientation, socioeconomic status, or the fact that a party might select the arbitrator to serve as an arbitrator in additional cases. After accepting appointment, an arbitrator should avoid entering into any relationship or acquiring any interest that might reasonably create the appearance of partiality, bias, or prejudice. An arbitrator does not become partial, biased, or prejudiced simply by having acquired knowledge of the parties, the issues or arguments, or the applicable law.

Standard 6. Duty to refuse appointment

Notwithstanding any contrary request, consent, or waiver by the parties, a proposed arbitrator must decline appointment if he or she is not able to be impartial.

Standard 7. Disclosure

(a) Intent

This standard is intended to identify the matters that must be disclosed by a person nominated or appointed as an arbitrator. To the extent that this standard addresses matters that are also addressed by statute, it is intended to include those statutory disclosure requirements, not to eliminate, reduce, or otherwise limit them.

(b) General provisions For purposes of this standard:

(1) *Collective bargaining cases excluded* The terms "cases" and "any arbitration" do not include collective bargaining cases or arbitrations conducted under or arising out of collective bargaining agreements between employers and employees or between their respective representatives.

(2) *Offers of employment or professional relationship* If an arbitrator has disclosed to the parties in an arbitration that he or she will entertain offers of employment or of professional relationships from a party or lawyer for a party while the arbitration is pending as required by subdivision (b) of standard 12, the arbitrator is not required to disclose to the parties in that arbitration any such offer from a party or lawyer for a party that he or she subsequently receives or accepts while that arbitration is pending.

(3) *Names of parties in cases* When making disclosures about other pending or prior cases, in order to preserve confidentiality, it is sufficient to give the name of any party who is not a party to the pending arbitration as "claimant" or "respondent" if the party is an individual and not a business or corporate entity.

(c) Time and manner of disclosure Within ten calendar days of service of

notice of the proposed nomination or appointment, a proposed arbitrator must disclose to all parties in writing all matters listed in subdivisions (d) and (e) of this standard of which the arbitrator is then aware. If an arbitrator subsequently becomes aware of a matter that must be disclosed under either subdivision (d) or (e) of this standard, the arbitrator must disclose that matter to the parties in writing within 10 calendar days after the arbitrator becomes aware of the matter.

(d) Required disclosures A person who is nominated or appointed as an arbitrator must disclose all matters that could cause a person aware of the facts to reasonably entertain a doubt that the proposed arbitrator would be able to be impartial, including all of the following:

(1) *Family relationships with party* The arbitrator or a member of the arbitrator's immediate or extended family is a party, a party's spouse or domestic partner, or an officer, director, or trustee of a party.

(2) *Family relationships with lawyer in the arbitration* The arbitrator, or the spouse, former spouse, domestic partner, child, sibling, or parent of the arbitrator or the arbitrator's spouse or domestic partner is:

(A) A lawyer in the arbitration;

(B) The spouse or domestic partner of a lawyer in the arbitration; or

(C) Currently associated in the private practice of law with a lawyer in the arbitration.

(3) *Significant personal relationship with party or lawyer for a party* The arbitrator or a member of the arbitrator's immediate family has or has had a significant personal relationship with any party or lawyer for a party.

(4) *Service as arbitrator for a party or lawyer for party*

(A) The arbitrator is serving or, within the preceding five years, has served:

(i) As a neutral arbitrator in another prior or pending noncollective bargaining case involving a party to the current arbitration or a lawyer for a party.

(ii) As a party-appointed arbitrator in another prior or pending noncollective bargaining case for either a party to the current arbitration or a lawyer for a party.

(iii) As a neutral arbitrator in another prior or pending noncollective bargaining case in which he or she was selected by a person serving as a party-appointed arbitrator in the current arbitration.

(B) Case information

If the arbitrator is serving or has served in any of the capacities listed under (A), he or she must disclose:

(i) The names of the parties in each prior or pending case and, where applicable, the name of the attorney representing the party in the current arbitration who is involved in the pending case, who was involved in the prior case, or whose current associate is involved in the pending case or was involved in the prior case.

(ii) The results of each prior case arbitrated to conclusion, including the date of the arbitration award, identification of the prevailing party, the amount of monetary damages awarded, if any, and the names of the parties' attorneys.

(C)   Summary of case information

If the total number of the cases disclosed under (A) is greater than five, the arbitrator must provide a summary of these cases that states:

(i) The number of pending cases in which the arbitrator is currently serving in each capacity;

(ii) The number of prior cases in which the arbitrator previously served in each capacity;

(iii) The number of prior cases arbitrated to conclusion; and

(iv) The number of such prior cases in which the party to the current arbitration, the party represented by the lawyer for a party in the current arbitration or the party represented by the party arbitrator in the current arbitration was the prevailing party.

(5)   *Compensated service as other dispute resolution neutral* The arbitrator is serving or has served as a dispute resolution neutral other than an arbitrator in another pending or prior noncollective bargaining case involving a party or lawyer for a party and the arbitrator received or expects to receive any form of compensation for serving in this capacity.

(A)   Time frame

For purposes of this paragraph (5), "prior case" means any case in which the arbitrator concluded his or her service as a dispute resolution neutral within two years before the date of the arbitrator's proposed nomination or appointment, but does not include any case in which the arbitrator concluded his or her service before January 1, 2002.

(B)   Case information

If the arbitrator is serving or has served in any of the capacities listed under this paragraph (5), he or she must disclose:

(i) The names of the parties in each prior or pending case and, where applicable, the name of the attorney in the current arbitration who is involved in the pending case, who was involved in the prior case, or whose current associate is involved in the pending case or was involved in the prior case;

(ii) The dispute resolution neutral capacity (mediator, referee, etc.) in which the arbitrator is serving or served in the case; and

(iii) In each such case in which the arbitrator rendered a decision as a temporary judge or referee, the date of the decision, the prevailing party, the amount of monetary damages awarded, if any, and the names of the parties' attorneys.

(C)   Summary of case information

If the total number of cases disclosed under this paragraph (5) is greater than five, the arbitrator must also provide a summary of the cases that states:

(i) The number of pending cases in which the arbitrator is currently serving in each capacity;

(ii) The number of prior cases in which the arbitrator previously served in each capacity;

(iii) The number of prior cases in which the arbitrator rendered a decision as a temporary judge or referee; and

(iv) The number of such prior cases in which the party to the current arbitration or the party represented by the lawyer for a party in the current arbitration was the prevailing party.

(6)   *Current arrangements for prospective neutral service* Whether the arbitrator has any current arrangement with a party concerning prospective employment or other compensated service as a dispute resolution neutral or is participating in or, within the last two years, has participated in discussions regarding such prospective employment or service with a party.

(7)   *Attorney-client relationships* Any attorney-client relationship the arbitrator has or has had with a party or lawyer for a party. Attorney-client relationships include the following:

(A) An officer, a director, or a trustee of a party is or, within the preceding two years, was a client of the arbitrator in the arbitrator's private practice of law or a client of a lawyer with whom the arbitrator is or was associated in the private practice of law;

(B) In any other proceeding involving the same issues, the arbitrator gave advice to a party or a lawyer in the arbitration concerning any matter involved in the arbitration; and

(C) The arbitrator served as a lawyer for or as an officer of a public agency which is a party and personally advised or in any way represented the public agency concerning the factual or legal issues in the arbitration.

(8)   *Other professional relationships* Any other professional relationship not already disclosed under paragraphs (2)-(7) that the arbitrator or a member of the arbitrator's immediate family has or has had with a party or lawyer for a party, including the following:

(A) The arbitrator was associated in the private practice of law with a lawyer in the arbitration within the last two years;

(B) The arbitrator or a member of the arbitrator's immediate family is or, within the preceding two years, was an employee of or an expert witness or a consultant for a party; and

(C) The arbitrator or a member of the arbitrator's immediate family is or, within the preceding two years, was an employee of or an expert witness or a consultant for a lawyer in the arbitration.

(9) *Financial interests in party* The arbitrator or a member of the arbitrator's immediate family has a financial interest in a party.

(10) *Financial interests in subject of arbitration* The arbitrator or a member of the arbitrator's immediate family has a financial interest in the subject matter of the arbitration.

(11) *Affected interest* The arbitrator or a member of the arbitrator's immediate family has an interest that could be substantially affected by the outcome of the arbitration.

(12) *Knowledge of disputed facts* The arbitrator or a member of the arbitrator's immediate or extended family has personal knowledge of disputed evidentiary facts relevant to the arbitration. A person who is likely to be a material witness in the proceeding is deemed to have personal knowledge of disputed evidentiary facts concerning the proceeding.

(13) *Membership in organizations practicing discrimination* The arbitrator's membership in any organization that practices invidious discrimination on the basis of race, sex, religion, national origin, or sexual orientation. Membership in a religious organization, an official military organization of the United States, or a nonprofit youth organization need not be disclosed unless it would interfere with the arbitrator's proper conduct of the proceeding or would cause a person aware of the fact to reasonably entertain a doubt concerning the arbitrator's ability to act impartially.

(14) Any other matter that:

(A) Might cause a person aware of the facts to reasonably entertain a doubt that the arbitrator would be able to be impartial;

(B) Leads the proposed arbitrator to believe there is a substantial doubt as to his or her capacity to be impartial, including, but not limited to, bias or prejudice toward a party, lawyer, or law firm in the arbitration; or

(C) Otherwise leads the arbitrator to believe that his or her disqualification will further the interests of justice.

(e) **Inability to conduct or timely complete proceedings** In addition to the matters that must be disclosed under subdivision (d), an arbitrator must also disclose:

(1) If the arbitrator is not able to properly perceive the evidence or properly conduct the proceedings because of a permanent or temporary physical impairment; and

(2) Any constraints on his or her availability known to the arbitrator that will interfere with his or her ability to commence or complete the arbitration in a timely manner.

(f) **Continuing duty** An arbitrator's duty to disclose the matters described in subdivisions (d) and (e) of this standard is a continuing duty, applying from service of the notice of the arbitrator's proposed nomination or appointment until the conclusion of the arbitration proceeding.

Comment to Standard 7

This standard requires arbitrators to disclose to all parties, in writing within 10 days of service of notice of their proposed nomination or appointment, all matters they are aware of at that time that could cause a person aware of the facts to reasonably entertain a doubt that the proposed arbitrator would be able to be impartial and to disclose any additional such matters within 10 days of becoming aware of them.

Timely disclosure to the parties is the primary means of ensuring the impartiality of an arbitrator. It provides the parties with the necessary information to make an informed selection of an arbitrator by disqualifying or ratifying the proposed arbitrator following disclosure. See also standard 10, concerning disclosure and disqualification requirements relating to concurrent and subsequent employment or professional relationships between an arbitrator and a party or attorney in the arbitration. A party may disqualify an arbitrator for failure to comply with statutory disclosure obligations (see Code Civ. Proc., § 1281.91(a)). Failure to disclose, within the time required for disclosure, a ground for disqualification of which the arbitrator was then aware is a ground for *vacatur* of the arbitrator's award (see Code Civ. Proc., § 1286.2(a)(6)(A)).

The arbitrator's overarching duty under this standard, which mirrors the duty set forth in Code of Civil Procedure section 1281.9, is to inform parties about matters that could cause a person aware of the facts to reasonably entertain a doubt that the proposed arbitrator would be able to be impartial. While the remaining subparagraphs of (d) require the disclosure of specific interests, relationships, or affiliations, these are only examples of common matters that could cause a person aware of the facts to reasonably entertain a doubt that the arbitrator would be able to be impartial. The absence of the particular interests, relationships, or affiliations listed in the subparagraphs does not necessarily mean that there is no matter that could reasonably raise a question about the arbitrator's ability to be impartial and that therefore must be disclosed. An arbitrator must make determinations concerning disclosure on a case-by-case basis, applying the general criteria for disclosure under paragraph (d).

Code of Civil Procedure section 1281.85 specifically requires that the ethical standards adopted by the Judicial Council address the disclosure of interests, relationships, or affiliations that may constitute conflicts of interest, including prior service as an arbitrator or other dispute resolution neutral entity. Section 1281.85 further provides that the standards "shall be consistent with the standards established for arbitrators in the judicial arbitration program and may expand but may not limit the disclosure and disqualification requirements established by this chapter [chapter 2 of title 9 of part III, Code of Civil Procedure, sections 1281–1281.95]."

Code of Civil Procedure section 1281.9 already establishes detailed requirements concerning disclosures by arbitrators, including a specific requirement that arbitrators disclose the existence of any ground specified in Code of Civil Procedure section 170.1 for disqualification of a judge. This standard does not eliminate or otherwise limit those requirements; in large part, it simply consolidates and integrates those existing statutory disclosure requirements by topic area. This standard does, however, expand upon or clarify the existing statutory disclosure requirements in the following ways:

- Requiring arbitrators to disclose to the parties any matter about which they become aware after the time for making an initial disclosure has expired, within 10 calendar days after the arbitrator becomes aware of the matter (subdivision (f)).

- Expanding required disclosures about the relationships or affiliations of an arbitrator's family members to include those of an arbitrator's domestic partner (subdivisions (d)(1) and (2); see also definitions of immediate and extended family in standard 2).

- Requiring arbitrators, in addition to making statutorily required disclosures regarding prior service as an arbitrator for a party or attorney for a party, to disclose prior services both as neutral arbitrator selected by a party arbitrator in the current arbitration and as any other type of dispute resolution neutral for a party or attorney in the arbitration (e.g., temporary judge, mediator, or referee) (subdivisions (d)(4)(C) and (5)).

- Requiring the arbitrator to disclose if he or she or a member of his or her immediate family is or was an employee, expert witness, or consultant for a party or a lawyer in the arbitration (subdivisions (d)(8)(A) and (B)).

- Requiring the arbitrator to disclose if he or she or a member of his or her immediate family has an interest that could be substantially affected by the outcome of the arbitration (subdivision (d)(11)).

- If a disclosure includes information about five or more cases, requiring arbitrators to provide a summary of that information (subdivisions (d)(4) and (5)).

- Requiring arbitrators to disclose membership in organizations that practice invidious discrimination on the basis of race, sex, religion, national origin, or sexual orientation (subdivision (d)(13)).

- Requiring the arbitrator to disclose any constraints on his or her availability known to the arbitrator that will interfere with his or her ability to commence or complete the arbitration in a timely manner (subdivision (d)).

- Clarifying that the duty to make disclosures is a continuing obligation, requiring disclosure of matters that were not known at the time of nomination or appointment but that become known afterward (subdivision (e)).

It is good practice for an arbitrator to ask each participant to make an effort to disclose any matters that may affect the arbitrator's ability to be impartial.

Standard 8. Additional disclosures in consumer arbitrations administered by a provider organization

(a) General provisions

(1) *Reliance on information provided by provider organization* Except as to the information in (c)(1), an arbitrator may rely on information supplied by the

administering provider organization in making the disclosures required by this standard. If the information that must be disclosed is available on the Internet, the arbitrator may comply with the obligation to disclose this information by providing the Internet address at which the information is located and notifying the party that the arbitrator will supply hard copies of this information upon request.

(2) *Reliance on representation that not a consumer arbitration* An arbitrator is not required to make the disclosures required by this standard if he or she reasonably believes that the arbitration is not a consumer arbitration based on reasonable reliance on a consumer party's representation that the arbitration is not a consumer arbitration.

(b) Additional disclosures required In addition to the disclosures required under standard 7, in a consumer arbitration as defined in standard 2 in which a dispute resolution provider organization is coordinating, administering, or providing the arbitration services, a person who is nominated or appointed as an arbitrator on or after January 1, 2003 must disclose the following within the time and in the same manner as the disclosures required under standard 7(c):

(1) *Relationships between the provider organization and party or lawyer in arbitration* Any significant past, present, or currently expected financial or professional relationship or affiliation between the administering dispute resolution provider organization and a party or lawyer in the arbitration. Information that must be disclosed under this standard includes:

(A) A party, a lawyer in the arbitration, or a law firm with which a lawyer in the arbitration is currently associated is a member of the provider organization.

(B) Within the preceding two years the provider organization has received a gift, bequest, or favor from a party, a lawyer in the arbitration, or a law firm with which a lawyer in the arbitration is currently associated.

(C) The provider organization has entered into, or the arbitrator currently expects that the provider organization will enter into, an agreement or relationship with any party or lawyer in the arbitration or a law firm with which a lawyer in the arbitration is currently associated under which the provider organization will administer, coordinate, or provide dispute resolution services in other non-collective bargaining matters or will provide other consulting services for that party, lawyer, or law firm.

(D) The provider organization is coordinating, administering, or providing dispute resolution services or has coordinated, administered, or provided such services in another pending or prior noncollective bargaining case in which a party or lawyer in the arbitration was a party or a lawyer. For purposes of this paragraph, "prior case" means a case in which the dispute resolution neutral affiliated with the provider organization concluded his or her service within the two years before the date of the arbitrator's proposed nomination or appointment, but does not include any case in which the dispute resolution neutral concluded his or her service before July 1, 2002.

(2) *Case information* If the provider organization is acting or has acted in any of the capacities described in paragraph (1)(D), the arbitrator must disclose:

(A) The names of the parties in each prior or pending case and, where applicable, the name of the attorney in the current arbitration who is involved in the pending case or who was involved in the prior case;

(B) The type of dispute resolution services (arbitration, mediation, reference, etc.) coordinated, administered, or provided by the provider organization in the case; and

(C) In each prior case in which a dispute resolution neutral affiliated with the provider organization rendered a decision as an arbitrator, a temporary judge appointed under article VI, § 4 of the California Constitution, or a referee appointed under Code of Civil Procedure sections 638 or 639, the date of the decision, the prevailing party, the amount of monetary damages awarded, if any, and the names of the parties' attorneys.

(3) *Summary of case information* If the total number of cases disclosed under paragraph (1)(D) is greater than five, the arbitrator must also provide a summary of these cases that states:

(A) The number of pending cases in which the provider organization is currently providing each type of dispute resolution services;

(B) The number of prior cases in which the provider organization previously provided each type of dispute resolution services;

(C) The number of such prior cases in which a neutral affiliated with the provider organization rendered a decision as an arbitrator, a temporary judge, or a referee; and

(D) The number of prior cases in which the party to the current arbitration or the party represented by the lawyer in the current arbitration was the prevailing party.

(c) **Relationship between provider organization and arbitrator.** If a relationship or affiliation is disclosed under paragraph (b), the arbitrator must also provide information about the following:

(1) Any financial relationship or affiliation the arbitrator has with the provider organization other than receiving referrals of cases, including whether the arbitrator has a financial interest in the provider organization or is an employee of the provider organization;

(2) The provider organization's process and criteria for recruiting, screening, and training the panel of arbitrators from which the arbitrator in this case is to be selected;

(3) The provider organization's process for identifying, recommending, and selecting potential arbitrators for specific cases; and

(4) Any role the provider organization plays in ruling on requests for disqualification of the arbitrator.

(d) Effective date The provisions of this standard take effect on January 1, 2003. Persons who are serving in arbitrations in which they were appointed to serve as arbitrators before January 1, 2003, are not subject to this standard in those pending arbitrations.

Comment to Standard 8

This standard only applies in consumer arbitrations in which a dispute resolution provider organization is administering the arbitration. Like standard 7, this standard expands upon the existing statutory disclosure requirements. Code of Civil Procedure section 1281.95 requires arbitrators in certain construction defect arbitrations to make disclosures concerning relationships between their employers or arbitration services and the parties in the arbitration. This standard requires arbitrators in all consumer arbitrations to disclose any financial or professional relationship between the administering provider organization and any party, attorney, or law firm in the arbitration and, if any such relationship exists, then the arbitrator must also disclose his or her relationship with the dispute resolution provider organization. This standard does not require an arbitrator to disclose if the provider organization has a financial interest in a party or lawyer in the arbitration or if a party or lawyer in the arbitration has a financial interest in the provider organization because provider organizations are prohibited under Code of Civil Procedure section 1281.92 from administering any consumer arbitration where any such relationship exists.

Subdivision (b). Currently expected relationships or affiliations that must be disclosed include all relationships or affiliations that the arbitrator, at the time the disclosure is made, expects will be formed. For example, if the arbitrator knows that the administering provider organization has agreed in concept to enter into a business relationship with a party, but they have not yet signed a written agreement formalizing that relationship, this would be a "currently expected" relationship that the arbitrator would be required to disclose.

Standard 9. Arbitrators' duty to inform themselves about matters to be disclosed

(a) General duty to inform him or herself A person who is nominated or appointed as an arbitrator must make a reasonable effort to inform himself or herself of matters that must be disclosed under standards 7 and 8.

(b) Obligation regarding extended family An arbitrator can fulfill the obligation under this standard to inform himself or herself of relationships or other matters involving his or her extended family and former spouse that are required to be disclosed under standard 7 by:

(1) Seeking information about these relationships and matters from the members of his or her immediate family and any members of his or her extended family living in his or her household; and

(2) Declaring in writing that he or she has made the inquiry in (1).

(c) Obligation regarding relationships with associates of lawyer in the arbitration An arbitrator can fulfill the obligation under this standard to inform himself or herself of relationships with any lawyer associated in the practice of law with the lawyer in the arbitration that are required to be disclosed under standard 7 by:

(1) Informing the lawyer in the arbitration, in writing, of all such relationships within the arbitrator's knowledge and asking the lawyer if the lawyer is aware of any other such relationships;

(2) Declaring in writing that he or she has made the inquiry in (1) and attaching to the declaration copies of his or her inquiry and any response from the lawyer in the arbitration.

(d)   Obligation regarding service as a neutral other than an arbitrator before July 1, 2002 An arbitrator can fulfill the obligation under this standard to inform himself or herself of his or her service as a dispute resolution neutral other than as an arbitrator in cases that commenced prior to July 1, 2002 by:

(1) Asking any dispute resolution provider organization that administered those prior services for this information; and

(2) Declaring in writing that he or she has made the inquiry in (1) and attaching to this declaration copies of his or her inquiry and any response from the provider organization.

(e)   Obligation regarding relationships with provider organization An arbitrator can fulfill his or her obligation under this standard to inform himself or herself of the information that is required to be disclosed under standard 8 by:

(1) Asking the dispute resolution provider organization for this information; and

(2) Declaring in writing that he or she has made the inquiry in (1) and attaching to this declaration copies of his or her inquiry and any response from the provider organization.

Comment to Standard 9

This standard expands arbitrators' existing duty of reasonable inquiry that applies with respect to financial interests under Code of Civil Procedure section 170.1(a)(3), to require arbitrators to make a reasonable effort to inform themselves about all matters that must be disclosed. This standard also clarifies what constitutes a reasonable effort by an arbitrator to inform himself or herself about specified matters, including relationships or other matters concerning his or her extended family and relationships with attorneys associated in the practice of law with the attorney in the arbitration (such as associates encompassed within the term "lawyer for a party").

Standard 10. Disqualification

(a) An arbitrator is disqualified if:

(1) The arbitrator fails to comply with his or her obligation to make disclosures and a party serves a notice of disqualification in the manner and within the time specified in Code of Civil Procedure section 1281.91;

(2) The arbitrator complies with his or her obligation to make disclosures

within 10 calendar days of service of notice of the proposed nomination or appointment and, based on that disclosure, a party serves a notice of disqualification in the manner and within the time specified in Code of Civil Procedure section 1281.91;

(3) The arbitrator makes a required disclosure more than 10 calendar days after service of notice of the proposed nomination or appointment and, based on that disclosure, a party serves a notice of disqualification in the manner and within the time specified in Code of Civil Procedure section 1281.91; or

(4) A party becomes aware that an arbitrator has made a material omission or material misrepresentation in his or her disclosure and, within 15 days after becoming aware of the omission or misrepresentation and within the time specified in Code of Civil Procedure section1281.91(c), the party serves a notice of disqualification that clearly describes the material omission or material misrepresentation and how and when the party became aware of this omission or misrepresentation; or

(5) If any ground specified in Code of Civil Procedure section 170.1 exists and the party makes a demand that the arbitrator disqualify himself or herself in the manner and within the time specified in Code of Civil Procedure section 1281.91(d).

(b) For purposes of this standard, "obligation to make disclosure" means an arbitrator's obligation to make disclosures under standards 7 or 8 or Code of Civil Procedure section 1281.9.

(c) Notwithstanding any contrary request, consent, or waiver by the parties, an arbitrator must disqualify himself or herself if he or she concludes at any time during the arbitration that he or she is not able to conduct the arbitration impartially.

Comment to Standard 10

Code of Civil Procedure section 1281.91 already establishes requirements concerning disqualification of arbitrators. This standard does not eliminate or otherwise limit those requirements or change existing authority or procedures for challenging an arbitrator's failure to disqualify himself or herself. The provisions of subdivisions (a)(1), (2), and (5) restate existing disqualification procedures under section 1281.91; (b) and (d) when an arbitrator makes, or fails to make, initial disclosures or where a section 170.1 ground exists. The provisions of subdivisions (a)(3) and (4) clarify the requirements relating to disqualification based on disclosure made by the arbitrator after appointment or based on the discovery by the party of a material omission or misrepresentation in the arbitrator's disclosure.

Standard 11. Duty to refuse gift, bequest, or favor

(a) An arbitrator must not, under any circumstances, accept a gift, bequest, favor, or honoraria from a party or any other person or entity whose interests are reasonably likely to come before the arbitrator in the arbitration.

(b) From service of notice of appointment or appointment until two years after the conclusion of the arbitration, an arbitrator must not, under any circumstances, accept a gift, bequest, favor, or honoraria from a party or any other person or entity whose interests have come before the arbitrator in the arbitration.

(c) An arbitrator must discourage members of his or her family residing in his or her household from accepting a gift, bequest, favor, or honoraria that the arbitrator would be prohibited from accepting under subdivisions (a) or (b).

(d) This standard does not prohibit an arbitrator from demanding or receiving a fee for services or expenses.

Comment to Standard 11

Gifts and favors do not include any rebate or discount made available in the regular course of business to members of the public.

Standard 12. Duties and limitations regarding future professional relationships or employment

(a) **Offers as lawyer, expert witness, or consultant** From the time of appointment until the conclusion of the arbitration, an arbitrator must not entertain or accept any offers of employment or new professional relationships as a lawyer, an expert witness, or a consultant from a party or a lawyer for a party in the pending arbitration.

(b) **Offers for other employment or professional relationships** In addition to the disclosures required by standards 7 and 8, within ten calendar days of service of notice of the proposed nomination or appointment, a proposed arbitrator must disclose to all parties in writing if, while that arbitration is pending, he or she will entertain offers of employment or new professional relationships in any capacity other than as a lawyer, expert witness, or consultant from a party or a lawyer for a party, including offers to serve as a dispute resolution neutral in another case. A party may disqualify the arbitrator based on this disclosure by serving a notice of disqualification in the manner and within the time specified in Code of Civil Procedure section 1281.91(b).

(c) **Acceptance of offers prohibited unless intent disclosed** If an arbitrator fails to make the disclosure required by subdivision (b) of this standard, from the time of appointment until the conclusion of the arbitration the arbitrator must not entertain or accept any such offers of employment or new professional relationships, including offers to serve as a dispute resolution neutral.

(d) **Relationships and use of confidential information related to the arbitrated case** An arbitrator must not at any time:

(1) Without the informed written consent of all parties, enter into any professional relationship or accept any professional employment as a lawyer, an expert witness, or a consultant relating to the case arbitrated; or

(2) Without the informed written consent of the party, enter into any professional relationship or accept employment in another matter in which information that he or she has received in confidence from a party by reason of serving as an arbitrator in a case is material.

Standard 13. Conduct of proceeding

(a) An arbitrator must conduct the arbitration fairly, promptly, and diligently and in accordance with the applicable law relating to the conduct of arbitration proceedings.

(b) In making the decision, an arbitrator must not be swayed by partisan interests, public clamor, or fear of criticism.

Comment to Standard 13

Subdivision (a). The arbitrator's duty to dispose of matters promptly and diligently must not take precedence over the arbitrator's duty to dispose of matters fairly.

Conducting the arbitration in a procedurally fair manner includes conducting a balanced process in which each party is given an opportunity to participate. When one but not all parties are unrepresented, an arbitrator must ensure that the party appearing without counsel has an adequate opportunity to be heard and involved. Conducting the arbitration promptly and diligently requires expeditious management of all stages of the proceeding and concluding the case as promptly as the circumstances reasonably permit. During an arbitration, an arbitrator may discuss the issues, arguments, and evidence with the parties or their counsel, make interim rulings, and otherwise control or direct the arbitration. This standard is not intended to restrict these activities.

The arbitrator's duty to uphold the integrity and fairness of the arbitration process includes an obligation to make reasonable efforts to prevent delaying tactics, harassment of any participant, or other abuse of the arbitration process. It is recognized, however, that the arbitrator's reasonable efforts may not successfully control all conduct of the participants.

For the general law relating to the conduct of arbitration proceedings, see chapter 3 of title 9 of part III of the Code of Civil Procedure, sections 1282–1284.2, relating to the conduct of arbitration proceedings. See also Code of Civil Procedure section 1286.2 concerning an arbitrator's unreasonable refusal to grant a continuance as grounds for *vacatur* of the award.

Standard 14. Ex parte communications

(a) An arbitrator must not initiate, permit, or consider any ex parte communications or consider other communications made to the arbitrator outside the presence of all of the parties concerning a pending or impending arbitration, except as permitted by this standard, by agreement of the parties, or by applicable law.

(b) An arbitrator may communicate with a party in the absence of other parties about administrative matters, such as setting the time and place of hearings or making other arrangements for the conduct of the proceedings, as long as the arbitrator reasonably believes that the communication will not result in a procedural or tactical advantage for any party. When such a discussion occurs, the arbitrator must promptly inform the other parties of the communication and must give the other parties an opportunity to respond before making any final determination concerning the matter discussed.

(c) An arbitrator may obtain the advice of a disinterested expert on the subject matter of the arbitration if the arbitrator notifies the parties of the person consulted and the substance of the advice and affords the parties a reasonable opportunity to respond.

Comment to Standard 14

See also Code of Civil Procedure sections 1282.2(e) regarding the arbitrator's authority to hear a matter when a party fails to appear and 1282.2(g) regarding the procedures that must be followed if an arbitrator intends to base an award on information not obtained at the hearing.

Standard 15. Confidentiality

(a) An arbitrator must not use or disclose information that he or she received in confidence by reason of serving as an arbitrator in a case to gain personal advantage. This duty applies from acceptance of appointment and continues after the conclusion of the arbitration.

(b) An arbitrator must not inform anyone of the award in advance of the time that the award is given to all parties. This standard does not prohibit an arbitrator from providing all parties with a tentative or draft decision for review or from providing an award to an assistant or to the provider organization that is coordinating, administering, or providing the arbitration services in the case for purposes of copying and distributing the award to all parties.

Standard 16. Compensation

(a) An arbitrator must not charge any fee for services or expenses that is in any way contingent on the result or outcome of the arbitration.

(b) Before accepting appointment, an arbitrator, a dispute resolution provider organization, or another person or entity acting on the arbitrator's behalf must inform all parties in writing of the terms and conditions of the arbitrator's compensation. This information must include any basis to be used in determining fees and any special fees for cancellation, research and preparation time, or other purposes.

Standard 17. Marketing

(a) An arbitrator must be truthful and accurate in marketing his or her services and must not make any representation that directly or indirectly implies favoritism or a specific outcome. An arbitrator must ensure that his or her personal marketing activities and any activities carried out on his or her behalf, including any activities of a provider organization with which the arbitrator is affiliated, comply with this requirement.

(b) An arbitrator must not solicit business from a participant in the arbitration while the arbitration is pending.

Comment to Standard 17

Subdivision (b). This provision is not intended to prohibit an arbitrator from accepting another arbitration from a party or attorney in the arbitration while the first matter is pending, as long as the arbitrator complies with the provisions of standard 12 and there was no express solicitation of this business by the arbitrator.

UNCITRAL MODEL LAW ON INTERNATIONAL COMMERCIAL ARBITRATION

(United Nations documents A/40/17, Annex I and A/61/17, Annex I)

(As adopted by the United Nations Commission on International Trade Law on 21 June 1985 and as amended by the United Nations Commission on International Trade Law on 7 July 2006)

CHAPTER I   GENERAL PROVISIONS

Article 1.   Scope of application

(1) This Law applies to international commercial[2] arbitration, subject to any agreement in force between this State and any other State or States.

(2) The provisions of this Law, except articles 8, 9, 17 H, 17 I, 17 J, 35 and 36, apply only if the place of arbitration is in the territory of this State.

(3) An arbitration is international if:

(a) the parties to an arbitration agreement have, at the time of the conclusion of that agreement, their places of business in different States; or

(b) one of the following places is situated outside the State in which the parties have their places of business:

(i) the place of arbitration if determined in, or pursuant to, the arbitration agreement;

(ii) any place where a substantial part of the obligations of the commercial relationship is to be performed or the place with which the subject-matter of the dispute is most closely connected; or

(c) the parties have expressly agreed that the subject-matter of the arbitration agreement relates to more than one country.

(4) For the purposes of paragraph (3) of this article:

(a) if a party has more than one place of business, the place of business is that which has the closest relationship to the arbitration agreement;

(b) if a party does not have a place of business, reference is to be made to his habitual residence.

(5) This Law shall not affect any other law of this State by virtue of which certain disputes may not be submitted to arbitration or may be submitted to arbitration

---

[2] The term "commercial" should be given a wide interpretation so as to cover matters arising from all relationships of a commercial nature, whether contractual or not. Relationships of a commercial nature include, but are not limited to, the following transactions: any trade transaction for the supply or exchange of goods or services; distribution agreement; commercial representation or agency; factoring; leasing; construction of works; consulting; engineering; licensing; investment; financing; banking; insurance; exploitation agreement or concession; joint venture and other forms of industrial or business cooperation; carriage of goods or passengers by air, sea, rail or road.

only according to provisions other than those of this Law.

Article 2.   Definitions and rules of interpretation

For the purposes of this Law:

(a) "arbitration" means any arbitration whether or not administered by a permanent arbitral institution;

(b) "arbitral tribunal" means a sole arbitrator or a panel of arbitrators;

(c) "court" means a body or organ of the judicial system of a State;

(d) where a provision of this Law, except article 28, leaves the parties free to determine a certain issue, such freedom includes the right of the parties to authorize a third party, including an institution, to make that determination;

(e) where a provision of this Law refers to the fact that the parties have agreed or that they may agree or in any other way refers to an agreement of the parties, such agreement includes any arbitration rules referred to in that agreement;

(f) where a provision of this Law, other than in articles 25(a) and 32(2)(a), refers to a claim, it also applies to a counter-claim, and where it refers to a defence, it also applies to a defence to such counter-claim.

Article 2 A.   International origin and general principles

(1) In the interpretation of this Law, regard is to be had to its international origin and to the need to promote uniformity in its application and the observance of good faith.

(2) Questions concerning matters governed by this Law which are not expressly settled in it are to be settled in conformity with the general principles on which this Law is based.

Article 3.   Receipt of written communications

(1) Unless otherwise agreed by the parties:

(a) any written communication is deemed to have been received if it is delivered to the addressee personally or if it is delivered at his place of business, habitual residence or mailing address; if none of these can be found after making a reasonable inquiry, a written communication is deemed to have been received if it is sent to the addressee's last-known place of business, habitual residence or mailing address by registered letter or any other means which provides a record of the attempt to deliver it;

(b) the communication is deemed to have been received on the day it is so delivered.

(2) The provisions of this article do not apply to communications in court proceedings.

Article 4.   Waiver of right to object

A party who knows that any provision of this Law from which the parties may derogate or any requirement under the arbitration agreement has not been complied with and yet proceeds with the arbitration without stating his objection to such non-compliance without undue delay or, if a time-limit is provided therefor, within such period of time, shall be deemed to have waived his right to object.

Article 5.   Extent of court intervention

In matters governed by this Law, no court shall intervene except where so provided in this Law.

Article 6.   Court or other authority for certain functions of arbitration assistance and supervision

The functions referred to in articles 11(3), 11(4), 13(3), 14, 16(3) and 34(2) shall be performed by . . . [Each State enacting this model law specifies the court, courts or, where referred to therein, other authority competent to perform these functions.]

CHAPTER II.   ARBITRATION AGREEMENT

Option I

Article 7.   Definition and form of arbitration agreement

(1) "Arbitration agreement" is an agreement by the parties to submit to arbitration all or certain disputes which have arisen or which may arise between them in respect of a defined legal relationship, whether contractual or not. An arbitration agreement may be in the form of an arbitration clause in a contract or in the form of a separate agreement.

(2) The arbitration agreement shall be in writing.

(3) An arbitration agreement is in writing if its content is recorded in any form, whether or not the arbitration agreement or contract has been concluded orally, by conduct, or by other means.

(4) The requirement that an arbitration agreement be in writing is met by an electronic communication if the information contained therein is accessible so as to be useable for subsequent reference; "electronic communication" means any communication that the parties make by means of data messages; "data message" means information generated, sent, received or stored by electronic, magnetic, optical or similar means, including, but not limited to, electronic data interchange (EDI), electronic mail, telegram, telex or telecopy.

(5) Furthermore, an arbitration agreement is in writing if it is contained in an exchange of statements of claim and defence in which the existence of an agreement is alleged by one party and not denied by the other.

(6) The reference in a contract to any document containing an arbitration clause constitutes an arbitration agreement in writing, provided that the reference is such as to make that clause part of the contract.

Option II

Article 7.   Definition of arbitration agreement

"Arbitration agreement" is an agreement by the parties to submit to arbitration all or certain disputes which have arisen or which may arise between them in respect of a defined legal relationship, whether contractual or not.

Article 8.   Arbitration agreement and substantive claim before court

(1) A court before which an action is brought in a matter which is the subject of an arbitration agreement shall, if a party so requests not later than when submitting his first statement on the substance of the dispute, refer the parties to arbitration unless it finds that the agreement is null and void, inoperative or incapable of being performed.

(2) Where an action referred to in paragraph (1) of this article has been brought, arbitral proceedings may nevertheless be commenced or continued, and an award may be made, while the issue is pending before the court.

Article 9.   Arbitration agreement and interim measures by court

It is not incompatible with an arbitration agreement for a party to request, before or during arbitral proceedings, from a court an interim measure of protection and for a court to grant such measure.

CHAPTER III.   COMPOSITION OF ARBITRAL TRIBUNAL

Article 10.   Number of arbitrators

(1) The parties are free to determine the number of arbitrators.

(2) Failing such determination, the number of arbitrators shall be three.

Article 11.   Appointment of arbitrators

(1) No person shall be precluded by reason of his nationality from acting as an arbitrator, unless otherwise agreed by the parties.

(2) The parties are free to agree on a procedure of appointing the arbitrator or arbitrators, subject to the provisions of paragraphs (4) and (5) of this article.

(3) Failing such agreement,

   (a) in an arbitration with three arbitrators, each party shall appoint one arbitrator, and the two arbitrators thus appointed shall appoint the third arbitrator; if a party fails to appoint the arbitrator within thirty days of receipt of a request to do so from the other party, or if the two arbitrators fail to agree on the third arbitrator within thirty days of their appointment, the appointment shall be made, upon request of a party, by the court or other authority specified in article 6;

   (b) in an arbitration with a sole arbitrator, if the parties are unable to agree on the arbitrator, he shall be appointed, upon request of a party, by the court or other authority specified in article 6.

(4) Where, under an appointment procedure agreed upon by the parties,

(a) a party fails to act as required under such procedure, or

(b) the parties, or two arbitrators, are unable to reach an agreement expected of them under such procedure, or

(c) a third party, including an institution, fails to perform any function entrusted to it under such procedure, any party may request the court or other authority specified in article 6 to take the necessary measure, unless the agreement on the appointment procedure provides other means for securing the appointment.

(5) A decision on a matter entrusted by paragraph (3) or (4) of this article to the court or other authority specified in article 6 shall be subject to no appeal. The court or other authority, in appointing an arbitrator, shall have due regard to any qualifications required of the arbitrator by the agreement of the parties and to such considerations as are likely to secure the appointment of an independent and impartial arbitrator and, in the case of a sole or third arbitrator, shall take into account as well the advisability of appointing an arbitrator of a nationality other than those of the parties.

Article 12.   Grounds for challenge

(1) When a person is approached in connection with his possible appointment as an arbitrator, he shall disclose any circumstances likely to give rise to justifiable doubts as to his impartiality or independence. An arbitrator, from the time of his appointment and throughout the arbitral proceedings, shall without delay disclose any such circumstances to the parties unless they have already been informed of them by him.

(2) An arbitrator may be challenged only if circumstances exist that give rise to justifiable doubts as to his impartiality or independence, or if he does not possess qualifications agreed to by the parties. A party may challenge an arbitrator appointed by him, or in whose appointment he has participated, only for reasons of which he becomes aware after the appointment has been made.

Article 13.   Challenge procedure

(1) The parties are free to agree on a procedure for challenging an arbitrator, subject to the provisions of paragraph (3) of this article.

(2) Failing such agreement, a party who intends to challenge an arbitrator shall, within fifteen days after becoming aware of the constitution of the arbitral tribunal or after becoming aware of any circumstance referred to in article 12(2), send a written statement of the reasons for the challenge to the arbitral tribunal. Unless the challenged arbitrator withdraws from his office or the other party agrees to the challenge, the arbitral tribunal shall decide on the challenge.

(3) If a challenge under any procedure agreed upon by the parties or under the procedure of paragraph (2) of this article is not successful, the challenging party may request, within thirty days after having received notice of the decision rejecting the challenge, the court or other authority specified in article 6 to decide

on the challenge, which decision shall be subject to no appeal; while such a request is pending, the arbitral tribunal, including the challenged arbitrator, may continue the arbitral proceedings and make an award.

Article 14.   Failure or impossibility to act

(1) If an arbitrator becomes de jure or de facto unable to perform his functions or for other reasons fails to act without undue delay, his mandate terminates if he withdraws from his office or if the parties agree on the termination. Otherwise, if a controversy remains concerning any of these grounds, any party may request the court or other authority specified in article 6 to decide on the termination of the mandate, which decision shall be subject to no appeal.

(2) If, under this article or article 13(2), an arbitrator withdraws from his office or a party agrees to the termination of the mandate of an arbitrator, this does not imply acceptance of the validity of any ground referred to in this article or article 12(2).

Article 15.   Appointment of substitute arbitrator

Where the mandate of an arbitrator terminates under article 13 or 14 or because of his withdrawal from office for any other reason or because of the revocation of his mandate by agreement of the parties or in any other case of termination of his mandate, a substitute arbitrator shall be appointed according to the rules that were applicable to the appointment of the arbitrator being replaced.

Chapter IV.   JURISDICTION OF ARBITRAL TRIBUNAL

Article 16.   Competence of arbitral tribunal to rule on its jurisdiction

(1) The arbitral tribunal may rule on its own jurisdiction, including any objections with respect to the existence or validity of the arbitration agreement. For that purpose, an arbitration clause which forms part of a contract shall be treated as an agreement independent of the other terms of the contract. A decision by the arbitral tribunal that the contract is null and void shall not entail ipso jure the invalidity of the arbitration clause.

(2) A plea that the arbitral tribunal does not have jurisdiction shall be raised not later than the submission of the statement of defence. A party is not precluded from raising such a plea by the fact that he has appointed, or participated in the appointment of, an arbitrator. A plea that the arbitral tribunal is exceeding the scope of its authority shall be raised as soon as the matter alleged to be beyond the scope of its authority is raised during the arbitral proceedings. The arbitral tribunal may, in either case, admit a later plea if it considers the delay justified.

(3) The arbitral tribunal may rule on a plea referred to in paragraph (2) of this article either as a preliminary question or in an award on the merits. If the arbitral tribunal rules as a preliminary question that it has jurisdiction, any party may request, within thirty days after having received notice of that ruling, the court specified in article 6 to decide the matter, which decision shall be subject to no appeal; while such a request is pending, the arbitral tribunal may continue the arbitral proceedings and make an award.

Chapter IV A. INTERIM MEASURES AND PRELIMINARY ORDERS

Section 1. Interim measures

Article 17. Power of arbitral tribunal to order interim measures

(1) Unless otherwise agreed by the parties, the arbitral tribunal may, at the request of a party, grant interim measures.

(2) An interim measure is any temporary measure, whether in the form of an award or in another form, by which, at any time prior to the issuance of the award by which the dispute is finally decided, the arbitral tribunal orders a party to:

(a) Maintain or restore the status quo pending determination of the dispute;

(b) Take action that would prevent, or refrain from taking action that is likely to cause, current or imminent harm or prejudice to the arbitral process itself;

(c) Provide a means of preserving assets out of which a subsequent award may be satisfied; or

(d) Preserve evidence that may be relevant and material to the resolution of the dispute.

Article 17 A. Conditions for granting interim measures

(1) The party requesting an interim measure under article 17(2)(a), (b) and (c) shall satisfy the arbitral tribunal that:

(a) Harm not adequately reparable by an award of damages is likely to result if the measure is not ordered, and such harm substantially outweighs the harm that is likely to result to the party against whom the measure is directed if the measure is granted; and

(b) There is a reasonable possibility that the requesting party will succeed on the merits of the claim. The determination on this possibility shall not affect the discretion of the arbitral tribunal in making any subsequent determination.

(2) With regard to a request for an interim measure under article 17(2)(d), the requirements in paragraphs (1)(a) and (b) of this article shall apply only to the extent the arbitral tribunal considers appropriate.

Section 2. Preliminary orders

Article 17 B. Applications for preliminary orders and conditions for granting preliminary orders

(1) Unless otherwise agreed by the parties, a party may, without notice to any other party, make a request for an interim measure together with an application for a preliminary order directing a party not to frustrate the purpose of the interim measure requested.

(2) The arbitral tribunal may grant a preliminary order provided it considers that prior disclosure of the request for the interim measure to the party against whom

it is directed risks frustrating the purpose of the measure.

(3) The conditions defined under article 17A apply to any preliminary order, provided that the harm to be assessed under article 17A(1)*(a)*, is the harm likely to result from the order being granted or not.

Article 17 C.   Specific regime for preliminary orders

(1) Immediately after the arbitral tribunal has made a determination in respect of an application for a preliminary order, the arbitral tribunal shall give notice to all parties of the request for the interim measure, the application for the preliminary order, the preliminary order, if any, and all other communications, including by indicating the content of any oral communication, between any party and the arbitral tribunal in relation thereto.

(2) At the same time, the arbitral tribunal shall give an opportunity to any party against whom a preliminary order is directed to present its case at the earliest practicable time.

(3) The arbitral tribunal shall decide promptly on any objection to the preliminary order.

(4) A preliminary order shall expire after twenty days from the date on which it was issued by the arbitral tribunal. However, the arbitral tribunal may issue an interim measure adopting or modifying the preliminary order, after the party against whom the preliminary order is directed has been given notice and an opportunity to present its case.

(5) A preliminary order shall be binding on the parties but shall not be subject to enforcement by a court. Such a preliminary order does not constitute an award.

Section 3.   *Provisions applicable to interim measures and preliminary orders*

Article 17 D.   Modification, suspension, termination

The arbitral tribunal may modify, suspend or terminate an interim measure or a preliminary order it has granted, upon application of any party or, in exceptional circumstances and upon prior notice to the parties, on the arbitral tribunal's own initiative.

Article 17 E.   Provision of security

(1) The arbitral tribunal may require the party requesting an interim measure to provide appropriate security in connection with the measure.

(2) The arbitral tribunal shall require the party applying for a preliminary order to provide security in connection with the order unless the arbitral tribunal considers it inappropriate or unnecessary to do so.

Article 17 F.   Disclosure

(1) The arbitral tribunal may require any party promptly to disclose any material change in the circumstances on the basis of which the measure was requested or

granted.

(2) The party applying for a preliminary order shall disclose to the arbitral tribunal all circumstances that are likely to be relevant to the arbitral tribunal's determination whether to grant or maintain the order, and such obligation shall continue until the party against whom the order has been requested has had an opportunity to present its case. Thereafter, paragraph (1) of this article shall apply.

Article 17 G.   Costs and damages

The party requesting an interim measure or applying for a preliminary order shall be liable for any costs and damages caused by the measure or the order to any party if the arbitral tribunal later determines that, in the circumstances, the measure or the order should not have been granted. The arbitral tribunal may award such costs and damages at any point during the proceedings.

Section 4.   Recognition and enforcement of interim measures

Article 17 H.   Recognition and enforcement

(1) An interim measure issued by an arbitral tribunal shall be recognized as binding and, unless otherwise provided by the arbitral tribunal, enforced upon application to the competent court, irrespective of the country in which it was issued, subject to the provisions of article 17 I.

(2) The party who is seeking or has obtained recognition or enforcement of an interim measure shall promptly inform the court of any termination, suspension or modification of that interim measure.

(3) The court of the State where recognition or enforcement is sought may, if it considers it proper, order the requesting party to provide appropriate security if the arbitral tribunal has not already made a determination with respect to security or where such a decision is necessary to protect the rights of third parties.

Article 17 I.   Grounds for refusing recognition or enforcement[3]

(1) Recognition or enforcement of an interim measure may be refused only:

(a) At the request of the party against whom it is invoked if the court is satisfied that:

(i) Such refusal is warranted on the grounds set forth in article 36(1)*(a)*(i), (ii), (iii) or (iv); or

(ii) The arbitral tribunal's decision with respect to the provision of security in connection with the interim measure issued by the arbitral tribunal has not been complied with; or

(iii) The interim measure has been terminated or suspended by the arbitral

---

[3] The conditions set forth in article 17 I are intended to limit the number of circumstances in which the court may refuse to enforce an interim measure. It would not be contrary to the level of harmonization sought to be achieved by these model provisions if a State were to adopt fewer circumstances in which enforcement may be refused.

tribunal or, where so empowered, by the court of the State in which the arbitration takes place or under the law of which that interim measure was granted; or

(b) If the court finds that:

(i) The interim measure is incompatible with the powers conferred upon the court unless the court decides to reformulate the interim measure to the extent necessary to adapt it to its own powers and procedures for the purposes of enforcing that interim measure and without modifying its substance; or

(ii) Any of the grounds set forth in article 36(1)*(b)*(i) or (ii), apply to the recognition and enforcement of the interim measure.

(2) Any determination made by the court on any ground in paragraph (1) of this article shall be effective only for the purposes of the application to recognize and enforce the interim measure. The court where recognition or enforcement is sought shall not, in making that determination, undertake a review of the substance of the interim measure.

Section 5.   *Court-ordered interim measures*

Article 17 J.   Court-ordered interim measures

A court shall have the same power of issuing an interim measure in relation to arbitration proceedings, irrespective of whether their place is in the territory of this State, as it has in relation to proceedings in courts. The court shall exercise such power in accordance with its own procedures in consideration of the specific features of international arbitration.

Chapter V.   CONDUCT OF ARBITRAL PROCEEDINGS

Article 18.   Equal treatment of parties

The parties shall be treated with equality and each party shall be given a full opportunity of presenting his case.

Article 19.   Determination of rules of procedure

(1) Subject to the provisions of this Law, the parties are free to agree on the procedure to be followed by the arbitral tribunal in conducting the proceedings.

(2) Failing such agreement, the arbitral tribunal may, subject to the provisions of this Law, conduct the arbitration in such manner as it considers appropriate. The power conferred upon the arbitral tribunal includes the power to determine the admissibility, relevance, materiality and weight of any evidence.

Article 20.   Place of arbitration

(1) The parties are free to agree on the place of arbitration. Failing such agreement, the place of arbitration shall be determined by the arbitral tribunal having regard to the circumstances of the case, including the convenience of the parties.

(2) Notwithstanding the provisions of paragraph (1) of this article, the arbitral tribunal may, unless otherwise agreed by the parties, meet at any place it considers appropriate for consultation among its members, for hearing witnesses, experts or the parties, or for inspection of goods, other property or documents.

Article 21.   Commencement of arbitral proceedings

Unless otherwise agreed by the parties, the arbitral proceedings in respect of a particular dispute commence on the date on which a request for that dispute to be referred to arbitration is received by the respondent.

Article 22.   Language

(1) The parties are free to agree on the language or languages to be used in the arbitral proceedings. Failing such agreement, the arbitral tribunal shall determine the language or languages to be used in the proceedings. This agreement or determination, unless otherwise specified therein, shall apply to any written statement by a party, any hearing and any award, decision or other communication by the arbitral tribunal.

(2) The arbitral tribunal may order that any documentary evidence shall be accompanied by a translation into the language or languages agreed upon by the parties or determined by the arbitral tribunal.

Article 23.   Statements of claim and defence

(1) Within the period of time agreed by the parties or determined by the arbitral tribunal, the claimant shall state the facts supporting his claim, the points at issue and the relief or remedy sought, and the respondent shall state his defence in respect of these particulars, unless the parties have otherwise agreed as to the required elements of such statements. The parties may submit with their statements all documents they consider to be relevant or may add a reference to the documents or other evidence they will submit.

(2) Unless otherwise agreed by the parties, either party may amend or supplement his claim or defence during the course of the arbitral proceedings, unless the arbitral tribunal considers it inappropriate to allow such amendment having regard to the delay in making it.

Article 24.   Hearings and written proceedings

(1) Subject to any contrary agreement by the parties, the arbitral tribunal shall decide whether to hold oral hearings for the presentation of evidence or for oral argument, or whether the proceedings shall be conducted on the basis of documents and other materials. However, unless the parties have agreed that no hearings shall be held, the arbitral tribunal shall hold such hearings at an appropriate stage of the proceedings, if so requested by a party.

(2) The parties shall be given sufficient advance notice of any hearing and of any meeting of the arbitral tribunal for the purposes of inspection of goods, other property or documents.

(3) All statements, documents or other information supplied to the arbitral

tribunal by one party shall be communicated to the other party. Also any expert report or evidentiary document on which the arbitral tribunal may rely in making its decision shall be communicated to the parties.

Article 25.   Default of a party

Unless otherwise agreed by the parties, if, without showing sufficient cause,

(a) the claimant fails to communicate his statement of claim in accordance with article 23(1), the arbitral tribunal shall terminate the proceedings;

(b) the respondent fails to communicate his statement of defence in accordance with article 23(1), the arbitral tribunal shall continue the proceedings without treating such failure in itself as an admission of the claimant's allegations;

(c) any party fails to appear at a hearing or to produce documentary evidence, the arbitral tribunal may continue the proceedings and make the award on the evidence before it.

Article 26.   Expert appointed by arbitral tribunal

(1) Unless otherwise agreed by the parties, the arbitral tribunal

(a) may appoint one or more experts to report to it on specific issues to be determined by the arbitral tribunal;

(b) may require a party to give the expert any relevant information or to produce, or to provide access to, any relevant documents, goods or other property for his inspection.

(2) Unless otherwise agreed by the parties, if a party so requests or if the arbitral tribunal considers it necessary, the expert shall, after delivery of his written or oral report, participate in a hearing where the parties have the opportunity to put questions to him and to present expert witnesses in order to testify on the points at issue.

Article 27.   Court assistance in taking evidence

The arbitral tribunal or a party with the approval of the arbitral tribunal may request from a competent court of this State assistance in taking evidence. The court may execute the request within its competence and according to its rules on taking evidence.

Chapter VI.   MAKING OF AWARD AND TERMINATION OF PROCEEDINGS

Article 28.   Rules applicable to substance of dispute

(1) The arbitral tribunal shall decide the dispute in accordance with such rules of law as are chosen by the parties as applicable to the substance of the dispute. Any designation of the law or legal system of a given State shall be construed, unless otherwise expressed, as directly referring to the substantive law of that State and not to its conflict of laws rules.

(2) Failing any designation by the parties, the arbitral tribunal shall apply the law

determined by the conflict of laws rules which it considers applicable.

(3) The arbitral tribunal shall decide ex aequo et bono or as amiable compositeur only if the parties have expressly authorized it to do so.

(4) In all cases, the arbitral tribunal shall decide in accordance with the terms of the contract and shall take into account the usages of the trade applicable to the transaction.

Article 29.   Decision making by panel of arbitrators

In arbitral proceedings with more than one arbitrator, any decision of the arbitral tribunal shall be made, unless otherwise agreed by the parties, by a majority of all its members. However, questions of procedure may be decided by a presiding arbitrator, if so authorized by the parties or all members of the arbitral tribunal.

Article 30.   Settlement

(1) If, during arbitral proceedings, the parties settle the dispute, the arbitral tribunal shall terminate the proceedings and, if requested by the parties and not objected to by the arbitral tribunal, record the settlement in the form of an arbitral award on agreed terms.

(2) An award on agreed terms shall be made in accordance with the provisions of article 31 and shall state that it is an award. Such an award has the same status and effect as any other award on the merits of the case.

Article 31.   Form and contents of award

(1) The award shall be made in writing and shall be signed by the arbitrator or arbitrators. In arbitral proceedings with more than one arbitrator, the signatures of the majority of all members of the arbitral tribunal shall suffice, provided that the reason for any omitted signature is stated.

(2) The award shall state the reasons upon which it is based, unless the parties have agreed that no reasons are to be given or the award is an award on agreed terms under article 30.

(3) The award shall state its date and the place of arbitration as determined in accordance with article 20(1). The award shall be deemed to have been made at that place.

(4) After the award is made, a copy signed by the arbitrators in accordance with paragraph (1) of this article shall be delivered to each party.

Article 32.   Termination of proceedings

(1) The arbitral proceedings are terminated by the final award or by an order of the arbitral tribunal in accordance with paragraph (2) of this article.

(2) The arbitral tribunal shall issue an order for the termination of the arbitral proceedings when:

(a) the claimant withdraws his claim, unless the respondent objects thereto and the arbitral tribunal recognizes a legitimate interest on his part in obtaining a final settlement of the dispute;

(b) the parties agree on the termination of the proceedings;

(c) the arbitral tribunal finds that the continuation of the proceedings has for any other reason become unnecessary or impossible.

(3) The mandate of the arbitral tribunal terminates with the termination of the arbitral proceedings, subject to the provisions of articles 33 and 34(4).

Article 33.   Correction and interpretation of award; additional award

(1) Within thirty days of receipt of the award, unless another period of time has been agreed upon by the parties:

(a) a party, with notice to the other party, may request the arbitral tribunal to correct in the award any errors in computation, any clerical or typographical errors or any errors of similar nature;

(b) if so agreed by the parties, a party, with notice to the other party, may request the arbitral tribunal to give an interpretation of a specific point or part of the award.

If the arbitral tribunal considers the request to be justified, it shall make the correction or give the interpretation within thirty days of receipt of the request. The interpretation shall form part of the award.

(2) The arbitral tribunal may correct any error of the type referred to in paragraph (1)(a) of this article on its own initiative within thirty days of the date of the award.

(3) Unless otherwise agreed by the parties, a party, with notice to the other party, may request, within thirty days of receipt of the award, the arbitral tribunal to make an additional award as to claims presented in the arbitral proceedings but omitted from the award. If the arbitral tribunal considers the request to be justified, it shall make the additional award within sixty days.

(4) The arbitral tribunal may extend, if necessary, the period of time within which it shall make a correction, interpretation or an additional award under paragraph (1) or (3) of this article.

(5) The provisions of article 31 shall apply to a correction or interpretation of the award or to an additional award.

Chapter VII.   RECOURSE AGAINST AWARD

Article 34.   Application for setting aside as exclusive recourse against arbitral award

(1) Recourse to a court against an arbitral award may be made only by an application for setting aside in accordance with paragraphs (2) and (3) of this article.

(2) An arbitral award may be set aside by the court specified in article 6 only if:

(a) the party making the application furnishes proof that:

(i) a party to the arbitration agreement referred to in article 7 was under some incapacity; or the said agreement is not valid under the law to which the parties have subjected it or, failing any indication thereon, under the law of this State; or

(ii) the party making the application was not given proper notice of the appointment of an arbitrator or of the arbitral proceedings or was otherwise unable to present his case; or

(iii) the award deals with a dispute not contemplated by or not falling within the terms of the submission to arbitration, or contains decisions on matters beyond the scope of the submission to arbitration, provided that, if the decisions on matters submitted to arbitration can be separated from those not so submitted, only that part of the award which contains decisions on matters not submitted to arbitration may be set aside; or

(iv) the composition of the arbitral tribunal or the arbitral procedure was not in accordance with the agreement of the parties, unless such agreement was in conflict with a provision of this Law from which the parties cannot derogate, or, failing such agreement, was not in accordance with this Law; or

(b) the court finds that:

(i) the subject-matter of the dispute is not capable of settlement by arbitration under the law of this State; or

(ii) the award is in conflict with the public policy of this State.

(3) An application for setting aside may not be made after three months have elapsed from the date on which the party making that application had received the award or, if a request had been made under article 33, from the date on which that request had been disposed of by the arbitral tribunal.

(4) The court, when asked to set aside an award, may, where appropriate and so requested by a party, suspend the setting aside proceedings for a period of time determined by it in order to give the arbitral tribunal an opportunity to resume the arbitral proceedings or to take such other action as in the arbitral tribunal's opinion will eliminate the grounds for setting aside.

Chapter VIII. RECOGNITION AND ENFORCEMENT OF AWARDS

Article 35. Recognition and enforcement

(1) An arbitral award, irrespective of the country in which it was made, shall be recognized as binding and, upon application in writing to the competent court, shall be enforced subject to the provisions of this article and of article 36.

(2) The party relying on an award or applying for its enforcement shall supply the duly authenticated original award or a duly certified copy thereof, and the original arbitration agreement referred to in article 7 or a duly certified copy thereof. If the award or agreement is not made in an official language of this State, the court may request the party to shall supply a duly certified translation thereof into such

language.[4]

Article 36.   Grounds for refusing recognition or enforcement

(1) Recognition or enforcement of an arbitral award, irrespective of the country in which it was made, may be refused only:

(a) at the request of the party against whom it is invoked, if that party furnishes to the competent court where recognition or enforcement is sought proof that:

(i) a party to the arbitration agreement referred to in article 7 was under some incapacity; or the said agreement is not valid under the law to which the parties have subjected it or, failing any indication thereon, under the law of the country where the award was made; or

(ii) the party against whom the award is invoked was not given proper notice of the appointment of an arbitrator or of the arbitral proceedings or was otherwise unable to present his case; or

(iii) the award deals with a dispute not contemplated by or not falling within the terms of the submission to arbitration, or it contains decisions on matters beyond the scope of the submission to arbitration, provided that, if the decisions on matters submitted to arbitration can be separated from those not so submitted, that part of the award which contains decisions on matters submitted to arbitration may be recognized and enforced; or

(iv) the composition of the arbitral tribunal or the arbitral procedure was not in accordance with the agreement of the parties or, failing such agreement, was not in accordance with the law of the country where the arbitration took place; or

(v) the award has not yet become binding on the parties or has been set aside or suspended by a court of the country in which, or under the law of which, that award was made; or

(b) if the court finds that:

(i) the subject-matter of the dispute is not capable of settlement by arbitration under the law of this State; or

(ii) the recognition or enforcement of the award would be contrary to the public policy of this State.

(2) If an application for setting aside or suspension of an award has been made to a court referred to in paragraph (1)(a)(v) of this article, the court where recognition or enforcement is sought may, if it considers it proper, adjourn its decision and may also, on the application of the party claiming recognition or enforcement of the award, order the other party to provide appropriate security.

---

[4] The conditions set forth in this paragraph are intended to set maximum standards. It would, thus, not be contrary to the harmonization to be achieved by the model law if a State retained even less onerous conditions.

Explanatory Note by the UNCITRAL secretariat on the 1985 Model Law on International Commercial Arbitration as amended in 2006

1. The UNCITRAL Model Law on International Commercial Arbitration ("the Model Law") was adopted by the United Nations Commission on International Trade Law (UNCITRAL) on 21 June 1985, at the end of the eighteenth session of the Commission. The General Assembly, in its resolution 40/72 of 11 December 1985, recommended "that all States give due consideration to the Model Law on International Commercial Arbitration, in view of the desirability of uniformity of the law of arbitral procedures and the specific needs of international commercial arbitration practice". The Model Law was amended by UNCITRAL on 7 July 2006, at the thirty-ninth session of the Commission (see below, paragraphs 4, 19, 20, 27, 29 and 53). The General Assembly, in its resolution 61/33 of 4 December 2006, recommended "that all States give favourable consideration to the enactment of the revised articles of the UNCITRAL Model Law on International Commercial Arbitration, or the revised UNCITRAL Model Law on International Commercial Arbitration, when they enact or revise their laws (. . .)".

2. The Model Law constitutes a sound basis for the desired harmonization and improvement of national laws. It covers all stages of the arbitral process from the arbitration agreement to the recognition and enforcement of the arbitral award and reflects a worldwide consensus on the principles and important issues of international arbitration practice. It is acceptable to States of all regions and the different legal or economic systems of the world. Since its adoption by UNCITRAL, the Model Law has come to represent the accepted international legislative standard for a modern arbitration law and a significant number of jurisdictions have enacted arbitration legislation based on the Model Law.

3. The form of a model law was chosen as the vehicle for harmonization and modernization in view of the flexibility it gives to States in preparing new arbitration laws. Notwithstanding that flexibility, and in order to increase the likelihood of achieving a satisfactory degree of harmonization, States are encouraged to make as few changes as possible when incorporating the Model Law into their legal systems. Efforts to minimize variation from the text adopted by UNCITRAL are also expected to increase the visibility of harmonization, thus enhancing the confidence of foreign parties, as the primary users of international arbitration, in the reliability of arbitration law in the enacting State.

4. The revision of the Model Law adopted in 2006 includes article 2 A, which is designed to facilitate interpretation by reference to internationally accepted principles and is aimed at promoting a uniform understanding of the Model Law. Other substantive amendments to the Model Law relate to the form of the arbitration agreement and to interim measures. The original 1985 version of the provision on the form of the arbitration agreement (article 7) was modelled on the language used in article II (2) of the Convention on the Recognition and Enforcement of Foreign Arbitral Awards (New York, 1958) ("the New York Convention"). The revision of

article 7 is intended to address evolving practice in international trade and technological developments. The extensive revision of article 17 on interim measures was considered necessary in light of the fact that such measures are increasingly relied upon in the practice of international commercial arbitration. The revision also includes an enforcement regime for such measures in recognition of the fact that the effectiveness of arbitration frequently depends upon the possibility of enforcing interim measures. The new provisions are contained in a new chapter of the Model Law on interim measures and preliminary orders (chapter IV A).

A. Background to the Model Law

5. The Model Law was developed to address considerable disparities in national laws on arbitration. The need for improvement and harmonization was based on findings that national laws were often particularly inappropriate for international cases.

1. Inadequacy of domestic laws

6. Recurrent inadequacies to be found in outdated national laws include provisions that equate the arbitral process with court litigation and fragmentary provisions that fail to address all relevant substantive law issues. Even most of those laws that appear to be up-to-date and comprehensive were drafted with domestic arbitration primarily, if not exclusively, in mind. While this approach is understandable in view of the fact that even today the bulk of cases governed by arbitration law would be of a purely domestic nature, the unfortunate consequence is that traditional local concepts are imposed on international cases and the needs of modern practice are often not met.

7. The expectations of the parties as expressed in a chosen set of arbitration rules or a "one-off" arbitration agreement may be frustrated, especially by mandatory provisions of applicable law. Unexpected and undesired restrictions found in national laws may prevent the parties, for example, from submitting future disputes to arbitration, from selecting the arbitrator freely, or from having the arbitral proceedings conducted according to agreed rules of procedure and with no more court involvement than appropriate. Frustration may also ensue from non-mandatory provisions that may impose undesired requirements on unwary parties who may not think about the need to provide otherwise when drafting the arbitration agreement. Even the absence of any legislative provision may cause difficulties simply by leaving unanswered some of the many procedural issues relevant in arbitration and not always settled in the arbitration agreement. The Model Law is intended to reduce the risk of such possible frustration, difficulties or surprise.

2. Disparity between national laws

8. Problems stemming from inadequate arbitration laws or from the absence of specific legislation governing arbitration are aggravated by the fact that national laws differ widely. Such differences are a frequent source of concern in international arbitration, where at least one of the parties is,

and often both parties are, confronted with foreign and unfamiliar provisions and procedures. Obtaining a full and precise account of the law applicable to the arbitration is, in such circumstances often expensive, impractical or impossible.

9. Uncertainty about the local law with the inherent risk of frustration may adversely affect the functioning of the arbitral process and also impact on the selection of the place of arbitration. Due to such uncertainty, a party may hesitate or refuse to agree to a place, which for practical reasons would otherwise be appropriate. The range of places of arbitration acceptable to parties is thus widened and the smooth functioning of the arbitral proceedings is enhanced where States adopt the Model Law, which is easily recognizable, meets the specific needs of international commercial arbitration and provides an international standard based on solutions acceptable to parties from different legal systems.

B. Salient features of the Model Law

1. Special procedural regime for international commercial arbitration

10. The principles and solutions adopted in the Model Law aim at reducing or eliminating the above-mentioned concerns and difficulties. As a response to the inadequacies and disparities of national laws, the Model Law presents a special legal regime tailored to international commercial arbitration, without affecting any relevant treaty in force in the State adopting the Model Law. While the Model Law was designed with international commercial arbitration in mind, it offers a set of basic rules that are not, in and of themselves, unsuitable to any other type of arbitration. States may thus consider extending their enactment of the Model Law to cover also domestic disputes, as a number of enacting States already have.

(a) Substantive and territorial scope of application

11. Article 1 defines the scope of application of the Model Law by reference to the notion of "international commercial arbitration". The Model Law defines an arbitration as international if "the parties to an arbitration agreement have, at the time of the conclusion of that agreement, their places of business in different States" (article 1 (3)). The vast majority of situations commonly regarded as international will meet this criterion. In addition, article 1 (3) broadens the notion of internationality so that the Model Law also covers cases where the place of arbitration, the place of contract performance, or the place of the subject-matter of the dispute is situated outside the State where the parties have their place of business, or cases where the parties have expressly agreed that the subject-matter of the arbitration agreement relates to more than one country. Article 1 thus recognizes extensively the freedom of the parties to submit a dispute to the legal regime established pursuant to the Model Law.

12. In respect of the term "commercial", the Model Law provides no strict definition. The footnote to article 1 (1) calls for "a wide interpretation"

and offers an illustrative and open-ended list of relationships that might be described as commercial in nature, "whether contractual or not". The purpose of the footnote is to circumvent any technical difficulty that may arise, for example, in determining which transactions should be governed by a specific body of "commercial law" that may exist in some legal systems.

13. Another aspect of applicability is the territorial scope of application. The principle embodied in article 1 (2) is that the Model Law as enacted in a given State applies only if the place of arbitration is in the territory of that State. However, article 1 (2) also contains important exceptions to that principle, to the effect that certain articles apply, irrespective of whether the place of arbitration is in the enacting State or elsewhere (or, as the case may be, even before the place of arbitration is determined). These articles are the following: articles 8 (1) and 9, which deal with the recognition of arbitration agreements, including their compatibility with interim measures ordered by a court, article 17 J on court-ordered interim measures, articles 17 H and 17 I on the recognition and enforcement of interim measures ordered by an arbitral tribunal, and articles 35 and 36 on the recognition and enforcement of arbitral awards.

14. The territorial criterion governing most of the provisions of the Model Law was adopted for the sake of certainty and in view of the following facts. In most legal systems, the place of arbitration is the exclusive criterion for determining the applicability of national law and, where the national law allows parties to choose the procedural law of a State other than that where the arbitration takes place, experience shows that parties rarely make use of that possibility. Incidentally, enactment of the Model Law reduces any need for the parties to choose a "foreign" law, since the Model Law grants the parties wide freedom in shaping the rules of the arbitral proceedings. In addition to designating the law governing the arbitral procedure, the territorial criterion is of considerable practical importance in respect of articles 11, 13, 14, 16, 27 and 34, which entrust State courts at the place of arbitration with functions of supervision and assistance to arbitration. It should be noted that the territorial criterion legally triggered by the parties' choice regarding the place of arbitration does not limit the arbitral tribunal's ability to meet at any place it considers appropriate for the conduct of the proceedings, as provided by article 20 (2).

(b) *Delimitation of court assistance and supervision*

15. Recent amendments to arbitration laws reveal a trend in favour of limiting and clearly defining court involvement in international commercial arbitration. This is justified in view of the fact that the parties to an arbitration agreement make a conscious decision to exclude court jurisdiction and prefer the finality and expediency of the arbitral process.

16. In this spirit, the Model Law envisages court involvement in the following instances. A first group comprises issues of appointment, challenge and termination of the mandate of an arbitrator (articles 11, 13 and 14), jurisdiction of the arbitral tribunal (article 16) and setting aside of the

arbitral award (article 34). These instances are listed in article 6 as functions that should be entrusted, for the sake of centralization, specialization and efficiency, to a specially designated court or, with respect to articles 11, 13 and 14, possibly to another authority (for example, an arbitral institution or a chamber of commerce). A second group comprises issues of court assistance in taking evidence (article 27), recognition of the arbitration agreement, including its compatibility with court-ordered interim measures (articles 8 and 9), court-ordered interim measures (article 17 J), and recognition and enforcement of interim measures (articles 17 H and 17 I) and of arbitral awards (articles 35 and 36).

17. Beyond the instances in these two groups, "no court shall intervene, in matters governed by this Law". Article 5 thus guarantees that all instances of possible court intervention are found in the piece of legislation enacting the Model Law, except for matters not regulated by it (for example, consolidation of arbitral proceedings, contractual relationship between arbitrators and parties or arbitral institutions, or fixing of costs and fees, including deposits). Protecting the arbitral process from unpredictable or disruptive court interference is essential to parties who choose arbitration (in particular foreign parties).

2. Arbitration agreement

18. Chapter II of the Model Law deals with the arbitration agreement, including its recognition by courts.

(a) Definition and form of arbitration agreement

19. The original 1985 version of the provision on the definition and form of arbitration agreement (article 7) closely followed article II (2) of the New York Convention, which requires that an arbitration agreement be in writing. If the parties have agreed to arbitrate, but they entered into the arbitration agreement in a manner that does not meet the form requirement, any party may have grounds to object to the jurisdiction of the arbitral tribunal. It was pointed out by practitioners that, in a number of situations, the drafting of a written document was impossible or impractical. In such cases, where the willingness of the parties to arbitrate was not in question, the validity of the arbitration agreement should be recognized. For that reason, article 7 was amended in 2006 to better conform to international contract practices. In amending article 7, the Commission adopted two options, which reflect two different approaches on the question of definition and form of arbitration agreement. The first approach follows the detailed structure of the original 1985 text. It confirms the validity and effect of a commitment by the parties to submit to arbitration an existing dispute ("*compromis*") or a future dispute ("*clause compromissoire*"). It follows the New York Convention in requiring the written form of the arbitration agreement but recognizes a record of the "contents" of the agreement "in any form" as equivalent to traditional "writing". The agreement to arbitrate may be entered into in any form (e.g. including orally) as long as the content of the agreement is recorded. This new rule is significant in that it no longer requires signatures of the parties or an

exchange of messages between the parties. It modernizes the language referring to the use of electronic commerce by adopting wording inspired from the 1996 UNCITRAL Model Law on Electronic Commerce and the 2005 United Nations Convention on the Use of Electronic Communications in International Contracts. It covers the situation of "an exchange of statements of claim and defence in which the existence of an agreement is alleged by one party and not denied by another". It also states that "the reference in a contract to any document" (for example, general conditions) "containing an arbitration clause constitutes an arbitration agreement in writing provided that the reference is such as to make that clause part of the contract". It thus clarifies that applicable contract law remains available to determine the level of consent necessary for a party to become bound by an arbitration agreement allegedly made "by reference". The second approach defines the arbitration agreement in a manner that omits any form requirement. No preference was expressed by the Commission in favour of either option I or II, both of which are offered for enacting States to consider, depending on their particular needs, and by reference to the legal context in which the Model Law is enacted, including the general contract law of the enacting State. Both options are intended to preserve the enforceability of arbitration agreements under the New York Convention.

20. In that respect, the Commission also adopted, at its thirty-ninth session in 2006, a "Recommendation regarding the interpretation of article II, paragraph 2, and article VII, paragraph 1, of the Convention on the Recognition and Enforcement of Foreign Arbitral Awards, done in New York, 10 June 1958" (A/61/17, Annex 2).2 The General Assembly, in its resolution 61/33 of 4 December 2006 noted that "in connection with the modernization of articles of the Model Law, the promotion of a uniform interpretation and application of the Convention on the Recognition and Enforcement of Foreign Arbitral Awards, done in New York, 10 June 1958, is particularly timely". The Recommendation was drafted in recognition of the widening use of electronic commerce and enactments of domestic legislation as well as case law, which are more favourable than the New York Convention in respect of the form requirement governing arbitration agreements, arbitration proceedings, and the enforcement of arbitral awards. The Recommendation encourages States to apply article II (2) of the New York Convention "recognizing that the circumstances described therein are not exhaustive". In addition, the Recommendation encourages States to adopt the revised article 7 of the Model Law. Both options of the revised article 7 establish a more favourable regime for the recognition and enforcement of arbitral awards than that provided under the New York Convention. By virtue of the "more favourable law provision" contained in article VII (1) of the New York Convention, the Recommendation clarifies that "any interested party" should be allowed "to avail itself of rights it may have, under the law or treaties of the country where an arbitration agreement is sought to be relied upon, to seek recognition of the validity of such an arbitration agreement".

(b) Arbitration agreement and the courts

21. Articles 8 and 9 deal with two important aspects of the complex relationship between the arbitration agreement and the resort to courts. Modelled on article II (3) of the New York Convention, article 8 (1) of the Model Law places any court under an obligation to refer the parties to arbitration if the court is seized with a claim on the same subject-matter unless it finds that the arbitration agreement is null and void, inoperative or incapable of being performed. The referral is dependent on a request, which a party may make not later than when submitting its first statement on the substance of the dispute. This provision, where adopted by a State enacting the Model Law, is by its nature binding only on the courts of that State. However, since article 8 is not limited in scope to agreements providing for arbitration to take place in the enacting State, it promotes the universal recognition and effect of international commercial arbitration agreements.

22. Article 9 expresses the principle that any interim measures of protection that may be obtained from courts under their procedural law (for example, pre-award attachments) are compatible with an arbitration agreement. That provision is ultimately addressed to the courts of any State, insofar as it establishes the compatibility between interim measures possibly issued by any court and an arbitration agreement, irrespective of the place of arbitration. Wherever a request for interim measures may be made to a court, it may not be relied upon, under the Model Law, as a waiver or an objection against the existence or effect of the arbitration agreement.

3. Composition of arbitral tribunal

23. Chapter III contains a number of detailed provisions on appointment, challenge, termination of mandate and replacement of an arbitrator. The chapter illustrates the general approach taken by the Model Law in eliminating difficulties that arise from inappropriate or fragmentary laws or rules. First, the approach recognizes the freedom of the parties to determine, by reference to an existing set of arbitration rules or by an ad hoc agreement, the procedure to be followed, subject to the fundamental requirements of fairness and justice. Secondly, where the parties have not exercised their freedom to lay down the rules of procedure or they have failed to cover a particular issue, the Model Law ensures, by providing a set of suppletive rules, that the arbitration may commence and proceed effectively until the dispute is resolved.

24. Where under any procedure, agreed upon by the parties or based upon the suppletive rules of the Model Law, difficulties arise in the process of appointment, challenge or termination of the mandate of an arbitrator, articles 11, 13 and 14 provide for assistance by courts or other competent authorities designated by the enacting State. In view of the urgency of matters relating to the composition of the arbitral tribunal or its ability to function, and in order to reduce the risk and effect of any dilatory tactics, short time-periods are set and decisions rendered by courts or other

authorities on such matters are not appealable.

4. Jurisdiction of arbitral tribunal

(a) Competence to rule on own jurisdiction

25. Article 16 (1) adopts the two important (not yet generally recognized) principles of *"Kompetenz-Kompetenz"* and of separability or autonomy of the arbitration clause. *"Kompetenz-Kompetenz"* means that the arbitral tribunal may independently rule on the question of whether it has jurisdiction, including any objections with respect to the existence or validity of the arbitration agreement, without having to resort to a court. Separability means that an arbitration clause shall be treated as an agreement independent of the other terms of the contract. As a consequence, a decision by the arbitral tribunal that the contract is null and void shall not entail *ipso jure* the invalidity of the arbitration clause. Detailed provisions in paragraph (2) require that any objections relating to the arbitrators' jurisdiction be made at the earliest possible time.

26. The competence of the arbitral tribunal to rule on its own jurisdiction (i.e. on the foundation, content and extent of its mandate and power) is, of course, subject to court control. Where the arbitral tribunal rules as a preliminary question that it has jurisdiction, article 16 (3) allows for immediate court control in order to avoid waste of time and money. However, three procedural safeguards are added to reduce the risk and effect of dilatory tactics: short time-period for resort to court (30 days), court decision not appealable, and discretion of the arbitral tribunal to continue the proceedings and make an award while the matter is pending before the court. In those cases where the arbitral tribunal decides to combine its decision on jurisdiction with an award on the merits, judicial review on the question of jurisdiction is available in setting aside proceedings under article 34 or in enforcement proceedings under article 36.

(b) Power to order interim measures and preliminary orders

27. Chapter IV A on interim measures and preliminary orders was adopted by the Commission in 2006. It replaces article 17 of the original 1985 version of the Model Law. Section 1 provides a generic definition of interim measures and sets out the conditions for granting such measures. An important innovation of the revision lies in the establishment (in section 4) of a regime for the recognition and enforcement of interim measures, which was modelled, as appropriate, on the regime for the recognition and enforcement of arbitral awards under articles 35 and 36 of the Model Law.

28. Section 2 of chapter IV A deals with the application for, and conditions for the granting of, preliminary orders. Preliminary orders provide a means for preserving the status quo until the arbitral tribunal issues an interim measure adopting or modifying the preliminary order. Article 17 B (1) provides that "a party may, without notice to any other party, make a request for an interim measure together with an application for a preliminary order directing a party not to frustrate the purpose of the interim measure requested". Article 17 B (2) permits an arbitral tribunal to

grant a preliminary order if "it considers that prior disclosure of the request for the interim measure to the party against whom it is directed risks frustrating the purpose of the measure". Article 17 C contains carefully drafted safeguards for the party against whom the preliminary order is directed, such as prompt notification of the application for the preliminary order and of the preliminary order itself (if any), and an opportunity for that party to present its case "at the earliest practicable time". In any event, a preliminary order has a maximum duration of twenty days and, while binding on the parties, is not subject to court enforcement and does not constitute an award. The term "preliminary order" is used to emphasize its limited nature.

29. Section 3 sets out rules applicable to both preliminary orders and interim measures.

30. Section 5 includes article 17 J on interim measures ordered by courts in support of arbitration, and provides that "a court shall have the same power of issuing an interim measure in relation to arbitration proceedings irrespective of whether their place is in the territory of the enacting State, as it has in relation to proceedings in courts". That article has been added in 2006 to put it beyond any doubt that the existence of an arbitration agreement does not infringe on the powers of the competent court to issue interim measures and that the party to such an arbitration agreement is free to approach the court with a request to order interim measures.

5. Conduct of arbitral proceedings

31. Chapter V provides the legal framework for a fair and effective conduct of the arbitral proceedings. Article 18, which sets out fundamental requirements of procedural justice, and article 19 on the rights and powers to determine the rules of procedure, express principles that are central to the Model Law.

(a) Fundamental procedural rights of a party

32. Article 18 embodies the principles that the parties shall be treated with equality and given a full opportunity of presenting their case. A number of provisions illustrate those principles. For example, article 24 (1) provides that, unless the parties have agreed that no oral hearings be held for the presentation of evidence or for oral argument, the arbitral tribunal shall hold such hearings at an appropriate stage of the proceedings, if so requested by a party. It should be noted that article 24 (1) deals only with the general entitlement of a party to oral hearings (as an alternative to proceedings conducted on the basis of documents and other materials) and not with the procedural aspects, such as the length, number or timing of hearings.

33. Another illustration of those principles relates to evidence by an expert appointed by the arbitral tribunal. Article 26 (2) requires the expert, after delivering his or her written or oral report, to participate in a hearing where the parties may put questions to the expert and present expert witnesses to testify on the points at issue, if such a hearing is requested by a party or deemed necessary by the arbitral tribunal. As another provision

aimed at ensuring fairness, objectivity and impartiality, article 24 (3) provides that all statements, documents and other information supplied to the arbitral tribunal by one party shall be communicated to the other party, and that any expert report or evidentiary document on which the arbitral tribunal may rely in making its decision shall be communicated to the parties. In order to enable the parties to be present at any hearing and at any meeting of the arbitral tribunal for inspection purposes, they shall be given sufficient notice in advance (article 24 (2)).

(b) Determination of rules of procedure

34. Article 19 guarantees the parties' freedom to agree on the procedure to be followed by the arbitral tribunal in conducting the proceedings, subject to a few mandatory provisions on procedure, and empowers the arbitral tribunal, failing agreement by the parties, to conduct the arbitration in such a manner as it considers appropriate. The power conferred upon the arbitral tribunal includes the power to determine the admissibility, relevance, materiality and weight of any evidence.

35. Autonomy of the parties in determining the rules of procedure is of special importance in international cases since it allows the parties to select or tailor the rules according to their specific wishes and needs, unimpeded by traditional and possibly conflicting domestic concepts, thus obviating the earlier mentioned risk of frustration or surprise (see above, paras. 7 and 9). The supplementary discretion of the arbitral tribunal is equally important in that it allows the tribunal to tailor the conduct of the proceedings to the specific features of the case without being hindered by any restraint that may stem from traditional local law, including any domestic rule on evidence. Moreover, it provides grounds for displaying initiative in solving any procedural question not regulated in the arbitration agreement or the Model Law.

36. In addition to the general provisions of article 19, other provisions in the Model Law recognize party autonomy and, failing agreement, empower the arbitral tribunal to decide on certain matters. Examples of particular practical importance in international cases are article 20 on the place of arbitration and article 22 on the language to be used in the proceedings.

(c) Default of a party

37. The arbitral proceedings may be continued in the absence of a party, provided that due notice has been given. This applies, in particular, to the failure of the respondent to communicate its statement of defence (article 25 *(b)*). The arbitral tribunal may also continue the proceedings where a party fails to appear at a hearing or to produce documentary evidence without showing sufficient cause for the failure (article 25 *(c)*). However, if the claimant fails to submit its statement of claim, the arbitral tribunal is obliged to terminate the proceedings (article 25 *(a)*).

38. Provisions that empower the arbitral tribunal to carry out its task even if one of the parties does not participate are of considerable practical importance. As experience shows, it is not uncommon for one of the parties to have little interest in cooperating or expediting matters. Such provisions

therefore provide international commercial arbitration its necessary effectiveness, within the limits of fundamental requirements of procedural justice.

6. Making of award and termination of proceedings

(a) Rules applicable to substance of dispute

39. Article 28 deals with the determination of the rules of law governing the substance of the dispute. Under paragraph (1), the arbitral tribunal decides the dispute in accordance with the rules of law chosen by the parties. This provision is significant in two respects. It grants the parties the freedom to choose the applicable substantive law, which is important where the national law does not clearly or fully recognize that right. In addition, by referring to the choice of "rules of law" instead of "law", the Model Law broadens the range of options available to the parties as regards the designation of the law applicable to the substance of the dispute. For example, parties may agree on rules of law that have been elaborated by an international forum but have not yet been incorporated into any national legal system. Parties could also choose directly an instrument such as the United Nations Convention on Contracts for the International Sale of Goods as the body of substantive law governing the arbitration, without having to refer to the national law of any State party to that Convention. The power of the arbitral tribunal, on the other hand, follows more traditional lines. When the parties have not chosen the applicable law, the arbitral tribunal shall apply the law (i.e., the national law) determined by the conflict-of-laws rules that it considers applicable.

40. Article 28 (3) recognizes that the parties may authorize the arbitral tribunal to decide the dispute *ex aequo et bono* or as *amiables compositeur*. This type of arbitration (where the arbitral tribunal may decide the dispute on the basis of principles it believes to be just, without having to refer to any particular body of law) is currently not known or used in all legal systems. The Model Law does not intend to regulate this area. It simply calls the attention of the parties on the need to provide clarification in the arbitration agreement and specifically to empower the arbitral tribunal. However, paragraph (4) makes it clear that in all cases where the dispute relates to a contract (including arbitration *ex aequo et bono*) the arbitral tribunal must decide in accordance with the terms of the contract and shall take into account the usages of the trade applicable to the transaction.

(b) Making of award and other decisions

41. In its rules on the making of the award (articles 29-31), the Model Law focuses on the situation where the arbitral tribunal consists of more than one arbitrator. In such a situation, any award and other decision shall be made by a majority of the arbitrators, except on questions of procedure, which may be left to a presiding arbitrator. The majority principle applies also to the signing of the award, provided that the reason for any omitted signature is stated.

42. Article 31 (3) provides that the award shall state the place of arbitration and shall be deemed to have been made at that place. The effect of the deeming provision is to emphasize that the final making of the award constitutes a legal act, which in practice does not necessarily coincide with one factual event. For the same reason that the arbitral proceedings need not be carried out at the place designated as the legal "place of arbitration", the making of the award may be completed through deliberations held at various places, by telephone or correspondence. In addition, the award does not have to be signed by the arbitrators physically gathering at the same place.

43. The arbitral award must be in writing and state its date. It must also state the reasons on which it is based, unless the parties have agreed otherwise or the award is "on agreed terms" (i.e., an award that records the terms of an amicable settlement by the parties). It may be added that the Model Law neither requires nor prohibits "dissenting opinions".

7. Recourse against award

44. The disparity found in national laws as regards the types of recourse against an arbitral award available to the parties presents a major difficulty in harmonizing international arbitration legislation. Some outdated laws on arbitration, by establishing parallel regimes for recourse against arbitral awards or against court decisions, provide various types of recourse, various (and often long) time periods for exercising the recourse, and extensive lists of grounds on which recourse may be based. That situation (of considerable concern to those involved in international commercial arbitration) is greatly improved by the Model Law, which provides uniform grounds upon which (and clear time periods within which) recourse against an arbitral award may be made.

(a) Application for setting aside as exclusive recourse

45. The first measure of improvement is to allow only one type of recourse, to the exclusion of any other recourse regulated in any procedural law of the State in question. Article 34 (1) provides that the sole recourse against an arbitral award is by application for setting aside, which must be made within three months of receipt of the award (article 34 (3)). In regulating "recourse" (i.e., the means through which a party may actively "attack" the award), article 34 does not preclude a party from seeking court control by way of defence in enforcement proceedings (articles 35 and 36). Article 34 is limited to action before a court (i.e., an organ of the judicial system of a State). However, a party is not precluded from appealing to an arbitral tribunal of second instance if the parties have agreed on such a possibility (as is common in certain commodity trades).

(b) Grounds for setting aside

46. As a further measure of improvement, the Model Law lists exhaustively the grounds on which an award may be set aside. This list essentially mirrors that contained in article 36 (1), which is taken from article V of the New York Convention. The grounds provided in article 34 (2) are set out in

two categories. Grounds which are to be proven by one party are as follows: lack of capacity of the parties to conclude an arbitration agreement; lack of a valid arbitration agreement; lack of notice of appointment of an arbitrator or of the arbitral proceedings or inability of a party to present its case; the award deals with matters not covered by the submission to arbitration; the composition of the arbitral tribunal or the conduct of arbitral proceedings are contrary to the effective agreement of the parties or, failing such agreement, to the Model Law. Grounds that a court may consider of its own initiative are as follows: non-arbitrability of the subject-matter of the dispute or violation of public policy (which is to be understood as serious departures from fundamental notions of procedural justice).

47. The approach under which the grounds for setting aside an award under the Model Law parallel the grounds for refusing recognition and enforcement of the award under article V of the New York Convention is reminiscent of the approach taken in the European Convention on International Commercial Arbitration (Geneva, 1961). Under article IX of the latter Convention, the decision of a foreign court to set aside an award for a reason other than the ones listed in article V of the New York Convention does not constitute a ground for refusing enforcement. The Model Law takes this philosophy one step further by directly limiting the reasons for setting aside.

48. Although the grounds for setting aside as set out in article 34 (2) are almost identical to those for refusing recognition or enforcement as set out in article 36 (1), a practical difference should be noted. An application for setting aside under article 34 (2) may only be made to a court in the State where the award was rendered whereas an application for enforcement might be made in a court in any State. For that reason, the grounds relating to public policy and non-arbitrability may vary in substance with the law applied by the court (in the State of setting aside or in the State of enforcement).

8. Recognition and enforcement of awards

49. The eighth and last chapter of the Model Law deals with the recognition and enforcement of awards. Its provisions reflect the significant policy decision that the same rules should apply to arbitral awards whether made in the country of enforcement or abroad, and that those rules should follow closely the New York Convention.

(a) Towards uniform treatment of all awards irrespective of country of origin

50. By treating awards rendered in international commercial arbitration in a uniform manner irrespective of where they were made, the Model Law distinguishes between "international" and "non-international" awards instead of relying on the traditional distinction between "foreign" and "domestic" awards. This new line is based on substantive grounds rather than territorial borders, which are inappropriate in view of the limited importance of the place of arbitration in international cases. The place of arbitration is often chosen for reasons of convenience of the parties and the dispute may have little or no connection with the State where the

arbitration legally takes place. Consequently, the recognition and enforcement of "international" awards, whether "foreign" or "domestic", should be governed by the same provisions.

51. By modelling the recognition and enforcement rules on the relevant provisions of the New York Convention, the Model Law supplements, without conflicting with, the regime of recognition and enforcement created by that successful Convention.

(b) Procedural conditions of recognition and enforcement

52. Under article 35 (1) any arbitral award, irrespective of the country in which it was made, shall be recognized as binding and enforceable, subject to the provisions of article 35 (2) and of article 36 (the latter of which sets forth the grounds on which recognition or enforcement may be refused). Based on the above consideration of the limited importance of the place of arbitration in international cases and the desire of overcoming territorial restrictions, reciprocity is not included as a condition for recognition and enforcement.

53. The Model Law does not lay down procedural details of recognition and enforcement, which are left to national procedural laws and practices. The Model Law merely sets certain conditions for obtaining enforcement under article 35 (2). It was amended in 2006 to liberalize formal requirements and reflect the amendment made to article 7 on the form of the arbitration agreement. Presentation of a copy of the arbitration agreement is no longer required under article 35 (2).

(c) Grounds for refusing recognition or enforcement

54. Although the grounds on which recognition or enforcement may be refused under the Model Law are identical to those listed in article V of the New York Convention, the grounds listed in the Model Law are relevant not only to foreign awards but to all awards rendered in the sphere of application of the piece of legislation enacting the Model Law. Generally, it was deemed desirable to adopt, for the sake of harmony, the same approach and wording as this important Convention. However, the first ground on the list as contained in the New York Convention (which provides that recognition and enforcement may be refused if "the parties to the arbitration agreement were, under the law applicable to them, under some incapacity") was modified since it was viewed as containing an incomplete and potentially misleading conflict-of-laws rule.

AMERICAN ARBITRATION ASSOCIATION, COMMERCIAL ARBITRATION RULES*

Amended and Effective June 1, 2009

Fee Schedule Amended and Effective June 1, 2010

R-1. Agreement of Parties⁺*

(a) The parties shall be deemed to have made these rules a part of their arbitration agreement whenever they have provided for arbitration by the American Arbitration Association (hereinafter AAA) under its Commercial Arbitration Rules or for arbitration by the AAA of a domestic commercial dispute without specifying particular rules. These rules and any amendment of them shall apply in the form in effect at the time the administrative requirements are met for a demand for arbitration or submission agreement received by the AAA. The parties, by written agreement, may vary the procedures set forth in these rules. After appointment of the arbitrator, such modifications may be made only with the consent of the arbitrator.

(b) Unless the parties or the AAA determines otherwise, the Expedited Procedures shall apply in any case in which no disclosed claim or counterclaim exceeds $75,000, exclusive of interest and arbitration fees and costs. Parties may also agree to use these procedures in larger cases. Unless the parties agree otherwise, these procedures will not apply in cases involving more than two parties. The Expedited Procedures shall be applied as described in Sections E-1 through E-10 of these rules, in addition to any other portion of these rules that is not in conflict with the Expedited Procedures.

(c) Unless the parties agree otherwise, the Procedures for Large, Complex Commercial Disputes shall apply to all cases in which the disclosed claim or counterclaim of any party is at least $500,000, exclusive of claimed interest, arbitration fees and costs. Parties may also agree to use the Procedures in cases involving claims or counterclaims under $500,000, or in nonmonetary cases. The Procedures for Large, Complex Commercial Disputes shall be applied as described in Sections L-1 through L-4 of these rules, in addition to any other portion of these rules that is not in conflict with the Procedures for Large, Complex Commercial Disputes.

⁺ The AAA applies the *Supplementary Procedures for Consumer-Related Disputes* to arbitration clauses in agreements between individual consumers and businesses where the business has a standardized, systematic application of arbitration clauses with customers and where the terms and conditions of the purchase of standardized, consumable goods or services are non-negotiable or primarily non-negotiable in most or all of its terms, conditions, features, or choices. The product or service must be for personal or household use. The AAA will have the discretion to apply or not to apply the Supplementary Procedures and the parties will be able to bring any disputes concerning the application or non-application to the attention of the arbitrator. Consumers are not prohibited from seeking relief in a small claims court for disputes or claims within the scope of its jurisdiction, even in consumer arbitration cases filed by the business.

* A dispute arising out of an employer promulgated plan will be administered under the AAA's National Rules for the Resolution of Employment Disputes.

(d) All other cases shall be administered in accordance with Sections R-1 through R-54 of these rules.

R-2. AAA and Delegation of Duties

When parties agree to arbitrate under these rules, or when they provide for arbitration by the AAA and an arbitration is initiated under these rules, they thereby authorize the AAA to administer the arbitration. The authority and duties of the AAA are prescribed in the agreement of the parties and in these rules, and may be carried out through such of the AAA's representatives as it may direct. The AAA may, in its discretion, assign the administration of an arbitration to any of its offices.

R-3. National Roster of Arbitrators

The AAA shall establish and maintain a National Roster of Commercial Arbitrators ("National Roster") and shall appoint arbitrators as provided in these rules. The term "arbitrator" in these rules refers to the arbitration panel, constituted for a particular case, whether composed of one or more arbitrators, or to an individual arbitrator, as the context requires.

R-4. Initiation under an Arbitration Provision in a Contract

(a) Arbitration under an arbitration provision in a contract shall be initiated in the following manner:

(i) The initiating party (the "claimant") shall, within the time period, if any, specified in the contract(s), give to the other party (the "respondent") written notice of its intention to arbitrate (the "demand"), which demand shall contain a statement setting forth the nature of the dispute, the names and addresses of all other parties, the amount involved, if any, the remedy sought, and the hearing locale requested.

(ii) The claimant shall file at any office of the AAA two copies of the demand and two copies of the arbitration provisions of the contract, together with the appropriate filing fee as provided in the schedule included with these rules.

(iii) The AAA shall confirm notice of such filing to the parties.

(b) A respondent may file an answering statement in duplicate with the AAA within 15 days after confirmation of notice of filing of the demand is sent by the AAA. The respondent shall, at the time of any such filing, send a copy of the answering statement to the claimant. If a counterclaim is asserted, it shall contain a statement setting forth the nature of the counterclaim, the amount involved, if any, and the remedy sought. If a counterclaim is made, the party making the counterclaim shall forward to the AAA with the answering statement the appropriate fee provided in the schedule included with these rules.

(c) If no answering statement is filed within the stated time, respondent will be deemed to deny the claim. Failure to file an answering statement shall not operate to delay the arbitration.

(d) When filing any statement pursuant to this section, the parties are encouraged to provide descriptions of their claims in sufficient detail to make the circumstances of the dispute clear to the arbitrator.

R-5.   Initiation under a Submission

Parties to any existing dispute may commence an arbitration under these rules by filing at any office of the AAA two copies of a written submission to arbitrate under these rules, signed by the parties. It shall contain a statement of the nature of the dispute, the names and addresses of all parties, any claims and counterclaims, the amount involved, if any, the remedy sought, and the hearing locale requested, together with the appropriate filing fee as provided in the schedule included with these rules. Unless the parties state otherwise in the submission, all claims and counterclaims will be deemed to be denied by the other party.

R-6.   Changes of Claim

After filing of a claim, if either party desires to make any new or different claim or counterclaim, it shall be made in writing and filed with the AAA. The party asserting such a claim or counterclaim shall provide a copy to the other party, who shall have 15 days from the date of such transmission within which to file an answering statement with the AAA. After the arbitrator is appointed, however, no new or different claim may be submitted except with the arbitrator's consent.

R-7.   Jurisdiction

(a) The arbitrator shall have the power to rule on his or her own jurisdiction, including any objections with respect to the existence, scope or validity of the arbitration agreement.

(b) The arbitrator shall have the power to determine the existence or validity of a contract of which an arbitration clause forms a part. Such an arbitration clause shall be treated as an agreement independent of the other terms of the contract. A decision by the arbitrator that the contract is null and void shall not for that reason alone render invalid the arbitration clause.

(c) A party must object to the jurisdiction of the arbitrator or to the arbitrability of a claim or counterclaim no later than the filing of the answering statement to the claim or counterclaim that gives rise to the objection. The arbitrator may rule on such objections as a preliminary matter or as part of the final award.

R-8.   Mediation

At any stage of the proceedings, the parties may agree to conduct a mediation conference under the Commercial Mediation Procedures in order to facilitate settlement. The mediator shall not be an arbitrator appointed to the case. Where the parties to a pending arbitration agree to mediate under the AAA's rules, no additional administrative fee is required to initiate the mediation.

R-9.   Administrative Conference

At the request of any party or upon the AAA's own initiative, the AAA may conduct an administrative conference, in person or by telephone, with the parties and/or their representatives. The conference may address such issues as arbitrator selection, potential mediation of the dispute, potential exchange of information, a timetable for hearings and any other administrative matters.

R-10. Fixing of Locale

The parties may mutually agree on the locale where the arbitration is to be held. If any party requests that the hearing be held in a specific locale and the other party files no objection thereto within 15 days after notice of the request has been sent to it by the AAA, the locale shall be the one requested. If a party objects to the locale requested by the other party, the AAA shall have the power to determine the locale, and its decision shall be final and binding.

R-11. Appointment from National Roster

(a) If the parties have not appointed an arbitrator and have not provided any other method of appointment, the arbitrator shall be appointed in the following manner: Immediately after the filing of the submission or the answering statement or the expiration of the time within which the answering statement is to be filed, the AAA shall send simultaneously to each party to the dispute an identical list of 10 (unless the AAA decides that a different number is appropriate) names of persons chosen from the National Roster. The parties are encouraged to agree to an arbitrator from the submitted list and to advise the AAA of their agreement.

(b) If the parties are unable to agree upon an arbitrator, each party to the dispute shall have 15 days from the transmittal date in which to strike names objected to, number the remaining names in order of preference, and return the list to the AAA. If a party does not return the list within the time specified, all persons named therein shall be deemed acceptable. From among the persons who have been approved on both lists, and in accordance with the designated order of mutual preference, the AAA shall invite the acceptance of an arbitrator to serve. If the parties fail to agree on any of the persons named, or if acceptable arbitrators are unable to act, or if for any other reason the appointment cannot be made from the submitted lists, the AAA shall have the power to make the appointment from among other members of the National Roster without the submission of additional lists.

(c) Unless the parties agree otherwise when there are two or more claimants or two or more respondents, the AAA may appoint all the arbitrators.

R-12. Direct Appointment by a Party

(a) If the agreement of the parties names an arbitrator or specifies a method of appointing an arbitrator, that designation or method shall be followed. The notice of appointment, with the name and address of the arbitrator, shall be filed with the AAA by the appointing party. Upon the request of any appointing party, the AAA shall submit a list of members of the National Roster from which the party may, if it so desires, make the appointment.

(b) Where the parties have agreed that each party is to name one arbitrator, the arbitrators so named must meet the standards of Section R-17 with respect to impartiality and independence unless the parties have specifically agreed pursuant to Section R-17(a) that the party-appointed arbitrators are to be non-neutral and need not meet those standards.

(c) If the agreement specifies a period of time within which an arbitrator shall be appointed and any party fails to make the appointment within that period, the AAA shall make the appointment.

(d) If no period of time is specified in the agreement, the AAA shall notify the party to make the appointment. If within 15 days after such notice has been sent, an arbitrator has not been appointed by a party, the AAA shall make the appointment.

R-13. Appointment of Chairperson by Party-Appointed Arbitrators or Parties

(a) If, pursuant to Section R-12, either the parties have directly appointed arbitrators, or the arbitrators have been appointed by the AAA, and the parties have authorized them to appoint a chairperson within a specified time and no appointment is made within that time or any agreed extension, the AAA may appoint the chairperson.

(b) If no period of time is specified for appointment of the chairperson and the party-appointed arbitrators or the parties do not make the appointment within 15 days from the date of the appointment of the last party appointed arbitrator, the AAA may appoint the chairperson.

(c) If the parties have agreed that their party-appointed arbitrators shall appoint the chairperson from the National Roster, the AAA shall furnish to the party-appointed arbitrators, in the manner provided in Section R-11, a list selected from the National Roster, and the appointment of the chairperson shall be made as provided in that Section.

R-14. Nationality of Arbitrator

Where the parties are nationals of different countries, the AAA, at the request of any party or on its own initiative, may appoint as arbitrator a national of a country other than that of any of the parties. The request must be made before the time set for the appointment of the arbitrator as agreed by the parties or set by these rules.

R-15. Number of Arbitrators

If the arbitration agreement does not specify the number of arbitrators, the dispute shall be heard and determined by one arbitrator, unless the AAA, in its discretion, directs that three arbitrators be appointed. A party may request three arbitrators in the demand or answer, which request the AAA will consider in exercising its discretion regarding the number of arbitrators appointed to the dispute.

R-16. Disclosure

(a) Any person appointed or to be appointed as an arbitrator shall disclose to the AAA any circumstance likely to give rise to justifiable doubt as to the arbitrator's impartiality or independence, including any bias or any financial or personal interest in the result of the arbitration or any past or present relationship with the parties or their representatives. Such obligation shall remain in effect throughout the arbitration.

(b) Upon receipt of such information from the arbitrator or another source, the AAA shall communicate the information to the parties and, if it deems it appropriate to do so, to the arbitrator and others.

(c) In order to encourage disclosure by arbitrators, disclosure of information pursuant to this Section R-16 is not to be construed as an indication that the arbitrator considers that the disclosed circumstance is likely to affect impartiality or independence.

R-17.   Disqualification of Arbitrator

(a) Any arbitrator shall be impartial and independent and shall perform his or her duties with diligence and in good faith, and shall be subject to disqualification for

(i) partiality or lack of independence,

(ii) inability or refusal to perform his or her duties with diligence and in good faith, and

(iii) any grounds for disqualification provided by applicable law. The parties may agree in writing, however, that arbitrators directly appointed by a party pursuant to Section R-12 shall be nonneutral, in which case such arbitrators need not be impartial or independent and shall not be subject to disqualification for partiality or lack of independence.

(b) Upon objection of a party to the continued service of an arbitrator, or on its own initiative, the AAA shall determine whether the arbitrator should be disqualified under the grounds set out above, and shall inform the parties of its decision, which decision shall be conclusive.

R-18.   Communication with Arbitrator

(a) No party and no one acting on behalf of any party shall communicate ex parte with an arbitrator or a candidate for arbitrator concerning the arbitration, except that a party, or someone acting on behalf of a party, may communicate ex parte with a candidate for direct appointment pursuant to Section R-12 in order to advise the candidate of the general nature of the controversy and of the anticipated proceedings and to discuss the candidate's qualifications, availability, or independence in relation to the parties or to discuss the suitability of candidates for selection as a third arbitrator where the parties or party-designated arbitrators are to participate in that selection.

(b) Section R-18(a) does not apply to arbitrators directly appointed by the parties who, pursuant to Section R-17(a), the parties have agreed in writing are nonneutral. Where the parties have so agreed under Section R-17(a), the AAA shall as an administrative practice suggest to the parties that they agree further that Section R-18(a) should nonetheless apply prospectively.

R-19.   Vacancies

(a) If for any reason an arbitrator is unable to perform the duties of the office, the AAA may, on proof satisfactory to it, declare the office vacant. Vacancies shall be filled in accordance with the applicable provisions of these rules.

(b) In the event of a vacancy in a panel of neutral arbitrators after the hearings have commenced, the remaining arbitrator or arbitrators may continue with the hearing and determination of the controversy, unless the parties agree otherwise.

(c) In the event of the appointment of a substitute arbitrator, the panel of arbitrators shall determine in its sole discretion whether it is necessary to repeat all or part of any prior hearings.

R-20. Preliminary Hearing

(a) At the request of any party or at the discretion of the arbitrator or the AAA, the arbitrator may schedule as soon as practicable a preliminary hearing with the parties and/or their representatives. The preliminary hearing may be conducted by telephone at the arbitrator's discretion.

(b) During the preliminary hearing, the parties and the arbitrator should discuss the future conduct of the case, including clarification of the issues and claims, a schedule for the hearings and any other preliminary matters.

R-21. Exchange of Information

(a) At the request of any party or at the discretion of the arbitrator, consistent with the expedited nature of arbitration, the arbitrator may direct

(i) the production of documents and other information, and

(ii) the identification of any witnesses to be called.

(b) At least five business days prior to the hearing, the parties shall exchange copies of all exhibits they intend to submit at the hearing.

(c) The arbitrator is authorized to resolve any disputes concerning the exchange of information.

R-22. Date, Time, and Place of Hearing

The arbitrator shall set the date, time, and place for each hearing. The parties shall respond to requests for hearing dates in a timely manner, be cooperative in scheduling the earliest practicable date, and adhere to the established hearing schedule. The AAA shall send a notice of hearing to the parties at least 10 days in advance of the hearing date, unless otherwise agreed by the parties.

R-23. Attendance at Hearings

The arbitrator and the AAA shall maintain the privacy of the hearings unless the law provides to the contrary. Any person having a direct interest in the arbitration is entitled to attend hearings. The arbitrator shall otherwise have the power to require the exclusion of any witness, other than a party or other essential person, during the testimony of any other witness. It shall be discretionary with the arbitrator to determine the propriety of the attendance of any other person other than a party and its representatives.

R-24. Representation

Any party may be represented by counsel or other authorized representative. A party intending to be so represented shall notify the other party and the AAA of the name and address of the representative at least three days prior to the date set for the hearing at which that person is first to appear. When such a representative initiates an arbitration or responds for a party, notice is deemed to have been given.

R-25. Oaths

Before proceeding with the first hearing, each arbitrator may take an oath of office and, if required by law, shall do so. The arbitrator may require witnesses to testify under oath administered by any duly qualified person and, if it is required by law or requested by any party, shall do so.

R-26. Stenographic Record

Any party desiring a stenographic record shall make arrangements directly with a stenographer and shall notify the other parties of these arrangements at least three days in advance of the hearing. The requesting party or parties shall pay the cost of the record. If the transcript is agreed by the parties, or determined by the arbitrator to be the official record of the proceeding, it must be provided to the arbitrator and made available to the other parties for inspection, at a date, time, and place determined by the arbitrator.

R-27. Interpreters

Any party wishing an interpreter shall make all arrangements directly with the interpreter and shall assume the costs of the service.

R-28. Postponements

The arbitrator may postpone any hearing upon agreement of the parties, upon request of a party for good cause shown, or upon the arbitrator's own initiative.

R-29. Arbitration in the Absence of a Party or Representative

Unless the law provides to the contrary, the arbitration may proceed in the absence of any party or representative who, after due notice, fails to be present or fails to obtain a postponement. An award shall not be made solely on the default of a party. The arbitrator shall require the party who is present to submit such evidence as the arbitrator may require for the making of an award.

R-30. Conduct of Proceedings

(a) The claimant shall present evidence to support its claim. The respondent shall then present evidence to support its defense. Witnesses for each party shall also submit to questions from the arbitrator and the adverse party. The arbitrator has the discretion to vary this procedure, provided that the parties are treated with equality and that each party has the right to be heard and is given a fair opportunity to present its case.

(b) The arbitrator, exercising his or her discretion, shall conduct the proceedings with a view to expediting the resolution of the dispute and may direct the order of proof, bifurcate proceedings and direct the parties to focus their presentations on issues the decision of which could dispose of all or part of the case.

(c) The parties may agree to waive oral hearings in any case.

R-31. Evidence

(a) The parties may offer such evidence as is relevant and material to the dispute and shall produce such evidence as the arbitrator may deem necessary to an understanding and determination of the dispute. Conformity to legal rules of evidence shall not be necessary. All evidence shall be taken in the presence of all of the arbitrators and all of the parties, except where any of the parties is absent, in default or has waived the right to be present.

(b) The arbitrator shall determine the admissibility, relevance, and materiality of the evidence offered and may exclude evidence deemed by the arbitrator to be cumulative or irrelevant.

(c) The arbitrator shall take into account applicable principles of legal privilege, such as those involving the confidentiality of communications between a lawyer and client.

(d) An arbitrator or other person authorized by law to subpoena witnesses or documents may do so upon the request of any party or independently.

R-32. Evidence by Affidavit and Post-hearing Filing of Documents or Other Evidence

(a) The arbitrator may receive and consider the evidence of witnesses by declaration or affidavit, but shall give it only such weight as the arbitrator deems it entitled to after consideration of any objection made to its admission.

(b) If the parties agree or the arbitrator directs that documents or other evidence be submitted to the arbitrator after the hearing, the documents or other evidence shall be filed with the AAA for transmission to the arbitrator. All parties shall be afforded an opportunity to examine and respond to such documents or other evidence.

R-33. Inspection or Investigation

An arbitrator finding it necessary to make an inspection or investigation in connection with the arbitration shall direct the AAA to so advise the parties. The arbitrator shall set the date and time and the AAA shall notify the parties. Any party who so desires may be present at such an inspection or investigation. In the event that one or all parties are not present at the inspection or investigation, the arbitrator shall make an oral or written report to the parties and afford them an opportunity to comment.

R-34. Interim Measures**

(a) The arbitrator may take whatever interim measures he or she deems necessary, including injunctive relief and measures for the protection or conservation of property and disposition of perishable goods.

(b) Such interim measures may take the form of an interim award, and the arbitrator may require security for the costs of such measures.

** The Optional Rules for Emergency Measures of Protection can be found below.

(c) A request for interim measures addressed by a party to a judicial authority shall not be deemed incompatible with the agreement to arbitrate or a waiver of the right to arbitrate.

R-35. Closing of Hearing

The arbitrator shall specifically inquire of all parties whether they have any further proofs to offer or witnesses to be heard. Upon receiving negative replies or if satisfied that the record is complete, the arbitrator shall declare the hearing closed. If briefs are to be filed, the hearing shall be declared closed as of the final date set by the arbitrator for the receipt of briefs. If documents are to be filed as provided in Section R-32 and the date set for their receipt is later than that set for the receipt of briefs, the later date shall be the closing date of the hearing. The time limit within which the arbitrator is required to make the award shall commence, in the absence of other agreements by the parties, upon the closing of the hearing.

R-36. Reopening of Hearing

The hearing may be reopened on the arbitrator's initiative, or upon application of a party, at any time before the award is made. If reopening the hearing would prevent the making of the award within the specific time agreed on by the parties in the contract(s) out of which the controversy has arisen, the matter may not be reopened unless the parties agree on an extension of time. When no specific date is fixed in the contract, the arbitrator may reopen the hearing and shall have 30 days from the closing of the reopened hearing within which to make an award.

R-37. Waiver of Rules

Any party who proceeds with the arbitration after knowledge that any provision or requirement of these rules has not been complied with and who fails to state an objection in writing shall be deemed to have waived the right to object.

R-38. Extensions of Time

The parties may modify any period of time by mutual agreement. The AAA or the arbitrator may for good cause extend any period of time established by these rules, except the time for making the award. The AAA shall notify the parties of any extension.

R-39. Serving of Notice

(a) Any papers, notices, or process necessary or proper for the initiation or continuation of an arbitration under these rules, for any court action in connection therewith, or for the entry of judgment on any award made under these rules may be served on a party by mail addressed to the party, or its representative at the last known address or by personal service, in or outside the state where the arbitration is to be held, provided that reasonable opportunity to be heard with regard to the dispute is or has been granted to the party.

(b) The AAA, the arbitrator and the parties may also use overnight delivery or electronic facsimile transmission (fax), to give the notices required by these rules. Where all parties and the arbitrator agree, notices may be transmitted by electronic mail (E-mail), or other methods of communication.

(c) Unless otherwise instructed by the AAA or by the arbitrator, any documents submitted by any party to the AAA or to the arbitrator shall simultaneously be provided to the other party or parties to the arbitration.

R-40. Majority Decision

When the panel consists of more than one arbitrator, unless required by law or by the arbitration agreement, a majority of the arbitrators must make all decisions.

R-41. Time of Award

The award shall be made promptly by the arbitrator and, unless otherwise agreed by the parties or specified by law, no later than 30 days from the date of closing the hearing, or, if oral hearings have been waived, from the date of the AAA's transmittal of the final statements and proofs to the arbitrator.

R-42. Form of Award

(a) Any award shall be in writing and signed by a majority of the arbitrators. It shall be executed in the manner required by law.

(b) The arbitrator need not render a reasoned award unless the parties request such an award in writing prior to appointment of the arbitrator or unless the arbitrator determines that a reasoned award is appropriate.

R-43. Scope of Award

(a) The arbitrator may grant any remedy or relief that the arbitrator deems just and equitable and within the scope of the agreement of the parties, including, but not limited to, specific performance of a contract.

(b) In addition to a final award, the arbitrator may make other decisions, including interim, interlocutory, or partial rulings, orders, and awards. In any interim, interlocutory, or partial award, the arbitrator may assess and apportion the fees, expenses, and compensation related to such award as the arbitrator determines is appropriate.

(c) In the final award, the arbitrator shall assess the fees, expenses, and compensation provided in Sections R-49, R-50, and R-51. The arbitrator may apportion such fees, expenses, and compensation among the parties in such amounts as the arbitrator determines is appropriate.

(d) The award of the arbitrator(s) may include:

(i) interest at such rate and from such date as the arbitrator(s) may deem appropriate; and

(ii) an award of attorneys' fees if all parties have requested such an award or it is authorized by law or their arbitration agreement.

R-44. Award upon Settlement

If the parties settle their dispute during the course of the arbitration and if the parties so request, the arbitrator may set forth the terms of the settlement in a "consent award." A consent award must include an allocation of arbitration costs, including administrative fees and expenses as well as arbitrator fees and expenses.

R-45.   Delivery of Award to Parties

Parties shall accept as notice and delivery of the award the placing of the award or a true copy thereof in the mail addressed to the parties or their representatives at the last known addresses, personal or electronic service of the award, or the filing of the award in any other manner that is permitted by law.

R-46.   Modification of Award

Within 20 days after the transmittal of an award, any party, upon notice to the other parties, may request the arbitrator, through the AAA, to correct any clerical, typographical, or computational errors in the award. The arbitrator is not empowered to redetermine the merits of any claim already decided. The other parties shall be given 10 days to respond to the request. The arbitrator shall dispose of the request within 20 days after transmittal by the AAA to the arbitrator of the request and any response thereto.

R-47.   Release of Documents for Judicial Proceedings

The AAA shall, upon the written request of a party, furnish to the party, at the party's expense, certified copies of any papers in the AAA's possession that may be required in judicial proceedings relating to the arbitration.

R-48.   Applications to Court and Exclusion of Liability

(a) No judicial proceeding by a party relating to the subject matter of the arbitration shall be deemed a waiver of the party's right to arbitrate.

(b) Neither the AAA nor any arbitrator in a proceeding under these rules is a necessary or proper party in judicial proceedings relating to the arbitration.

(c) Parties to an arbitration under these rules shall be deemed to have consented that judgment upon the arbitration award may be entered in any federal or state court having jurisdiction thereof.

(d) Parties to an arbitration under these rules shall be deemed to have consented that neither the AAA nor any arbitrator shall be liable to any party in any action for damages or injunctive relief for any act or omission in connection with any arbitration under these rules.

R-49.   Administrative Fees

As a not-for-profit organization, the AAA shall prescribe an initial filing fee and a case service fee to compensate it for the cost of providing administrative services. The fees in effect when the fee or charge is incurred shall be applicable. The filing fee shall be advanced by the party or parties making a claim or counterclaim, subject to final apportionment by the arbitrator in the award. The AAA may, in the event of extreme hardship on the part of any party, defer or reduce the administrative fees.

R-50.   Expenses

The expenses of witnesses for either side shall be paid by the party producing such witnesses. All other expenses of the arbitration, including required travel and other expenses of the arbitrator, AAA representatives, and any witness and the cost of any proof produced at the direct request of the arbitrator, shall be borne equally by the parties, unless they agree otherwise or unless the arbitrator in the award assesses such expenses or any part thereof against any specified party or parties.

R-51. Neutral Arbitrator's Compensation

(a) Arbitrators shall be compensated at a rate consistent with the arbitrator's stated rate of compensation.

(b) If there is disagreement concerning the terms of compensation, an appropriate rate shall be established with the arbitrator by the AAA and confirmed to the parties.

(c) Any arrangement for the compensation of a neutral arbitrator shall be made through the AAA and not directly between the parties and the arbitrator.

R-52. Deposits

The AAA may require the parties to deposit in advance of any hearings such sums of money as it deems necessary to cover the expense of the arbitration, including the arbitrator's fee, if any, and shall render an accounting to the parties and return any unexpended balance at the conclusion of the case.

R-53. Interpretation and Application of Rules

The arbitrator shall interpret and apply these rules insofar as they relate to the arbitrator's powers and duties. When there is more than one arbitrator and a difference arises among them concerning the meaning or application of these rules, it shall be decided by a majority vote. If that is not possible, either an arbitrator or a party may refer the question to the AAA for final decision. All other rules shall be interpreted and applied by the AAA.

R-54. Suspension for Nonpayment

If arbitrator compensation or administrative charges have not been paid in full, the AAA may so inform the parties in order that one of them may advance the required payment. If such payments are not made, the arbitrator may order the suspension or termination of the proceedings. If no arbitrator has yet been appointed, the AAA may suspend the proceedings.

EXPEDITED PROCEDURES

E-1. Limitation on Extensions

Except in extraordinary circumstances, the AAA or the arbitrator may grant a party no more than one seven-day extension of time to respond to the demand for arbitration or counterclaim as provided in Section R-4.

E-2. Changes of Claim or Counterclaim

A claim or counterclaim may be increased in amount, or a new or different claim or counterclaim added, upon the agreement of the other party, or the consent of the arbitrator. After the arbitrator is appointed, however, no new or different claim or counterclaim may be submitted except with the arbitrator's consent. If an increased claim or counterclaim exceeds $75,000, the case will be administered under the regular procedures unless all parties and the arbitrator agree that the case may continue to be processed under the Expedited Procedures.

E-3. Serving of Notices

In addition to notice provided by Section R-39(b), the parties shall also accept notice by telephone. Telephonic notices by the AAA shall subsequently be confirmed in writing to the parties. Should there be a failure to confirm in writing any such oral notice, the proceeding shall nevertheless be valid if notice has, in fact, been given by telephone.

E-4. Appointment and Qualifications of Arbitrator

(a) The AAA shall simultaneously submit to each party an identical list of five proposed arbitrators drawn from its National Roster from which one arbitrator shall be appointed.

(b) The parties are encouraged to agree to an arbitrator from this list and to advise the AAA of their agreement. If the parties are unable to agree upon an arbitrator, each party may strike two names from the list and return it to the AAA within seven days from the date of the AAA's mailing to the parties. If for any reason the appointment of an arbitrator cannot be made from the list, the AAA may make the appointment from other members of the panel without the submission of additional lists.

(c) The parties will be given notice by the AAA of the appointment of the arbitrator, who shall be subject to disqualification for the reasons specified in Section R-17. The parties shall notify the AAA within seven days of any objection to the arbitrator appointed. Any such objection shall be for cause and shall be confirmed in writing to the AAA with a copy to the other party or parties.

E-5. Exchange of Exhibits

At least two business days prior to the hearing, the parties shall exchange copies of all exhibits they intend to submit at the hearing. The arbitrator shall resolve disputes concerning the exchange of exhibits.

E-6. Proceedings on Documents

Where no party's claim exceeds $10,000, exclusive of interest and arbitration costs, and other cases in which the parties agree, the dispute shall be resolved by submission of documents, unless any party requests an oral hearing, or the arbitrator determines that an oral hearing is necessary. The arbitrator shall establish a fair and equitable procedure for the submission of documents.

E-7. Date, Time, and Place of Hearing

In cases in which a hearing is to be held, the arbitrator shall set the date, time, and place of the hearing, to be scheduled to take place within 30 days of confirmation of the arbitrator's appointment. The AAA will notify the parties in advance of the hearing date.

E-8. The Hearing

(a) Generally, the hearing shall not exceed one day. Each party shall have equal opportunity to submit its proofs and complete its case. The arbitrator shall determine the order of the hearing, and may require further submission of documents within two days after the hearing. For good cause shown, the arbitrator may schedule additional hearings within seven business days after the initial day of hearings.

(b) Generally, there will be no stenographic record. Any party desiring a stenographic record may arrange for one pursuant to the provisions of Section R-26.

E-9. Time of Award

Unless otherwise agreed by the parties, the award shall be rendered not later than 14 days from the date of the closing of the hearing or, if oral hearings have been waived, from the date of the AAA's transmittal of the final statements and proofs to the arbitrator.

E-10. Arbitrator's Compensation

Arbitrators will receive compensation at a rate to be suggested by the AAA regional office.

PROCEDURES FOR LARGE, COMPLEX COMMERCIAL DISPUTES

L-1. Administrative Conference

Prior to the dissemination of a list of potential arbitrators, the AAA shall, unless the parties agree otherwise, conduct an administrative conference with the parties and/or their attorneys or other representatives by conference call. The conference will take place within 14 days after the commencement of the arbitration. In the event the parties are unable to agree on a mutually acceptable time for the conference, the AAA may contact the parties individually to discuss the issues contemplated herein. Such administrative conference shall be conducted for the following purposes and for such additional purposes as the parties or the AAA may deem appropriate:

(a) to obtain additional information about the nature and magnitude of the dispute and the anticipated length of hearing and scheduling;

(b) to discuss the views of the parties about the technical and other qualifications of the arbitrators;

(c) to obtain conflicts statements from the parties; and

(d) to consider, with the parties, whether mediation or other non-adjudicative methods of dispute resolution might be appropriate.

L-2. Arbitrators

(a) Large, Complex Commercial Cases shall be heard and determined by either one or three arbitrators, as may be agreed upon by the parties. If the parties are unable to agree upon the number of arbitrators and a claim or counterclaim involves at least $1,000,000, then three arbitrator(s) shall hear and determine the case. If the parties are unable to agree on the number of arbitrators and each claim and counterclaim is less than $1,000,000, then one arbitrator shall hear and determine the case.

(b) The AAA shall appoint arbitrator(s) as agreed by the parties. If they are unable to agree on a method of appointment, the AAA shall appoint arbitrators from the Large, Complex Commercial Case Panel, in the manner provided in the Regular Commercial Arbitration Rules. Absent agreement of the parties, the arbitrator(s) shall not have served as the mediator in the mediation phase of the instant proceeding.

L-3. Preliminary Hearing

As promptly as practicable after the selection of the arbitrator(s), a preliminary hearing shall be held among the parties and/or their attorneys or other representatives and the arbitrator(s). Unless the parties agree otherwise, the preliminary hearing will be conducted by telephone conference call rather than in person. At the preliminary hearing the matters to be considered shall include, without limitation:

(a) service of a detailed statement of claims, damages and defenses, a statement of the issues asserted by each party and positions with respect thereto, and any legal authorities the parties may wish to bring to the attention of the arbitrator(s);

(b) stipulations to uncontested facts;

(c) the extent to which discovery shall be conducted;

(d) exchange and premarking of those documents which each party believes may be offered at the hearing;

(e) the identification and availability of witnesses, including experts, and such matters with respect to witnesses including their biographies and expected testimony as may be appropriate;

(f) whether, and the extent to which, any sworn statements and/or depositions may be introduced;

(g) the extent to which hearings will proceed on consecutive days;

(h) whether a stenographic or other official record of the proceedings shall be maintained;

(i) the possibility of utilizing mediation or other non-adjudicative methods of dispute resolution; and

(j) the procedure for the issuance of subpoenas.

By agreement of the parties and/or order of the arbitrator(s), the prehearing activities and the hearing procedures that will govern the arbitration will be memorialized in a Scheduling and Procedure Order.

L-4. Management of Proceedings

(a) Arbitrator(s) shall take such steps as they may deem necessary or desirable to avoid delay and to achieve a just, speedy and cost-effective resolution of Large,

Complex Commercial Cases.

(b) Parties shall cooperate in the exchange of documents, exhibits and information within such party's control if the arbitrator(s) consider such production to be consistent with the goal of achieving a just, speedy and cost-effective resolution of a Large, Complex Commercial Case.

(c) The parties may conduct such discovery as may be agreed to by all the parties provided, however, that the arbitrator(s) may place such limitations on the conduct of such discovery as the arbitrator(s) shall deem appropriate. If the parties cannot agree on production of documents and other information, the arbitrator(s), consistent with the expedited nature of arbitration, may establish the extent of the discovery.

(d) At the discretion of the arbitrator(s), upon good cause shown and consistent with the expedited nature of arbitration, the arbitrator(s) may order depositions of, or the propounding of interrogatories to, such persons who may possess information determined by the arbitrator(s) to be necessary to determination of the matter.

(e) The parties shall exchange copies of all exhibits they intend to submit at the hearing 10 business days prior to the hearing unless the arbitrator(s) determine otherwise.

(f) The exchange of information pursuant to this rule, as agreed by the parties and/or directed by the arbitrator(s), shall be included within the Scheduling and Procedure Order.

(g) The arbitrator is authorized to resolve any disputes concerning the exchange of information.

(h) Generally hearings will be scheduled on consecutive days or in blocks of consecutive days in order to maximize efficiency and minimize costs.

OPTIONAL RULES FOR EMERGENCY MEASURES OF PROTECTION

O-1. Applicability

Where parties by special agreement or in their arbitration clause have adopted these rules for emergency measures of protection, a party in need of emergency relief prior to the constitution of the panel shall notify the AAA and all other parties in writing of the nature of the relief sought and the reasons why such relief is required on an emergency basis. The application shall also set forth the reasons why the party is entitled to such relief. Such notice may be given by facsimile transmission, or other reliable means, but must include a statement certifying that all other parties have been notified or an explanation of the steps taken in good faith to notify other parties.

O-2. Appointment of Emergency Arbitrator

Within one business day of receipt of notice as provided in Section O-1, the AAA shall appoint a single emergency arbitrator from a special AAA panel of emergency arbitrators designated to rule on emergency applications. The emergency arbitrator shall immediately disclose any circumstance likely, on the basis of the facts disclosed in the application, to affect such arbitrator's impartiality or independence. Any challenge to the appointment of the emergency arbitrator must be made within one business day of the communication by the AAA to the parties of the appointment of the emergency arbitrator and the circumstances disclosed.

O-3. Schedule

The emergency arbitrator shall as soon as possible, but in any event within two business days of appointment, establish a schedule for consideration of the application for emergency relief. Such schedule shall provide a reasonable opportunity to all parties to be heard, but may provide for proceeding by telephone conference or on written submissions as alternatives to a formal hearing.

O-4. Interim Award

If after consideration the emergency arbitrator is satisfied that the party seeking the emergency relief has shown that immediate and irreparable loss or damage will result in the absence of emergency relief, and that such party is entitled to such relief, the emergency arbitrator may enter an interim award granting the relief and stating the reasons therefore.

O-5. Constitution of the Panel

Any application to modify an interim award of emergency relief must be based on changed circumstances and may be made to the emergency arbitrator until the panel is constituted; thereafter such a request shall be addressed to the panel. The emergency arbitrator shall have no further power to act after the panel is constituted unless the parties agree that the emergency arbitrator is named as a member of the panel.

O-6. Security

Any interim award of emergency relief may be conditioned on provision by the party seeking such relief of appropriate security.

O-7. Special Master

A request for interim measures addressed by a party to a judicial authority shall not be deemed incompatible with the agreement to arbitrate or a waiver of the right to arbitrate. If the AAA is directed by a judicial authority to nominate a special master to consider and report on an application for emergency relief, the AAA shall proceed as provided in Section O-1 of this article and the references to the emergency arbitrator shall be read to mean the special master, except that the special master shall issue a report rather than an interim award.

O-8. Costs

The costs associated with applications for emergency relief shall initially be apportioned by the emergency arbitrator or special master, subject to the power of the panel to determine finally the apportionment of such costs.

ADMINISTRATIVE FEES

Administrative Fee Schedules (Standard and Flexible Fee)

The AAA has two administrative fee options for parties filing claims or counter-claims, the Standard Fee Schedule and Flexible Fee Schedule. The Standard Fee Schedule has a two payment schedule, and the Flexible Fee Schedule has a three payment schedule which offers lower initial filing fees, but potentially higher total administrative fees of approximately 12% to 19% for cases that proceed to a hearing. The administrative fees of the AAA are based on the amount of the claim or counterclaim. Arbitrator compensation is not included in this schedule. Unless the parties agree otherwise, arbitrator compensation and administrative fees are subject to allocation by the arbitrator in the award.

In an effort to make arbitration costs reasonable for consumers, the AAA has a separate fee schedule for consumer-related disputes. Please refer to Section C-8 of the Supplementary Procedures for Consumer-Related Disputes when filing a consumer-related claim. Note that the Flexible Fee Schedule is not available on cases administered under these supplementary procedures.

The AAA applies the Supplementary Procedures for Consumer-Related Disputes to arbitration clauses in agreements between individual consumers and businesses where the business has a standardized, systematic application of arbitration clauses with customers and where the terms and conditions of the purchase of standard-ized, consumable goods or services are non-negotiable or primarily non-negotiable in most or all of its terms, conditions, features, or choices. The product or service must be for personal or household use. The AAA will have the discretion to apply or not to apply the Supplementary Procedures and the parties will be able to bring any disputes concerning the application or non-application to the attention of the arbitrator. Consumers are not prohibited from seeking relief in a small claims court for disputes or claims within the scope of its jurisdiction, even in consumer arbitration cases filed by the business.

Fees for incomplete or deficient filings: Where the applicable arbitration agree-ment does not reference the AAA, the AAA will attempt to obtain the agreement of the other parties to the dispute to have the arbitration administered by the AAA. However, where the AAA is unable to obtain the agreement of the parties to have the AAA administer the arbitration, the AAA will administratively close the case and will not proceed with the administration of the arbitration. In these cases, the AAA will return the filing fees to the filing party, less the amount specified in the fee schedule below for deficient filings.

Parties that file demands for arbitration that are incomplete or otherwise do not meet the filing requirements contained in these Rules shall also be charged the amount specified below for deficient filings if they fail or are unable to respond to the AAA's request to correct the deficiency.

Fees for additional services: The AAA reserves the right to assess additional administrative fees for services performed by the AAA beyond those provided for in these Rules which may be required by the parties' agreement or stipulation.

Standard Fee Schedule

An Initial Filing Fee is payable in full by a filing party when a claim, counterclaim, or additional claim is filed. A Final Fee will be incurred for all cases that proceed to their first hearing. This fee will be payable in advance at the time that the first hearing is scheduled. This fee will be refunded at the conclusion of the case if no hearings have occurred. However, if the Association is not notified at least 24 hours before the time of the scheduled hearing, the Final Fee will remain due and will not be refunded.

These fees will be billed in accordance with the following schedule:

Amount of Claim	Initial Filing Fee	Final Fee
Above $0 to $10,000	$775	$200
Above $10,000 to $75,000	$975	$300
Above $75,000 to $150,000	$1,850	$750
Above $150,000 to $300,000	$2,800	$1,250
Above $300,000 to $500,000	$4,350	$1,750
Above $500,000 to $1,000,000	$6,200	$2,500
Above $1,000,000 to $5,000,000	$8,200	$3,250
Above $5,000,000 to $10,000,000	$10,200	$4,000
Above $10,000,000	Base fee of $12,800 plus.01% of the amount above $10,000,000 Fee Capped at $65,000	$6,000
Nonmonetary Claims[1]	$3,350	$1,250
Deficient Claim Filing Fee[2]	$350	
Additional Services[3]		

Fees are subject to increase if the amount of a claim or counterclaim is modified after the initial filing date. Fees are subject to decrease if the amount of a claim or counterclaim is modified before the first hearing.

The minimum fees for any case having three or more arbitrators are $2,800 for the Initial Filing Fee, plus a $1,250 Final Fee. Expedited Procedures are applied in any case where no disclosed claim or counterclaim exceeds $75,000, exclusive of interest and arbitration costs.

Parties on cases filed under either the Flexible Fee Schedule or the Standard Fee Schedule that are held in abeyance for one year will be assessed an annual abeyance fee of $300. If a party refuses to pay the assessed fee, the other party or parties may

---

[1] This fee is applicable when a claim or counterclaim is not for a monetary amount. Where a monetary claim amount is not known, parties will be required to state a range of claims or be subject to a filing fee of $10,200.

[2] The Deficient Claim Filing Fee shall not be charged in cases filed by a consumer in an arbitration governed by the Supplementary Procedures for the Resolution of Consumer-Related Disputes, or in cases filed by an Employee who is submitting their dispute to arbitration pursuant to an employer promulgated plan.

[3] The AAA may assess additional fees where procedures or services outside the Rules sections are required under the parties' agreement or by stipulation.

pay the entire fee on behalf of all parties, otherwise the matter will be administratively closed.

. . .

Refund Schedule for Standard Fee Schedule

The AAA offers a refund schedule on filing fees connected with the Standard Fee Schedule. For cases with claims up to $75,000, a minimum filing fee of $350 will not be refunded. For all other cases, a minimum fee of $600 will not be refunded. Subject to the minimum fee requirements, refunds will be calculated as follows:

> 100% of the filing fee, above the minimum fee, will be refunded if the case is settled or withdrawn within five calendar days of filing.

> 50% of the filing fee, will be refunded if the case is settled or withdrawn between six and 30 calendar days of filing.

> 25% of the filing fee will be refunded if the case is settled or withdrawn between 31 and 60 calendar days of filing.

No refund will be made once an arbitrator has been appointed (this includes one arbitrator on a three-arbitrator panel). No refunds will be granted on awarded cases.

Note: The date of receipt of the demand for arbitration with the AAA will be used to calculate refunds of filing fees for both claims and counterclaims.

Flexible Fee Schedule

A non-refundable Initial Filing Fee is payable in full by a filing party when a claim, counterclaim, or additional claim is filed. Upon receipt of the Demand for Arbitration, the AAA will promptly initiate the case and notify all parties as well as establish the due date for filing of an Answer, which may include a Counterclaim. In order to proceed with the further administration of the arbitration and appointment of the arbitrator(s), the appropriate, non-refundable Proceed Fee outlined below must be paid.

If a Proceed Fee is not submitted within ninety (90) days of the filing of the Claimant's Demand for Arbitration, the Association will administratively close the file and notify all parties.

No refunds or refund schedule will apply to the Filing or Proceed Fees once received.

The Flexible Fee Schedule below also may be utilized for the filing of counterclaims. However, as with the Claimant's claim, the counterclaim will not be presented to the arbitrator until the Proceed Fee is paid.

A Final Fee will be incurred for all claims and/or counterclaims that proceed to their first hearing. This fee will be payable in advance when the first hearing is scheduled, but will be refunded at the conclusion of the case if no hearings have occurred. However, if the Association is not notified of a cancellation at least 24 hours before the time of the scheduled hearing, the Final Fee will remain due and will not be refunded.

All fees will be billed in accordance with the following schedule:

Amount of Claim	Initial Filing Fee	Proceed Fee	Final Fee
Above $0 to $10,000	$400	$475	$200
Above $10,000 to $75,000	$625	$500	$300
Above $75,000 to $150,000	$850	$1250	$750
Above $150,000 to $300,000	$1,000	$2125	$1,250
Above $300,000 to $500,000	$1,500	$3,400	$1,750
Above $500,000 to $1,000,000	$2,500	$4,500	$2,500
Above $1,000,000 to $5,000,000	$2,500	$6,700	$3,250
Above $5,000,000 to $10,000,000	$3,500	$8,200	$4,000
Above $10,000,000	$4,500	$10,300 plus .01% of claim amount over $10,000,000 up to $65,000	$6,000
Nonmonetary[1]	$2,000	$2,000	$1,250
Deficient Claim Filing Fee	$350		
Additional Services[2]			

. . .

All fees are subject to increase if the amount of a claim or counterclaim is modified after the initial filing date. Fees are subject to decrease if the amount of a claim or counterclaim is modified before the first hearing.

The minimum fees for any case having three or more arbitrators are $1,000 for the Initial Filing Fee; $2,125 for the Proceed Fee; and $1,250 for the Final Fee.

Under the Flexible Fee Schedule, a party's obligation to pay the Proceed Fee shall remain in effect regardless of any agreement of the parties to stay, postpone or otherwise modify the arbitration proceedings. Parties that, through mutual agreement, have held their case in abeyance for one year will be assessed an annual abeyance fee of $300. If a party refuses to pay the assessed fee, the other party or parties may pay the entire fee on behalf of all parties, otherwise the matter will be closed.

Note: The date of receipt by the AAA of the demand for arbitration will be used

---

[1] This fee is applicable when a claim or counterclaim is not for a monetary amount. Where a monetary claim amount is not known, parties will be required to state a range of claims or be subject to a filing fee of $3,500 and a proceed fee of $8,200.

[2] The AAA reserves the right to assess additional administrative fees for services performed by the AAA beyond those provided for in these Rules and which may be required by the parties' agreement or stipulation.

to calculate the ninety (90) day time limit for payment of the Proceed Fee.

There is no Refund Schedule in the Flexible Fee Schedule.

Hearing Room Rental

The fees described above do not cover the cost of hearing rooms, which are available on a rental basis. Check with the AAA for availability and rates.

AMERICAN ARBITRATION ASSOCIATION, CONSUMER-RELATED DISPUTES SUPPLEMENTARY PROCEDURES*

Rules Effective September 15, 2005

Fees Effective January 1, 2010

GLOSSARY OF TERMS

Claimant

A Claimant is the party who files the claim or starts the arbitration. Either the consumer or the business may be the Claimant.

Respondent

A Respondent is the party against whom the claim is filed. If a Respondent states a claim in arbitration, it is called a counterclaim. Either the consumer or the business may be the Respondent.

ADR Process

An ADR (Alternative Dispute Resolution) Process is a method of resolving a dispute out of court. Mediation and Arbitration are the most widely used ADR processes.

Arbitration

In arbitration, the parties submit disputes to an impartial person (the arbitrator) for a decision. Each party can present evidence to the arbitrator. Arbitrators do not have to follow the Rules of Evidence used in court. Arbitrators decide cases with written decisions or "awards." An award is usually binding on the parties. A court may enforce an arbitration award, but the court's review of arbitration awards is limited.

Desk Arbitration

In a Desk Arbitration, the parties submit their arguments and evidence to the arbitrator in writing. The arbitrator then makes an award based only on the documents. No hearing is held.

Telephone Hearing

In a Telephone Hearing, the parties have the opportunity to tell the arbitrator about their case during a conference call. Often this is done after the parties have sent in documents for the arbitrator to review. A Telephone Hearing can be cheaper and easier than an In Person Hearing.

In Person Hearing

During an In Person Hearing, the parties and the arbitrator meet in a conference

---

room or office and the parties present their evidence in a process that is similar to going to court. However, an In Person Hearing is not as formal as going to court.

Mediation

In Mediation, an impartial person (the mediator) helps the parties try to settle their dispute by reaching an agreement together. A mediator's role is to help the parties come to an agreement. A mediator does not arbitrate or decide the outcome.

Neutral

A Neutral is a word that is used to describe someone who is a mediator, arbitrator, or other independent, impartial person selected to serve as the independent third party in an ADR process.

Case Manager

The Case Manager is the AAA's employee assigned to handle the administrative aspects of the case. He or she does not decide the case. He or she only manages the case's administrative steps, such as exchanging documents, matching schedules, and setting up hearings. The Case Manager is the parties' contact point for almost all aspects of the case outside of any hearings.

ADR Agreement

An ADR Agreement is an agreement between a business and a consumer to submit disputes to mediation, arbitration, or other ADR processes.

ADR Program

An ADR Program is any program or service set up or used by a business to resolve disputes out of court.

Independent ADR Institution

An Independent ADR Institution is an organization that provides independent and impartial administration of ADR programs for consumers and businesses. The American Arbitration Association is an Independent ADR Institution.

SUPPLEMENTARY PROCEDURES FOR THE RESOLUTION OF CONSUMER-RELATED DISPUTES

C-1. Agreement of Parties and Applicability

(a) The Commercial Dispute Resolution Procedures and these Supplementary Procedures for Consumer-Related Disputes shall apply whenever the American Arbitration Association (AAA) or its rules are used in an agreement between a consumer and a business where the business has a standardized, systematic application of arbitration clauses with customers and where the terms and conditions of the purchase of standardized, consumable goods or services are non-negotiable or primarily non-negotiable in most or all of its terms, conditions, features, or choices. The product or service must be for personal or household use. The AAA will have the discretion to apply or not to apply the Supplementary

Procedures and the parties will be able to bring any disputes concerning the application or non-application to the attention of the arbitrator. The AAA's most current rules will be used when the arbitration is started. If there is a difference between the Commercial Dispute Resolution Procedures and the Supplementary Procedures, the Supplementary Procedures will be used. The Commercial Dispute Resolution Procedures may be found on our Web site. . . . They may also be obtained from the Case Manager.

(b) The Expedited Procedures will be used unless there are three arbitrators. In such cases, the Commercial Dispute Resolution Procedures shall apply.

(c) The AAA may substitute another set of rules, such as the Real Estate or the Wireless Industry Arbitration Rules, for the Commercial Dispute Resolution Procedures in some cases.

(d) Parties can still take their claims to a small claims court.

C-2. Initiation Under an Arbitration Agreement

(a) The filing party (the "claimant") must notify the other party (the "respondent"), in writing, that it wishes to arbitrate a dispute. This notification is referred to as the "demand" for arbitration. The demand should:

- briefly explain the dispute,
- list the names and addresses of the consumer and the business,
- specify the amount of money involved,
- state what the claimant wants.

The claimant must also send two copies of the demand to the AAA at the time it sends the demand to the respondent. When sending a demand to the AAA, the claimant must attach a copy of the arbitration agreement from the consumer contract with the business. The claimant must also send the appropriate administrative fees and deposits. A fee schedule can be found in Section C-8 at the end of this Supplement.

(b) The AAA shall confirm receipt of the demand to the parties.

(c) The respondent may answer the demand and may also file a counterclaim. The answer must be sent to the AAA within ten calendar days after the AAA acknowledges receipt of claimant's demand. The answer must:

- be in writing,
- be sent, in duplicate, to the AAA,
- be sent to the claimant at the same time.
- If the respondent has a counterclaim, it must state the nature of the counterclaim, the amount involved, and the remedy sought.

(d) If no answer is filed within the stated time, the AAA will assume that the respondent denies the claim.

(e) The respondent must also send the appropriate administrative fees and deposits. A fee schedule can be found in Section C-8 at the end of this Supplement. Payment is due ten calendar days after the AAA acknowledges receipt of claimant's demand.

C-3. Initiation Under a Submission

Where no agreement to arbitrate exists in the contract between the consumer and the business, the parties may agree to arbitrate a dispute. To begin arbitration, the parties must send the AAA a submission agreement. The submission agreement must:

- be in writing,
- be signed by both parties,
- briefly explain the dispute,
- list the names and addresses of the consumer and the business,
- specify the amount of money involved,
- state the solution sought.

The parties should send two copies of the submission to the AAA. They must also send the administrative fees and deposits. A fee schedule can be found in Section C-8 at the end of this Supplement.

C-4. Appointment of Arbitrator

Immediately after the filing of the submission or the answer, or after the deadline for filing the answer, the AAA will appoint an arbitrator. The parties will have seven calendar days from the time the AAA notifies them, to submit any factual objections to that arbitrator's service.

C-5. Proceedings on Documents ("Desk Arbitration")

Where no claims or counterclaims exceed $10,000, the dispute shall be resolved by the submission of documents. Any party, however, may ask for a hearing. The arbitrator may also decide that a hearing is necessary.

The arbitrator will establish a fair process for submitting the documents. Documents must be sent to the AAA. These will be forwarded to the arbitrator.

C-6. Expedited Hearing Procedures

A party may request that the arbitrator hold a hearing. This hearing may be by telephone or in person. The hearing may occur even if the other party does not attend. A request for a hearing should be made in writing within ten calendar days after the AAA acknowledges receipt of a claimant's demand for arbitration. Requests received after that date will be allowed at the discretion of the arbitrator.

In a case where any party's claim exceeds $10,000, the arbitrator will conduct a hearing unless the parties agree not to have one.

Any hearings will be conducted in accordance with the Expedited Procedures of the Commercial Dispute Resolution Procedures. These procedures may be found on our Web site. . . . They may also be obtained from the Case Manager.

C-7. The Award

(a) Unless the parties agree otherwise, the arbitrator must make his or her award within fourteen calendar days from the date of the closing of the hearing. For Desk Arbitrations, the arbitrator has fourteen calendar days from when the AAA sends the final documents to the arbitrator.

(b) Awards shall be in writing and shall be executed as required by law.

(c) In the award, the arbitrator should apply any identified pertinent contract terms, statutes, and legal precedents. The arbitrator may grant any remedy, relief or outcome that the parties could have received in court. The award shall be final and binding. The award is subject to review in accordance with applicable statutes governing arbitration awards.

C-8. Administrative Fees and Arbitrator Fees*

Administrative fees and arbitrator compensation deposits are due from the claimant at the time a case is filed. They are due from the respondent at the time the answer is due. The amounts paid by the consumer and the business are set forth below.

Administrative Fees

Administrative fees are based on the size of the claim and counterclaim in a dispute. They are based only on the actual damages and not on any additional damages, such as attorneys' fees or punitive damages. Portions of these fees are refundable pursuant to the Commercial Fee Schedule.

Arbitrator Fees

For cases in which no claim exceeds $75,000, arbitrators are paid based on the type of proceeding that is used. The parties make deposits as set forth below. Any unused deposits are returned at the end of the case.

Desk Arbitration or Telephone Hearing	$250 for service on the case
In Person Hearing	$750 per day of hearing

For cases in which a claim or counterclaim exceeds $75,000, arbitrators are compensated at the rates set forth on their panel biographies.

Fees and Deposits to be Paid by the Consumer:

If the consumer's claim or counterclaim does not exceed $10,000, then the

---

* Pursuant to Section 1284.3 of the California Code of Civil Procedure, consumers with a gross monthly income of less than 300% of the federal poverty guidelines are entitled to a waiver of arbitration fees and costs, exclusive of arbitrator fees. This law applies to all consumer agreements subject to the California Arbitration Act, and to all consumer arbitrations conducted in California. If you believe that you meet these requirements, you must submit to the AAA a declaration under of oath regarding your monthly income and the number of persons in your household. Please contact the AAA's Western Case Management Center at 1-877-528-0879, if you have any questions regarding the waiver of administrative fees. (Effective January 1, 2003)

consumer is responsible for one-half the arbitrator's fees up to a maximum of $125. This deposit is used to pay the arbitrator. It is refunded if not used.

If the consumer's claim or counterclaim is greater than $10,000, but does not exceed $75,000, then the consumer is responsible for one-half the arbitrator's fees up to a maximum of $375. This deposit is used to pay the arbitrator. It is refunded if not used.

If the consumer's claim or counterclaim exceeds $75,000, or if the consumer's claim or counterclaim is non-monetary, then the consumer must pay an Administrative Fee in accordance with the Commercial Fee Schedule. A portion of this fee is refundable pursuant to the Commercial Fee Schedule. The consumer must also deposit one-half of the arbitrator's compensation. This deposit is used to pay the arbitrator. This deposit is refunded if not used. The arbitrator's compensation rate is set forth on the panel biography provided to the parties when the arbitrator is appointed.

Fees and Deposits to be Paid by the Business:

Administrative Fees:

If neither party's claim or counterclaim exceeds $10,000, the business must pay $775 and a Case Service Fee of $200 if a hearing is held. A portion of this fee is refundable pursuant to the Commercial Fee Schedule.

If either party's claim or counterclaim exceeds $10,000, but does not exceed $75,000, the business must pay $975 and a Case Service Fee of $300 if a hearing is held. A portion of this fee is refundable pursuant to the Commercial Fee Schedule.

If the business's claim or counterclaim exceeds $75,000 or if the business's claim or counterclaim is non-monetary, the business must pay an Administrative Fee in accordance with the Commercial Fee Schedule. A portion of this fee is refundable pursuant to the Commercial Fee Schedule.

Arbitrator Fees:

The business must pay for all arbitrator compensation deposits beyond those that are the responsibility of the consumer. These deposits are refunded if not used.

If a party fails to pay its fees and share of the administrative fee or the arbitrator compensation deposit, the other party may advance such funds. The arbitrator may assess these costs in the award.

AMERICAN ARBITRATION ASSOCIATION, SUPPLEMENTARY RULES FOR CLASS ARBITRATIONS*

Rules Effective October 8, 2003

Fees Effective January 1, 2010

1. Applicability

(a) These Supplementary Rules for Class Arbitrations ("Supplementary Rules") shall apply to any dispute arising out of an agreement that provides for arbitration pursuant to any of the rules of the American Arbitration Association ("AAA") where a party submits a dispute to arbitration on behalf of or against a class or purported class, and shall supplement any other applicable AAA rules. These Supplementary Rules shall also apply whenever a court refers a matter pleaded as a class action to the AAA for administration, or when a party to a pending AAA arbitration asserts new claims on behalf of or against a class or purported class.

(b) Where inconsistencies exist between these Supplementary Rules and other AAA rules that apply to the dispute, these Supplementary Rules will govern. The arbitrator shall have the authority to resolve any inconsistency between any agreement of the parties and these Supplementary Rules, and in doing so shall endeavor to avoid any prejudice to the interests of absent members of a class or purported class.

(c) Whenever a court has, by order, addressed and resolved any matter that would otherwise be decided by an arbitrator under these Supplementary Rules, the arbitrator shall follow the order of the court.

2. Class Arbitration Roster and Number of Arbitrators

(a) In any arbitration conducted pursuant to these Supplementary Rules, at least one of the arbitrators shall be appointed from the AAA's national roster of class arbitration arbitrators.

(b) If the parties cannot agree upon the number of arbitrators to be appointed, the dispute shall be heard by a sole arbitrator unless the AAA, in its discretion, directs that three arbitrators be appointed. As used in these Supplementary Rules, the term "arbitrator" includes both one and three arbitrators.

3. Construction of the Arbitration Clause

Upon appointment, the arbitrator shall determine as a threshold matter, in a reasoned, partial final award on the construction of the arbitration clause, whether the applicable arbitration clause permits the arbitration to proceed on behalf of or against a class (the "Clause Construction Award"). The arbitrator shall stay all proceedings following the issuance of the Clause Construction Award for a period of at least 30 days to permit any party to move a court of competent jurisdiction to confirm or to vacate the Clause Construction Award. Once all parties inform the arbitrator in writing during the period of the stay that they do not intend to seek judicial review of the Clause Construction Award, or once the requisite time period expires without any party having informed the arbitrator that it has done so, the arbitrator may proceed with the arbitration on the basis stated in the Clause Construction Award. If any party informs the arbitrator within the period provided that it has sought judicial review, the arbitrator may stay further proceedings, or some part of them, until the arbitrator is informed of the ruling of the court.

In construing the applicable arbitration clause, the arbitrator shall not consider the existence of these Supplementary Rules, or any other AAA rules, to be a factor either in favor of or against permitting the arbitration to proceed on a class basis.

4. Class Certification

(a) Prerequisites to a Class Arbitration

If the arbitrator is satisfied that the arbitration clause permits the arbitration to proceed as a class arbitration, as provided in Rule 3, or where a court has ordered that an arbitrator determine whether a class arbitration may be maintained, the arbitrator shall determine whether the arbitration should proceed as a class arbitration. For that purpose, the arbitrator shall consider the criteria enumerated in this Rule 4 and any law or agreement of the parties the arbitrator determines applies to the arbitration. In doing so, the arbitrator shall determine whether one or more members of a class may act in the arbitration as representative parties on behalf of all members of the class described. The arbitrator shall permit a representative to do so only if each of the following conditions is met:

(1) the class is so numerous that joinder of separate arbitrations on behalf of all members is impracticable;

(2) there are questions of law or fact common to the class;

(3) the claims or defenses of the representative parties are typical of the claims or defenses of the class;

(4) the representative parties will fairly and adequately protect the interests of the class;

(5) counsel selected to represent the class will fairly and adequately protect the interests of the class; and

(6) each class member has entered into an agreement containing an arbitration clause which is substantially similar to that signed by the class representative(s) and each of the other class members.

(b) Class Arbitrations Maintainable

An arbitration may be maintained as a class arbitration if the prerequisites of subdivision (a) are satisfied, and in addition, the arbitrator finds that the questions of law or fact common to the members of the class predominate over any questions affecting only individual members, and that a class arbitration is superior to other available methods for the fair and efficient adjudication of the controversy. The matters pertinent to the findings include:

(1) the interest of members of the class in individually controlling the prosecution or defense of separate arbitrations;

(2) the extent and nature of any other proceedings concerning the controversy already commenced by or against members of the class;

(3) the desirability or undesirability of concentrating the determination of the claims in a single arbitral forum; and

(4) the difficulties likely to be encountered in the management of a class arbitration.

5.   Class Determination Award

(a) The arbitrator's determination concerning whether an arbitration should proceed as a class arbitration shall be set forth in a reasoned, partial final award (the "Class Determination Award"), which shall address each of the matters set forth in Rule 4.

(b) A Class Determination Award certifying a class arbitration shall define the class, identify the class representative(s) and counsel, and shall set forth the class claims, issues, or defenses. A copy of the proposed Notice of Class Determination (see Rule 6), specifying the intended mode of delivery of the Notice to the class members, shall be attached to the award.

(c) The Class Determination Award shall state when and how members of the class may be excluded from the class arbitration. If an arbitrator concludes that some exceptional circumstance, such as the need to resolve claims seeking injunctive relief or claims to a limited fund, makes it inappropriate to allow class members to request exclusion, the Class Determination Award shall explain the reasons for that conclusion.

(d) The arbitrator shall stay all proceedings following the issuance of the Class Determination Award for a period of at least 30 days to permit any party to move a court of competent jurisdiction to confirm or to vacate the Class Determination Award. Once all parties inform the arbitrator in writing during the period of the stay that they do not intend to seek judicial review of the Class Determination Award, or once the requisite time period expires without any party having informed the arbitrator that it has done so, the arbitrator may proceed with the arbitration on the basis stated in the Class Determination Award. If any party informs the arbitrator within the period provided that it has sought judicial review, the arbitrator may stay further proceedings, or some part of them, until the arbitrator is informed of the ruling of the court.

(e) A Class Determination Award may be altered or amended by the arbitrator before a final award is rendered.

6.   Notice of Class Determination

(a) In any arbitration administered under these Supplementary Rules, the arbitrator shall, after expiration of the stay following the Class Determination Award, direct that class members be provided the best notice practicable under the circumstances (the "Notice of Class Determination"). The Notice of Class Determination shall be given to all members who can be identified through reasonable effort.

(b) The Notice of Class Determination must concisely and clearly state in plain, easily understood language:

(1) the nature of the action;

(2) the definition of the class certified;

(3) the class claims, issues, or defenses;

(4) that a class member may enter an appearance through counsel if the member so desires, and that any class member may attend the hearings;

(5) that the arbitrator will exclude from the class any member who requests exclusion, stating when and how members may elect to be excluded;

(6) the binding effect of a class judgment on class members;

(7) the identity and biographical information about the arbitrator, the class representative(s) and class counsel that have been approved by the arbitrator to represent the class; and

(8) how and to whom a class member may communicate about the class arbitration, including information about the AAA Class Arbitration Docket (see Rule 9).

7. Final Award

The final award on the merits in a class arbitration, whether or not favorable to the class, shall be reasoned and shall define the class with specificity. The final award shall also specify or describe those to whom the notice provided in Rule 6 was directed, those the arbitrator finds to be members of the class, and those who have elected to opt out of the class.

8. Settlement, Voluntary Dismissal, or Compromise

(a) (1) Any settlement, voluntary dismissal, or compromise of the claims, issues, or defenses of an arbitration filed as a class arbitration shall not be effective unless approved by the arbitrator.

(2) The arbitrator must direct that notice be provided in a reasonable manner to all class members who would be bound by a proposed settlement, voluntary dismissal, or compromise.

(3) The arbitrator may approve a settlement, voluntary dismissal, or compromise that would bind class members only after a hearing and on finding that the settlement, voluntary dismissal, or compromise is fair, reasonable, and adequate.

(b) The parties seeking approval of a settlement, voluntary dismissal, or compromise under this Rule must submit to the arbitrator any agreement made in connection with the proposed settlement, voluntary dismissal, or compromise.

(c) The arbitrator may refuse to approve a settlement unless it affords a new opportunity to request exclusion to individual class members who had an earlier opportunity to request exclusion but did not do so.

(d) Any class member may object to a proposed settlement, voluntary dismissal, or compromise that requires approval under this Rule. Such an objection may be withdrawn only with the approval of the arbitrator.

9. Confidentiality; Class Arbitration Docket

(a) The presumption of privacy and confidentiality in arbitration proceedings shall not apply in class arbitrations. All class arbitration hearings and filings may be made public, subject to the authority of the arbitrator to provide otherwise in special circumstances. However, in no event shall class members, or their individual counsel, if any, be excluded from the arbitration hearings.

(b) The AAA shall maintain on its Web site a Class Arbitration Docket of arbitrations filed as class arbitrations. The Class Arbitration Docket will provide certain information about the arbitration to the extent known to the AAA, including:

(1) a copy of the demand for arbitration;

(2) the identities of the parties;

(3) the names and contact information of counsel for each party;

(4) a list of awards made in the arbitration by the arbitrator; and

(5) the date, time and place of any scheduled hearings.

10. Form and Publication of Awards

(a) Any award rendered under these Supplementary Rules shall be in writing, shall be signed by the arbitrator or a majority of the arbitrators, and shall provide reasons for the award.

(b) All awards rendered under these Supplementary Rules shall be publicly available, on a cost basis.

11. Administrative Fees and Suspension for Nonpayment

(a) A preliminary filing fee of $3,350 is payable in full by a party making a demand for treatment of a claim, counterclaim, or additional claim as a class arbitration. The preliminary filing fee shall cover all AAA administrative fees through the rendering of the Clause Construction Award. If the arbitrator determines that the arbitration shall proceed beyond the Clause Construction Award, a supplemental filing fee shall be paid by the requesting party. The supplemental filing fee shall be calculated based on the amount claimed in the class arbitration and in accordance with the fee schedule contained in the AAA's Commercial Arbitration Rules.

(b) Disputes regarding the parties' obligation to pay administrative fees or arbitrator's compensation pursuant to applicable law or the parties' agreement may be determined by the arbitrator. Upon the joint application of the parties, however, an arbitrator other than the arbitrator appointed to decide the merits of the arbitration, shall be appointed by the AAA to render a partial final award solely related to any disputes regarding the parties' obligations to pay administrative fees or arbitrator's compensation.

(c) If an invoice for arbitrator compensation or administrative charges has not been paid in full, the AAA may so inform the parties in order that one of them may advance the required deposit. If such payments are not made, the arbitrator may order the suspension or termination of the proceedings. If no arbitrator has yet been appointed, the AAA may suspend the proceedings.

(d) If an arbitration conducted pursuant to these Supplementary Rules is suspended for nonpayment, a notice that the case has been suspended shall be published on the AAA's Class Arbitration Docket.

12. Applications to Court and Exclusion of Liability

(a) No judicial proceeding initiated by a party relating to a class arbitration shall be deemed a waiver of the party's right to arbitrate.

(b) Neither the AAA nor any arbitrator in a class arbitration or potential class arbitration under these Supplementary Rules is a necessary or proper party in or to judicial proceedings relating to the arbitration. It is the policy of the AAA to comply with any order of a court directed to the parties to an arbitration or with respect to the conduct of an arbitration, whether or not the AAA is named as a party to the judicial proceeding in which the order is issued.

(c) Parties to a class arbitration under these Supplementary Rules shall be deemed to have consented that judgment upon each of the awards rendered in the arbitration may be entered in any federal or state court having jurisdiction thereof.

(d) Parties to an arbitration under these Supplementary Rules shall be deemed to have consented that neither the AAA nor any arbitrator shall be liable to any party in any action seeking damages or injunctive relief for any act or omission in connection with any arbitration under these Supplementary Rules.

JAMS EMPLOYMENT ARBITRATION RULES AND PROCEDURES*

Effective July 15, 2009

Rule 1. Scope of Rules

(a) The JAMS Employment Arbitration Rules and Procedures ("Rules") govern binding Arbitrations of disputes or claims that are administered by JAMS and in which the Parties agree to use these Rules or, in the absence of such agreement, the disputes or claims are employment-related, unless other Rules are prescribed.

(b) The Parties shall be deemed to have made these Rules a part of their Arbitration agreement ("Agreement") whenever they have provided for Arbitration by JAMS under its Employment Rules or for Arbitration by JAMS without specifying any particular JAMS Rules and the disputes or claims meet the criteria of the first paragraph of this Rule.

(c) The authority and duties of JAMS are prescribed in the Agreement of the Parties and in these Rules, and may be carried out through such representatives as it may direct.

(d) JAMS may, in its discretion, assign the administration of an Arbitration to any of its Resolution Centers.

(e) The term "Party" as used in these Rules includes Parties to the Arbitration and their counsel or representatives.

(f) "Electronic filing" (e-file) means the electronic transmission of documents to and from JAMS and other Parties for the purpose of filing via the Internet. "Electronic service" (e-service) means the electronic transmission of documents via JAMS Electronic Filing System to a party, attorney or representative under these Rules.

Rule 2. Party-Agreed Procedures

The Parties may agree on any procedures not specified herein or in lieu of these Rules that are consistent with the applicable law and JAMS policies including, without limitation, the JAMS Policy on Employment Arbitration Minimum Standards of Procedural Fairness, and Rules 15(i), 30 and 31. The Parties shall promptly notify JAMS of any such Party-agreed procedures and shall confirm such procedures in writing. The Party-agreed procedures shall be enforceable as if contained in these Rules.

Rule 3. Amendment of Rules

JAMS may amend these Rules without notice. The Rules in effect on the date of the commencement of an Arbitration (as defined in Rule 5) shall apply to that Arbitration, unless the Parties have agreed upon another version of the Rules.

Rule 4. Conflict with Law

---

* Reprinted with permission. Copyright © 2009 by JAMS. All rights reserved.

If any of these Rules, or modification of these Rules agreed on by the Parties, is determined to be in conflict with a provision of applicable law, the provision of law will govern over the Rule in conflict, and no other Rule will be affected.

Rule 5.   Commencing an Arbitration

(a) The Arbitration is deemed commenced when JAMS confirms in a Commencement Letter its receipt of one of the following:

(i) A post-dispute Arbitration agreement fully executed by all Parties and that specifies JAMS administration or use of any JAMS Rules; or

(ii) A pre-dispute written contractual provision requiring the Parties to arbitrate the employment dispute or claim and which specifies JAMS administration or use of any JAMS Rules or which the Parties agree shall be administered by JAMS; or

(iii) A written confirmation of an oral agreement of all Parties to participate in an Arbitration administered by JAMS or conducted pursuant to any JAMS Rules; or

(iv) A copy of a court order compelling Arbitration at JAMS.

(b) The Commencement Letter shall confirm which one of the above requirements for commencement has been met, that JAMS has received all payments required under the applicable fee schedule, and that the claimant has provided JAMS with contact information for all Parties along with evidence that the Demand has been served on all Parties.

(c) If a Party that is obligated to arbitrate in accordance with subparagraph (a) of this Rule fails to agree to participate in the Arbitration process, JAMS shall confirm in writing that Party's failure to respond or participate and, pursuant to Rule 19, the Arbitrator, once appointed, shall schedule, and provide appropriate notice of a Hearing or other opportunity for the Party demanding the Arbitration to demonstrate its entitlement to relief.

(d) The date of commencement of the Arbitration is the date of the Commencement Letter, but it is not intended to be applicable to any legal requirements such as the statute of limitations, any contractual limitations period, or claims notice requirements. The term "commencement" as used in this Rule is intended only to pertain to the operation of this and other rules (such as Rule 3, 9(a), 9(c), 13(a), 17(a), 31(a).)

Rule 6.   Preliminary and Administrative Matters

(a) JAMS may convene, or the Parties may request, administrative conferences to discuss any procedural matter relating to the administration of the Arbitration.

(b) If no Arbitrator has yet been appointed, at the request of a Party and in the absence of Party agreement, JAMS may determine the location of the Hearing, subject to Arbitrator review. In determining the location of the Hearing, such factors as the subject matter of the dispute, the convenience of the Parties and witnesses and the relative resources of the Parties shall be considered, but in no event will the Hearing be scheduled in a location that precludes attendance by the

Employee.

(c) If, at any time, any Party has failed to pay fees or expenses in full, JAMS may order the suspension or termination of the proceedings. JAMS may so inform the Parties in order that one of them may advance the required payment. If one Party advances the payment owed by a non-paying Party, the Arbitration shall proceed and the Arbitrator may allocate the non-paying Party's share of such costs, in accordance with Rules 24(f) and 31(c). An administrative suspension shall toll any other time limits contained in these Rules or the Parties' Agreement.

(d) JAMS does not maintain an official record of documents filed in the Arbitration. If the Parties wish to have any documents returned to them, they must advise JAMS in writing within 30 days of the conclusion of the Arbitration. If special arrangements are required regarding file maintenance or document retention, they must be agreed to in writing and JAMS reserves the right to impose an additional fee for such special arrangements. Documents that are submitted for e-filing are retained for 30 days following the conclusion of the Arbitration.

(e) Unless the Parties' agreement or applicable law provides otherwise, JAMS, if it determines that the Arbitrations so filed have common issues of fact or law, may consolidate Arbitrations in the following instances:

(i) If a Party files more than one Arbitration with JAMS, JAMS may consolidate the Arbitrations into a single arbitration.

(ii) Where a Demand or Demands for Arbitration is or are submitted naming Parties already involved in another Arbitration or Arbitrations pending under these Rules, JAMS may decide that the new case or cases shall be consolidated into one or more of the pending proceedings and referred to one of the Arbitrators or panels of Arbitrators already appointed.

(iii) Where a Demand or Demands for Arbitration is or are submitted naming parties that are not identical to the Parties in the existing Arbitration or Arbitrations, JAMS may decide that the new case or cases shall be consolidated into one or more of the pending proceedings and referred to one of the Arbitrators or panels of Arbitrators already appointed.

When rendering its decision, JAMS will take into account all circumstances, including the links between the cases and the progress already made in the existing Arbitrations.

Unless applicable law provides otherwise, where JAMS decides to consolidate a proceeding into a pending Arbitration, the Parties to the consolidated case or cases will be deemed to have waived their right to designate an Arbitrator as well as any contractual provision with respect to the site of the Arbitration.

(f) Where a third party seeks to participate in an Arbitration already pending under these Rules or where a Party to an Arbitration under these Rules seeks to compel a third party to participate in a pending Arbitration, the Arbitrator shall determine such request, taking into account all circumstances the Arbitrator deems relevant and applicable.

Rule 7.   Number of Arbitrators and Appointment of Chairperson

(a) The Arbitration shall be conducted by one neutral Arbitrator unless all Parties agree otherwise. In these Rules, the term "Arbitrator" shall mean, as the context requires, the Arbitrator or the panel of Arbitrators in a tripartite Arbitration.

(b) In cases involving more than one Arbitrator the Parties shall agree on, or in the absence of agreement JAMS shall designate, the Chairperson of the Arbitration Panel. If the Parties and the Arbitrators agree, a single member of the Arbitration Panel may, acting alone, decide discovery and procedural matters, including the conduct of hearings to receive documents and testimony from third parties who have been subpoenaed to produce documents.

(c) Where the Parties have agreed that each Party is to name one Arbitrator, the Arbitrators so named shall be neutral and independent of the appointing Party unless the Parties have agreed that they shall be non-neutral.

Rule 8.   Service

(a) The Arbitrator may at any time require electronic filing and service of documents in an Arbitration. If an Arbitrator requires electronic filing, the Parties shall maintain and regularly monitor a valid, usable and live email address for the receipt of all documents filed through JAMS Electronic Filing System. Any document filed electronically shall be considered as filed with JAMS when the transmission to JAMS Electronic Filing System is complete. Any document e-filed by 11:59 p.m. (of the sender's time zone) shall be deemed filed on that date. Upon completion of filing, JAMS Electronic Filing System shall issue a confirmation receipt that includes the date and time of receipt. The confirmation receipt shall serve as proof of filing.

(b) Every document filed with JAMS Electronic Filing System shall be deemed to have been signed by the Arbitrator, Case Manager, attorney or declarant who submits the document to JAMS Electronic Filing System, and shall bear the typed name, address, telephone number, and Bar number of a signing attorney. Documents containing signatures of third-parties (i.e., unopposed motions, affidavits, stipulations, etc.) may also be filed electronically by indicating that the original signatures are maintained by the filing Party in paper-format.

(c) Delivery of e-service documents through JAMS Electronic Filing System to other registered users shall be considered as valid and effective service and shall have the same legal effect as an original paper document. Recipients of e-service documents shall access their documents through JAMS Electronic Filing System. E-service shall be deemed complete when the party initiating e-service completes the transmission of the electronic document(s) to JAMS Electronic Filing System for e-filing and/or e-service. Upon actual or constructive receipt of the electronic document(s) by the party to be served, a Certificate of Electronic Service shall be issued by JAMS Electronic Filing System to the party initiating e-service and that Certificate shall serve as proof of service. Any party who ignores or attempts to refuse e-service shall be deemed to have received the electronic document(s) 72 hours following the transmission of the electronic document(s) to JAMS Electronic Filing System.

(d) If an electronic filing or service does not occur because of (1) an error in the transmission of the document to JAMS Electronic Filing System or served Party which was unknown to the sending Party, (2) a failure to process the electronic document when received by JAMS Electronic Filing System, (3) the Party was erroneously excluded from the service list, or (4) other technical problems experienced by the filer, the Arbitrator or JAMS may for good cause shown permit the document to be filed *nunc pro tunc* to the date it was first attempted to be sent electronically. Or in the case of service, the Party shall, absent extraordinary circumstances, be entitled to an order extending the date for any response or the period within which any right, duty or other act must be performed.

(e) For documents that are not filed electronically, service by a Party under these Rules is effected by providing one signed copy of the document to each Party and two copies in the case of a sole Arbitrator and four copies in the case of a tripartite panel to JAMS. Service may be made by hand-delivery, overnight delivery service or U.S. mail. Service by any of these means is considered effective upon the date of deposit of the document. Service by electronic mail or facsimile transmission is considered effective upon transmission, but only if followed within one week of delivery by service of an appropriate number of copies and originals by one of the other service methods.

In computing any period of time prescribed or allowed by these Rules for a Party to do some act within a prescribed period after the service of a notice or other paper on the Party and the notice or paper is served on the Party only by U.S. Mail, three (3) calendar days shall be added to the prescribed period.

Rule 9.   Notice of Claims

(a) Each Party shall afford all other Parties reasonable and timely notice of its claims, affirmative defenses or counterclaims. Any such notice shall include a short statement of its factual basis. No claim, remedy, counterclaim, or affirmative defense will be considered by the Arbitrator in the absence of such prior notice to the other Parties, unless the Arbitrator determines that no Party has been unfairly prejudiced by such lack of formal notice or all Parties agree that such consideration is appropriate notwithstanding the lack of prior notice.

(b) Within fourteen (14) calendar days after the commencement of an Arbitration, Claimant shall submit to JAMS and serve on the other Parties a notice of its claim and remedies sought. Such notice shall consist of either a Demand for Arbitration or a copy of a Complaint previously filed with a court. (In the latter case, Claimant may accompany the Complaint with a copy of any Answer to that Complaint filed by any Respondent.)

(c) Within fourteen (14) calendar days of service of the notice of claim, a Respondent may submit to JAMS and serve on other Parties a response and must so submit and serve a statement of any affirmative defenses (including jurisdictional challenges) or counterclaims it may have.

(d) Within fourteen (14) calendar days of service of a counterclaim, a claimant may submit to JAMS and serve on other Parties a response to such counterclaim and must so submit and serve a statement of any affirmative defenses (including jurisdictional challenges) it may have.

(e) Any claim or counterclaim to which no response has been served will be deemed denied.

Rule 10.   Changes of Claims

After the filing of a claim and before the Arbitrator is appointed, any Party may make a new or different claim against a Party or any third Party that is subject to Arbitration in the proceeding. Such claim shall be made in writing, filed with JAMS and served on the other Parties. Any response to the new claim shall be made within fourteen (14) calendar days after service of such claim. After the Arbitrator is appointed, no new or different claim may be submitted except with the Arbitrator's approval. A Party may request a Hearing on this issue. Each Party has the right to respond to any new or amended claim in accordance with Rule 9(d).

Rule 11.   Interpretation of Rules and Jurisdictional Challenges

(a) Once appointed, the Arbitrator shall resolve disputes about the interpretation and applicability of these Rules and conduct of the Arbitration Hearing. The resolution of the issue by the Arbitrator shall be final.

(b) Whenever in these Rules a matter is to be determined by "JAMS" (such as in Rules 6; 11 (d); 15(d), (f), (g) or (i)), such determination shall be made in accordance with JAMS administrative procedures.

(c) Jurisdictional and arbitrability disputes, including disputes over the formation, existence, validity, interpretation or scope of the agreement under which Arbitration is sought, and who are proper Parties to the Arbitration, shall be submitted to and ruled on by the Arbitrator. Unless the relevant law requires otherwise, the Arbitrator has the authority to determine jurisdiction and arbitrability issues as a preliminary matter.

(d) Disputes concerning the appointment of the Arbitrator shall be resolved by JAMS.

(e) The Arbitrator may, upon a showing of good cause or *sua sponte*, when necessary to facilitate the Arbitration, extend any deadlines established in these Rules, provided that the time for rendering the Award may only be altered in accordance with Rules 22(i) or 24.

Rule 12.   Representation

(a) The Parties may be represented by counsel or any other person of the Party's choice. Each Party shall give prompt written notice to the Case Manager and the other Parties of the name, address, telephone and fax numbers, and email address of its representative. The representative of a Party may act on the Party's behalf in complying with these Rules.

(b) Changes in Representation. A Party shall give prompt written notice to the Case Manager and the other Parties of any change in its representation, including the name, address, telephone and fax numbers, and email address of the new representative. Such notice shall state that the written consent of the former representative, if any, and of the new representative, has been obtained and shall state the effective date of the new representation.

Rule 13.   Withdrawal from Arbitration

(a) No Party may terminate or withdraw from an Arbitration after the issuance of the Commencement Letter (see Rule 5) except by written agreement of all Parties to the Arbitration.

(b) A Party that asserts a claim or counterclaim may unilaterally withdraw that claim or counterclaim without prejudice by serving written notice on the other Parties and on the Arbitrator. However, the opposing Parties may, within fourteen (14) calendar days of service of notice of the withdrawal of the claim or counterclaim, request that the Arbitrator order that the withdrawal be with prejudice. If such a request is made, it shall be determined by the Arbitrator.

Rule 14.   *Ex Parte* Communications

(a) No Party may have any *ex parte* communication with a neutral Arbitrator jointly selected by the Parties. The Arbitrator(s) may authorize any Party to communicate directly with the Arbitrator(s) by email or other written correspondence, so long as copies are simultaneously forwarded to the JAMS Case Manager and the other Parties.

(b) A Party may have *ex parte* communication with its appointed neutral or non-neutral Arbitrator as necessary to secure the Arbitrator's services and to assure the absence of conflicts and in connection with the selection of the Chairperson of the arbitral panel.

(c) The Parties may agree to permit more extensive *ex parte* communication between a Party and a non-neutral Arbitrator. More extensive communications with a non-neutral arbitrator may also be permitted by applicable law and rules of ethics.

Rule 15.   Arbitrator Selection and Replacement

(a) Unless the Arbitrator has been previously selected by agreement of the Parties, JAMS may attempt to facilitate agreement among the Parties regarding selection of the Arbitrator.

(b) If the Parties do not agree on an Arbitrator, JAMS shall send the Parties a list of at least five (5) Arbitrator candidates in the case of a sole Arbitrator and ten (10) Arbitrator candidates in the case of a tripartite panel. JAMS shall also provide each Party with a brief description of the background and experience of each Arbitrator candidate. JAMS may replace any or all names on the list of Arbitrator candidates for reasonable cause at any time before the Parties have submitted their choice pursuant to subparagraph (c) below.

(c) Within seven (7) calendar days of service by the Parties of the list of names, each Party may strike two (2) names in the case of a sole Arbitrator and three (3) names in the case of a tripartite panel, and shall rank the remaining Arbitrator candidates in order of preference. The remaining Arbitrator candidate with the highest composite ranking shall be appointed the Arbitrator. JAMS may grant a reasonable extension of the time to strike and rank the Arbitrator candidates to any Party without the consent of the other Parties.

(d) If this process does not yield an Arbitrator or a complete panel, JAMS shall designate the sole Arbitrator or as many members of the tripartite panel as are necessary to complete the panel.

(e) If a Party fails to respond to a list of Arbitrator candidates within seven (7) calendar days after its service, JAMS shall deem that Party to have accepted all of the Arbitrator candidates.

(f) Entities whose interests are not adverse with respect to the issues in dispute shall be treated as a single Party for purposes of the Arbitrator selection process. JAMS shall determine whether the interests between entities are adverse for purposes of Arbitrator selection, considering such factors as whether the entities are represented by the same attorney and whether the entities are presenting joint or separate positions at the Arbitration.

(g) If, for any reason, the Arbitrator who is selected is unable to fulfill the Arbitrator's duties, a successor Arbitrator shall be chosen in accordance with this Rule. If a member of a panel of Arbitrators becomes unable to fulfill his or her duties after the beginning of a Hearing but before the issuance of an Award, a new Arbitrator will be chosen in accordance with this Rule unless, in the case of a tripartite panel, the Parties agree to proceed with the remaining two Arbitrators. JAMS will make the final determination as to whether an Arbitrator is unable to fulfill his or her duties, and that decision shall be final.

(h) Any disclosures regarding the selected Arbitrator shall be made as required by law or within ten (10) calendar days from the date of appointment. The obligation of the Arbitrator to make all required disclosures continues throughout the Arbitration process. Such disclosures may be provided in electronic format, provided that JAMS will produce a hard copy to any Party that requests it.

(i) At any time during the Arbitration process, a Party may challenge the continued service of an Arbitrator for cause. The challenge must be based upon information that was not available to the Parties at the time the Arbitrator was selected. A challenge for cause must be in writing and exchanged with opposing Parties who may respond within seven (7) days of service of the challenge. JAMS shall make the final determination as to such challenge. Such determination shall take into account the materiality of the facts and any prejudice to the Parties. That decision will be final.

(j) Where the Parties have agreed that a Party-appointed Arbitrator is to be non-neutral, that Party-appointed Arbitrator is not obliged to withdraw if requested to do so only by the party who did not appoint that Arbitrator.

Rule 16. Preliminary Conference

At the request of any Party or at the direction of the Arbitrator, a Preliminary Conference shall be conducted with the Parties or their counsel or representatives. The Preliminary Conference may address any or all of the following subjects:

(a) The exchange of information in accordance with Rule 17 or otherwise;

(b) The schedule for discovery as permitted by the Rules, as agreed by the Parties or as required or authorized by applicable law;

(c) The pleadings of the Parties and any agreement to clarify or narrow the issues or structure the Arbitration Hearing;

(d) The scheduling of the Hearing and any pre-Hearing exchanges of information, exhibits, motions or briefs;

(e) The attendance of witnesses as contemplated by Rule 21;

(f) The scheduling of any dispositive motion pursuant to Rule 18;

(g) The premarking of exhibits; preparation of joint exhibit lists and the resolution of the admissibility of exhibits;

(h) The form of the Award; and

(i) Such other matters as may be suggested by the Parties or the Arbitrator.

The Preliminary Conference may be conducted telephonically and may be resumed from time to time as warranted.

Rule 17.   Exchange of Information

(a) The Parties shall cooperate in good faith in the voluntary and informal exchange of all non-privileged documents and other information (including electronically stored information ("ESI")) relevant to the dispute or claim immediately after commencement of the Arbitration. They shall complete an initial exchange of all relevant, non-privileged documents, including, without limitation, copies of all documents in their possession or control on which they rely in support of their positions, names of individuals whom they may call as witnesses at the Arbitration Hearing, and names of all experts who may be called to testify at the Arbitration Hearing, together with each expert's report that may be introduced at the Arbitration Hearing, within twenty-one (21) calendar days after all pleadings or notice of claims have been received. The Arbitrator may modify these obligations at the Preliminary Conference.

(b) Each Party may take at least one deposition of an opposing Party or an individual under the control of the opposing Party. The Parties shall attempt to agree on the number, time, location, and duration of the deposition(s). Absent agreement, the Arbitrator shall determine these issues including whether to grant a request for additional depositions, based upon the reasonable need for the requested information, the availability of other discovery, and the burdensomeness of the request on the opposing Parties and witness.

(c) As they become aware of new documents or information, including experts who may be called upon to testify, all Parties continue to be obligated to provide relevant, non-privileged documents, to supplement their identification of witnesses and experts and to honor any informal agreements or understandings between the Parties regarding documents or information to be exchanged. Documents that were not previously exchanged, or witnesses and experts that were not previously identified, may not be considered by the Arbitrator at the Hearing, unless agreed by the Parties or upon a showing of good cause.

(d) The Parties shall promptly notify JAMS when a dispute exists regarding discovery issues. A conference shall be arranged with the Arbitrator, either by telephone or in person, and the Arbitrator shall decide the dispute. With the written consent of all Parties, and in accordance with an agreed written procedure, the Arbitrator may appoint a special master to assist in resolving a discovery dispute.

Rule 18.   Summary Disposition of a Claim or Issue

The Arbitrator may permit any Party to file a Motion for Summary Disposition of a particular claim or issue, either by agreement of all interested Parties or at the request of one Party, provided other interested Parties have reasonable notice to respond to the motion.

Rule 19.   Scheduling and Location of Hearing

(a) The Arbitrator, after consulting with the Parties that have appeared, shall determine the date, time and location of the Hearing. The Arbitrator and the Parties shall attempt to schedule consecutive Hearing days if more than one day is necessary.

(b) If a Party has failed to participate in the Arbitration process, and the Arbitrator reasonably believes that the Party will not participate in the Hearing, the Arbitrator may set the Hearing without consulting with that Party. The non-participating Party shall be served with a Notice of Hearing at least thirty (30) calendar days prior to the scheduled date unless the law of the relevant jurisdiction allows for or the Parties have agreed to shorter notice.

(c) The Arbitrator, in order to hear a third party witness, or for the convenience of the Parties or the witnesses, may conduct the Hearing at any location. Any JAMS Resolution Center may be designated a Hearing location for purposes of the issuance of a subpoena or subpoena *duces tecum* to a third party witness.

Rule 20.   Pre-Hearing Submissions

(a) Except as set forth in any scheduling order that may be adopted, at least fourteen (14) calendar days before the Arbitration Hearing, the Parties shall file with JAMS and serve and exchange (1) a list of the witnesses they intend to call, including any experts, (2) a short description of the anticipated testimony of each such witness and an estimate of the length of the witness' direct testimony, and (3) a list of all exhibits intended to be used at the Hearing. The Parties should exchange with each other a copy of any such exhibits to the extent that it has not been previously exchanged. The Parties should pre-mark exhibits and shall attempt to resolve any disputes regarding the admissibility of exhibits prior to the Hearing.

(b) The Arbitrator may require that each Party submit concise written statements of position, including summaries of the facts and evidence a Party intends to present, discussion of the applicable law and the basis for the requested Award or denial of relief sought. The statements, which may be in the form of a letter, shall be filed with JAMS and served upon the other Parties, at least seven (7) calendar days before the Hearing date. Rebuttal statements or other pre-Hearing written submissions may be permitted or required at the discretion of the Arbitrator.

Rule 21.   Securing Witnesses and Documents for the Arbitration Hearing

At the written request of a Party, all other Parties shall produce for the Arbitration Hearing all specified witnesses in their employ or under their control without need of subpoena. The Arbitrator may issue subpoenas for the attendance of witnesses or the production of documents either prior to or at the Hearing pursuant to this Rule or Rule 19(c). The subpoena or subpoena *duces tecum* shall be issued in accordance with the applicable law. Pre-issued subpoenas may be used in jurisdictions that permit them. In the event a Party or a subpoenaed person objects to the production of a witness or other evidence, the Party or subpoenaed person may file an objection with the Arbitrator, who shall promptly rule on the objection, weighing both the burden on the producing Party and witness and the need of the proponent for the witness or other evidence.

Rule 22.   The Arbitration Hearing

(a) The Arbitrator will ordinarily conduct the Arbitration Hearing in the manner set forth in these Rules. The Arbitrator may vary these procedures if it is determined reasonable and appropriate to do so. It is expected that the Employee will attend the Arbitration Hearing, as will any other individual Party with information about a significant issue.

(b) The Arbitrator shall determine the order of proof, which will generally be similar to that of a court trial.

(c) The Arbitrator shall require witnesses to testify under oath if requested by any Party, or otherwise in the discretion of the Arbitrator.

(d) Strict conformity to the rules of evidence is not required, except that the Arbitrator shall apply applicable law relating to privileges and work product. The Arbitrator shall consider evidence that he or she finds relevant and material to the dispute, giving the evidence such weight as is appropriate. The Arbitrator may be guided in that determination by principles contained in the Federal Rules of Evidence or any other applicable rules of evidence. The Arbitrator may limit testimony to exclude evidence that would be immaterial or unduly repetitive, provided that all Parties are afforded the opportunity to present material and relevant evidence.

(e) The Arbitrator shall receive and consider relevant deposition testimony recorded by transcript or videotape, provided that the other Parties have had the opportunity to attend and cross-examine. The Arbitrator may in his or her discretion consider witness affidavits or other recorded testimony even if the other Parties have not had the opportunity to cross-examine, but will give that evidence only such weight as the Arbitrator deems appropriate.

(f) The Parties will not offer as evidence, and the Arbitrator shall neither admit into the record nor consider, prior settlement offers by the Parties or statements or recommendations made by a mediator or other person in connection with efforts to resolve the dispute being arbitrated, except to the extent that applicable law permits the admission of such evidence.

(g) The Hearing or any portion thereof may be conducted telephonically with the agreement of the Parties or in the discretion of the Arbitrator.

(h) When the Arbitrator determines that all relevant and material evidence and arguments have been presented, and any interim or partial awards have been issued, the Arbitrator shall declare the Hearing closed. The Arbitrator may defer the closing of the Hearing until a date agreed upon by the Arbitrator and the Parties, to permit the Parties to submit post-Hearing briefs, which may be in the form of a letter, and/or to make closing arguments. If post-Hearing briefs are to be submitted, or closing arguments are to be made, the Hearing shall be deemed closed upon receipt by the Arbitrator of such briefs or at the conclusion of such closing arguments.

(i) At any time before the Award is rendered, the Arbitrator may, *sua sponte* or on application of a Party for good cause shown, re-open the Hearing. If the Hearing is re-opened and the re-opening prevents the rendering of the Award within the time limits specified by these Rules, the time limits will be extended until the reopened Hearing is declared closed by the Arbitrator.

(j) The Arbitrator may proceed with the Hearing in the absence of a Party that, after receiving notice of the Hearing pursuant to Rule 19, fails to attend. The Arbitrator may not render an Award solely on the basis of the default or absence of the Party, but shall require any Party seeking relief to submit such evidence as the Arbitrator may require for the rendering of an Award. If the Arbitrator reasonably believes that a Party will not attend the Hearing, the Arbitrator may schedule the Hearing as a telephonic Hearing and may receive the evidence necessary to render an Award by affidavit. The notice of Hearing shall specify if it will be in person or telephonic.

(k) (i) Any Party may arrange for a stenographic or other record to be made of the Hearing and shall inform the other Parties in advance of the Hearing. The requesting Party shall bear the cost of such stenographic record. If all other Parties agree to share the cost of the stenographic record, it shall be made available to the Arbitrator and may be used in the proceeding.

(ii) If there is no agreement to share the cost, the stenographic record may not be provided to the Arbitrator and may not be used in the proceeding unless the Party arranging for the stenographic record either agrees to provide access to the stenographic record at no charge or on terms that are acceptable to the Parties and the reporting service.

(iii) If the Parties agree to an Optional Arbitration Appeal Procedure (see Rule 34), they shall ensure that a stenographic or other record is made of the Hearing.

(iv) The Parties may agree that the cost of the stenographic record shall or shall not be allocated by the Arbitrator in the Award.

Rule 23.   Waiver of Hearing

The Parties may agree to waive the oral Hearing and submit the dispute to the Arbitrator for an Award based on written submissions and other evidence as the Parties may agree.

Rule 24.   Awards

(a) The Arbitrator shall render a Final Award or a Partial Final Award within thirty (30) calendar days after the date of the close of the Hearing as defined in Rule 22(h) or, if a Hearing has been waived, within thirty (30) calendar days after the receipt by the Arbitrator of all materials specified by the Parties, except (i) by the agreement of the Parties, (ii) upon good cause for an extension of time to render the Award, or (iii) as provided in Rule 22(i). The Arbitrator shall provide the Final Award or the Partial Final Award to JAMS for issuance in accordance with this Rule.

(b) Where a panel of Arbitrators has heard the dispute, the decision and Award of a majority of the panel shall constitute the Arbitration Award.

(c) In determining the merits of the dispute the Arbitrator shall be guided by the rules of law agreed upon by the Parties. In the absence of such agreement, the Arbitrator will be guided by the law or the rules of law that the Arbitrator deems to be most appropriate. The Arbitrator may grant any remedy or relief that is just and equitable and within the scope of the Parties' agreement, including but not limited to specific performance of a contract or any other equitable or legal remedy.

(d) In addition to a Final Award or Partial Final Award, the Arbitrator may make other decisions, including interim or partial rulings, orders and Awards.

(e) Interim Measures. The Arbitrator may grant whatever interim measures are deemed necessary, including injunctive relief and measures for the protection or conservation of property and disposition of disposable goods. Such interim measures may take the form of an interim Award, and the Arbitrator may require security for the costs of such measures. Any recourse by a Party to a court for interim or provisional relief shall not be deemed incompatible with the agreement to arbitrate or a waiver of the right to arbitrate.

(f) The Award of the Arbitrator may allocate Arbitration fees and Arbitrator compensation and expenses unless such an allocation is expressly prohibited by the Parties' agreement or by applicable law. (Such a prohibition may not limit the power of the Arbitrator to allocate Arbitration fees and Arbitrator compensation and expenses pursuant to Rule 31(c)).

(g) The Award of the Arbitrator may allocate attorneys' fees and expenses and interest (at such rate and from such date as the Arbitrator may deem appropriate) if provided by the Parties' agreement or allowed by applicable law.

(h) The Award will consist of a written statement signed by the Arbitrator regarding the disposition of each claim and the relief, if any, as to each claim. The Award shall also contain a concise written statement of the reasons for the Award, stating the essential findings and conclusions on which the award is based. The Parties may agree to any other form of award, unless the arbitration is based on an arbitration agreement that is required as a condition of employment.

(i) After the Award has been rendered, and provided the Parties have complied with Rule 31, the Award shall be issued by serving copies on the Parties. Service may be made by U.S. Mail. It need not be sent certified or registered.

(j) Within seven (7) calendar days after service of the Award by JAMS, any Party may serve upon the other Parties and on JAMS a request that the Arbitrator correct any computational, typographical or other similar error in an Award (including the reallocation of fees pursuant to Rule 31), or the Arbitrator may *sua sponte* propose to correct such errors in an Award. A Party opposing such correction shall have seven (7) calendar days thereafter in which to file any objection. The

Arbitrator may make any necessary and appropriate correction to the Award within twenty-one (21) calendar days of receiving a request or fourteen (14) calendar days after the Arbitrator's proposal to do so. The Arbitrator may extend the time within which to make corrections upon good cause. The corrected Award shall be served upon the Parties in the same manner as the Award.

(k) The Award is considered final, for purposes of either an Optional Arbitration Appeal Procedure pursuant to Rule 34 or a judicial proceeding to enforce, modify or vacate the Award pursuant to Rule 25, fourteen (14) calendar days after service is deemed effective if no request for a correction is made, or as of the effective date of service of a corrected Award.

Rule 25. Enforcement of the Award

Proceedings to enforce, confirm, modify or vacate an Award will be controlled by and conducted in conformity with the Federal Arbitration Act, 9 U.S.C. Sec 1 et seq. or applicable state law. The Parties to an Arbitration under these Rules shall be deemed to have consented that judgment upon the Award may be entered in any court having jurisdiction thereof.

Rule 26. Confidentiality and Privacy

(a) JAMS and the Arbitrator shall maintain the confidential nature of the Arbitration proceeding and the Award, including the Hearing, except as necessary in connection with a judicial challenge to or enforcement of an Award, or unless otherwise required by law or judicial decision.

(b) The Arbitrator may issue orders to protect the confidentiality of proprietary information, trade secrets or other sensitive information.

(c) Subject to the discretion of the Arbitrator or agreement of the Parties, any person having a direct interest in the Arbitration may attend the Arbitration Hearing. The Arbitrator may exclude any non-Party from any part of a Hearing.

Rule 27. Waiver

(a) If a Party becomes aware of a violation of or failure to comply with these Rules and fails promptly to object in writing, the objection will be deemed waived, unless the Arbitrator determines that waiver will cause substantial injustice or hardship.

(b) If any Party becomes aware of information that could be the basis of a challenge for cause to the continued service of the Arbitrator, such challenge must be made promptly, in writing, to the Arbitrator or JAMS. Failure to do so shall constitute a waiver of any objection to continued service by the Arbitrator.

Rule 28. Settlement and Consent Award

(a) The Parties may agree, at any stage of the Arbitration process, to submit the case to JAMS for mediation. The JAMS mediator assigned to the case may not be the Arbitrator or a member of the Appeal Panel, unless the Parties so agree pursuant to Rule 28(b).

(b) The Parties may agree to seek the assistance of the Arbitrator in reaching settlement. By their written agreement to submit the matter to the Arbitrator for settlement assistance, the Parties will be deemed to have agreed that the assistance of the Arbitrator in such settlement efforts will not disqualify the Arbitrator from continuing to serve as Arbitrator if settlement is not reached; nor shall such assistance be argued to a reviewing court as the basis for vacating or modifying an Award.

(c) If, at any stage of the Arbitration process, all Parties agree upon a settlement of the issues in dispute and request the Arbitrator to embody the agreement in a Consent Award, the Arbitrator shall comply with such request unless the Arbitrator believes the terms of the agreement are illegal or undermine the integrity of the Arbitration process. If the Arbitrator is concerned about the possible consequences of the proposed Consent Award, he or she shall inform the Parties of that concern and may request additional specific information from the Parties regarding the proposed Consent Award. The Arbitrator may refuse to enter the proposed Consent Award and may withdraw from the case.

Rule 29.   Sanctions

The Arbitrator may order appropriate sanctions for failure of a Party to comply with its obligations under any of these Rules. These sanctions may include, but are not limited to, assessment of Arbitration fees and Arbitrator compensation and expenses, any other costs occasioned by the actionable conduct including reasonable attorney's fees, exclusion of certain evidence, drawing adverse inferences, or in extreme cases determining an issue or issues submitted to Arbitration adversely to the Party that has failed to comply.

Rule 30.   Disqualification of the Arbitrator as a Witness or Party and Exclusion of Liability

(a) The Parties may not call the Arbitrator, the Case Manager or any other JAMS employee or agent as a witness or as an expert in any pending or subsequent litigation or other proceeding involving the Parties and relating to the dispute that is the subject of the Arbitration. The Arbitrator, Case Manager and other JAMS employees and agents are also incompetent to testify as witnesses or experts in any such proceeding.

(b) The Parties shall defend and/or pay the cost (including any attorneys' fees) of defending the Arbitrator, Case Manager and/or JAMS from any subpoenas from outside Parties arising from the Arbitration.

(c) The Parties agree that neither the Arbitrator, Case Manager nor JAMS is a necessary Party in any litigation or other proceeding relating to the Arbitration or the subject matter of the Arbitration, and neither the Arbitrator, Case Manager nor JAMS, including its employees or agents, shall be liable to any Party for any act or omission in connection with any Arbitration conducted under these Rules, including but not limited to any disqualification of or recusal by the Arbitrator.

Rule 31.   Fees

(a) Except as provided in paragraph (c) below, unless the Parties have agreed to a different allocation, each Party shall pay its *pro-rata* share of JAMS fees and expenses as set forth in the JAMS fee schedule in effect at the time of the commencement of the Arbitration. To the extent possible, the allocation of such fees and expenses shall not be disclosed to the Arbitrator. JAMS agreement to render services is jointly with the Party and the attorney or other representative of the Party in the Arbitration. The non-payment of fees may result in an administrative suspension of the case in accordance with Rule 6(c).

(b) JAMS requires that the Parties deposit the fees and expenses for the Arbitration prior to the Hearing and the Arbitrator may preclude a Party that has failed to deposit its *pro-rata* or agreed-upon share of the fees and expenses from offering evidence of any affirmative claim at the Hearing.

(c) If an arbitration is based on a clause or agreement that is required as a condition of employment, the only fee that an employee may be required to pay is the initial JAMS Case Management Fee. JAMS does not preclude an employee from contributing to administrative and arbitrator fees and expenses. If an arbitration is not based on a clause or agreement that is required as a condition of employment, the Parties are jointly and severally liable for the payment of JAMS Arbitration fees and Arbitrator compensation and expenses. In the event that one Party has paid more than its share of such fees, compensation and expenses, the Arbitrator may award against any other Party any such fees, compensation and expenses that such Party owes with respect to the Arbitration.

(d) Entities whose interests are not adverse with respect to the issues in dispute shall be treated as a single Party for purposes of JAMS assessment of fees. JAMS shall determine whether the interests between entities are adverse for purpose of fees, considering such factors as whether the entities are represented by the same attorney and whether the entities are presenting joint or separate positions at the Arbitration.

Rule 32.   Bracketed (or High-Low) Arbitration Option

(a) At any time before the issuance of the Arbitration Award, the Parties may agree, in writing, on minimum and maximum amounts of damages that may be awarded on each claim or on all claims in the aggregate. The Parties shall promptly notify JAMS, and provide to JAMS a copy of their written agreement setting forth the agreed-upon maximum and minimum amounts.

(b) JAMS shall not inform the Arbitrator of the agreement to proceed with this option or of the agreed-upon minimum and maximum levels without the consent of the Parties.

(c) The Arbitrator shall render the Award in accordance with Rule 24.

(d) In the event that the Award of the Arbitrator is between the agreed-upon minimum and maximum amounts, the Award shall become final as is. In the event that the Award is below the agreed-upon minimum amount, the final Award issued shall be corrected to reflect the agreed-upon minimum amount. In the event that the Award is above the agreed-upon maximum amount, the final Award issued shall be corrected to reflect the agreed-upon maximum amount.

Rule 33.   Final Offer (or Baseball) Arbitration Option

(a) Upon agreement of the Parties to use the option set forth in this Rule, at least seven (7) calendar days before the Arbitration Hearing, the Parties shall exchange and provide to JAMS written proposals for the amount of money damages they would offer or demand, as applicable, and that they believe to be appropriate based on the standard set forth in Rule 24(c). JAMS shall promptly provide a copy of the Parties' proposals to the Arbitrator, unless the Parties agree that they should not be provided to the Arbitrator. At any time prior to the close of the Arbitration Hearing, the Parties may exchange revised written proposals or demands, which shall supersede all prior proposals. The revised written proposals shall be provided to JAMS, which shall promptly provide them to the Arbitrator, unless the Parties agree otherwise.

(b) If the Arbitrator has been informed of the written proposals, in rendering the Award the Arbitrator shall choose between the Parties' last proposals, selecting the proposal that the Arbitrator finds most reasonable and appropriate in light of the standard set forth in Rule 24(c). This provision modifies Rule 24(h) in that no written statement of reasons shall accompany the Award.

(c) If the Arbitrator has not been informed of the written proposals, the Arbitrator shall render the Award as if pursuant to Rule 24, except that the Award shall thereafter be corrected to conform to the closest of the last proposals, and the closest of the last proposals will become the Award.

(d) Other than as provided herein, the provisions of Rule 24 shall be applicable.

Rule 34.   Optional Arbitration Appeal Procedure

At any time before the Award becomes final pursuant to Rule 24, the Parties may agree to the JAMS Optional Arbitration Appeal Procedure. All Parties must agree in writing for such procedure to be effective. Once a Party has agreed to the Optional Arbitration Appeal Procedure, it cannot unilaterally withdraw from it, unless it withdraws, pursuant to Rule 13, from the Arbitration.

UNCITRAL ARBITRATION RULES

(as revised in 2010)

Section I. Introductory rules

Article 1 Scope of application*

1. Where parties have agreed that disputes between them in respect of a defined legal relationship, whether contractual or not, shall be referred to arbitration under the UNCITRAL Arbitration Rules, then such disputes shall be settled in accordance with these Rules subject to such modification as the parties may agree.

2. The parties to an arbitration agreement concluded after 15 August 2010 shall be presumed to have referred to the Rules in effect on the date of commencement of the arbitration, unless the parties have agreed to apply a particular version of the Rules. That presumption does not apply where the arbitration agreement has been concluded by accepting after 15 August 2010 an offer made before that date.

3. These Rules shall govern the arbitration except that where any of these Rules is in conflict with a provision of the law applicable to the arbitration from which the parties cannot derogate, that provision shall prevail.

Article 2 Notice and calculation of periods of time

1. A notice, including a notification, communication or proposal, may be transmitted by any means of communication that provides or allows for a record of its transmission.

2. If an address has been designated by a party specifically for this purpose or authorized by the arbitral tribunal, any notice shall be delivered to that party at that address, and if so delivered shall be deemed to have been received. Delivery by electronic means such as facsimile or email may only be made to an address so designated or authorized.

3. In the absence of such designation or authorization, a notice is:

(a) received if it is physically delivered to the addressee; or

(b) deemed to have been received if it is delivered at the place of business, habitual residence or mailing address of the addressee.

4. If, after reasonable efforts, delivery cannot be effected in accordance with paragraphs 2 or 3, a notice is deemed to have been received if it is sent to the addressee's last-known place of business, habitual residence or mailing address by registered letter or any other means that provides a record of delivery or of attempted delivery.

5. A notice shall be deemed to have been received on the day it is delivered in accordance with paragraphs 2, 3 or 4, or attempted to be delivered in accordance with paragraph 4. A notice transmitted by electronic means is deemed to have been received on the day it is sent, except that a notice of arbitration so transmitted is

---

* A model arbitration clause for contracts can be found in the annex to the Rules.

only deemed to have been received on the day when it reaches the addressee's electronic address.

6. For the purpose of calculating a period of time under these Rules, such period shall begin to run on the day following the day when a notice is received. If the last day of such period is an official holiday or a non-business day at the residence or place of business of the addressee, the period is extended until the first business day which follows. Official holidays or non-business days occurring during the running of the period of time are included in calculating the period.

Article 3   Notice of arbitration

1. The party or parties initiating recourse to arbitration (hereinafter called the "claimant") shall communicate to the other party or parties (hereinafter called the "respondent") a notice of arbitration.

2. Arbitral proceedings shall be deemed to commence on the date on which the notice of arbitration is received by the respondent.

3. The notice of arbitration shall include the following:

(a) A demand that the dispute be referred to arbitration;

(b) The names and contact details of the parties;

(c) Identification of the arbitration agreement that is invoked;

(d) Identification of any contract or other legal instrument out of or in relation to which the dispute arises or, in the absence of such contract or instrument, a brief description of the relevant relationship;

(e) A brief description of the claim and an indication of the amount involved, if any;

(f) The relief or remedy sought;

(g) A proposal as to the number of arbitrators, language and place of arbitration, if the parties have not previously agreed thereon.

4. The notice of arbitration may also include:

(a) A proposal for the designation of an appointing authority referred to in article 6, paragraph 1;

(b) A proposal for the appointment of a sole arbitrator referred to in article 8, paragraph 1;

(c) Notification of the appointment of an arbitrator referred to in articles 9 or 10.

5. The constitution of the arbitral tribunal shall not be hindered by any controversy with respect to the sufficiency of the notice of arbitration, which shall be finally resolved by the arbitral tribunal.

Article 4   Response to the notice of arbitration

1. Within 30 days of the receipt of the notice of arbitration, the respondent shall

communicate to the claimant a response to the notice of arbitration, which shall include:

(a) The name and contact details of each respondent;

(b) A response to the information set forth in the notice of arbitration, pursuant to article 3, paragraphs 3 (c) to (g).

2. The response to the notice of arbitration may also include:

(a) Any plea that an arbitral tribunal to be constituted under these Rules lacks jurisdiction;

(b) A proposal for the designation of an appointing authority referred to in article 6, paragraph 1;

(c) A proposal for the appointment of a sole arbitrator referred to in article 8, paragraph 1;

(d) Notification of the appointment of an arbitrator referred to in articles 9 or 10;

(e) A brief description of counterclaims or claims for the purpose of a set-off, if any, including where relevant, an indication of the amounts involved, and the relief or remedy sought;

(f) A notice of arbitration in accordance with article 3 in case the respondent formulates a claim against a party to the arbitration agreement other than the claimant.

3. The constitution of the arbitral tribunal shall not be hindered by any controversy with respect to the respondent's failure to communicate a response to the notice of arbitration, or an incomplete or late response to the notice of arbitration, which shall be finally resolved by the arbitral tribunal.

Article 5   Representation and assistance

Each party may be represented or assisted by persons chosen by it. The names and addresses of such persons must be communicated to all parties and to the arbitral tribunal. Such communication must specify whether the appointment is being made for purposes of representation or assistance. Where a person is to act as a representative of a party, the arbitral tribunal, on its own initiative or at the request of any party, may at any time require proof of authority granted to the representative in such a form as the arbitral tribunal may determine.

Article 6   Designating and appointing authorities

1. Unless the parties have already agreed on the choice of an appointing authority, a party may at any time propose the name or names of one or more institutions or persons, including the Secretary-General of the Permanent Court of Arbitration at The Hague (hereinafter called the "PCA"), one of whom would serve as appointing authority.

2. If all parties have not agreed on the choice of an appointing authority within 30 days after a proposal made in accordance with paragraph 1 has been received by all

other parties, any party may request the Secretary-General of the PCA to designate the appointing authority.

3. Where these Rules provide for a period of time within which a party must refer a matter to an appointing authority and no appointing authority has been agreed on or designated, the period is suspended from the date on which a party initiates the procedure for agreeing on or designating an appointing authority until the date of such agreement or designation.

4. Except as referred to in article 41, paragraph (4), if the appointing authority refuses to act, or if it fails to appoint an arbitrator within 30 days after it receives a party's request to do so, fails to act within any other period provided by these Rules, or fails to decide on a challenge to an arbitrator within a reasonable time after receiving a party's request to do so, any party may request the Secretary-General of the PCA to designate a substitute appointing authority.

5. In exercising their functions under these Rules, the appointing authority and the Secretary-General of the PCA may require from any party and the arbitrators the information they deem necessary and they shall give the parties and, where appropriate, the arbitrators, an opportunity to present their views in any manner they consider appropriate. All such communications to and from the appointing authority and the Secretary-General of the PCA shall also be provided by the sender to all other parties.

6. When the appointing authority is requested to appoint an arbitrator pursuant to articles 8, 9, 10 or 14, the party making the request shall send to the appointing authority copies of the notice of arbitration and, if it exists, any response to the notice of arbitration.

7. The appointing authority shall have regard to such considerations as are likely to secure the appointment of an independent and impartial arbitrator and shall take into account the advisability of appointing an arbitrator of a nationality other than the nationalities of the parties.

Section II. Composition of the arbitral tribunal

Article 7   Number of arbitrators

1. If the parties have not previously agreed on the number of arbitrators, and if within 30 days after the receipt by the respondent of the notice of arbitration the parties have not agreed that there shall be only one arbitrator, three arbitrators shall be appointed.

2. Notwithstanding paragraph 1, if no other parties have responded to a party's proposal to appoint a sole arbitrator within the time limit provided for in paragraph 1 and the party or parties concerned have failed to appoint a second arbitrator in accordance with articles 9 or 10, the appointing authority may, at the request of a party, appoint a sole arbitrator pursuant to the procedure provided for in article 8, paragraph 2 if it determines that, in view of the circumstances of the case, this is more appropriate.

Article 8   Appointment of arbitrators (articles 8 to 10)

1. If the parties have agreed that a sole arbitrator is to be appointed and if within 30 days after receipt by all other parties of a proposal for the appointment of a sole arbitrator the parties have not reached agreement thereon, a sole arbitrator shall, at the request of a party, be appointed by the appointing authority.

2. The appointing authority shall appoint the sole arbitrator as promptly as possible. In making the appointment, the appointing authority shall use the following list-procedure, unless the parties agree that the list-procedure should not be used or unless the appointing authority determines in its discretion that the use of the list-procedure is not appropriate for the case:

(a) The appointing authority shall communicate to each of the parties an identical list containing at least three names;

(b) Within 15 days after the receipt of this list, each party may return the list to the appointing authority after having deleted the name or names to which it objects and numbered the remaining names on the list in the order of its preference;

(c) After the expiration of the above period of time the appointing authority shall appoint the sole arbitrator from among the names approved on the lists returned to it and in accordance with the order of preference indicated by the parties;

(d) If for any reason the appointment cannot be made according to this procedure, the appointing authority may exercise its discretion in appointing the sole arbitrator.

Article 9

1. If three arbitrators are to be appointed, each party shall appoint one arbitrator. The two arbitrators thus appointed shall choose the third arbitrator who will act as the presiding arbitrator of the arbitral tribunal.

2. If within 30 days after the receipt of a party's notification of the appointment of an arbitrator the other party has not notified the first party of the arbitrator it has appointed, the first party may request the appointing authority to appoint the second arbitrator.

3. If within 30 days after the appointment of the second arbitrator the two arbitrators have not agreed on the choice of the presiding arbitrator, the presiding arbitrator shall be appointed by the appointing authority in the same way as a sole arbitrator would be appointed under article 8.

Article 10

1. For the purposes of article 9, paragraph 1, where three arbitrators are to be appointed and there are multiple parties as claimant or as respondent, unless the parties have agreed to another method of appointment of arbitrators, the multiple parties jointly, whether as claimant or as respondent, shall appoint an arbitrator.

2. If the parties have agreed that the arbitral tribunal is to be composed of a

number of arbitrators other than one or three, the arbitrators shall be appointed according to the method agreed upon by the parties.

3. In the event of any failure to constitute the arbitral tribunal under these Rules, the appointing authority shall, at the request of any party, constitute the arbitral tribunal and, in doing so, may revoke any appointment already made and appoint or reappoint each of the arbitrators and designate one of them as the presiding arbitrator.

Article 11   Disclosures by and challenge of arbitrators** (articles 11 to 13)

When a person is approached in connection with his or her possible appointment as an arbitrator, he or she shall disclose any circumstances likely to give rise to justifiable doubts as to his or her impartiality or independence. An arbitrator, from the time of his or her appointment and throughout the arbitral proceedings, shall without delay disclose any such circumstances to the parties and the other arbitrators unless they have already been informed by him or her of these circumstances.

Article 12

1. Any arbitrator may be challenged if circumstances exist that give rise to justifiable doubts as to the arbitrator's impartiality or independence.

2. A party may challenge the arbitrator appointed by it only for reasons of which it becomes aware after the appointment has been made.

3. In the event that an arbitrator fails to act or in the event of the de jure or de facto impossibility of his or her performing his or her functions, the procedure in respect of the challenge of an arbitrator as provided in article 13 shall apply.

Article 13

1. A party that intends to challenge an arbitrator shall send notice of its challenge within 15 days after it has been notified of the appointment of the challenged arbitrator, or within 15 days after the circumstances mentioned in articles 11 and 12 became known to that party.

2. The notice of challenge shall be communicated to all other parties, to the arbitrator who is challenged and to the other arbitrators. The notice of challenge shall state the reasons for the challenge.

3. When an arbitrator has been challenged by a party, all parties may agree to the challenge. The arbitrator may also, after the challenge, withdraw from his or her office. In neither case does this imply acceptance of the validity of the grounds for the challenge.

4. If, within 15 days from the date of the notice of challenge, all parties do not agree to the challenge or the challenged arbitrator does not withdraw, the party making the challenge may elect to pursue it. In that case, within 30 days from the

---

** Model statements of independence pursuant to article 11 can be found in the annex to the Rules.

date of the notice of challenge, it shall seek a decision on the challenge by the appointing authority.

Article 14   Replacement of an arbitrator

1. Subject to paragraph (2), in any event where an arbitrator has to be replaced during the course of the arbitral proceedings, a substitute arbitrator shall be appointed or chosen pursuant to the procedure provided for in articles 8 to 11 that was applicable to the appointment or choice of the arbitrator being replaced. This procedure shall apply even if during the process of appointing the arbitrator to be replaced, a party had failed to exercise its right to appoint or to participate in the appointment.

2. If, at the request of a party, the appointing authority determines that, in view of the exceptional circumstances of the case, it would be justified for a party to be deprived of its right to appoint a substitute arbitrator, the appointing authority may, after giving an opportunity to the parties and the remaining arbitrators to express their views: (a) appoint the substitute arbitrator; or (b) after the closure of the hearings, authorize the other arbitrators to proceed with the arbitration and make any decision or award.

Article 15   Repetition of hearings in the event of the replacement of an arbitrator

If an arbitrator is replaced, the proceedings shall resume at the stage where the arbitrator who was replaced ceased to perform his or her functions, unless the arbitral tribunal decides otherwise.

Article 16   Exclusion of liability

Save for intentional wrongdoing, the parties waive, to the fullest extent permitted under the applicable law, any claim against the arbitrators, the appointing authority and any person appointed by the arbitral tribunal based on any act or omission in connection with the arbitration.

Section III.   Arbitral proceedings

Article 17   General provisions

1. Subject to these Rules, the arbitral tribunal may conduct the arbitration in such manner as it considers appropriate, provided that the parties are treated with equality and that at an appropriate stage of the proceedings each party is given a reasonable opportunity of presenting its case. The arbitral tribunal, in exercising its discretion, shall conduct the proceedings so as to avoid unnecessary delay and expense and to provide a fair and efficient process for resolving the parties' dispute.

2. As soon as practicable after its constitution and after inviting the parties to express their views, the arbitral tribunal shall establish the provisional timetable of the arbitration. The arbitral tribunal may, at any time, after inviting the parties to express their views, extend or abridge any period of time prescribed under these Rules or agreed by the parties.

3. If at an appropriate stage of the proceedings any party so requests, the arbitral

tribunal shall hold hearings for the presentation of evidence by witnesses, including expert witnesses, or for oral argument. In the absence of such a request, the arbitral tribunal shall decide whether to hold such hearings or whether the proceedings shall be conducted on the basis of documents and other materials.

4. All communications to the arbitral tribunal by one party shall be communicated by that party to all other parties. Such communications shall be made at the same time, except as otherwise permitted by the arbitral tribunal if it may do so under applicable law.

5. The arbitral tribunal may, at the request of any party, allow one or more third persons to be joined in the arbitration as a party provided such person is a party to the arbitration agreement, unless the arbitral tribunal finds, after giving all parties, including the person or persons to be joined, the opportunity to be heard, that joinder should not be permitted because of prejudice to any of those parties. The arbitral tribunal may make a single award or several awards in respect of all parties so involved in the arbitration.

Article 18   Place of arbitration

1. If the parties have not previously agreed on the place of arbitration, the place of arbitration shall be determined by the arbitral tribunal having regard to the circumstances of the case. The award shall be deemed to have been made at the place of arbitration.

2. The arbitral tribunal may meet at any location it considers appropriate for deliberations. Unless otherwise agreed by the parties, the arbitral tribunal may also meet at any location it considers appropriate for any other purpose, including hearings.

Article 19   Language

1. Subject to an agreement by the parties, the arbitral tribunal shall, promptly after its appointment, determine the language or languages to be used in the proceedings. This determination shall apply to the statement of claim, the statement of defence, and any further written statements and, if oral hearings take place, to the language or languages to be used in such hearings.

2. The arbitral tribunal may order that any documents annexed to the statement of claim or statement of defence, and any supplementary documents or exhibits submitted in the course of the proceedings, delivered in their original language, shall be accompanied by a translation into the language or languages agreed upon by the parties or determined by the arbitral tribunal.

Article 20   Statement of claim

1. The claimant shall communicate its statement of claim in writing to the respondent and to each of the arbitrators within a period of time to be determined by the arbitral tribunal. The claimant may elect to treat its notice of arbitration referred to in article 3 as a statement of claim, provided that the notice of arbitration also complies with the requirements of paragraphs 2 to 4 of this article.

2. The statement of claim shall include the following particulars:

(a) The names and contact details of the parties;

(b) A statement of the facts supporting the claim;

(c) The points at issue;

(d) The relief or remedy sought;

(e) The legal grounds or arguments supporting the claim.

3. A copy of any contract or other legal instrument out of or in relation to which the dispute arises and of the arbitration agreement shall be annexed to the statement of claim.

4. The statement of claim should, as far as possible, be accompanied by all documents and other evidence relied upon by the claimant, or contain references to them.

Article 21   Statement of defence

1. The respondent shall communicate its statement of defence in writing to the claimant and to each of the arbitrators within a period of time to be determined by the arbitral tribunal. The respondent may elect to treat its response to the notice of arbitration referred to in article 4 as a statement of defence, provided that the response to the notice of arbitration also complies with the requirements of paragraph 2 of this article.

2. The statement of defence shall reply to the particulars (b) to (e) of the statement of claim (article 20, paragraph 2). The statement of defence should, as far as possible, be accompanied by all documents and other evidence relied upon by the respondent, or contain references to them.

3. In its statement of defence, or at a later stage in the arbitral proceedings if the arbitral tribunal decides that the delay was justified under the circumstances, the respondent may make a counterclaim or rely on a claim for the purpose of a set-off provided that the arbitral tribunal has jurisdiction over it.

4. The provisions of article 20, paragraphs 2 to 4 shall apply to a counterclaim, a claim under article 4, paragraph (2) (f) and a claim relied on for the purpose of a set-off.

Article 22   Amendments to the claim or defence

During the course of the arbitral proceedings, a party may amend or supplement its claim or defence, including a counterclaim or a claim for the purpose of a set-off, unless the arbitral tribunal considers it inappropriate to allow such amendment or supplement having regard to the delay in making it or prejudice to other parties or any other circumstances. However, a claim or defence, including a counterclaim or a claim for the purpose of a set-off, may not be amended or supplemented in such a manner that the amended or supplemented claim or defence falls outside the jurisdiction of the arbitral tribunal.

Article 23   Pleas as to the jurisdiction of the arbitral tribunal

1. The arbitral tribunal shall have the power to rule on its own jurisdiction,

including any objections with respect to the existence or validity of the arbitration agreement. For that purpose, an arbitration clause that forms part of a contract shall be treated as an agreement independent of the other terms of the contract. A decision by the arbitral tribunal that the contract is null shall not entail automatically the invalidity of the arbitration clause.

2. A plea that the arbitral tribunal does not have jurisdiction shall be raised no later than in the statement of defence or, with respect to a counterclaim or a claim for the purpose of a set-off, in the reply to the counterclaim or to the claim for the purpose of a set-off. A party is not precluded from raising such a plea by the fact that it has appointed, or participated in the appointment of, an arbitrator. A plea that the arbitral tribunal is exceeding the scope of its authority shall be raised as soon as the matter alleged to be beyond the scope of its authority is raised during the arbitral proceedings. The arbitral tribunal may, in either case, admit a later plea if it considers the delay justified.

3. The arbitral tribunal may rule on a plea referred to in paragraph 2 either as a preliminary question or in an award on the merits. The arbitral tribunal may continue the arbitral proceedings and make an award, notwithstanding any pending challenge to its jurisdiction before a court.

Article 24   Further written statements

The arbitral tribunal shall decide which further written statements, in addition to the statement of claim and the statement of defence, shall be required from the parties or may be presented by them and shall fix the periods of time for communicating such statements.

Article 25   Periods of time

The periods of time fixed by the arbitral tribunal for the communication of written statements (including the statement of claim and statement of defence) should not exceed 45 days. However, the arbitral tribunal may extend the time limits if it concludes that an extension is justified.

Article 26   Interim measures

1. The arbitral tribunal may, at the request of a party, grant interim measures.

2. An interim measure is any temporary measure by which, at any time prior to the issuance of the award by which the dispute is finally decided, the arbitral tribunal orders a party, for example and without limitation, to:

(a) Maintain or restore the status quo pending determination of the dispute;

(b) Take action that would prevent, or refrain from taking action that is likely to cause, (i) current or imminent harm or (ii) prejudice to the arbitral process itself;

(c) Provide a means of preserving assets out of which a subsequent award may be satisfied; or

(d) Preserve evidence that may be relevant and material to the resolution of the dispute.

3. The party requesting an interim measure under paragraphs 2 (a) to (c) shall satisfy the arbitral tribunal that:

(a) Harm not adequately reparable by an award of damages is likely to result if the measure is not ordered, and such harm substantially outweighs the harm that is likely to result to the party against whom the measure is directed if the measure is granted; and

(b) There is a reasonable possibility that the requesting party will succeed on the merits of the claim. The determination on this possibility shall not affect the discretion of the arbitral tribunal in making any subsequent determination.

4. With regard to a request for an interim measure under paragraph 2 (d), the requirements in paragraphs 3 (a) and (b) shall apply only to the extent the arbitral tribunal considers appropriate.

5. The arbitral tribunal may modify, suspend or terminate an interim measure it has granted, upon application of any party or, in exceptional circumstances and upon prior notice to the parties, on the arbitral tribunal's own initiative.

6. The arbitral tribunal may require the party requesting an interim measure to provide appropriate security in connection with the measure.

7. The arbitral tribunal may require any party promptly to disclose any material change in the circumstances on the basis of which the interim measure was requested or granted.

8. The party requesting an interim measure may be liable for any costs and damages caused by the measure to any party if the arbitral tribunal later determines that, in the circumstances then prevailing, the measure should not have been granted. The arbitral tribunal may award such costs and damages at any point during the proceedings.

9. A request for interim measures addressed by any party to a judicial authority shall not be deemed incompatible with the agreement to arbitrate, or as a waiver of that agreement.

Article 27   Evidence

1. Each party shall have the burden of proving the facts relied on to support its claim or defence.

2. Witnesses, including expert witnesses, who are presented by the parties to testify to the arbitral tribunal on any issue of fact or expertise may be any individual, notwithstanding that the individual is a party to the arbitration or in any way related to a party. Unless otherwise directed by the arbitral tribunal, statements by witnesses, including expert witnesses, may be presented in writing and signed by them.

3. At any time during the arbitral proceedings the arbitral tribunal may require the parties to produce documents, exhibits or other evidence within such a period of time as the arbitral tribunal shall determine.

4. The arbitral tribunal shall determine the admissibility, relevance, materiality and weight of the evidence offered.

Article 28   Hearings

1. In the event of an oral hearing, the arbitral tribunal shall give the parties adequate advance notice of the date, time and place thereof.

2. Witnesses, including expert witnesses, may be heard under the conditions and examined in the manner set by the arbitral tribunal.

3. Hearings shall be held in camera unless the parties agree otherwise. The arbitral tribunal may require the retirement of any witness or witnesses, including expert witnesses, during the testimony of such other witnesses, except that a witness, including an expert witness, who is a party to the arbitration shall not, in principle, be asked to retire.

4. The arbitral tribunal may direct that witnesses, including expert witnesses, be examined through means of telecommunication that do not require their physical presence at the hearing (such as video conference).

Article 29   Experts appointed by the arbitral tribunal

1. After consultation with the parties, the arbitral tribunal may appoint one or more independent experts to report to it, in writing, on specific issues to be determined by the arbitral tribunal. A copy of the expert's terms of reference, established by the arbitral tribunal, shall be communicated to the parties.

2. The expert shall, in principle before accepting appointment, submit to the arbitral tribunal and to the parties a description of his or her qualifications and a statement of his or her impartiality and independence. Within the time ordered by the arbitral tribunal, the parties shall inform the arbitral tribunal whether they have any objections as to the expert's qualifications, impartiality or independence. The arbitral tribunal shall decide promptly whether to accept any such objections. After an expert's appointment, a party may object to the expert's qualifications, impartiality or independence only if the objection is for reasons of which the party becomes aware after the appointment has been made. The arbitral tribunal shall decide promptly what, if any, action to take.

3. The parties shall give the expert any relevant information or produce for his or her inspection any relevant documents or goods that he or she may require of them. Any dispute between a party and such expert as to the relevance of the required information or production shall be referred to the arbitral tribunal for decision.

4. Upon receipt of the expert's report, the arbitral tribunal shall communicate a copy of the report to the parties, which shall be given the opportunity to express, in writing, their opinion on the report. A party shall be entitled to examine any document on which the expert has relied in his or her report.

5. At the request of any party, the expert, after delivery of the report, may be heard at a hearing where the parties shall have the opportunity to be present and to interrogate the expert. At this hearing, any party may present expert witnesses in order to testify on the points at issue. The provisions of article 28 shall be applicable to such proceedings.

Article 30 Default

1. If, within the period of time fixed by these Rules or the arbitral tribunal, without showing sufficient cause:

(a) The claimant has failed to communicate its statement of claim, the arbitral tribunal shall issue an order for the termination of the arbitral proceedings, unless there are remaining matters that may need to be decided and the arbitral tribunal considers it appropriate to do so;

(b) The respondent has failed to communicate its response to the notice of arbitration or its statement of defence, the arbitral tribunal shall order that the proceedings continue, without treating such failure in itself as an admission of the claimant's allegations; the provisions of this subparagraph also apply to a claimant's failure to submit a defence to a counterclaim or to a claim for the purpose of a set-off.

2. If a party, duly notified under these Rules, fails to appear at a hearing, without showing sufficient cause for such failure, the arbitral tribunal may proceed with the arbitration.

3. If a party, duly invited by the arbitral tribunal to produce documents, exhibits or other evidence, fails to do so within the established period of time, without showing sufficient cause for such failure, the arbitral tribunal may make the award on the evidence before it.

Article 31 Closure of hearings

1. The arbitral tribunal may inquire of the parties if they have any further proof to offer or witnesses to be heard or submissions to make and, if there are none, it may declare the hearings closed.

2. The arbitral tribunal may, if it considers it necessary owing to exceptional circumstances, decide, on its own initiative or upon application of a party, to reopen the hearings at any time before the award is made.

Article 32 Waiver of right to object

A failure by any party to object promptly to any noncompliance with these Rules or with any requirement of the arbitration agreement shall be deemed to be a waiver of the right of such party to make such an objection, unless such party can show that, under the circumstances, its failure to object was justified.

Section IV. The award

Article 33 Decisions

1. When there is more than one arbitrator, any award or other decision of the arbitral tribunal shall be made by a majority of the arbitrators.

2. In the case of questions of procedure, when there is no majority or when the arbitral tribunal so authorizes, the presiding arbitrator may decide alone, subject to revision, if any, by the arbitral tribunal.

Article 34   Form and effect of the award

1. The arbitral tribunal may make separate awards on different issues at different times.

2. All awards shall be made in writing and shall be final and binding on the parties. The parties shall carry out all awards without delay.

3. The arbitral tribunal shall state the reasons upon which the award is based, unless the parties have agreed that no reasons are to be given.

4. An award shall be signed by the arbitrators and it shall contain the date on which the award was made and indicate the place of arbitration. Where there is more than one arbitrator and any of them fails to sign, the award shall state the reason for the absence of the signature.

5. An award may be made public with the consent of all parties or where and to the extent disclosure is required of a party by legal duty, to protect or pursue a legal right or in relation to legal proceedings before a court or other competent authority.

6. Copies of the award signed by the arbitrators shall be communicated to the parties by the arbitral tribunal.

Article 35   Applicable law, amiable compositeur

1. The arbitral tribunal shall apply the rules of law designated by the parties as applicable to the substance of the dispute. Failing such designation by the parties, the arbitral tribunal shall apply the law which it determines to be appropriate.

2. The arbitral tribunal shall decide as amiable compositeur or ex aequo et bono only if the parties have expressly authorized the arbitral tribunal to do so.

3. In all cases, the arbitral tribunal shall decide in accordance with the terms of the contract, if any, and shall take into account any usage of trade applicable to the transaction.

Article 36   Settlement or other grounds for termination

1. If, before the award is made, the parties agree on a settlement of the dispute, the arbitral tribunal shall either issue an order for the termination of the arbitral proceedings or, if requested by the parties and accepted by the arbitral tribunal, record the settlement in the form of an arbitral award on agreed terms. The arbitral tribunal is not obliged to give reasons for such an award.

2. If, before the award is made, the continuation of the arbitral proceedings becomes unnecessary or impossible for any reason not mentioned in paragraph 1, the arbitral tribunal shall inform the parties of its intention to issue an order for the termination of the proceedings. The arbitral tribunal shall have the power to issue such an order unless there are remaining matters that may need to be decided and the arbitral tribunal considers it appropriate to do so.

3. Copies of the order for termination of the arbitral proceedings or of the arbitral award on agreed terms, signed by the arbitrators, shall be communicated by the arbitral tribunal to the parties. Where an arbitral award on agreed terms is made, the provisions of article 34, paragraphs 2, 4 and 5 shall apply.

Article 37 Interpretation of the award

1. Within 30 days after the receipt of the award, a party, with notice to the other parties, may request that the arbitral tribunal give an interpretation of the award.

2. The interpretation shall be given in writing within 45 days after the receipt of the request. The interpretation shall form part of the award and the provisions of article 34, paragraphs 2 to 6, shall apply.

Article 38 Correction of the award

1. Within 30 days after the receipt of the award, a party, with notice to the other parties, may request the arbitral tribunal to correct in the award any error in computation, any clerical or typographical error, or any error or omission of a similar nature. If the arbitral tribunal considers that the request is justified, it shall make the correction within 45 days of receipt of the request.

2. The arbitral tribunal may within 30 days after the communication of the award make such corrections on its own initiative.

3. Such corrections shall be in writing and shall form part of the award. The provisions of article 34, paragraphs 2 to 6, shall apply.

Article 39 Additional award

1. Within 30 days after the receipt of the termination order or the award, a party, with notice to the other parties, may request the arbitral tribunal to make an award or an additional award as to claims presented in the arbitral proceedings but not decided by the arbitral tribunal.

2. If the arbitral tribunal considers the request for an award or additional award to be justified, it shall render or complete its award within 60 days after the receipt of the request. The arbitral tribunal may extend, if necessary, the period of time within which it shall make the award.

3. When such an award or additional award is made, the provisions of article 34, paragraphs 2 to 6, shall apply.

Article 40 Definition of costs

1. The arbitral tribunal shall fix the costs of arbitration in the final award and, if it deems appropriate, in another decision.

2. The term "costs" includes only:

(a) The fees of the arbitral tribunal to be stated separately as to each arbitrator and to be fixed by the tribunal itself in accordance with article 41;

(b) The reasonable travel and other expenses incurred by the arbitrators;

(c) The reasonable costs of expert advice and of other assistance required by the arbitral tribunal;

(d) The reasonable travel and other expenses of witnesses to the extent such expenses are approved by the arbitral tribunal;

(e) The legal and other costs incurred by the parties in relation to the arbitration to the extent that the arbitral tribunal determines that the amount of such costs is reasonable;

(f) Any fees and expenses of the appointing authority as well as the fees and expenses of the Secretary-General of the PCA.

3. In relation to interpretation, correction or completion of any award under articles 37 to 39, the arbitral tribunal may charge the costs referred to in paragraphs 2 (b) to (f), but no additional fees.

Article 41   Fees and expenses of arbitrators

1. The fees and expenses of the arbitrators shall be reasonable in amount, taking into account the amount in dispute, the complexity of the subject matter, the time spent by the arbitrators and any other relevant circumstances of the case.

2. If there is an appointing authority and it applies or has stated that it will apply a schedule or particular method for determining the fees for arbitrators in international cases, the arbitral tribunal in fixing its fees shall take that schedule or method into account to the extent that it considers appropriate in the circumstances of the case.

3. Promptly after its constitution, the arbitral tribunal shall inform the parties as to how it proposes to determine its fees and expenses, including any rates it intends to apply. Within 15 days of receiving that proposal, any party may refer the proposal to the appointing authority for review. If, within 45 days of receipt of such a referral, the appointing authority finds that the proposal of the arbitral tribunal is inconsistent with paragraph 1, it shall make any necessary adjustments thereto, which shall be binding upon the arbitral tribunal.

4. (a) When informing the parties of the arbitrators' fees and expenses that have been fixed pursuant to article 40, paragraphs 2 (a) and (b), the arbitral tribunal shall also explain the manner in which the corresponding amounts have been calculated.

(b) Within 15 days of receiving the arbitral tribunal's determination of fees and expenses, any party may refer for review such determination to the appointing authority. If no appointing authority has been agreed upon or designated, or if the appointing authority fails to act within the time specified in these Rules, then the review shall be made by the Secretary-General of the PCA.

(c) If the appointing authority or the Secretary-General of the PCA finds that the arbitral tribunal's determination is inconsistent with the arbitral tribunal's proposal (and any adjustment thereto) under paragraph 3 or is otherwise manifestly excessive, it shall, within 45 days of receiving such a referral, make any adjustments to the arbitral tribunal's determination that are necessary to satisfy the criteria in paragraph 1. Any such adjustments shall be binding upon the arbitral tribunal.

(d) Any such adjustments shall either be included by the arbitral tribunal in its award or, if the award has already been issued, be implemented in a correction to the award, to which the procedure of article 38, paragraph 3 shall apply.

5. Throughout the procedure under paragraphs 3 and 4, the arbitral tribunal shall

proceed with the arbitration, in accordance with article 17, paragraph 1.

6. A referral under paragraph 4 shall not affect any determination in the award other than the arbitral tribunal's fees and expenses; nor shall it delay the recognition and enforcement of all parts of the award other than those relating to the determination of the arbitral tribunal's fees and expenses.

Article 42   Allocation of costs

1. The costs of the arbitration shall in principle be borne by the unsuccessful party or parties. However, the arbitral tribunal may apportion each of such costs between the parties if it determines that apportionment is reasonable, taking into account the circumstances of the case.

2. The arbitral tribunal shall in the final award or, if it deems appropriate, in any other award, determine any amount that a party may have to pay to another party as a result of the decision on allocation of costs.

Article 43   Deposit of costs

1. The arbitral tribunal, on its establishment, may request the parties to deposit an equal amount as an advance for the costs referred to in article 40, paragraphs 2 (a) to (c).

2. During the course of the arbitral proceedings the arbitral tribunal may request supplementary deposits from the parties.

3. If an appointing authority has been agreed upon or designated, and when a party so requests and the appointing authority consents to perform the function, the arbitral tribunal shall fix the amounts of any deposits or supplementary deposits only after consultation with the appointing authority, which may make any comments to the arbitral tribunal that it deems appropriate concerning the amount of such deposits and supplementary deposits.

4. If the required deposits are not paid in full within 30 days after the receipt of the request, the arbitral tribunal shall so inform the parties in order that one or more of them may make the required payment. If such payment is not made, the arbitral tribunal may order the suspension or termination of the arbitral proceedings.

5. After a termination order or final award has been made, the arbitral tribunal shall render an accounting to the parties of the deposits received and return any unexpended balance to the parties.

Annex   Model arbitration clause for contracts

Any dispute, controversy or claim arising out of or relating to this contract, or the breach, termination or invalidity thereof, shall be settled by arbitration in accordance with the UNCITRAL Arbitration Rules.

Note — Parties should consider adding:

(a)   The appointing authority shall be . . . (name of institution or person);

(b)   The number of arbitrators shall be . . . (one or three);

(c)   The place of arbitration shall be . . . (town and country);

(d)   The language to be used in the arbitral proceedings shall be . . . .

Possible waiver statement

Note — If the parties wish to exclude recourse against the arbitral award that may be available under the applicable law, they may consider adding a provision to that effect as suggested below, considering, however, that the effectiveness and conditions of such an exclusion depend on the applicable law.

Waiver: The parties hereby waive their right to any form of recourse against an award to any court or other competent authority, insofar as such waiver can validly be made under the applicable law.

Model statements of independence pursuant to article 11 of the Rules

No circumstances to disclose: I am impartial and independent of each of the parties and intend to remain so. To the best of my knowledge, there are no circumstances, past or present, likely to give rise to justifiable doubts as to my impartiality or independence. I shall promptly notify the parties and the other arbitrators of any such circumstances that may subsequently come to my attention during this arbitration.

Circumstances to disclose: I am impartial and independent of each of the parties and intend to remain so. Attached is a statement made pursuant to article 11 of the UNCITRAL Arbitration Rules of (a) my past and present professional, business and other relationships with the parties and (b) any other relevant circumstances. [Include statement] I confirm that those circumstances do not affect my independence and impartiality. I shall promptly notify the parties and the other arbitrators of any such further relationships or circumstances that may subsequently come to my attention during this arbitration.

Note — Any party may consider requesting from the arbitrator the following addition to the statement of independence:

I confirm, on the basis of the information presently available to me, that I can devote the time necessary to conduct this arbitration diligently, efficiently and in accordance with the time limits in the Rules.

AMERICAN ARBITRATION ASSOCIATION INTERNATIONAL CENTRE FOR DISPUTE RESOLUTION INTERNATIONAL ARBITRATION RULES*

Rules Amended and Effective June 1, 2009

Fee Schedule Amended and Effective June 1, 2010

Article 1

1. Where parties have agreed in writing to arbitrate disputes under these International Arbitration Rules or have provided for arbitration of an international dispute by the International Centre for Dispute Resolution or the American Arbitration Association without designating particular Rules, the arbitration shall take place in accordance with these Rules, as in effect at the date of commencement of the arbitration, subject to whatever modifications the parties may adopt in writing.

2. These Rules govern the arbitration, except that, where any such rule is in conflict with any provision of the law applicable to the arbitration from which the parties cannot derogate, that provision shall prevail.

3. These Rules specify the duties and responsibilities of the administrator, the International Centre for Dispute Resolution, a division of the American Arbitration Association. The administrator may provide services through its Centre, located in New York, or through the facilities of arbitral institutions with which it has agreements of cooperation.

Article 2 Commencing the Arbitration
Notice of Arbitration and Statement of Claim

1. The party initiating arbitration ("claimant") shall give written notice of arbitration to the administrator and at the same time to the party against whom a claim is being made ("respondent").

2. Arbitral proceedings shall be deemed to commence on the date on which the administrator receives the notice of arbitration.

3. The notice of arbitration shall contain a statement of claim including the following:

    (a) a demand that the dispute be referred to arbitration;

    (b) the names, addresses and telephone numbers of the parties;

    (c) a reference to the arbitration clause or agreement that is invoked;

    (d) a reference to any contract out of or in relation to which the dispute arises;

    (e) a description of the claim and an indication of the facts supporting it;

    (f) the relief or remedy sought and the amount claimed; and

---

(g) may include proposals as to the means of designating and the number of arbitrators, the place of arbitration and the language(s) of the arbitration.

4. Upon receipt of the notice of arbitration, the administrator shall communicate with all parties with respect to the arbitration and shall acknowledge the commencement of the arbitration.

Article 3   Statement of Defense and Counterclaim

1. Within 30 days after the commencement of the arbitration, a respondent shall submit a written statement of defense, responding to the issues raised in the notice of arbitration, to the claimant and any other parties, and to the administrator.

2. At the time a respondent submits its statement of defense, a respondent may make counterclaims or assert setoffs as to any claim covered by the agreement to arbitrate, as to which the claimant shall within 30 days submit a written statement of defense to the respondent and any other parties and to the administrator.

3. A respondent shall respond to the administrator, the claimant and other parties within 30 days after the commencement of the arbitration as to any proposals the claimant may have made as to the number of arbitrators, the place of the arbitration or the language(s) of the arbitration, except to the extent that the parties have previously agreed as to these matters.

4. The arbitral tribunal, or the administrator if the arbitral tribunal has not yet been formed, may extend any of the time limits established in this article if it considers such an extension justified.

Article 4   Amendments to Claims

During the arbitral proceedings, any party may amend or supplement its claim, counterclaim or defense, unless the tribunal considers it inappropriate to allow such amendment or supplement because of the party's delay in making it, prejudice to the other parties or any other circumstances. A party may not amend or supplement a claim or counterclaim if the amendment or supplement would fall outside the scope of the agreement to arbitrate.

THE TRIBUNAL

Article 5   Number of Arbitrators

If the parties have not agreed on the number of arbitrators, one arbitrator shall be appointed unless the administrator determines in its discretion that three arbitrators are appropriate because of the large size, complexity or other circumstances of the case.

Article 6   Appointment of Arbitrators

1. The parties may mutually agree upon any procedure for appointing arbitrators and shall inform the administrator as to such procedure.

2. The parties may mutually designate arbitrators, with or without the assistance of the administrator. When such designations are made, the parties shall notify the administrator so that notice of the appointment can be communicated to the

arbitrators, together with a copy of these Rules.

3. If within 45 days after the commencement of the arbitration, all of the parties have not mutually agreed on a procedure for appointing the arbitrator(s) or have not mutually agreed on the designation of the arbitrator(s), the administrator shall, at the written request of any party, appoint the arbitrator(s) and designate the presiding arbitrator. If all of the parties have mutually agreed upon a procedure for appointing the arbitrator(s), but all appointments have not been made within the time limits provided in that procedure, the administrator shall, at the written request of any party, perform all functions provided for in that procedure that remain to be performed.

4. In making such appointments, the administrator, after inviting consultation with the parties, shall endeavor to select suitable arbitrators. At the request of any party or on its own initiative, the administrator may appoint nationals of a country other than that of any of the parties.

5. Unless the parties have agreed otherwise no later than 45 days after the commencement of the arbitration, if the notice of arbitration names two or more claimants or two or more respondents, the administrator shall appoint all the arbitrators.

Article 7   Impartiality and Independence of Arbitrators

1. Arbitrators acting under these Rules shall be impartial and independent. Prior to accepting appointment, a prospective arbitrator shall disclose to the administrator any circumstance likely to give rise to justifiable doubts as to the arbitrator's impartiality or independence. If, at any stage during the arbitration, new circumstances arise that may give rise to such doubts, an arbitrator shall promptly disclose such circumstances to the parties and to the administrator. Upon receipt of such information from an arbitrator or a party, the administrator shall communicate it to the other parties and to the tribunal.

2. No party or anyone acting on its behalf shall have any ex parte communication relating to the case with any arbitrator, or with any candidate for appointment as party-appointed arbitrator except to advise the candidate of the general nature of the controversy and of the anticipated proceedings and to discuss the candidate's qualifications, availability or independence in relation to the parties, or to discuss the suitability of candidates for selection as a third arbitrator where the parties or party designated arbitrators are to participate in that selection. No party or anyone acting on its behalf shall have any ex parte communication relating to the case with any candidate for presiding arbitrator.

Article 8   Challenge of Arbitrators

1. A party may challenge any arbitrator whenever circumstances exist that give rise to justifiable doubts as to the arbitrator's impartiality or independence. A party wishing to challenge an arbitrator shall send notice of the challenge to the administrator within 15 days after being notified of the appointment of the arbitrator or within 15 days after the circumstances giving rise to the challenge become known to that party.

2. The challenge shall state in writing the reasons for the challenge.

3. Upon receipt of such a challenge, the administrator shall notify the other parties of the challenge. When an arbitrator has been challenged by one party, the other party or parties may agree to the acceptance of the challenge and, if there is agreement, the arbitrator shall withdraw. The challenged arbitrator may also withdraw from office in the absence of such agreement. In neither case does withdrawal imply acceptance of the validity of the grounds for the challenge.

Article 9

If the other party or parties do not agree to the challenge or the challenged arbitrator does not withdraw, the administrator in its sole discretion shall make the decision on the challenge.

Article 10   Replacement of an Arbitrator

If an arbitrator withdraws after a challenge, or the administrator sustains the challenge, or the administrator determines that there are sufficient reasons to accept the resignation of an arbitrator, or an arbitrator dies, a substitute arbitrator shall be appointed pursuant to the provisions of Article 6, unless the parties otherwise agree.

Article 11

1. If an arbitrator on a three-person tribunal fails to participate in the arbitration for reasons other than those identified in Article 10, the two other arbitrators shall have the power in their sole discretion to continue the arbitration and to make any decision, ruling or award, notwithstanding the failure of the third arbitrator to participate. In determining whether to continue the arbitration or to render any decision, ruling or award without the participation of an arbitrator, the two other arbitrators shall take into account the stage of the arbitration, the reason, if any, expressed by the third arbitrator for such nonparticipation and such other matters as they consider appropriate in the circumstances of the case. In the event that the two other arbitrators determine not to continue the arbitration without the participation of the third arbitrator, the administrator on proof satisfactory to it shall declare the office vacant, and a substitute arbitrator shall be appointed pursuant to the provisions of Article 6, unless the parties otherwise agree.

2. If a substitute arbitrator is appointed under either Article 10 or Article 11, the tribunal shall determine at its sole discretion whether all or part of any prior hearings shall be repeated.

GENERAL CONDITIONS

Article 12   Representation

Any party may be represented in the arbitration. The names, addresses and telephone numbers of representatives shall be communicated in writing to the other parties and to the administrator. Once the tribunal has been established, the parties or their representatives may communicate in writing directly with the tribunal.

Article 13   Place of Arbitration

1. If the parties disagree as to the place of arbitration, the administrator may initially determine the place of arbitration, subject to the power of the tribunal to determine finally the place of arbitration within 60 days after its constitution. All such determinations shall be made having regard for the contentions of the parties and the circumstances of the arbitration.

2. The tribunal may hold conferences or hear witnesses or inspect property or documents at any place it deems appropriate. The parties shall be given sufficient written notice to enable them to be present at any such proceedings.

Article 14   Language

If the parties have not agreed otherwise, the language(s) of the arbitration shall be that of the documents containing the arbitration agreement, subject to the power of the tribunal to determine otherwise based upon the contentions of the parties and the circumstances of the arbitration. The tribunal may order that any documents delivered in another language shall be accompanied by a translation into the language(s) of the arbitration.

Article 15   Pleas as to Jurisdiction

1. The tribunal shall have the power to rule on its own jurisdiction, including any objections with respect to the existence, scope or validity of the arbitration agreement.

2. The tribunal shall have the power to determine the existence or validity of a contract of which an arbitration clause forms a part. Such an arbitration clause shall be treated as an agreement independent of the other terms of the contract. A decision by the tribunal that the contract is null and void shall not for that reason alone render invalid the arbitration clause.

3. A party must object to the jurisdiction of the tribunal or to the arbitrability of a claim or counterclaim no later than the filing of the statement of defense, as provided in Article 3, to the claim or counterclaim that gives rise to the objection. The tribunal may rule on such objections as a preliminary matter or as part of the final award.

Article 16   Conduct of the Arbitration

1. Subject to these Rules, the tribunal may conduct the arbitration in whatever manner it considers appropriate, provided that the parties are treated with equality and that each party has the right to be heard and is given a fair opportunity to present its case.

2. The tribunal, exercising its discretion, shall conduct the proceedings with a view to expediting the resolution of the dispute. It may conduct a preparatory conference with the parties for the purpose of organizing, scheduling and agreeing to procedures to expedite the subsequent proceedings.

3. The tribunal may in its discretion direct the order of proof, bifurcate proceedings, exclude cumulative or irrelevant testimony or other evidence and direct the parties to focus their presentations on issues the decision of which could

dispose of all or part of the case.

4. Documents or information supplied to the tribunal by one party shall at the same time be communicated by that party to the other party or parties.

Article 17   Further Written Statements

1. The tribunal may decide whether the parties shall present any written statements in addition to statements of claims and counterclaims and statements of defense, and it shall fix the periods of time for submitting any such statements.

2. The periods of time fixed by the tribunal for the communication of such written statements should not exceed 45 days. However, the tribunal may extend such time limits if it considers such an extension justified.

Article 18   Notices

1. Unless otherwise agreed by the parties or ordered by the tribunal, all notices, statements and written communications may be served on a party by air mail, air courier, facsimile transmission, telex, telegram or other written forms of electronic communication addressed to the party or its representative at its last known address or by personal service.

2. For the purpose of calculating a period of time under these Rules, such period shall begin to run on the day following the day when a notice, statement or written communication is received. If the last day of such period is an official holiday at the place received, the period is extended until the first business day which follows. Official holidays occurring during the running of the period of time are included in calculating the period.

Article 19   Evidence

1. Each party shall have the burden of proving the facts relied on to support its claim or defense.

2. The tribunal may order a party to deliver to the tribunal and to the other parties a summary of the documents and other evidence which that party intends to present in support of its claim, counterclaim or defense.

3. At any time during the proceedings, the tribunal may order parties to produce other documents, exhibits or other evidence it deems necessary or appropriate.

Article 20   Hearings

1. The tribunal shall give the parties at least 30 days advance notice of the date, time and place of the initial oral hearing. The tribunal shall give reasonable notice of subsequent hearings.

2. At least 15 days before the hearings, each party shall give the tribunal and the other parties the names and addresses of any witnesses it intends to present, the subject of their testimony and the languages in which such witnesses will give their testimony.

3. At the request of the tribunal or pursuant to mutual agreement of the parties, the administrator shall make arrangements for the interpretation of oral testimony

or for a record of the hearing.

4. Hearings are private unless the parties agree otherwise or the law provides to the contrary. The tribunal may require any witness or witnesses to retire during the testimony of other witnesses. The tribunal may determine the manner in which witnesses are examined.

5. Evidence of witnesses may also be presented in the form of written statements signed by them.

6. The tribunal shall determine the admissibility, relevance, materiality and weight of the evidence offered by any party. The tribunal shall take into account applicable principles of legal privilege, such as those involving the confidentiality of communications between a lawyer and client.

Article 21   Interim Measures of Protection

1. At the request of any party, the tribunal may take whatever interim measures it deems necessary, including injunctive relief and measures for the protection or conservation of property.

2. Such interim measures may take the form of an interim award, and the tribunal may require security for the costs of such measures.

3. A request for interim measures addressed by a party to a judicial authority shall not be deemed incompatible with the agreement to arbitrate or a waiver of the right to arbitrate.

4. The tribunal may in its discretion apportion costs associated with applications for interim relief in any interim award or in the final award.

Article 22   Experts

1. The tribunal may appoint one or more independent experts to report to it, in writing, on specific issues designated by the tribunal and communicated to the parties.

2. The parties shall provide such an expert with any relevant information or produce for inspection any relevant documents or goods that the expert may require. Any dispute between a party and the expert as to the relevance of the requested information or goods shall be referred to the tribunal for decision.

3. Upon receipt of an expert's report, the tribunal shall send a copy of the report to all parties and shall give the parties an opportunity to express, in writing, their opinion on the report. A party may examine any document on which the expert has relied in such a report.

4. At the request of any party, the tribunal shall give the parties an opportunity to question the expert at a hearing. At this hearing, parties may present expert witnesses to testify on the points at issue.

Article 23   Default

1. If a party fails to file a statement of defense within the time established by the tribunal without showing sufficient cause for such failure, as determined by the

tribunal, the tribunal may proceed with the arbitration.

2. If a party, duly notified under these Rules, fails to appear at a hearing without showing sufficient cause for such failure, as determined by the tribunal, the tribunal may proceed with the arbitration.

3. If a party, duly invited to produce evidence or take any other steps in the proceedings, fails to do so within the time established by the tribunal without showing sufficient cause for such failure, as determined by the tribunal, the tribunal may make the award on the evidence before it.

Article 24   Closure of Hearing

1. After asking the parties if they have any further testimony or evidentiary submissions and upon receiving negative replies or if satisfied that the record is complete, the tribunal may declare the hearings closed.

2. The tribunal in its discretion, on its own motion or upon application of a party, may reopen the hearings at any time before the award is made.

Article 25   Waiver of Rules

A party who knows that any provision of the Rules or requirement under the Rules has not been complied with, but proceeds with the arbitration without promptly stating an objection in writing thereto, shall be deemed to have waived the right to object.

Article 26   Awards, Decisions and Rulings

1. When there is more than one arbitrator, any award, decision or ruling of the arbitral tribunal shall be made by a majority of the arbitrators. If any arbitrator fails to sign the award, it shall be accompanied by a statement of the reason for the absence of such signature.

2. When the parties or the tribunal so authorize, the presiding arbitrator may make decisions or rulings on questions of procedure, subject to revision by the tribunal.

Article 27   Form and Effect of the Award

1. Awards shall be made in writing, promptly by the tribunal, and shall be final and binding on the parties. The parties undertake to carry out any such award without delay.

2. The tribunal shall state the reasons upon which the award is based, unless the parties have agreed that no reasons need be given.

3. The award shall contain the date and the place where the award was made, which shall be the place designated pursuant to Article 13.

4. An award may be made public only with the consent of all parties or as required by law.

5. Copies of the award shall be communicated to the parties by the administrator.

6. If the arbitration law of the country where the award is made requires the

award to be filed or registered, the tribunal shall comply with such requirement.

7. In addition to making a final award, the tribunal may make interim, interlocutory or partial orders and awards.

8. Unless otherwise agreed by the parties, the administrator may publish or otherwise make publicly available selected awards, decisions and rulings that have been edited to conceal the names of the parties and other identifying details or that have been made publicly available in the course of enforcement or otherwise.

Article 28   Applicable Laws and Remedies

1. The tribunal shall apply the substantive law(s) or rules of law designated by the parties as applicable to the dispute. Failing such a designation by the parties, the tribunal shall apply such law(s) or rules of law as it determines to be appropriate.

2. In arbitrations involving the application of contracts, the tribunal shall decide in accordance with the terms of the contract and shall take into account usages of the trade applicable to the contract.

3. The tribunal shall not decide as *amiable compositeur* or *ex aequo et bono* unless the parties have expressly authorized it to do so.

4. A monetary award shall be in the currency or currencies of the contract unless the tribunal considers another currency more appropriate, and the tribunal may award such pre-award and post-award interest, simple or compound, as it considers appropriate, taking into consideration the contract and applicable law.

5. Unless the parties agree otherwise, the parties expressly waive and forego any right to punitive, exemplary or similar damages unless a statute requires that compensatory damages be increased in a specified manner. This provision shall not apply to any award of arbitration costs to a party to compensate for dilatory or bad faith conduct in the arbitration.

Article 29   Settlement or Other Reasons for Termination

1. If the parties settle the dispute before an award is made, the tribunal shall terminate the arbitration and, if requested by all parties, may record the settlement in the form of an award on agreed terms. The tribunal is not obliged to give reasons for such an award.

2. If the continuation of the proceedings becomes unnecessary or impossible for any other reason, the tribunal shall inform the parties of its intention to terminate the proceedings. The tribunal shall thereafter issue an order terminating the arbitration, unless a party raises justifiable grounds for objection.

Article 30   Interpretation or Correction of the Award

1. Within 30 days after the receipt of an award, any party, with notice to the other parties, may request the tribunal to interpret the award or correct any clerical, typographical or computation errors or make an additional award as to claims presented but omitted from the award.

2. If the tribunal considers such a request justified, after considering the

contentions of the parties, it shall comply with such a request within 30 days after the request.

Article 31   Costs

The tribunal shall fix the costs of arbitration in its award. The tribunal may apportion such costs among the parties if it determines that such apportionment is reasonable, taking into account the circumstances of the case.

Such costs may include:

(a) the fees and expenses of the arbitrators;

(b) the costs of assistance required by the tribunal, including its experts;

(c) the fees and expenses of the administrator;

(d) the reasonable costs for legal representation of a successful party; and

(e) any such costs incurred in connection with an application for interim or emergency relief pursuant to Article 21.

Article 32   Compensation of Arbitrators

Arbitrators shall be compensated based upon their amount of service, taking into account their stated rate of compensation and the size and complexity of the case. The administrator shall arrange an appropriate daily or hourly rate, based on such considerations, with the parties and with each of the arbitrators as soon as practicable after the commencement of the arbitration. If the parties fail to agree on the terms of compensation, the administrator shall establish an appropriate rate and communicate it in writing to the parties.

Article 33   Deposit of Costs

1. When a party files claims, the administrator may request the filing party to deposit appropriate amounts as an advance for the costs referred to in Article 31, paragraphs (a.), (b.) and (c.).

2. During the course of the arbitral proceedings, the tribunal may request supplementary deposits from the parties.

3. If the deposits requested are not paid in full within 30 days after the receipt of the request, the administrator shall so inform the parties, in order that one or the other of them may make the required payment. If such payments are not made, the tribunal may order the suspension or termination of the proceedings.

4. After the award has been made, the administrator shall render an accounting to the parties of the deposits received and return any unexpended balance to the parties.

Article 34   Confidentiality

Confidential information disclosed during the proceedings by the parties or by witnesses shall not be divulged by an arbitrator or by the administrator. Except as provided in Article 27, unless otherwise agreed by the parties, or required by applicable law, the members of the tribunal and the administrator shall keep confidential all matters relating to the arbitration or the award.

Article 35   Exclusion of Liability

The members of the tribunal and the administrator shall not be liable to any party for any act or omission in connection with any arbitration conducted under these Rules, except that they may be liable for the consequences of conscious and deliberate wrongdoing.

Article 36   Interpretation of Rules

The tribunal shall interpret and apply these Rules insofar as they relate to its powers and duties. The administrator shall interpret and apply all other Rules.

Article 37   Emergency Measures of Protection

1. Unless the parties agree otherwise, the provisions of this Article 37 shall apply to arbitrations conducted under arbitration clauses or agreements entered on or after May 1, 2006.

2. A party in need of emergency relief prior to the constitution of the tribunal shall notify the administrator and all other parties in writing of the nature of the relief sought and the reasons why such relief is required on an emergency basis. The application shall also set forth the reasons why the party is entitled to such relief. Such notice may be given by e-mail, facsimile transmission or other reliable means, but must include a statement certifying that all other parties have been notified or an explanation of the steps taken in good faith to notify other parties.

3. Within one business day of receipt of notice as provided in paragraph 2, the administrator shall appoint a single emergency arbitrator from a special panel of emergency arbitrators designated to rule on emergency applications. Prior to accepting appointment, a prospective emergency arbitrator shall disclose to the administrator any circumstance likely to give rise to justifiable doubts to the arbitrator's impartiality or independence. Any challenge to the appointment of the emergency arbitrator must be made within one business day of the communication by the administrator to the parties of the appointment of the emergency arbitrator and the circumstances disclosed.

4. The emergency arbitrator shall as soon as possible, but in any event within two business days of appointment, establish a schedule for consideration of the application for emergency relief. Such schedule shall provide a reasonable opportunity to all parties to be heard, but may provide for proceedings by telephone conference or on written submissions as alternatives to a formal hearing. The emergency arbitrator shall have the authority vested in the tribunal under Article 15, including the authority to rule on her/his own jurisdiction, and shall resolve any disputes over the applicability of this Article 37.

5. The emergency arbitrator shall have the power to order or award any interim or conservancy measure the emergency arbitrator deems necessary, including injunctive relief and measures for the protection or conservation of property. Any such measure may take the form of an interim award or of an order. The emergency arbitrator shall give reasons in either case. The emergency arbitrator may modify or vacate the interim award or order for good cause shown.

6. The emergency arbitrator shall have no further power to act after the tribunal is constituted. Once the tribunal has been constituted, the tribunal may reconsider, modify or vacate the interim award or order of emergency relief issued by the emergency arbitrator. The emergency arbitrator may not serve as a member of the tribunal unless the parties agree otherwise.

7. Any interim award or order of emergency relief may be conditioned on provision by the party seeking such relief of appropriate security.

8. A request for interim measures addressed by a party to a judicial authority shall not be deemed incompatible with this Article 37 or with the agreement to arbitrate or a waiver of the right to arbitrate. If the administrator is directed by a judicial authority to nominate a special master to consider and report on an application for emergency relief, the administrator shall proceed as in Paragraph 2 of this article and the references to the emergency arbitrator shall be read to mean the special master, except that the special master shall issue a report rather than an interim award.

9. The costs associated with applications for emergency relief shall initially be apportioned by the emergency arbitrator or special master, subject to the power of the tribunal to determine finally the apportionment of such costs.

ADMINISTRATIVE FEES

Administrative Fee Schedules (Standard and Flexible Fee)

The ICDR has two administrative fee options for parties filing claims or counterclaims, the Standard Fee Schedule and Flexible Fee Schedule. The Standard Fee Schedule has a two payment schedule, and the Flexible Fee Schedule has a three payment schedule which offers lower initial filing fees, but potentially higher total administrative fees of approximately 12% to 19% for cases that proceed to a hearing. The administrative fees of the ICDR are based on the amount of the claim or counterclaim. Arbitrator compensation is not included in this schedule. Unless the parties agree otherwise, arbitrator compensation and administrative fees are subject to allocation by the arbitrator in the award.

Fees for incomplete or deficient filings: Where the applicable arbitration agreement does not reference the ICDR or the AAA, the ICDR will attempt to obtain the agreement of the other parties to the dispute to have the arbitration administered by the ICDR. However, where the ICDR is unable to obtain the agreement of the parties to have the ICDR administer the arbitration, the ICDR will administratively close the case and will not proceed with the administration of the arbitration. In these cases, the ICDR will return the filing fees to the filing party, less the amount specified in the fee schedule below for deficient filings.

Parties that file demands for arbitration that are incomplete or otherwise do not meet the filing requirements contained in these Rules shall also be charged the amount specified below for deficient filings if they fail or are unable to respond to the ICDR's request to correct the deficiency.

Fees for additional services: The ICDR reserves the right to assess additional administrative fees for services performed by the ICDR beyond those provided for in these Rules which may be required by the parties' agreement or stipulation.

Suspension for Nonpayment: If arbitrator compensation or administrative charges have not been paid in full, the administrator may so inform the parties in order that one of them may advance the required payment. If such payments are not made, the tribunal may order the suspension or termination of the proceedings. If no arbitrator has yet been appointed, the ICDR may suspend the proceedings.

Standard Fee Schedule

An Initial Filing Fee is payable in full by a filing party when a claim, counterclaim, or additional claim is filed. A Final Fee will be incurred for all cases that proceed to their first hearing. This fee will be payable in advance at the time that the first hearing is scheduled. This fee will be refunded at the conclusion of the case if no hearings have occurred. However, if the administrator is not notified at least 24 hours before the time of the scheduled hearing, the Final Fee will remain due and will not be refunded.

These fees will be billed in accordance with the following schedule:

Amount of Claim	Initial Filing Fee	Final Fee
Above $0 to $10,000	$775	$200
Above $10,000 to $75,000	$975	$300
Above $75,000 to $150,000	$1,850	$750
Above $150,000 to $300,000	$2,800	$1,250
Above $300,000 to $500,000	$4,350	$1,750
Above $500,000 to $1,000,000	$6,200	$2,500
Above $1,000,000 to $5,000,000	$8,200	$3,250
Above $5,000,000 to $10,000,000	$10,200	$4,000
Above $10,000,000	Base fee of $12,800 plus .01% of the amount of claim above $10,000,000 Fee Capped at $65,000	$6,000
Nonmonetary Claims[1]	$3,350	$1,250
Deficient Claim Filing[2]	$350	
Additional Services[3]		

Fees are subject to increase if the amount of a claim or counterclaim is modified after the initial filing date. Fees are subject to decrease if the amount of a claim or counterclaim is modified before the first hearing.

The minimum fees for any case having three or more arbitrators are $2,800 for the filing fee, plus a $1,250 Case Service Fee.

Parties on cases filed under either the Flexible Fee Schedule or the Standard Fee Schedule that are held in abeyance for one year will be assessed an annual abeyance fee of $300. If a party refuses to pay the assessed fee, the other party or parties may pay the entire fee on behalf of all parties, otherwise the matter will be administratively closed.

. . .

Refund Schedule for Standard Fee Schedule

The ICDR offers a refund schedule on filing fees connected with the Standard Fee Schedule. For cases with claims up to $75,000, a minimum filing fee of $350 will not be refunded. For all other cases, a minimum fee of $600 will not be refunded. Subject to the minimum fee requirements, refunds will be calculated as follows:

> 100% of the filing fee, above the minimum fee, will be refunded if the case is settled or withdrawn within five calendar days of filing.

---

[1] This fee is applicable when a claim or counterclaim is not for a monetary amount. Where a monetary claim amount is not known, parties will be required to state a range of claims or be subject to a filing fee of $10,200.

[2] The Deficient Claim Filing Fee shall not be charged in cases filed by a consumer in an arbitration governed by the Supplementary Procedures for the Resolution of Consumer-Related Disputes, or in cases filed by an Employee who is submitting their dispute to arbitration pursuant to an employer promulgated plan.

[3] The ICDR may assess additional fees where procedures or services outside the Rules sections are required under the parties' agreement or by stipulation.

> 50% of the filing fee will be refunded if the case is settled or withdrawn between six and 30 calendar days of filing.

> 25% of the filing fee will be refunded if the case is settled or withdrawn between 31 and 60 calendar days of filing.

No refund will be made once an arbitrator has been appointed (this includes one arbitrator on a three-arbitrator panel). No refunds will be granted on awarded cases.

Note: The date of receipt of the demand for arbitration with the ICDR will be used to calculate refunds of filing fees for both claims and counterclaims.

Flexible Fee Schedule

A non-refundable Initial Filing Fee is payable in full by a filing party when a claim, counterclaim, or additional claim is filed. Upon receipt of the Demand for Arbitration, the ICDR will promptly initiate the case and notify all parties as well as establish the due date for filing of an Answer, which may include a Counterclaim. In order to proceed with the further administration of the arbitration and appointment of the arbitrator(s), the appropriate, non-refundable Proceed Fee outlined below must be paid.

If a Proceed Fee is not submitted within ninety (90) days of the filing of the Claimant's Demand for Arbitration, the ICDR will administratively close the file and notify all parties.

No refunds or refund schedule will apply to the Filing or Proceed Fees once received.

The Flexible Fee Schedule below also may be utilized for the filing of counter-claims. However, as with the Claimant's claim, the counterclaim will not be presented to the arbitrator until the Proceed Fee is paid.

A Final Fee will be incurred for all claims and/or counterclaims that proceed to their first hearing. This fee will be payable in advance when the first hearing is scheduled, but will be refunded at the conclusion of the case if no hearings have occurred. However, if the administrator is not notified of a cancellation at least 24 hours before the time of the scheduled hearing, the Final Fee will remain due and will not be refunded.

All fees will be billed in accordance with the following schedule:

Amount of Claim	Initial Filing Fee	Proceed Fee	Final Fee
Above $0 to $10,000	$400	475	$200
Above $10,000 to $75,000	$625	$500	$300
Above $75,000 to $150,000	$850	$1250	$750
Above $150,000 to $300,000	$1,000	$2125	$1,250
Above $300,000 to $500,000	$1,500	$3,400	$1,750
Above $500,000 to $1,000,000	$2,500	$4,500	$2,500
Above $1,000,000 to $5,000,000	$2,500	$6,700	$3,250
Above $5,000,000 to $10,000,000	$3,500	$8,200	$4,000
Above $10,000,000	$4,500	$10,300 plus .01% of claim amount over $10,000,000 up to $65,000	$6,000
Nonmonetary[1]	$2,000	$2,000	$1,250
Deficient Claim Filing Fee Additional Services[2]	$350		

All fees are subject to increase if the amount of a claim or counterclaim is modified after the initial filing date. Fees are subject to decrease if the amount of a claim or counterclaim is modified before the first hearing.

The minimum fees for any case having three or more arbitrators are $1,000 for the Initial Filing Fee; $2,125 for the Proceed Fee; and $1,250 for the Final Fee.

Under the Flexible Fee Schedule, a party's obligation to pay the Proceed Fee shall remain in effect regardless of any agreement of the parties to stay, postpone or otherwise modify the arbitration proceedings. Parties that, through mutual agreement, have held their case in abeyance for one year will be assessed an annual abeyance fee of $300. If a party refuses to pay the assessed fee, the other party or parties may pay the entire fee on behalf of all parties, otherwise the matter will be closed.

Note: The date of receipt by the ICDR of the demand/notice for arbitration will be used to calculate the ninety(90)-day time limit for payment of the Proceed Fee.

. . .

There is no Refund Schedule in the Flexible Fee Schedule.

Hearing Room Rental

The fees described above do not cover the cost of hearing rooms, which are

---

[1] This fee is applicable when a claim or counterclaim is not for a monetary amount. Where a monetary claim amount is not known, parties will be required to state a range of claims or be subject to a filing fee of $3,500 and a proceed fee of $8,200.

[2] The ICDR reserves the right to assess additional administrative fees for services performed by the ICDR beyond those provided for in these Rules and which may be required by the parties' agreement or stipulation.

available on a rental basis. Check with the ICDR for availability and rates.

RULES OF ARBITRATION OF THE INTERNATIONAL CHAMBER OF COMMERCE*

In force as of 1 January 2012

INTRODUCTORY PROVISIONS

Article 1   International Court of Arbitration

1. The International Court of Arbitration (the "Court") of the International Chamber of Commerce (the "ICC") is the independent arbitration body of the ICC. The statutes of the Court are set forth in Appendix I.

2. The Court does not itself resolve disputes. It administers the resolution of disputes by arbitral tribunals, in accordance with the Rules of Arbitration of the ICC (the "Rules"). The Court is the only body authorized to administer arbitrations under the Rules, including the scrutiny and approval of awards rendered in accordance with the Rules. It draws up its own internal rules, which are set forth in Appendix II (the "Internal Rules").

3. The President of the Court (the "President") or, in the President's absence or otherwise at the President's request, one of its Vice-Presidents shall have the power to take urgent decisions on behalf of the Court, provided that any such decision is reported to the Court at its next session.

4. As provided for in the Internal Rules, the Court may delegate to one or more committees composed of its members the power to take certain decisions, provided that any such decision is reported to the Court at its next session.

5. The Court is assisted in its work by the Secretariat of the Court (the "Secretariat") under the direction of its Secretary General (the "Secretary General").

Article 2   Definitions

In the Rules:

   (i) "arbitral tribunal" includes one or more arbitrators;

   (ii) "claimant" includes one or more claimants, "respondent" includes one or more respondents, and "additional party" includes one or more additional parties;

   (iii) "party" or "parties" include claimants, respondents or additional parties;

   (iv) "claim" or "claims" include any claim by any party against any other party;

   (v) "award" includes, *inter alia*, an interim, partial or final award.

Article 3   Written Notifications or Communications; Time Limits

1. All pleadings and other written communications submitted by any party, as well as all documents annexed thereto, shall be supplied in a number of copies sufficient to provide one copy for each party, plus one for each arbitrator, and one for the Secretariat. A copy of any notification or communication from the arbitral tribunal to the parties shall be sent to the Secretariat.

2. All notifications or communications from the Secretariat and the arbitral tribunal shall be made to the last address of the party or its representative for whom the same are intended, as notified either by the party in question or by the other party. Such notification or communication may be made by delivery against receipt, registered post, courier, email, or any other means of telecommunication that provides a record of the sending thereof.

3. A notification or communication shall be deemed to have been made on the day it was received by the party itself or by its representative, or would have been received if made in accordance with Article 3(2).

4. Periods of time specified in or fixed under the Rules shall start to run on the day following the date a notification or communication is deemed to have been made in accordance with Article 3(3). When the day next following such date is an official holiday, or a non-business day in the country where the notification or communication is deemed to have been made, the period of time shall commence on the first following business day. Official holidays and non-business days are included in the calculation of the period of time. If the last day of the relevant period of time granted is an official holiday or a non-business day in the country where the notification or communication is deemed to have been made, the period of time shall expire at the end of the first following business day.

COMMENCING THE ARBITRATION

Article 4   Request for Arbitration

1. A party wishing to have recourse to arbitration under the Rules shall submit its Request for Arbitration (the "Request") to the Secretariat at any of the offices specified in the Internal Rules. The Secretariat shall notify the claimant and respondent of the receipt of the Request and the date of such receipt.

2. The date on which the Request is received by the Secretariat shall, for all purposes, be deemed to be the date of the commencement of the arbitration.

3. The Request shall contain the following information:

   a) the name in full, description, address and other contact details of each of the parties;

   b) the name in full, address and other contact details of any person(s) representing the claimant in the arbitration;

   c) a description of the nature and circumstances of the dispute giving rise to the claims and of the basis upon which the claims are made;

   d) a statement of the relief sought, together with the amounts of any quantified claims and, to the extent possible, an estimate of the monetary value of any other claims;

e) any relevant agreements and, in particular, the arbitration agreement(s);

f) where claims are made under more than one arbitration agreement, an indication of the arbitration agreement under which each claim is made;

g) all relevant particulars and any observations or proposals concerning the number of arbitrators and their choice in accordance with the provisions of Articles 12 and 13, and any nomination of an arbitrator required thereby; and

h) all relevant particulars and any observations or proposals as to the place of the arbitration, the applicable rules of law and the language of the arbitration.

The claimant may submit such other documents or information with the Request as it considers appropriate or as may contribute to the efficient resolution of the dispute.

4. Together with the Request, the claimant shall:

a) submit the number of copies thereof required by Article 3(1); and

b) make payment of the filing fee required by Appendix III ("Arbitration Costs and Fees") in force on the date the Request is submitted. In the event that the claimant fails to comply with either of these requirements, the Secretariat may fix a time limit within which the claimant must comply, failing which the file shall be closed without prejudice to the claimant's right to submit the same claims at a later date in another Request.

5. The Secretariat shall transmit a copy of the Request and the documents annexed thereto to the respondent for its Answer to the Request once the Secretariat has sufficient copies of the Request and the required filing fee.

Article 5   Answer to the Request; Counterclaims

1. Within 30 days from the receipt of the Request from the Secretariat, the respondent shall submit an Answer (the "Answer") which shall contain the following information:

a) its name in full, description, address and other contact details;

b) the name in full, address and other contact details of any person(s) representing the respondent in the arbitration;

c) its comments as to the nature and circumstances of the dispute giving rise to the claims and the basis upon which the claims are made;

d) its response to the relief sought;

e) any observations or proposals concerning the number of arbitrators and their choice in light of the claimant's proposals and in accordance with the provisions of Articles 12 and 13, and any nomination of an arbitrator required thereby; and

f) any observations or proposals as to the place of the arbitration, the applicable rules of law and the language of the arbitration. The respondent may submit such other documents or information with the Answer as it considers appropriate or as may contribute to the efficient resolution of the dispute.

2. The Secretariat may grant the respondent an extension of the time for submitting the Answer, provided the application for such an extension contains the respondent's observations or proposals concerning the number of arbitrators and their choice and, where required by Articles 12 and 13, the nomination of an arbitrator. If the respondent fails to do so, the Court shall proceed in accordance with the Rules.

3. The Answer shall be submitted to the Secretariat in the number of copies specified by Article 3(1).

4. The Secretariat shall communicate the Answer and the documents annexed thereto to all other parties.

5. Any counterclaims made by the respondent shall be submitted with the Answer and shall provide:

a) a description of the nature and circumstances of the dispute giving rise to the counterclaims and of the basis upon which the counterclaims are made;

b) a statement of the relief sought together with the amounts of any quantified counterclaims and, to the extent possible, an estimate of the monetary value of any other counterclaims;

c) any relevant agreements and, in particular, the arbitration agreement(s); and

d) where counterclaims are made under more than one arbitration agreement, an indication of the arbitration agreement under which each counterclaim is made.

The respondent may submit such other documents or information with the counterclaims as it considers appropriate or as may contribute to the efficient resolution of the dispute.

6. The claimant shall submit a reply to any counterclaim within 30 days from the date of receipt of the counterclaims communicated by the Secretariat. Prior to the transmission of the file to the arbitral tribunal, the Secretariat may grant the claimant an extension of time for submitting the reply.

Article 6   Effect of the Arbitration Agreement

1. Where the parties have agreed to submit to arbitration under the Rules, they shall be deemed to have submitted *ipso facto* to the Rules in effect on the date of commencement of the arbitration, unless they have agreed to submit to the Rules in effect on the date of their arbitration agreement.

2. By agreeing to arbitration under the Rules, the parties have accepted that the arbitration shall be administered by the Court.

3. If any party against which a claim has been made does not submit an Answer, or raises one or more pleas concerning the existence, validity or scope of the arbitration agreement or concerning whether all of the claims made in the

arbitration may be determined together in a single arbitration, the arbitration shall proceed and any question of jurisdiction or of whether the claims may be determined together in that arbitration shall be decided directly by the arbitral tribunal, unless the Secretary General refers the matter to the Court for its decision pursuant to Article 6(4).

4. In all cases referred to the Court under Article 6(3), the Court shall decide whether and to what extent the arbitration shall proceed. The arbitration shall proceed if and to the extent that the Court is *prima facie* satisfied that an arbitration agreement under the Rules may exist. In particular:

(i) where there are more than two parties to the arbitration, the arbitration shall proceed between those of the parties, including any additional parties joined pursuant to Article 7, with respect to which the Court is *prima facie* satisfied that an arbitration agreement under the Rules that binds them all may exist; and

(ii) where claims pursuant to Article 9 are made under more than one arbitration agreement, the arbitration shall proceed as to those claims with respect to which the Court is *prima facie* satisfied (a) that the arbitration agreements under which those claims are made may be compatible, and (b) that all parties to the arbitration may have agreed that those claims can be determined together in a single arbitration. The Court's decision pursuant to Article 6(4) is without prejudice to the admissibility or merits of any party's plea or pleas.

5. In all matters decided by the Court under Article 6(4), any decision as to the jurisdiction of the arbitral tribunal, except as to parties or claims with respect to which the Court decides that the arbitration cannot proceed, shall then be taken by the arbitral tribunal itself.

6. Where the parties are notified of the Court's decision pursuant to Article 6(4) that the arbitration cannot proceed in respect of some or all of them, any party retains the right to ask any court having jurisdiction whether or not, and in respect of which of them, there is a binding arbitration agreement.

7. Where the Court has decided pursuant to Article 6(4) that the arbitration cannot proceed in respect of any of the claims, such decision shall not prevent a party from reintroducing the same claim at a later date in other proceedings.

8. If any of the parties refuses or fails to take part in the arbitration or any stage thereof, the arbitration shall proceed notwithstanding such refusal or failure.

9. Unless otherwise agreed, the arbitral tribunal shall not cease to have jurisdiction by reason of any allegation that the contract is non-existent or null and void, provided that the arbitral tribunal upholds the validity of the arbitration agreement. The arbitral tribunal shall continue to have jurisdiction to determine the parties' respective rights and to decide their claims and pleas even though the contract itself may be non-existent or null and void.

MULTIPLE PARTIES, MULTIPLE CONTRACTS AND CONSOLIDATION

Article 7   Joinder of Additional Parties

1. A party wishing to join an additional party to the arbitration shall submit its request for arbitration against the additional party (the request for Joinder) to the Secretariat. The date on which the Request for Joinder is received by the Secretariat shall, for all purposes, be deemed to be the date of the commencement of arbitration against the additional party. Any such joinder shall be subject to the provisions of Articles 6(3)–6(7) and 9. No additional party may be joined after the confirmation or appointment of any arbitrator, unless all parties, including the additional party, otherwise agree. The Secretariat may fix a time limit for the submission of a Request for Joinder.

2. The Request for Joinder shall contain the following information:

a) the case reference of the existing arbitration;

b) the name in full, description, address and other contact details of each of the parties, including the additional party; and

c) the information specified in Article 4(3) subparagraphs c), d), e) and f).

The party filing the Request for Joinder may submit therewith such other documents or information as it considers appropriate or as may contribute to the efficient resolution of the dispute.

3. The provisions of Articles 4(4) and 4(5) shall apply, *mutatis mutandis*, to the Request for Joinder.

4. The additional party shall submit an Answer in accordance, *mutatis mutandis*, with the provisions of Articles 5(1)-5(4). The additional party may make claims against any other party in accordance with the provisions of Article 8.

Article 8   Claims Between Multiple Parties

1. In an arbitration with multiple parties, claims may be made by any party against any other party, subject to the provisions of Articles 6(3)-6(7) and 9 and provided that no new claims may be made after the Terms of Reference are signed or approved by the Court without the authorization of the arbitral tribunal pursuant to Article 23(4).

2. Any party making a claim pursuant to Article 8(1) shall provide the information specified in Article 4(3) subparagraphs c), d), e) and f).

3. Before the Secretariat transmits the file to the arbitral tribunal in accordance with Article 16, the following provisions shall apply, *mutatis mutandis*, to any claim made: Article 4(4) subparagraph a); Article 4(5); Article 5(1) except for subparagraphs a), b), e) and f); Article 5(2); Article 5(3) and Article 5(4). Thereafter, the arbitral tribunal shall determine the procedure for making a claim.

Article 9   Multiple Contracts

Subject to the provisions of Articles 6(3)–6(7) and 23(4), claims arising out of or in connection with more than one contract may be made in a single arbitration, irrespective of whether such claims are made under one or more than one arbitration agreement under the Rules.

Article 10   Consolidation of Arbitrations

The Court may, at the request of a party, consolidate two or more arbitrations pending under the Rules into a single arbitration, where:

a) the parties have agreed to consolidation; or

b) all of the claims in the arbitrations are made under the same arbitration agreement; or

c) where the claims in the arbitrations are made under more than one arbitration agreement, the arbitrations are between the same parties, the disputes in the arbitrations arise in connection with the same legal relationship, and the Court finds the arbitration agreements to be compatible.

In deciding whether to consolidate, the Court may take into account any circumstances it considers to be relevant, including whether one or more arbitrators have been confirmed or appointed in more than one of the arbitrations and, if so, whether the same or different persons have been confirmed or appointed. When arbitrations are consolidated, they shall be consolidated into the arbitration that commenced first, unless otherwise agreed by all parties.

THE ARBITRAL TRIBUNAL

Article 11   General Provisions

1. Every arbitrator must be and remain impartial and independent of the parties involved in the arbitration.

2. Before appointment or confirmation, a prospective arbitrator shall sign a statement of acceptance, availability, impartiality and independence. The prospective arbitrator shall disclose in writing to the Secretariat any facts or circumstances which might be of such a nature as to call into question the arbitrator's independence in the eyes of the parties, as well as any circumstances that could give rise to reasonable doubts as to the arbitrator's impartiality. The Secretariat shall provide such information to the parties in writing and fix a time limit for any comments from them.

3. An arbitrator shall immediately disclose in writing to the Secretariat and to the parties any facts or circumstances of a similar nature to those referred to in Article 11(2) concerning the arbitrator's impartiality or independence which may arise during the arbitration.

4. The decisions of the Court as to the appointment, confirmation, challenge or replacement of an arbitrator shall be final, and the reasons for such decisions shall not be communicated.

5. By accepting to serve, arbitrators undertake to carry out their responsibilities in accordance with the Rules.

6. Insofar as the parties have not provided otherwise, the arbitral tribunal shall be constituted in accordance with the provisions of Articles 12 and 13.

Article 12   Constitution of the Arbitral Tribunal

Number of Arbitrators

1. The disputes shall be decided by a sole arbitrator or by three arbitrators.

2. Where the parties have not agreed upon the number of arbitrators, the Court shall appoint a sole arbitrator, save where it appears to the Court that the dispute is such as to warrant the appointment of three arbitrators. In such case, the claimant shall nominate an arbitrator within a period of 15 days from the receipt of the notification of the decision of the Court, and the respondent shall nominate an arbitrator within a period of 15 days from the receipt of the notification of the nomination made by the claimant. If a party fails to nominate an arbitrator, the appointment shall be made by the Court.

Sole Arbitrator

3. Where the parties have agreed that the dispute shall be resolved by a sole arbitrator, they may, by agreement, nominate the sole arbitrator for confirmation. If the parties fail to nominate a sole arbitrator within 30 days from the date when the claimant's Request for Arbitration has been received by the other party, or within such additional time as may be allowed by the Secretariat, the sole arbitrator shall be appointed by the Court.

Three Arbitrators

4. Where the parties have agreed that the dispute shall be resolved by three arbitrators, each party shall nominate in the Request and the Answer, respectively, one arbitrator for confirmation. If a party fails to nominate an arbitrator, the appointment shall be made by the Court.

5. Where the dispute is to be referred to three arbitrators, the third arbitrator, who will act as president of the arbitral tribunal, shall be appointed by the Court, unless the parties have agreed upon another procedure for such appointment, in which case the nomination will be subject to confirmation pursuant to Article 13. Should such procedure not result in a nomination within 30 days from the confirmation or appointment of the co-arbitrators or any other time limit agreed by the parties or fixed by the Court, the third arbitrator shall be appointed by the Court.

6. Where there are multiple claimants or multiple respondents, and where the dispute is to be referred to three arbitrators, the multiple claimants, jointly, and the multiple respondents, jointly, shall nominate an arbitrator for confirmation pursuant to Article 13.

7. Where an additional party has been joined, and where the dispute is to be referred to three arbitrators, the additional party may, jointly with the claimant(s) or with the respondent(s), nominate an arbitrator for confirmation pursuant to Article 13. 8 In the absence of a joint nomination pursuant to Articles 12(6) or 12(7) and where all parties are unable to agree to a method for the constitution of the arbitral tribunal, the Court may appoint each member of the

arbitral tribunal and shall designate one of them to act as president. In such case, the Court shall be at liberty to choose any person it regards as suitable to act as arbitrator, applying Article 13 when it considers this appropriate.

Article 13   Appointment and Confirmation of the Arbitrators

1. In confirming or appointing arbitrators, the Court shall consider the prospective arbitrator's nationality, residence and other relationships with the countries of which the parties or the other arbitrators are nationals and the prospective arbitrator's availability and ability to conduct the arbitration in accordance with the Rules. The same shall apply where the Secretary General confirms arbitrators pursuant to Article 13(2).

2. The Secretary General may confirm as co-arbitrators, sole arbitrators and presidents of arbitral tribunals persons nominated by the parties or pursuant to their particular agreements, provided that the statement they have submitted contains no qualification regarding impartiality or independence or that a qualified statement regarding impartiality or independence has not given rise to objections. Such confirmation shall be reported to the Court at its next session. If the Secretary General considers that a co-arbitrator, sole arbitrator or president of an arbitral tribunal should not be confirmed, the matter shall be submitted to the Court.

3. Where the Court is to appoint an arbitrator, it shall make the appointment upon proposal of a National Committee or Group of the ICC that it considers to be appropriate. If the Court does not accept the proposal made, or if the National Committee or Group fails to make the proposal requested within the time limit fixed by the Court, the Court may repeat its request, request a proposal from another National Committee or Group that it considers to be appropriate, or appoint directly any person whom it regards as suitable.

4. The Court may also appoint directly to act as arbitrator any person whom it regards as suitable where:

     a) one or more of the parties is a state or claims to be a state entity; or

     b) the Court considers that it would be appropriate to appoint an arbitrator from a country or territory where there is no National Committee or Group; or

     c) the President certifies to the Court that circumstances exist which, in the President's opinion, make a direct appointment necessary and appropriate.

5. The sole arbitrator or the president of the arbitral tribunal shall be of a nationality other than those of the parties. However, in suitable circumstances and provided that none of the parties objects within the time limit fixed by the Court, the sole arbitrator or the president of the arbitral tribunal may be chosen from a country of which any of the parties is a national.

Article 14   Challenge of Arbitrators

1. A challenge of an arbitrator, whether for an alleged lack of impartiality or independence, or otherwise, shall be made by the submission to the Secretariat of a written statement specifying the facts and circumstances on which the challenge is based.

2. For a challenge to be admissible, it must be submitted by a party either within 30 days from receipt by that party of the notification of the appointment or confirmation of the arbitrator, or within 30 days from the date when the party making the challenge was informed of the facts and circumstances on which the challenge is based if such date is subsequent to the receipt of such notification.

3. The Court shall decide on the admissibility and, at the same time, if necessary, on the merits of a challenge after the Secretariat has afforded an opportunity for the arbitrator concerned, the other party or parties and any other members of the arbitral tribunal to comment in writing within a suitable period of time. Such comments shall be communicated to the parties and to the arbitrators.

Article 15   Replacement of Arbitrators

1. An arbitrator shall be replaced upon death, upon acceptance by the Court of the arbitrator's resignation, upon acceptance by the Court of a challenge, or upon acceptance by the Court of a request of all the parties.

2. An arbitrator shall also be replaced on the Court's own initiative when it decides that the arbitrator is prevented *de jure* or *de facto* from fulfilling the arbitrator's functions, or that the arbitrator is not fulfilling those functions in accordance with the Rules or within the prescribed time limits.

3. When, on the basis of information that has come to its attention, the Court considers applying Article 15(2), it shall decide on the matter after the arbitrator concerned, the parties and any other members of the arbitral tribunal have had an opportunity to comment in writing within a suitable period of time. Such comments shall be communicated to the parties and to the arbitrators.

4. When an arbitrator is to be replaced, the Court has discretion to decide whether or not to follow the original nominating process. Once reconstituted, and after having invited the parties to comment, the arbitral tribunal shall determine if and to what extent prior proceedings shall be repeated before the reconstituted arbitral tribunal.

5. Subsequent to the closing of the proceedings, instead of replacing an arbitrator who has died or been removed by the Court pursuant to Articles 15(1) or 15(2), the Court may decide, when it considers it appropriate, that the remaining arbitrators shall continue the arbitration. In making such determination, the Court shall take into account the views of the remaining arbitrators and of the parties and such other matters that it considers appropriate in the circumstances.

THE ARBITRAL PROCEEDINGS

Article 16   Transmission of the File to the Arbitral Tribunal

The Secretariat shall transmit the file to the arbitral tribunal as soon as it has been constituted, provided the advance on costs requested by the Secretariat at this stage has been paid.

Article 17   Proof of Authority

At any time after the commencement of the arbitration, the arbitral tribunal or the Secretariat may require proof of the authority of any party representatives.

Article 18   Place of the Arbitration

1. The place of the arbitration shall be fixed by the Court, unless agreed upon by the parties.

2. The arbitral tribunal may, after consultation with the parties, conduct hearings and meetings at any location it considers appropriate, unless otherwise agreed by the parties.

3. The arbitral tribunal may deliberate at any location it considers appropriate.

Article 19   Rules Governing the Proceedings

The proceedings before the arbitral tribunal shall be governed by the Rules and, where the Rules are silent, by any rules which the parties or, failing them, the arbitral tribunal may settle on, whether or not reference is thereby made to the rules of procedure of a national law to be applied to the arbitration.

Article 20   Language of the Arbitration

In the absence of an agreement by the parties, the arbitral tribunal shall determine the language or languages of the arbitration, due regard being given to all relevant circumstances, including the language of the contract.

Article 21   Applicable Rules of Law

1. The parties shall be free to agree upon the rules of law to be applied by the arbitral tribunal to the merits of the dispute. In the absence of any such agreement, the arbitral tribunal shall apply the rules of law which it determines to be appropriate.

2. The arbitral tribunal shall take account of the provisions of the contract, if any, between the parties and of any relevant trade usages.

3. The arbitral tribunal shall assume the powers of an *amiable compositeur* or decide *ex aequo et bono* only if the parties have agreed to give it such powers.

Article 22   Conduct of the Arbitration

1. The arbitral tribunal and the parties shall make every effort to conduct the arbitration in an expeditious and cost-effective manner, having regard to the complexity and value of the dispute.

2. In order to ensure effective case management, the arbitral tribunal, after consulting the parties, may adopt such procedural measures as it considers appropriate, provided that they are not contrary to any agreement of the parties.

3. Upon the request of any party, the arbitral tribunal may make orders concerning the confidentiality of the arbitration proceedings or of any other matters in connection with the arbitration and may take measures for protecting trade secrets and confidential information.

4. In all cases, the arbitral tribunal shall act fairly and impartially and ensure that each party has a reasonable opportunity to present its case.

5. The parties undertake to comply with any order made by the arbitral tribunal.

Article 23   Terms of Reference

1. As soon as it has received the file from the Secretariat, the arbitral tribunal shall draw up, on the basis of documents or in the presence of the parties and in the light of their most recent submissions, a document defining its Terms of Reference. This document shall include the following particulars:

a) the names in full, description, address and other contact details of each of the parties and of any person(s) representing a party in the arbitration;

b) the addresses to which notifications and communications arising in the course of the arbitration may be made;

c) a summary of the parties' respective claims and of the relief sought by each party, together with the amounts of any quantified claims and, to the extent possible, an estimate of the monetary value of any other claims;

d) unless the arbitral tribunal considers it inappropriate, a list of issues to be determined;

e) the names in full, address and other contact details of each of the arbitrators;

f) the place of the arbitration; and

g) particulars of the applicable procedural rules and, if such is the case, reference to the power conferred upon the arbitral tribunal to act as *amiable compositeur* or to decide *ex aequo et bono*.

2. The Terms of Reference shall be signed by the parties and the arbitral tribunal. Within two months of the date on which the file has been transmitted to it, the arbitral tribunal shall transmit to the Court the Terms of Reference signed by it and by the parties. The Court may extend this time limit pursuant to a reasoned request from the arbitral tribunal or on its own initiative if it decides it is necessary to do so.

3. If any of the parties refuses to take part in the drawing up of the Terms of Reference or to sign the same, they shall be submitted to the Court for approval. When the Terms of Reference have been signed in accordance with Article 23(2) or approved by the Court, the arbitration shall proceed.

4. After the Terms of Reference have been signed or approved by the Court, no party shall make new claims which fall outside the limits of the Terms of Reference unless it has been authorized to do so by the arbitral tribunal, which shall consider the nature of such new claims, the stage of the arbitration and other relevant circumstances.

Article 24   Case Management Conference and Procedural Timetable

1. When drawing up the Terms of Reference or as soon as possible thereafter, the arbitral tribunal shall convene a case management conference to consult the parties on procedural measures that may be adopted pursuant to Article 22(2). Such measures may include one or more of the case management techniques described

in Appendix IV.

2. During or following such conference, the arbitral tribunal shall establish the procedural timetable that it intends to follow for the conduct of the arbitration. The procedural timetable and any modifications thereto shall be communicated to the Court and the parties.

3. To ensure continued effective case management, the arbitral tribunal, after consulting the parties by means of a further case management conference or otherwise, may adopt further procedural measures or modify the procedural timetable.

4. Case management conferences may be conducted through a meeting in person, by video conference, telephone or similar means of communication. In the absence of an agreement of the parties, the arbitral tribunal shall determine the means by which the conference will be conducted. The arbitral tribunal may request the parties to submit case management proposals in advance of a case management conference and may request the attendance at any case management conference of the parties in person or through an internal representative.

Article 25   Establishing the Facts of the Case

1. The arbitral tribunal shall proceed within as short a time as possible to establish the facts of the case by all appropriate means.

2. After studying the written submissions of the parties and all documents relied upon, the arbitral tribunal shall hear the parties together in person if any of them so requests or, failing such a request, it may of its own motion decide to hear them.

3. The arbitral tribunal may decide to hear witnesses, experts appointed by the parties or any other person, in the presence of the parties, or in their absence provided they have been duly summoned.

4. The arbitral tribunal, after having consulted the parties, may appoint one or more experts, define their terms of reference and receive their reports. At the request of a party, the parties shall be given the opportunity to question at a hearing any such expert.

5. At any time during the proceedings, the arbitral tribunal may summon any party to provide additional evidence.

6. The arbitral tribunal may decide the case solely on the documents submitted by the parties unless any of the parties requests a hearing.

Article 26   Hearings

1. When a hearing is to be held, the arbitral tribunal, giving reasonable notice, shall summon the parties to appear before it on the day and at the place fixed by it.

2. If any of the parties, although duly summoned, fails to appear without valid excuse, the arbitral tribunal shall have the power to proceed with the hearing.

3. The arbitral tribunal shall be in full charge of the hearings, at which all the parties shall be entitled to be present. Save with the approval of the arbitral tribunal and the parties, persons not involved in the proceedings shall not be admitted.

4. The parties may appear in person or through duly authorized representatives. In addition, they may be assisted by advisers.

Article 27 Closing of the Proceedings and Date for Submission of Draft Awards

As soon as possible after the last hearing concerning matters to be decided in an award or the filing of the last authorized submissions concerning such matters, whichever is later, the arbitral tribunal shall:

a) declare the proceedings closed with respect to the matters to be decided in the award; and

b) inform the Secretariat and the parties of the date by which it expects to submit its draft award to the Court for approval pursuant to Article 33.

After the proceedings are closed, no further submission or argument may be made, or evidence produced, with respect to the matters to be decided in the award, unless requested or authorized by the arbitral tribunal.

Article 28 Conservatory and Interim Measures

1. Unless the parties have otherwise agreed, as soon as the file has been transmitted to it, the arbitral tribunal may, at the request of a party, order any interim or conservatory measure it deems appropriate. The arbitral tribunal may make the granting of any such measure subject to appropriate security being furnished by the requesting party. Any such measure shall take the form of an order, giving reasons, or of an award, as the arbitral tribunal considers appropriate.

2. Before the file is transmitted to the arbitral tribunal, and in appropriate circumstances even thereafter, the parties may apply to any competent judicial authority for interim or conservatory measures. The application of a party to a judicial authority for such measures or for the implementation of any such measures ordered by an arbitral tribunal shall not be deemed to be an infringement or a waiver of the arbitration agreement and shall not affect the relevant powers reserved to the arbitral tribunal.

Any such application and any measures taken by the judicial authority must be notified without delay to the Secretariat. The Secretariat shall inform the arbitral tribunal thereof.

Article 29 Emergency Arbitrator

1. A party that needs urgent interim or conservatory measures that cannot await the constitution of an arbitral tribunal ("Emergency Measures") may make an application for such measures pursuant to the Emergency Arbitrator Rules in Appendix V. Any such application shall be accepted only if it is received by the Secretariat prior to the transmission of the file to the arbitral tribunal pursuant to Article 16 and irrespective of whether the party making the application has already submitted its Request for Arbitration.

2. The emergency arbitrator's decision shall take the form of an order. The parties undertake to comply with any order made by the emergency arbitrator.

3. The emergency arbitrator's order shall not bind the arbitral tribunal with

respect to any question, issue or dispute determined in the order. The arbitral tribunal may modify, terminate or annul the order or any modification thereto made by the emergency arbitrator.

4. The arbitral tribunal shall decide upon any party's requests or claims related to the emergency arbitrator proceedings, including the reallocation of the costs of such proceedings and any claims arising out of or in connection with the compliance or non-compliance with the order.

5. Articles 29(1)-29(4) and the Emergency Arbitrator Rules set forth in Appendix V (collectively the "Emergency Arbitrator Provisions") shall apply only to parties that are either signatories of the arbitration agreement under the Rules that is relied upon for the application or successors to such signatories.

6. The Emergency Arbitrator Provisions shall not apply if:

a) the arbitration agreement under the Rules was concluded before the date on which the Rules came into force;

b) the parties have agreed to opt out of the Emergency Arbitrator Provisions; or

c) the parties have agreed to another pre-arbitral procedure that provides for the granting of conservatory, interim or similar measures.

7. The Emergency Arbitrator Provisions are not intended to prevent any party from seeking urgent interim or conservatory measures from a competent judicial authority at any time prior to making an application for such measures, and in appropriate circumstances even thereafter, pursuant to the Rules. Any application for such measures from a competent judicial authority shall not be deemed to be an infringement or a waiver of the arbitration agreement. Any such application and any measures taken by the judicial authority must be notified without delay to the Secretariat.

AWARDS

Article 30 Time Limit for the Final Award

1. The time limit within which the arbitral tribunal must render its final award is six months. Such time limit shall start to run from the date of the last signature by the arbitral tribunal or by the parties of the Terms of Reference or, in the case of application of Article 23(3), the date of the notification to the arbitral tribunal by the Secretariat of the approval of the Terms of Reference by the Court. The Court may fix a different time limit based upon the procedural timetable established pursuant to Article 24(2).

2. The Court may extend the time limit pursuant to a reasoned request from the arbitral tribunal or on its own initiative if it decides it is necessary to do so.

Article 31 Making of the Award

1. When the arbitral tribunal is composed of more than one arbitrator, an award is made by a majority decision. If there is no majority, the award shall be made by

the president of the arbitral tribunal alone.

2. The award shall state the reasons upon which it is based.

3 The award shall be deemed to be made at the place of the arbitration and on the date stated therein.

Article 32   Award by Consent

If the parties reach a settlement after the file has been transmitted to the arbitral tribunal in accordance with Article 16, the settlement shall be recorded in the form of an award made by consent of the parties, if so requested by the parties and if the arbitral tribunal agrees to do so.

Article 33   Scrutiny of the Award by the Court

Before signing any award, the arbitral tribunal shall submit it in draft form to the Court. The Court may lay down modifications as to the form of the award and, without affecting the arbitral tribunal's liberty of decision, may also draw its attention to points of substance. No award shall be rendered by the arbitral tribunal until it has been approved by the Court as to its form.

Article 34   Notification, Deposit and Enforceability of the Award

1. Once an award has been made, the Secretariat shall notify to the parties the text signed by the arbitral tribunal, provided always that the costs of the arbitration have been fully paid to the ICC by the parties or by one of them.

2. Additional copies certified true by the Secretary General shall be made available on request and at any time to the parties, but to no one else.

3. By virtue of the notification made in accordance with Article 34(1), the parties waive any other form of notification or deposit on the part of the arbitral tribunal.

4. An original of each award made in accordance with the Rules shall be deposited with the Secretariat.

5. The arbitral tribunal and the Secretariat shall assist the parties in complying with whatever further formalities may be necessary.

6. Every award shall be binding on the parties. By submitting the dispute to arbitration under the Rules, the parties undertake to carry out any award without delay and shall be deemed to have waived their right to any form of recourse insofar as such waiver can validly be made.

Article 35   Correction and Interpretation of the Award; Remission of Awards

1. On its own initiative, the arbitral tribunal may correct a clerical, computational or typographical error, or any errors of similar nature contained in an award, provided such correction is submitted for approval to the Court within 30 days of the date of such award.

2. Any application of a party for the correction of an error of the kind referred to in Article 35(1), or for the interpretation of an award, must be made to the Secretariat within 30 days of the receipt of the award by such party, in a number of copies as stated in Article 3(1). After transmittal of the application to the arbitral

tribunal, the latter shall grant the other party a short time limit, normally not exceeding 30 days, from the receipt of the application by that party, to submit any comments thereon. The arbitral tribunal shall submit its decision on the application in draft form to the Court not later than 30 days following the expiration of the time limit for the receipt of any comments from the other party or within such other period as the Court may decide.

3. A decision to correct or to interpret the award shall take the form of an addendum and shall constitute part of the award. The provisions of Articles 31, 33 and 34 shall apply *mutatis mutandis*.

4. Where a court remits an award to the arbitral tribunal, the provisions of Articles 31, 33, 34 and this Article 35 shall apply *mutatis mutandis* to any addendum or award made pursuant to the terms of such remission. The Court may take any steps as may be necessary to enable the arbitral tribunal to comply with the terms of such remission and may fix an advance to cover any additional fees and expenses of the arbitral tribunal and any additional ICC administrative expenses.

COSTS

Article 36　Advance to Cover the Costs of the Arbitration

1. After receipt of the Request, the Secretary General may request the claimant to pay a provisional advance in an amount intended to cover the costs of the arbitration until the Terms of Reference have been drawn up. Any provisional advance paid will be considered as a partial payment by the claimant of any advance on costs fixed by the Court pursuant to this Article 36.

2. As soon as practicable, the Court shall fix the advance on costs in an amount likely to cover the fees and expenses of the arbitrators and the ICC administrative expenses for the claims which have been referred to it by the parties, unless any claims are made under Article 7 or 8 in which case Article 36(4) shall apply. The advance on costs fixed by the Court pursuant to this Article 36(2) shall be payable in equal shares by the claimant and the respondent.

3. Where counterclaims are submitted by the respondent under Article 5 or otherwise, the Court may fix separate advances on costs for the claims and the counterclaims. When the Court has fixed separate advances on costs, each of the parties shall pay the advance on costs corresponding to its claims.

4. Where claims are made under Article 7 or 8, the Court shall fix one or more advances on costs that shall be payable by the parties as decided by the Court. Where the Court has previously fixed any advance on costs pursuant to this Article 36, any such advance shall be replaced by the advance(s) fixed pursuant to this Article 36(4), and the amount of any advance previously paid by any party will be considered as a partial payment by such party of its share of the advance(s) on costs as fixed by the Court pursuant to this Article 36(4).

5. The amount of any advance on costs fixed by the Court pursuant to this Article 36 may be subject to readjustment at any time during the arbitration. In all cases, any party shall be free to pay any other party's share of any advance on costs should such other party fail to pay its share.

6. When a request for an advance on costs has not been complied with, and after consultation with the arbitral tribunal, the Secretary General may direct the arbitral tribunal to suspend its work and set a time limit, which must be not less than 15 days, on the expiry of which the relevant claims shall be considered as withdrawn. Should the party in question wish to object to this measure, it must make a request within the aforementioned period for the matter to be decided by the Court. Such party shall not be prevented, on the ground of such withdrawal, from reintroducing the same claims at a later date in another proceeding.

7. If one of the parties claims a right to a set-off with regard to any claim, such set-off shall be taken into account in determining the advance to cover the costs of the arbitration in the same way as a separate claim insofar as it may require the arbitral tribunal to consider additional matters.

Article 37   Decision as to the Costs of the Arbitration

1. The costs of the arbitration shall include the fees and expenses of the arbitrators and the ICC administrative expenses fixed by the Court, in accordance with the scale in force at the time of the commencement of the arbitration, as well as the fees and expenses of any experts appointed by the arbitral tribunal and the reasonable legal and other costs incurred by the parties for the arbitration.

2. The Court may fix the fees of the arbitrators at a figure higher or lower than that which would result from the application of the relevant scale should this be deemed necessary due to the exceptional circumstances of the case.

3. At any time during the arbitral proceedings, the arbitral tribunal may make decisions on costs, other than those to be fixed by the Court, and order payment.

4. The final award shall fix the costs of the arbitration and decide which of the parties shall bear them or in what proportion they shall be borne by the parties.

5. In making decisions as to costs, the arbitral tribunal may take into account such circumstances as it considers relevant, including the extent to which each party has conducted the arbitration in an expeditious and cost-effective manner.

6. In the event of the withdrawal of all claims or the termination of the arbitration before the rendering of a final award, the Court shall fix the fees and expenses of the arbitrators and the ICC administrative expenses. If the parties have not agreed upon the allocation of the costs of the arbitration or other relevant issues with respect to costs, such matters shall be decided by the arbitral tribunal. If the arbitral tribunal has not been constituted at the time of such withdrawal or termination, any party may request the Court to proceed with the constitution of the arbitral tribunal in accordance with the Rules so that the arbitral tribunal may make decisions as to costs.

MISCELLANEOUS

Article 38   Modified Time Limits

1. The parties may agree to shorten the various time limits set out in the Rules. Any such agreement entered into subsequent to the constitution of an arbitral

tribunal shall become effective only upon the approval of the arbitral tribunal.

2. The Court, on its own initiative, may extend any time limit which has been modified pursuant to Article 38(1) if it decides that it is necessary to do so in order that the arbitral tribunal and the Court may fulfil their responsibilities in accordance with the Rules.

Article 39   Waiver

A party which proceeds with the arbitration without raising its objection to a failure to comply with any provision of the Rules, or of any other rules applicable to the proceedings, any direction given by the arbitral tribunal, or any requirement under the arbitration agreement relating to the constitution of the arbitral tribunal or the conduct of the proceedings, shall be deemed to have waived its right to object.

Article 40   Limitation of Liability

The arbitrators, any person appointed by the arbitral tribunal, the emergency arbitrator, the Court and its members, the ICC and its employees, and the ICC National Committees and Groups and their employees and representatives shall not be liable to any person for any act or omission in connection with the arbitration, except to the extent such limitation of liability is prohibited by applicable law.

Article 41   General Rule

In all matters not expressly provided for in the Rules, the Court and the arbitral tribunal shall act in the spirit of the Rules and shall make every effort to make sure that the award is enforceable at law.

APPENDIX I – STATUTES OF THE INTERNATIONAL COURT OF ARBITRATION

Article 1   Function

1. The function of the International Court of Arbitration of the International Chamber of Commerce (the "Court") is to ensure the application of the Rules of Arbitration of the International Chamber of Commerce, and it has all the necessary powers for that purpose.

2. As an autonomous body, it carries out these functions in complete independence from the ICC and its organs.

3. Its members are independent from the ICC National Committees and Groups.

Article 2   Composition of the Court

The Court shall consist of a President,[1] Vice-Presidents,[2] and members and alternate members (collectively designated as members). In its work it is assisted by its Secretariat (Secretariat of the Court).

---

[1] Referred to as "Chairman of the International Court of Arbitration" in the Constitution of the International Chamber of Commerce.

[2] Referred to as "Vice-Chairmen of the International Court of Arbitration" in the Constitution of the International Chamber of Commerce.

Article 3   Appointment

1. The President is elected by the ICC World Council upon the recommendation of the Executive Board of the ICC.

2. The ICC World Council appoints the Vice-Presidents of the Court from among the members of the Court or otherwise.

3. Its members are appointed by the ICC World Council on the proposal of National Committees or Groups, one member for each National Committee or Group.

4. On the proposal of the President of the Court, the World Council may appoint alternate members.

5. The term of office of all members, including, for the purposes of this paragraph, the President and Vice- Presidents, is three years. If a member is no longer in a position to exercise the member's functions, a successor is appointed by the World Council for the remainder of the term. Upon the recommendation of the Executive Board, the duration of the term of office of any member may be extended beyond three years if the World Council so decides.

Article 4   Plenary Session of the Court

The Plenary Sessions of the Court are presided over by the President or, in the President's absence, by one of the Vice-Presidents designated by the President. The deliberations shall be valid when at least six members are present. Decisions are taken by a majority vote, the President or Vice-President, as the case may be, having a casting vote in the event of a tie.

Article 5   Committees

The Court may set up one or more Committees and establish the functions and organization of such Committees.

Article 6   Confidentiality

The work of the Court is of a confidential nature which must be respected by everyone who participates in that work in whatever capacity. The Court lays down the rules regarding the persons who can attend the meetings of the Court and its Committees and who are entitled to have access to materials related to the work of the Court and its Secretariat.

Article 7   Modification of the Rules of Arbitration

Any proposal of the Court for a modification of the Rules is laid before the Commission on Arbitration before submission to the Executive Board of the ICC for approval, provided, however, that the Court, in order to take account of developments in information technology, may propose to modify or supplement the provisions of Article 3 of the Rules or any related provisions in the Rules without laying any such proposal before the Commission.

APPENDIX II – INTERNAL RULES OF THE INTERNATIONAL COURT OF ARBITRATION

Article 1   Confidential Character of the Work of the International Court of Arbitration

1. For the purposes of this Appendix, members of the Court include the President and Vice-Presidents of the Court.

2. The sessions of the Court, whether plenary or those of a Committee of the Court, are open only to its members and to the Secretariat.

3. However, in exceptional circumstances, the President of the Court may invite other persons to attend. Such persons must respect the confidential nature of the work of the Court.

4. The documents submitted to the Court, or drawn up by it or the Secretariat in the course of the Court's proceedings, are communicated only to the members of the Court and to the Secretariat and to persons authorized by the President to attend Court sessions.

5. The President or the Secretary General of the Court may authorize researchers undertaking work of an academic nature to acquaint themselves with awards and other documents of general interest, with the exception of memoranda, notes, statements and documents remitted by the parties within the framework of arbitration proceedings.

6. Such authorization shall not be given unless the beneficiary has undertaken to respect the confidential character of the documents made available and to refrain from publishing anything based upon information contained therein without having previously submitted the text for approval to the Secretary General of the Court.

7. The Secretariat will in each case submitted to arbitration under the Rules retain in the archives of the Court all awards, Terms of Reference and decisions of the Court, as well as copies of the pertinent correspondence of the Secretariat.

8. Any documents, communications or correspondence submitted by the parties or the arbitrators may be destroyed unless a party or an arbitrator requests in writing within a period fixed by the Secretariat the return of such documents, communications or correspondence. All related costs and expenses for the return of those documents shall be paid by such party or arbitrator.

Article 2   Participation of Members of the International Court of Arbitration in ICC Arbitration

1. The President and the members of the Secretariat of the Court may not act as arbitrators or as counsel in cases submitted to ICC arbitration.

2. The Court shall not appoint Vice-Presidents or members of the Court as arbitrators. They may, however, be proposed for such duties by one or more of the parties, or pursuant to any other procedure agreed upon by the parties, subject to confirmation.

3. When the President, a Vice-President or a member of the Court or of the

Secretariat is involved in any capacity whatsoever in proceedings pending before the Court, such person must inform the Secretary General of the Court upon becoming aware of such involvement.

4. Such person must be absent from the Court session whenever the matter is considered by the Court and shall not participate in the discussions or in the decisions of the Court.

5. Such person will not receive any material documentation or information pertaining to such proceedings.

Article 3   Relations between the Members of the Court and the ICC National Committees and Groups

1. By virtue of their capacity, the members of the Court are independent of the ICC National Committees and Groups which proposed them for appointment by the ICC World Council.

2. Furthermore, they must regard as confidential, vis-à-vis the said National Committees and Groups, any information concerning individual cases with which they have become acquainted in their capacity as members of the Court, except when they have been requested by the President of the Court, by a Vice-President of the Court authorized by the President of the Court, or by the Court's Secretary General to communicate specific information to their respective National Committees or Groups.

Article 4   Committee of the Court

1. In accordance with the provisions of Article 1(4) of the Rules and Article 5 of its statutes (Appendix I), the Court hereby establishes a Committee of the Court.

2. The members of the Committee consist of a president and at least two other members. The President of the Court acts as the president of the Committee. In the President's absence or otherwise at the President's request, a Vice-President of the Court or, in exceptional circumstances, another member of the Court may act as president of the Committee.

3. The other two members of the Committee are appointed by the Court from among the Vice Presidents or the other members of the Court. At each Plenary Session the Court appoints the members who are to attend the meetings of the Committee to be held before the next Plenary Session.

4. The Committee meets when convened by its president. Two members constitute a quorum.

5. (a) The Court shall determine the decisions that may be taken by the Committee.

(b) The decisions of the Committee are taken unanimously.

(c) When the Committee cannot reach a decision or deems it preferable to abstain, it transfers the case to the next Plenary Session, making any suggestions it deems appropriate.

(d) The Committee's decisions are brought to the notice of the Court at its next

Plenary Session.

Article 5　Court Secretariat

1. In the Secretary General's absence or otherwise at the Secretary General's request, the Deputy Secretary General and/or the General Counsel shall have the authority to refer matters to the Court, confirm arbitrators, certify true copies of awards and request the payment of a provisional advance, respectively provided for in Articles 6(3), 13(2), 34(2) and 36(1) of the Rules.

2. The Secretariat may, with the approval of the Court, issue notes and other documents for the information of the parties and the arbitrators, or as necessary for the proper conduct of the arbitral proceedings.

3. Offices of the Secretariat may be established outside the headquarters of the ICC. The Secretariat shall keep a list of offices designated by the Secretary General. Requests for Arbitration may be submitted to the Secretariat at any of its offices, and the Secretariat's functions under the Rules may be carried out from any of its offices, as instructed by the Secretary General, Deputy Secretary General or General Counsel.

Article 6　Scrutiny of Arbitral Awards

When the Court scrutinizes draft awards in accordance with Article 33 of the Rules, it considers, to the extent practicable, the requirements of mandatory law at the place of the arbitration.

APPENDIX III – ARBITRATION COSTS AND FEES

Article 1　Advance on Costs

1. Each request to commence an arbitration pursuant to the Rules must be accompanied by a filing fee of US$3,000. Such payment is non-refundable and shall be credited to the claimant's portion of the advance on costs.

2. The provisional advance fixed by the Secretary General according to Article 36(1) of the Rules shall normally not exceed the amount obtained by adding together the ICC administrative expenses, the minimum of the fees (as set out in the scale hereinafter) based upon the amount of the claim and the expected reimbursable expenses of the arbitral tribunal incurred with respect to the drafting of the Terms of Reference. If such amount is not quantified, the provisional advance shall be fixed at the discretion of the Secretary General. Payment by the claimant shall be credited to its share of the advance on costs fixed by the Court.

3. In general, after the Terms of Reference have been signed or approved by the Court and the procedural timetable has been established, the arbitral tribunal shall, in accordance with Article 36(6) of the Rules, proceed only with respect to those claims or counterclaims in regard to which the whole of the advance on costs has been paid.

4. The advance on costs fixed by the Court according to Articles 36(2) or 36(4) of the Rules comprises the fees of the arbitrator or arbitrators (hereinafter referred to as "arbitrator"), any arbitration-related expenses of the arbitrator and the ICC

administrative expenses.

5. Each party shall pay its share of the total advance on costs in cash. However, if a party's share of the advance on costs is greater than US$ 500,000 (the "Threshold Amount"), such party may post a bank guarantee for any amount above the Threshold Amount. The Court may modify the Threshold Amount at any time at its discretion.

6. The Court may authorize the payment of advances on costs, or any party's share thereof, in instalments, subject to such conditions as the Court thinks fit, including the payment of additional ICC administrative expenses.

7. A party that has already paid in full its share of the advance on costs fixed by the Court may, in accordance with Article 36(5) of the Rules, pay the unpaid portion of the advance owed by the defaulting party by posting a bank guarantee.

8. When the Court has fixed separate advances on costs pursuant to Article 36(3) of the Rules, the Secretariat shall invite each party to pay the amount of the advance corresponding to its respective claim(s).

9. When, as a result of the fixing of separate advances on costs, the separate advance fixed for the claim of either party exceeds one half of such global advance as was previously fixed (in respect of the same claims and counterclaims that are the subject of separate advances), a bank guarantee may be posted to cover any such excess amount. In the event that the amount of the separate advance is subsequently increased, at least one half of the increase shall be paid in cash.

10. The Secretariat shall establish the terms governing all bank guarantees which the parties may post pursuant to the above provisions.

11. As provided in Article 36(5) of the Rules, the advance on costs may be subject to readjustment at any time during the arbitration, in particular to take into account fluctuations in the amount in dispute, changes in the amount of the estimated expenses of the arbitrator, or the evolving difficulty or complexity of arbitration proceedings.

12. Before any expertise ordered by the arbitral tribunal can be commenced, the parties, or one of them, shall pay an advance on costs fixed by the arbitral tribunal sufficient to cover the expected fees and expenses of the expert as determined by the arbitral tribunal. The arbitral tribunal shall be responsible for ensuring the payment by the parties of such fees and expenses.

13. The amounts paid as advances on costs do not yield interest for the parties or the arbitrator.

Article 2   Costs and Fees

1. Subject to Article 37(2) of the Rules, the Court shall fix the fees of the arbitrator in accordance with the scale hereinafter set out or, where the amount in dispute is not stated, at its discretion.

2. In setting the arbitrator's fees, the Court shall take into consideration the diligence and efficiency of the arbitrator, the time spent, the rapidity of the proceedings, the complexity of the dispute and the timeliness of the submission of

the draft award, so as to arrive at a figure within the limits specified or, in exceptional circumstances (Article 37(2) of the Rules), at a figure higher or lower than those limits.

3. When a case is submitted to more than one arbitrator, the Court, at its discretion, shall have the right to increase the total fees up to a maximum which shall normally not exceed three times the fees of one arbitrator.

4. The arbitrator's fees and expenses shall be fixed exclusively by the Court as required by the Rules. Separate fee arrangements between the parties and the arbitrator are contrary to the Rules.

5. The Court shall fix the ICC administrative expenses of each arbitration in accordance with the scale hereinafter set out or, where the amount in dispute is not stated, at its discretion. In exceptional circumstances, the Court may fix the ICC administrative expenses at a lower or higher figure than that which would result from the application of such scale, provided that such expenses shall normally not exceed the maximum amount of the scale.

6. At any time during the arbitration, the Court may fix as payable a portion of the ICC administrative expenses corresponding to services that have already been performed by the Court and the Secretariat.

7. The Court may require the payment of administrative expenses in addition to those provided in the scale of administrative expenses as a condition for holding an arbitration in abeyance at the request of the parties or of one of them with the acquiescence of the other.

8. If an arbitration terminates before the rendering of a final award, the Court shall fix the fees and expenses of the arbitrators and the ICC administrative expenses at its discretion, taking into account the stage attained by the arbitral proceedings and any other relevant circumstances.

9. Any amount paid by the parties as an advance on costs exceeding the costs of the arbitration fixed by the Court shall be reimbursed to the parties having regard to the amounts paid.

10. In the case of an application under Article 35(2) of the Rules or of a remission pursuant to Article 35(4) of the Rules, the Court may fix an advance to cover additional fees and expenses of the arbitral tribunal and additional ICC administrative expenses and may make the transmission of such application to the arbitral tribunal subject to the prior cash payment in full to the ICC of such advance. The Court shall fix at its discretion the costs of the procedure following an application or a remission, which shall include any possible fees of the arbitrator and ICC administrative expenses, when approving the decision of the arbitral tribunal.

11. The Secretariat may require the payment of administrative expenses in addition to those provided in the scale of administrative expenses for any expenses arising in relation to a request pursuant to Article 34(5) of the Rules.

12. When an arbitration is preceded by an attempt at amicable resolution pursuant to the ICC ADR Rules, one half of the ICC administrative expenses paid for such ADR proceedings shall be credited to the ICC administrative expenses of

the arbitration.

13. Amounts paid to the arbitrator do not include any possible value added tax (VAT) or other taxes or charges and imposts applicable to the arbitrator's fees. Parties have a duty to pay any such taxes or charges; however, the recovery of any such charges or taxes is a matter solely between the arbitrator and the parties.

14. Any ICC administrative expenses may be subject to value added tax (VAT) or charges of a similar nature at the prevailing rate.

Article 3   ICC as Appointing Authority

Any request received for an authority of the ICC to act as appointing authority will be treated in accordance with the Rules of ICC as Appointing Authority in UNCITRAL or Other *Ad Hoc* Arbitration Proceedings and shall be accompanied by a non-refundable filing fee of US$ 3,000. No request shall be processed unless accompanied by the said filing fee. For additional services, ICC may at its discretion fix ICC administrative expenses, which shall be commensurate with the services provided and shall normally not exceed the maximum amount of US$ 10,000.

Article 4   Scales of Administrative Expenses and Arbitrator's Fees

1. The Scales of Administrative Expenses and Arbitrator's Fees set forth below shall be effective as of 1 January 2012 in respect of all arbitrations commenced on or after such date, irrespective of the version of the Rules applying to such arbitrations.

2. To calculate the ICC administrative expenses and the arbitrator's fees, the amounts calculated for each successive tranche of the amount in dispute must be added together, except that where the amount in dispute is over US$ 500 million, a flat amount of US$ 113,215 shall constitute the entirety of the ICC administrative expenses.

3. All amounts fixed by the Court or pursuant to any of the appendices to the Rules are payable in US$ except where prohibited by law, in which case the ICC may apply a different scale and fee arrangement in another currency.

A. Administrative Expenses

Amount in dispute (in US Dollars)	Administrative expenses
up to 50,000	$3,000
from 50,001 to 100,000	4.73%
from 100,001 to 200,000	2.53%
from 200,001 to 500,000	2.09%
from 500,001 to 1,000,000	1.51%
from 1,000,001 to 2,000,000	0.95%
from 2,000,001 to 5,000,000	0.46%
from 5,000,001 to 10,000,000	0.25%
from 10,000,001 to 30,000,000	0.10%
from 30,000,001 to 50,000,000	0.09%
from 50,000,001 to 80,000,000	0.01%

Amount in dispute (in US Dollars)	Administrative expenses
from 80,000,001 to 500,000,000	0.0035%
over 500,000,000	$113,215

. . .

B. Arbitrator's Fees

Amount in dispute (in US Dollars)	Fees	
	minimum	maximum
up to 50,000	$3,000.00	18.0200%
from 50,001 to 100,000	2.6500%	13.5680%
from 100,001 to 200,000	1.4310%	7.6850%
from 200,001 to 500,000	1.3670%	6.8370%
from 500,001 to 1,000,000	0.9540%	4.0280%
from 1,000,001 to 2,000,000	0.6890%	3.6040%
from 2,000,001 to 5,000,000	0.3750%	1.3910%
from 5,000,001 to 10,000,000	0.1280%	0.9100%
from 10,000,001 to 30,000,000	0.0640%	0.2410%
from 30,000,001 to 50,000,000	0.0590%	0.2280%
from 50,000,001 to 80,000,000	0.0330%	0.1570%
from 80,000,001 to 100,000,000	0.0210%	0.1150%
from 100,000,001 to 500,000,000	0.0110%	0.0580%
over 500,000,000	0.0100%	0.0400%

[The previous two tables are for illustrative purposes only, and show the administrative expenses and arbitrator's fees in US$ when the calculations in the following two tables are done properly.]

AMOUNT IN DISPUTE (in US Dollars)	A. ADMINISTRATIVE EXPENSES (in US Dollars)
up to 50,000	3,000
from 50,001 to 100,000	3,000 + 4.73% of amt. over 50,000
from 100,001 to 200,000	5,365 + 2.53% of amt. over 100,000
from 200,001 to 500,000	7,895 + 2.09% of amt. over 200,000
from 500,001 to 1,000,000	14,165 + 1.51% of amt. over 500,000
from 1,000,001 to 2,000,000	21,715 + 0.95% of amt. over 1,000,000
from 2,000,001 to 5,000,000	31,215 + 0.46% of amt. over 2,000,000
from 5,000,001 to 10,000,000	45,015 + 0.25% of amt. over 5,000,000
from 10,000,001 to 30,000,000	57,515 + 0.10% of amt. over 10,000,000
from 30,000,001 to 50,000,000	77,515 + 0.09% of amt. over 30,000,000
from 50,000,001 to 80,000,000	95,515 + 0.01% of amt. over 50,000,000
from 80,000,001 to 100,000,000	98,515 + 0.0035% of amt. over 80,000,000
from 100,000,001 to 500,000,000	99,215 + 0.0035% of amt. over 100,000,000

AMOUNT IN DISPUTE (in US Dollars)	A. ADMINISTRATIVE EXPENSES (in US Dollars)
over 500,000,000	113,215

AMOUNT IN DISPUTE (in US Dollars)	B. ARBITRATOR'S FEES (in US Dollars)	
	Minimum	Maximum
up to 50,000	3000	18.0200% of amount in dispute
from 50,001 to 100,000	3,000 + 2.6500% of amt. over 50,000	9,010 + 13.5680% of amt. over 50,000
from 100,001 to 200,000	4,325 + 1.4310% of amt. over 100,000	15,794 + 7.6850% of amt. over 100,000
from 200,001 to 500,000	5,756 + 1.3670% of amt. over 200,000	23,479 + 6.8370% of amt. over 200,000
from 500,001 to 1,000,000	9,857 + 0.9540% of amt. over 500,000	43,990 + 4.0280% of amt. over 500,000
from 1,000,001 to 2,000,000	14,627 + 0.6890% of amt. over 1,000,000	64,130 + 3.6040% of amt. over 1,000,000
from 2,000,001 to 5,000,000	21,517 + 0.3750% of amt. over 2,000,000	100,170 + 1.3910% of amt. over 2,000,000
from 5,000,001 to 10,000,000	32,767 + 0.1280% of amt. over 5,000,000	141,900 + 0.9100% of amt. over 5,000,000
from 10,000,001 to 30,000,000	39,167 + 0.0640% of amt. over 10,000,000	187,400 + 0.2410% of amt. over 10,000,000
from 30,000,001 to 50,000,000	51,967 + 0.0590% of amt. over 30,000,000	235,600 + 0.2280% of amt. over 30,000,000
from 50,000,001 to 80,000,000	63,767 + 0.0330% of amt. over 50,000,000	281,200 + 0.1570% of amt. over 50,000,000
from 80,000,001 to 100,000,000	73,667 + 0.0210% of amt. over 80,000,000	328,300 + 0.1150% of amt. over 80,000,000
from 100,000,001 to 500,000,000	77,867 + 0.0110% of amt. over 100,000,000	351,300 + 0.0580% of amt. over 100,000,000
over 500,000,000	121,867 + 0.0100% of amt. over 500,000,000	583,300 + 0.0400% of amt. over 500,000,000

. . .

APPENDIX V – EMERGENCY ARBITRATOR RULES

Article 1   Application for Emergency Measures

1. A party wishing to have recourse to an emergency arbitrator pursuant to Article 29 of the Rules of Arbitration of the ICC (the "Rules") shall submit its Application for Emergency Measures (the Application) to the Secretariat at any of the offices specified in the Internal Rules of the Court in Appendix II to the Rules.

2. The Application shall be supplied in a number of copies sufficient to provide one copy for each party, plus one for the emergency arbitrator, and one for the Secretariat.

3. The Application shall contain the following information:

a) the name in full, description, address and other contact details of each of the parties;

b) the name in full, address and other contact details of any person(s) representing the applicant;

c) a description of the circumstances giving rise to the Application and of the underlying dispute referred or to be referred to arbitration;

d) a statement of the Emergency Measures sought;

e) the reasons why the applicant needs urgent interim or conservatory measures that cannot await the constitution of an arbitral tribunal;

f) any relevant agreements and, in particular, the arbitration agreement;

g) any agreement as to the place of the arbitration, the applicable rules of law or the language of the arbitration;

h) proof of payment of the amount referred to in Article 7(1) of this Appendix; and

i) any Request for Arbitration and any other submissions in connection with the underlying dispute, which have been filed with the Secretariat by any of the parties to the emergency arbitrator proceedings prior to the making of the Application.

The Application may contain such other documents or information as the applicant considers appropriate or as may contribute to the efficient examination of the Application.

4. The Application shall be drawn up in the language of the arbitration if agreed upon by the parties or, in the absence of any such agreement, in the language of the arbitration agreement.

5. If and to the extent that the President of the Court (the "President") considers, on the basis of the information contained in the Application, that the Emergency Arbitrator Provisions apply with reference to Article 29(5) and Article 29(6) of the Rules, the Secretariat shall transmit a copy of the Application and the documents annexed thereto to the responding party. If and to the extent that the President considers otherwise, the Secretariat shall inform the parties that the emergency

arbitrator proceedings shall not take place with respect to some or all of the parties and shall transmit a copy of the Application to them for information.

6. The President shall terminate the emergency arbitrator proceedings if a Request for Arbitration has not been received by the Secretariat from the applicant within 10 days of the Secretariat's receipt of the Application, unless the emergency arbitrator determines that a longer period of time is necessary.

Article 2   Appointment of the Emergency Arbitrator; Transmission of the File

1. The President shall appoint an emergency arbitrator within as short a time as possible, normally within two days from the Secretariat's receipt of the Application.

2. No emergency arbitrator shall be appointed after the file has been transmitted to the arbitral tribunal pursuant to Article 16 of the Rules. An emergency arbitrator appointed prior thereto shall retain the power to make an order within the time limit permitted by Article 6(4) of this Appendix.

3. Once the emergency arbitrator has been appointed, the Secretariat shall so notify the parties and shall transmit the file to the emergency arbitrator. Thereafter, all written communications from the parties shall be submitted directly to the emergency arbitrator with a copy to the other party and the Secretariat. A copy of any written communications from the emergency arbitrator to the parties shall be submitted to the Secretariat.

4. Every emergency arbitrator shall be and remain impartial and independent of the parties involved in the dispute.

5. Before being appointed, a prospective emergency arbitrator shall sign a statement of acceptance, availability, impartiality and independence. The Secretariat shall provide a copy of such statement to the parties.

6. An emergency arbitrator shall not act as an arbitrator in any arbitration relating to the dispute that gave rise to the Application.

Article 3   Challenge of an Emergency Arbitrator

1. A challenge against the emergency arbitrator must be made within three days from receipt by the party making the challenge of the notification of the appointment or from the date when that party was informed of the facts and circumstances on which the challenge is based if such date is subsequent to the receipt of such notification.

2. The challenge shall be decided by the Court after the Secretariat has afforded an opportunity for the emergency arbitrator and the other party or parties to provide comments in writing within a suitable period of time.

Article 4   Place of the Emergency Arbitrator Proceedings

1. If the parties have agreed upon the place of the arbitration, such place shall be the place of the emergency arbitrator proceedings. In the absence of such agreement, the President shall fix the place of the emergency arbitrator proceedings, without prejudice to the determination of the place of the arbitration pursuant to Article 18(1) of the Rules.

2. Any meetings with the emergency arbitrator may be conducted through a meeting in person at any location the emergency arbitrator considers appropriate or by video conference, telephone or similar means of communication.

Article 5   Proceedings

1. The emergency arbitrator shall establish a procedural timetable for the emergency arbitrator proceedings within as short a time as possible, normally within two days from the transmission of the file to the emergency arbitrator pursuant to Article 2(3) of this Appendix.

2. The emergency arbitrator shall conduct the proceedings in the manner which the emergency arbitrator considers to be appropriate, taking into account the nature and the urgency of the Application. In all cases, the emergency arbitrator shall act fairly and impartially and ensure that each party has a reasonable opportunity to present its case.

Article 6   Order

1. Pursuant to Article 29(2) of the Rules, the emergency arbitrator's decision shall take the form of an order (the "Order").

2. In the Order, the emergency arbitrator shall determine whether the Application is admissible pursuant to Article 29(1) of the Rules and whether the emergency arbitrator has jurisdiction to order Emergency Measures.

3. The Order shall be made in writing and shall state the reasons upon which it is based. It shall be dated and signed by the emergency arbitrator.

4. The Order shall be made no later than 15 days from the date on which the file was transmitted to the emergency arbitrator pursuant to Article 2(3) of this Appendix. The President may extend the time limit pursuant to a reasoned request from the emergency arbitrator or on the President's own initiative if the President decides it is necessary to do so.

5. Within the time limit established pursuant to Article 6(4) of this Appendix, the emergency arbitrator shall send the Order to the parties, with a copy to the Secretariat, by any of the means of communication permitted by Article 3(2) of the Rules that the emergency arbitrator considers will ensure prompt receipt.

6. The Order shall cease to be binding on the parties upon:

     a) the President's termination of the emergency arbitrator proceedings pursuant to Article 1(6) of this Appendix;

     b) the acceptance by the Court of a challenge against the emergency arbitrator pursuant to Article 3 of this Appendix;

     c) the arbitral tribunal's final award, unless the arbitral tribunal expressly decides otherwise; or

     d) the withdrawal of all claims or the termination of the arbitration before the rendering of a final award.

7. The emergency arbitrator may make the Order subject to such conditions as

the emergency arbitrator thinks fit, including requiring the provision of appropriate security.

8. Upon a reasoned request by a party made prior to the transmission of the file to the arbitral tribunal pursuant to Article 16 of the Rules, the emergency arbitrator may modify, terminate or annul the Order.

Article 7   Costs of the Emergency Arbitrator Proceedings

1. The applicant must pay an amount of US$ 40,000, consisting of US$ 10,000 for ICC administrative expenses and US$ 30 000 for the emergency arbitrator's fees and expenses. Notwithstanding Article 1(5) of this Appendix, the Application shall not be notified until the payment of US$ 40,000 is received by the Secretariat.

2. The President may, at any time during the emergency arbitrator proceedings, decide to increase the emergency arbitrator's fees or the ICC administrative expenses taking into account, *inter alia*, the nature of the case and the nature and amount of work performed by the emergency arbitrator, the Court, the President and the Secretariat. If the party which submitted the Application fails to pay the increased costs within the time limit fixed by the Secretariat, the Application shall be considered as withdrawn.

3. The emergency arbitrator's Order shall fix the costs of the emergency arbitrator proceedings and decide which of the parties shall bear them or in what proportion they shall be borne by the parties.

4. The costs of the emergency arbitrator proceedings include the ICC administrative expenses, the emergency arbitrator's fees and expenses and the reasonable legal and other costs incurred by the parties for the emergency arbitrator proceedings.

5. In the event that the emergency arbitrator proceedings do not take place pursuant to Article 1(5) of this Appendix or are otherwise terminated prior to the making of an Order, the President shall determine the amount to be reimbursed to the applicant, if any. An amount of US$ 5,000 for ICC administrative expenses is non-refundable in all cases.

Article 8   General Rule

1. The President shall have the power to decide, at the President's discretion, all matters relating to the administration of the emergency arbitrator proceedings not expressly provided for in this Appendix.

2. In the President's absence or otherwise at the President's request, any of the Vice-Presidents of the Court shall have the power to take decisions on behalf of the President.

3. In all matters concerning emergency arbitrator proceedings not expressly provided for in this Appendix, the Court, the President and the emergency arbitrator shall act in the spirit of the Rules and this Appendix.

STANDARD AND SUGGESTED CLAUSES

Below are standard and suggested clauses for use by parties who wish to have recourse to ICC arbitration and/or ICC ADR under the foregoing Rules.

Arbitration

All disputes arising out of or in connection with the present contract shall be finally settled under the Rules of Arbitration of the International Chamber of Commerce by one or more arbitrators appointed in accordance with the said Rules.

Arbitration without emergency arbitrator

All disputes arising out of or in connection with the present contract shall be finally settled under the Rules of Arbitration of the International Chamber of Commerce by one or more arbitrators appointed in accordance with the said Rules. The Emergency Arbitrator Provisions shall not apply.

Optional ADR

The parties may at any time, without prejudice to any other proceedings, seek to settle any dispute arising out of or in connection with the present contract in accordance with the ICC ADR Rules.

Obligation to consider ADR

In the event of any dispute arising out of or in connection with the present contract, the parties agree in the first instance to discuss and consider submitting the matter to settlement proceedings under the ICC ADR Rules.

Obligation to submit dispute to ADR with an automatic expiration mechanism

In the event of any dispute arising out of or in connection with the present contract, the parties agree to submit the matter to settlement proceedings under the ICC ADR Rules. If the dispute has not been settled pursuant to the said Rules within 45 days following the filing of a Request for ADR or within such other period as the parties may agree in writing, the parties shall have no further obligations under this paragraph.

Obligation to submit dispute to ADR, followed by arbitration if required

In the event of any dispute arising out of or in connection with the present contract, the parties agree to submit the matter to settlement proceedings under the ICC ADR Rules. If the dispute has not been settled pursuant to the said Rules within 45 days following the filing of a Request for ADR or within such other period as the parties may agree in writing, such dispute shall be finally settled under the Rules of Arbitration of the International Chamber of Commerce by one or more arbitrators appointed in accordance with the said Rules of Arbitration.

How to use these clauses

Parties wishing to use ICC arbitration and/or ICC ADR should choose one of the above clauses, which cover different situations and needs. If the parties do not want the Emergency Arbitrator Provisions to apply, they must expressly opt out by using the second of the two arbitration clauses. Parties are free to adapt the chosen clause to their particular circumstances. For instance, when providing for arbitration, they may wish to stipulate the number of arbitrators, given that the Rules of Arbitration contain a presumption in favour of a sole arbitrator. They may also wish to stipulate the language and place of the arbitration and the law applicable to the merits. When providing for ADR, they may wish to specify the settlement technique to be applied, failing which mediation, the default mechanism, will be used. The last clause above is a two-tiered clause providing for ADR followed by arbitration. Other combinations of services are also possible. Combined and multi-tiered dispute resolution clauses may help to facilitate dispute management. However, it is also possible for parties to file requests under the ICC ADR Rules or the ICC Rules for Expertise at any time, even after a dispute has arisen or in the course of other dispute resolution proceedings.

At all times, care must be taken to avoid any risk of ambiguity in the drafting of the clause. Unclear wording causes uncertainty and delay and can hinder or even compromise the dispute resolution process. When incorporating any of the above clauses in their contracts, parties are advised to take account of any factors that may affect their enforceability under applicable law. For instance, they should have regard to any mandatory requirements at the place of arbitration and the place of enforcement. Translations of the above clauses and clauses providing for other procedures and combinations of procedures can be found at <www.iccarbitration-.org>.

LCIA RULES OF ARBITRATION[*]

(effective 1 January 1998)

Where any agreement, submission or reference provides in writing and in whatsoever manner for arbitration under the rules of the LCIA or by the Court of the LCIA ("the LCIA Court"), the parties shall be taken to have agreed in writing that the arbitration shall be conducted in accordance with the following rules ("the Rules") or such amended rules as the LCIA may have adopted hereafter to take effect before the commencement of the arbitration. The Rules include the Schedule of Costs in effect at the commencement of the arbitration, as separately amended from time to time by the LCIA Court.

Article 1   The Request for Arbitration

1.1 Any party wishing to commence an arbitration under these Rules ("the Claimant") shall send to the Registrar of the LCIA Court ("the Registrar") a written request for arbitration ("the Request"), containing or accompanied by:

(a) the names, addresses, telephone, facsimile, telex and e-mail numbers (if known) of the parties to the arbitration and of their legal representatives;

(b) a copy of the written arbitration clause or separate written arbitration agreement invoked by the Claimant ("the Arbitration Agreement"), together with a copy of the contractual documentation in which the arbitration clause is contained or in respect of which the arbitration arises;

(c) a brief statement describing the nature and circumstances of the dispute, and specifying the claims advanced by the Claimant against another party to the arbitration ("the Respondent");

(d) a statement of any matters (such as the seat or language(s) of the arbitration, or the number of arbitrators, or their qualifications or identities) on which the parties have already agreed in writing for the arbitration or in respect of which the Claimant wishes to make a proposal;

(e) if the Arbitration Agreement calls for party nomination of arbitrators, the name, address, telephone, facsimile, telex and e-mail numbers (if known) of the Claimant's nominee;

(f) the fee prescribed in the Schedule of Costs (without which the Request shall be treated as not having been received by the Registrar and the arbitration as not having been commenced);

(g) confirmation to the Registrar that copies of the Request (including all accompanying documents) have been or are being served simultaneously on all other parties to the arbitration by one or more means of service to be identified in such confirmation.

1.2 The date of receipt by the Registrar of the Request shall be treated as the date on which the arbitration has commenced for all purposes. The Request (including all accompanying documents) should be submitted to the Registrar in two copies where a sole arbitrator should be appointed, or, if the parties have agreed or the Claimant considers that three arbitrators should be appointed, in four copies.

Article 2   The Response

2.1 Within 30 days of service of the Request on the Respondent, (or such lesser period fixed by the LCIA Court), the Respondent shall send to the Registrar a written response to the Request ("the Response"), containing or accompanied by:

(a) confirmation or denial of all or part of the claims advanced by the Claimant in the Request;

(b) a brief statement describing the nature and circumstances of any counter-claims advanced by the Respondent against the Claimant;

(c) comment in response to any statements contained in the Request, as called for under Article 1.1(d), on matters relating to the conduct of the arbitration;

(d) if the Arbitration Agreement calls for party nomination of arbitrators, the name, address, telephone, facsimile, telex and e-mail numbers (if known) of the Respondent's nominee; and

(e) confirmation to the Registrar that copies of the Response (including all accompanying documents) have been or are being served simultaneously on all other parties to the arbitration by one or more means of service to be identified in such confirmation.

2.2 The Response (including all accompanying documents) should be submitted to the Registrar in two copies, or if the parties have agreed or the Respondent considers that three arbitrators should be appointed, in four copies.

2.3 Failure to send a Response shall not preclude the Respondent from denying any claim or from advancing a counterclaim in the arbitration. However, if the Arbitration Agreement calls for party nomination of arbitrators, failure to send a Response or to nominate an arbitrator within time or at all shall constitute an irrevocable waiver of that party's opportunity to nominate an arbitrator.

Article 3   The LCIA Court and Registrar

3.1 The functions of the LCIA Court under these Rules shall be performed in its name by the President or a Vice-President of the LCIA Court or by a division of three or five members of the LCIA Court appointed by the President or a Vice-President of the LCIA Court, as determined by the President.

3.2 The functions of the Registrar under these Rules shall be performed by the Registrar or any deputy Registrar of the LCIA Court under the supervision of the LCIA Court.

3.3 All communications from any party or arbitrator to the LCIA Court shall be addressed to the Registrar.

Article 4   Notices and Periods of Time

4.1 Any notice or other communication that may be or is required to be given by a party under these Rules shall be in writing and shall be delivered by registered postal or courier service or transmitted by facsimile, telex, e-mail or any other means of telecommunication that provide a record of its transmission.

4.2 A party's last-known residence or place of business during the arbitration shall be a valid address for the purpose of any notice or other communication in the absence of any notification of a change to such address by that party to the other parties, the Arbitral Tribunal and the Registrar.

4.3 For the purpose of determining the date of commencement of a time limit, a notice or other communication shall be treated as having been received on the day it is delivered or, in the case of telecommunications, transmitted in accordance with Articles 4.1 and 4.2.

4.4 For the purpose of determining compliance with a time limit, a notice or other communication shall be treated as having been sent, made or transmitted if it is dispatched in accordance with Articles 4.1 and 4.2 prior to or on the date of the expiration of the time-limit.

4.5 Notwithstanding the above, any notice or communication by one party may be addressed to another party in the manner agreed in writing between them or, failing such agreement, according to the practice followed in the course of their previous dealings or in whatever manner ordered by the Arbitral Tribunal.

4.6 For the purpose of calculating a period of time under these Rules, such period shall begin to run on the day following the day when a notice or other communication is received. If the last day of such period is an official holiday or a non-business day at the residence or place of business of the addressee, the period is extended until the first business day which follows. Official holidays or non-business days occurring during the running of the period of time are included in calculating that period.

4.7 The Arbitral Tribunal may at any time extend (even where the period of time has expired) or abridge any period of time prescribed under these Rules or under the Arbitration Agreement for the conduct of the arbitration, including any notice or communication to be served by one party on any other party.

Article 5   Formation of the Arbitral Tribunal

5.1 The expression "the Arbitral Tribunal" in these Rules includes a sole arbitrator or all the arbitrators where more than one. All references to an arbitrator shall include the masculine and feminine. (References to the President, Vice-President and members of the LCIA Court, the Registrar or deputy Registrar, expert, witness, party and legal representative shall be similarly understood).

5.2 All arbitrators conducting an arbitration under these Rules shall be and remain at all times impartial and independent of the parties; and none shall act in the arbitration as advocates for any party. No arbitrator, whether before or after appointment, shall advise any party on the merits or outcome of the dispute.

5.3 Before appointment by the LCIA Court, each arbitrator shall furnish to the

Registrar a written résumé of his past and present professional positions; he shall agree in writing upon fee rates conforming to the Schedule of Costs; and he shall sign a declaration to the effect that there are no circumstances known to him likely to give rise to any justified doubts as to his impartiality or independence, other than any circumstances disclosed by him in the declaration. Each arbitrator shall thereby also assume a continuing duty forthwith to disclose any such circumstances to the LCIA Court, to any other members of the Arbitral Tribunal and to all the parties if such circumstances should arise after the date of such declaration and before the arbitration is concluded.

5.4 The LCIA Court shall appoint the Arbitral Tribunal as soon as practicable after receipt by the Registrar of the Response or after the expiry of 30 days following service of the Request upon the Respondent if no Response is received by the Registrar (or such lesser period fixed by the LCIA Court). The LCIA Court may proceed with the formation of the Arbitral Tribunal notwithstanding that the Request is incomplete or the Response is missing, late or incomplete. A sole arbitrator shall be appointed unless the parties have agreed in writing otherwise, or unless the LCIA Court determines that in view of all the circumstances of the case a three-member tribunal is appropriate.

5.5 The LCIA Court alone is empowered to appoint arbitrators. The LCIA Court will appoint arbitrators with due regard for any particular method or criteria of selection agreed in writing by the parties. In selecting arbitrators consideration will be given to the nature of the transaction, the nature and circumstances of the dispute, the nationality, location and languages of the parties and (if more than two) the number of parties.

5.6 In the case of a three-member Arbitral Tribunal, the chairman (who will not be a party-nominated arbitrator) shall be appointed by the LCIA Court.

Article 6   Nationality of Arbitrators

6.1 Where the parties are of different nationalities, a sole arbitrator or chairman of the Arbitral Tribunal shall not have the same nationality as any party unless the parties who are not of the same nationality as the proposed appointee all agree in writing otherwise.

6.2 The nationality of parties shall be understood to include that of controlling shareholders or interests.

6.3 For the purpose of this Article, a person who is a citizen of two or more states shall be treated as a national of each state; and citizens of the European Union shall be treated as nationals of its different Member States and shall not be treated as having the same nationality.

Article 7   Party and Other Nominations

7.1 If the parties have agreed that any arbitrator is to be appointed by one or more of them or by any third person, that agreement shall be treated as an agreement to nominate an arbitrator for all purposes. Such nominee may only be appointed by the LCIA Court as arbitrator subject to his prior compliance with Article 5.3. The LCIA Court may refuse to appoint any such nominee if it determines that he is not suitable or independent or impartial.

7.2 Where the parties have howsoever agreed that the Respondent or any third person is to nominate an arbitrator and such nomination is not made within time or at all, the LCIA Court may appoint an arbitrator notwithstanding the absence of the nomination and without regard to any late nomination. Likewise, if the Request for Arbitration does not contain a nomination by the Claimant where the parties have howsoever agreed that the Claimant or a third person is to nominate an arbitrator, the LCIA Court may appoint an arbitrator notwithstanding the absence of the nomination and without regard to any late nomination.

Article 8   Three or More Parties

8.1 Where the Arbitration Agreement entitles each party howsoever to nominate an arbitrator, the parties to the dispute number more than two and such parties have not all agreed in writing that the disputant parties represent two separate sides for the formation of the Arbitral Tribunal as Claimant and Respondent respectively, the LCIA Court shall appoint the Arbitral Tribunal without regard to any party's nomination.

8.2 In such circumstances, the Arbitration Agreement shall be treated for all purposes as a written agreement by the parties for the appointment of the Arbitral Tribunal by the LCIA Court.

Article 9   Expedited Formation

9.1 In exceptional urgency, on or after the commencement of the arbitration, any party may apply to the LCIA Court for the expedited formation of the Arbitral Tribunal, including the appointment of any replacement arbitrator under Articles 10 and 11 of these Rules.

9.2 Such an application shall be made in writing to the LCIA Court, copied to all other parties to the arbitration; and it shall set out the specific grounds for exceptional urgency in the formation of the Arbitral Tribunal.

9.3 The LCIA Court may, in its complete discretion, abridge or curtail any time-limit under these Rules for the formation of the Arbitral Tribunal, including service of the Response and of any matters or documents adjudged to be missing from the Request. The LCIA Court shall not be entitled to abridge or curtail any other time-limit.

Article 10   Revocation of Arbitrator's Appointment

10.1 If either (a) any arbitrator gives written notice of his desire to resign as arbitrator to the LCIA Court, to be copied to the parties and the other arbitrators (if any) or (b) any arbitrator dies, falls seriously ill, refuses, or becomes unable or unfit to act, either upon challenge by a party or at the request of the remaining arbitrators, the LCIA Court may revoke that arbitrator's appointment and appoint another arbitrator. The LCIA Court shall decide upon the amount of fees and expenses to be paid for the former arbitrator's services (if any) as it may consider appropriate in all the circumstances.

10.2 If any arbitrator acts in deliberate violation of the Arbitration Agreement (including these Rules) or does not act fairly and impartially as between the parties or does not conduct or participate in the arbitration proceedings with reasonable diligence, avoiding unnecessary delay or expense, that arbitrator may be considered unfit in the opinion of the LCIA Court.

10.3 An arbitrator may also be challenged by any party if circumstances exist that give rise to justifiable doubts as to his impartiality or independence. A party may challenge an arbitrator it has nominated, or in whose appointment it has participated, only for reasons of which it becomes aware after the appointment has been made.

10.4 A party who intends to challenge an arbitrator shall, within 15 days of the formation of the Arbitral Tribunal or (if later) after becoming aware of any circumstances referred to in Article 10.1, 10.2 or 10.3, send a written statement of the reasons for its challenge to the LCIA Court, the Arbitral Tribunal and all other parties. Unless the challenged arbitrator withdraws or all other parties agree to the challenge within 15 days of receipt of the written statement, the LCIA Court shall decide on the challenge.

Article 11   Nomination and Replacement of Arbitrators

11.1 In the event that the LCIA Court determines that any nominee is not suitable or independent or impartial or if an appointed arbitrator is to be replaced for any reason, the LCIA Court shall have a complete discretion to decide whether or not to follow the original nominating process.

11.2 If the LCIA Court should so decide, any opportunity given to a party to make a re-nomination shall be waived if not exercised within 15 days (or such lesser time as the LCIA Court may fix), after which the LCIA Court shall appoint the replacement arbitrator.

Article 12   Majority Power to Continue Proceedings

12.1 If any arbitrator on a three-member Arbitral Tribunal refuses or persistently fails to participate in its deliberations, the two other arbitrators shall have the power, upon their written notice of such refusal or failure to the LCIA Court, the parties and the third arbitrator, to continue the arbitration (including the making of any decision, ruling or award), notwithstanding the absence of the third arbitrator.

12.2 In determining whether to continue the arbitration, the two other arbitrators shall take into account the stage of the arbitration, any explanation made by the third arbitrator for his non-participation and such other matters as they consider appropriate in the circumstances of the case. The reasons for such determination shall be stated in any award, order or other decision made by the two arbitrators without the participation of the third arbitrator.

12.3 In the event that the two other arbitrators determine at any time not to continue the arbitration without the participation of the third arbitrator missing from their deliberations, the two arbitrators shall notify in writing the parties and the LCIA Court of such determination; and in that event, the two arbitrators or any party may refer the matter to the LCIA Court for the revocation of that third arbitrator's appointment and his replacement under Article 10.

Article 13   Communications between Parties and the Arbitral Tribunal

13.1 Until the Arbitral Tribunal is formed, all communications between parties and arbitrators shall be made through the Registrar.

13.2 Thereafter, unless and until the Arbitral Tribunal directs that communications shall take place directly between the Arbitral Tribunal and the parties (with simultaneous copies to the Registrar), all written communications between the parties and the Arbitral Tribunal shall continue to be made through the Registrar.

13.3 Where the Registrar sends any written communication to one party on behalf of the Arbitral Tribunal, he shall send a copy to each of the other parties. Where any party sends to the Registrar any communication (including Written Statements and Documents under Article 15), it shall include a copy for each arbitrator; and it shall also send copies direct to all other parties and confirm to the Registrar in writing that it has done or is doing so.

Article 14   Conduct of the Proceedings

14.1 The parties may agree on the conduct of their arbitral proceedings and they are encouraged to do so, consistent with the Arbitral Tribunal's general duties at all times:

(i) to act fairly and impartially as between all parties, giving each a reasonable opportunity of putting its case and dealing with that of its opponent; and

(ii) to adopt procedures suitable to the circumstances of the arbitration, avoiding unnecessary delay or expense, so as to provide a fair and efficient means for the final resolution of the parties' dispute.

Such agreements shall be made by the parties in writing or recorded in writing by the Arbitral Tribunal at the request of and with the authority of the parties.

14.2 Unless otherwise agreed by the parties under Article 14.1, the Arbitral Tribunal shall have the widest discretion to discharge its duties allowed under such law(s) or rules of law as the Arbitral Tribunal may determine to be applicable; and at all times the parties shall do everything necessary for the fair, efficient and expeditious conduct of the arbitration.

14.3 In the case of a three-member Arbitral Tribunal the chairman may, with the prior consent of the other two arbitrators, make procedural rulings alone.

Article 15   Submission of Written Statements and Documents

15.1 Unless the parties have agreed otherwise under Article 14.1 or the Arbitral Tribunal should determine differently, the written stage of the proceedings shall be as set out below.

15.2 Within 30 days of receipt of written notification from the Registrar of the formation of the Arbitral Tribunal, the Claimant shall send to the Registrar a Statement of Case setting out in sufficient detail the facts and any contentions of law on which it relies, together with the relief claimed against all other parties, save and insofar as such matters have not been set out in its Request.

15.3 Within 30 days of receipt of the Statement of Case or written notice from the

Claimant that it elects to treat the Request as its Statement of Case, the Respondent shall send to the Registrar a Statement of Defence setting out in sufficient detail which of the facts and contentions of law in the Statement of Case or Request (as the case may be) it admits or denies, on what grounds and on what other facts and contentions of law it relies. Any counterclaims shall be submitted with the Statement of Defence in the same manner as claims are to be set out in the Statement of Case.

15.4 Within 30 days of receipt of the Statement of Defence, the Claimant shall send to the Registrar a Statement of Reply which, where there are any counterclaims, shall include a Defence to Counterclaim in the same manner as a defence is to be set out in the Statement of Defence.

15.5 If the Statement of Reply contains a Defence to Counterclaim, within 30 days of its receipt the Respondent shall send to the Registrar a Statement of Reply to Counterclaim.

15.6 All Statements referred to in this Article shall be accompanied by copies (or, if they are especially voluminous, lists) of all essential documents on which the party concerned relies and which have not previously been submitted by any party, and (where appropriate) by any relevant samples and exhibits.

15.7 As soon as practicable following receipt of the Statements specified in this Article, the Arbitral Tribunal shall proceed in such manner as has been agreed in writing by the parties or pursuant to its authority under these Rules.

15.8 If the Respondent fails to submit a Statement of Defence or the Claimant a Statement of Defence to Counterclaim, or if at any point any party fails to avail itself of the opportunity to present its case in the manner determined by Article 15.2 to 15.6 or directed by the Arbitral Tribunal, the Arbitral Tribunal may nevertheless proceed with the arbitration and make an award.

Article 16   Seat of Arbitration and Place of Hearings

16.1 The parties may agree in writing the seat (or legal place) of their arbitration. Failing such a choice, the seat of arbitration shall be London, unless and until the LCIA Court determines in view of all the circumstances, and after having given the parties an opportunity to make written comment, that another seat is more appropriate.

16.2 The Arbitral Tribunal may hold hearings, meetings and deliberations at any convenient geographical place in its discretion; and if elsewhere than the seat of the arbitration, the arbitration shall be treated as an arbitration conducted at the seat of the arbitration and any award as an award made at the seat of the arbitration for all purposes.

16.3 The law applicable to the arbitration (if any) shall be the arbitration law of the seat of arbitration, unless and to the extent that the parties have expressly agreed in writing on the application of another arbitration law and such agreement is not prohibited by the law of the arbitral seat.

Article 17   Language of Arbitration

17.1 The initial language of the arbitration shall be the language of the Arbitration Agreement, unless the parties have agreed in writing otherwise and providing always that a non-participating or defaulting party shall have no cause for complaint if communications to and from the Registrar and the arbitration proceedings are conducted in English.

17.2 In the event that the Arbitration Agreement is written in more than one language, the LCIA Court may, unless the Arbitration Agreement provides that the arbitration proceedings shall be conducted in more than one language, decide which of those languages shall be the initial language of the arbitration.

17.3 Upon the formation of the Arbitral Tribunal and unless the parties have agreed upon the language or languages of the arbitration, the Arbitration Tribunal shall decide upon the language(s) of the arbitration, after giving the parties an opportunity to make written comment and taking into account the initial language of the arbitration and any other matter it may consider appropriate in all the circumstances of the case.

17.4 If any document is expressed in a language other than the language(s) of the arbitration and no translation of such document is submitted by the party relying upon the document, the Arbitral Tribunal or (if the Arbitral Tribunal has not been formed) the LCIA Court may order that party to submit a translation in a form to be determined by the Arbitral Tribunal or the LCIA Court, as the case may be.

Article 18   Party Representation

18.1 Any party may be represented by legal practitioners or any other representatives.

18.2 At any time the Arbitral Tribunal may require from any party proof of authority granted to its representative(s) in such form as the Arbitral Tribunal may determine.

Article 19   Hearings

19.1 Any party which expresses a desire to that effect has the right to be heard orally before the Arbitral Tribunal on the merits of the dispute, unless the parties have agreed in writing on documents-only arbitration.

19.2 The Arbitral Tribunal shall fix the date, time and physical place of any meetings and hearings in the arbitration, and shall give the parties reasonable notice thereof.

19.3 The Arbitral Tribunal may in advance of any hearing submit to the parties a list of questions which it wishes them to answer with special attention.

19.4 All meetings and hearings shall be in private unless the parties agree otherwise in writing or the Arbitral Tribunal directs otherwise.

19.5 The Arbitral Tribunal shall have the fullest authority to establish time limits for meetings and hearings, or for any parts thereof.

Article 20   Witnesses

20.1 Before any hearing, the Arbitral Tribunal may require any party to give notice of the identity of each witness that party wishes to call (including rebuttal witnesses), as well as the subject matter of that witness's testimony, its content and its relevance to the issues in the arbitration.

20.2 The Arbitral Tribunal may also determine the time, manner and form in which such materials should be exchanged between the parties and presented to the Arbitral Tribunal; and it has a discretion to allow, refuse, or limit the appearance of witnesses (whether witness of fact or expert witness).

20.3 Subject to any order otherwise by the Arbitral Tribunal, the testimony of a witness may be presented by a party in written form, either as a signed statement or as a sworn affidavit.

20.4 Subject to Article 14.1 and 14.2, any party may request that a witness, on whose testimony another party seeks to rely, should attend for oral questioning at a hearing before the Arbitral Tribunal. If the Arbitral Tribunal orders that other party to produce the witness and the witness fails to attend the oral hearing without good cause, the Arbitral Tribunal may place such weight on the written testimony (or exclude the same altogether) as it considers appropriate in the circumstances of the case.

20.5 Any witness who gives oral evidence at a hearing before the Arbitral Tribunal may be questioned by each of the parties under the control of the Arbitral Tribunal. The Arbitral Tribunal may put questions at any stage of his evidence.

20.6 Subject to the mandatory provisions of any applicable law, it shall not be improper for any party or its legal representatives to interview any witness or potential witness for the purpose of presenting his testimony in written form or producing him as an oral witness.

20.7 Any individual intending to testify to the Arbitral Tribunal on any issue of fact or expertise shall be treated as a witness under these Rules notwithstanding that the individual is a party to the arbitration or was or is an officer, employee or shareholder of any party.

Article 21   Experts to the Arbitral Tribunal

21.1 Unless otherwise agreed by the parties in writing, the Arbitral Tribunal:

(a) may appoint one or more experts to report to the Arbitral Tribunal on specific issues, who shall be and remain impartial and independent of the parties throughout the arbitration proceedings; and

(b) may require a party to give any such expert any relevant information or to provide access to any relevant documents, goods, samples, property or site for inspection by the expert.

21.2 Unless otherwise agreed by the parties in writing, if a party so requests or if the Arbitral Tribunal considers it necessary, the expert shall, after delivery of his written or oral report to the Arbitral Tribunal and the parties, participate in one or more hearings at which the parties shall have the opportunity to question the expert on his report and to present expert witnesses in order to testify on the points at issue.

21.3 The fees and expenses of any expert appointed by the Arbitral Tribunal under this Article shall be paid out of the deposits payable by the parties under Article 24 and shall form part of the costs of the arbitration.

Article 22   Additional Powers of the Arbitral Tribunal

22.1 Unless the parties at any time agree otherwise in writing, the Arbitral Tribunal shall have the power, on the application of any party or of its own motion, but in either case only after giving the parties a reasonable opportunity to state their views:

(a) to allow any party, upon such terms (as to costs and otherwise) as it shall determine, to amend any claim, counterclaim, defence and reply;

(b) to extend or abbreviate any time-limit provided by the Arbitration Agreement or these Rules for the conduct of the arbitration or by the Arbitral Tribunal's own orders;

(c) to conduct such enquiries as may appear to the Arbitral Tribunal to be necessary or expedient, including whether and to what extent the Arbitral Tribunal should itself take the initiative in identifying the issues and ascertaining the relevant facts and the law(s) or rules of law applicable to the arbitration, the merits of the parties' dispute and the Arbitration Agreement;

(d) to order any party to make any property, site or thing under its control and relating to the subject matter of the arbitration available for inspection by the Arbitral Tribunal, any other party, its expert or any expert to the Arbitral Tribunal;

(e) to order any party to produce to the Arbitral Tribunal, and to the other parties for inspection, and to supply copies of, any documents or classes of documents in their possession, custody or power which the Arbitral Tribunal determines to be relevant;

(f) to decide whether or not to apply any strict rules of evidence (or any other rules) as to the admissibility, relevance or weight of any material tendered by a party on any matter of fact or expert opinion; and to determine the time, manner and form in which such material should be exchanged between the parties and presented to the Arbitral Tribunal;

(g) to order the correction of any contract between the parties or the Arbitration Agreement, but only to the extent required to rectify any mistake which the Arbitral Tribunal determines to be common to the parties and then only if and to the extent to which the law(s) or rules of law applicable to the contract or Arbitration Agreement permit such correction; and

(h) to allow, only upon the application of a party, one or more third persons to be joined in the arbitration as a party provided any such third person and the applicant party have consented thereto in writing, and thereafter to make a single final award, or separate awards, in respect of all parties so implicated in the arbitration.

22.2 By agreeing to arbitration under these Rules, the parties shall be treated as having agreed not to apply to any state court or other judicial authority for any order available from the Arbitral Tribunal under Article 22.1, except with the agreement in writing of all parties.

22.3 The Arbitral Tribunal shall decide the parties' dispute in accordance with the law(s) or rules of law chosen by the parties as applicable to the merits of their dispute. If and to the extent that the Arbitral Tribunal determines that the parties have made no such choice, the Arbitral Tribunal shall apply the law(s) or rules of law which it considers appropriate.

22.4 The Arbitral Tribunal shall only apply to the merits of the dispute principles deriving from "ex aequo et bono," "amiable composition" or "honourable engagement" where the parties have so agreed expressly in writing.

Article 23   Jurisdiction of the Arbitral Tribunal

23.1 The Arbitral Tribunal shall have the power to rule on its own jurisdiction, including any objection to the initial or continuing existence, validity or effectiveness of the Arbitration Agreement. For that purpose, an arbitration clause which forms or was intended to form part of another agreement shall be treated as an arbitration agreement independent of that other agreement. A decision by the Arbitral Tribunal that such other agreement is non-existent, invalid or ineffective shall not entail ipso jure the non-existence, invalidity or ineffectiveness of the arbitration clause.

23.2 A plea by a Respondent that the Arbitral Tribunal does not have jurisdiction shall be treated as having been irrevocably waived unless it is raised not later than the Statement of Defence; and a like plea by a Respondent to Counterclaim shall be similarly treated unless it is raised no later than the Statement of Defence to Counterclaim. A plea that the Arbitral Tribunal is exceeding the scope of its authority shall be raised promptly after the Arbitral Tribunal has indicated its intention to decide on the matter alleged by any party to be beyond the scope of its authority, failing which such plea shall also be treated as having been waived irrevocably. In any case, the Arbitral Tribunal may nevertheless admit an untimely plea if it considers the delay justified in the particular circumstances.

23.3 The Arbitral Tribunal may determine the plea to its jurisdiction or authority in an award as to jurisdiction or later in an award on the merits, as it considers appropriate in the circumstances.

23.4 By agreeing to arbitration under these Rules, the parties shall be treated as having agreed not to apply to any state court or other judicial authority for any relief regarding the Arbitral Tribunal's jurisdiction or authority, except with the agreement in writing of all parties to the arbitration or the prior authorisation of the Arbitral Tribunal or following the latter's award ruling on the objection to its jurisdiction or authority.

Article 24   Deposits

24.1 The LCIA Court may direct the parties, in such proportions as it thinks appropriate, to make one or several interim or final payments on account of the costs of the arbitration. Such deposits shall be made to and held by the LCIA and from time to time may be released by the LCIA Court to the arbitrator(s), any expert appointed by the Arbitral Tribunal and the LCIA itself as the arbitration progresses.

24.2 The Arbitral Tribunal shall not proceed with the arbitration without ascertaining at all times from the Registrar or any deputy Registrar that the LCIA is in requisite funds.

24.3 In the event that a party fails or refuses to provide any deposit as directed by the LCIA Court, the LCIA Court may direct the other party or parties to effect a substitute payment to allow the arbitration to proceed (subject to any award on costs). In such circumstances, the party paying the substitute payment shall be entitled to recover that amount as a debt immediately due from the defaulting party.

24.4 Failure by a claimant or counterclaiming party to provide promptly and in full the required deposit may be treated by the LCIA Court and the Arbitral Tribunal as a withdrawal of the claim or counterclaim respectively.

Article 25   Interim and Conservatory Measures

25.1 The Arbitral Tribunal shall have the power, unless otherwise agreed by the parties in writing, on the application of any party:

(a) to order any respondent party to a claim or counterclaim to provide security for all or part of the amount in dispute, by way of deposit or bank guarantee or in any other manner and upon such terms as the Arbitral Tribunal considers appropriate. Such terms may include the provision by the claiming or counterclaiming party of a cross-indemnity, itself secured in such manner as the Arbitral Tribunal considers appropriate, for any costs or losses incurred by such respondent in providing security. The amount of any costs and losses payable under such cross-indemnity may be determined by the Arbitral Tribunal in one or more awards;

(b) to order the preservation, storage, sale or other disposal of any property or thing under the control of any party and relating to the subject matter of the arbitration; and

(c) to order on a provisional basis, subject to final determination in an award, any relief which the Arbitral Tribunal would have power to grant in an award, including a provisional order for the payment of money or the disposition of property as between any parties.

25.2 The Arbitral Tribunal shall have the power, upon the application of a party, to order any claiming or counterclaiming party to provide security for the legal or other costs of any other party by way of deposit or bank guarantee or in any other manner and upon such terms as the Arbitral Tribunal considers appropriate. Such terms may include the provision by that other party of a cross-indemnity, itself secured in such manner as the Arbitral Tribunal considers appropriate, for any costs and losses incurred by such claimant or counterclaimant in providing security. The amount of any costs and losses payable under such cross-indemnity may be determined by the Arbitral Tribunal in one or more awards. In the event that a claiming or counterclaiming party does not comply with any order to provide security, the Arbitral Tribunal may stay that party's claims or counterclaims or dismiss them in an award.

25.3 The power of the Arbitral Tribunal under Article 25.1 shall not prejudice howsoever any party's right to apply to any state court or other judicial authority for interim or conservatory measures before the formation of the Arbitral Tribunal and, in exceptional cases, thereafter. Any application and any order for such measures after the formation of the Arbitral Tribunal shall be promptly communicated by the applicant to the Arbitral Tribunal and all other parties. However, by agreeing to arbitration under these Rules, the parties shall be taken to have agreed not to apply to any state court or other judicial authority for any order for security for its legal or other costs available from the Arbitral Tribunal under Article 25.2.

Article 26   The Award

26.1 The Arbitral Tribunal shall make its award in writing and, unless all parties agree in writing otherwise, shall state the reasons upon which its award is based. The award shall also state the date when the award is made and the seat of the arbitration; and it shall be signed by the Arbitral Tribunal or those of its members assenting to it.

26.2 If any arbitrator fails to comply with the mandatory provisions of any applicable law relating to the making of the award, having been given a reasonable opportunity to do so, the remaining arbitrators may proceed in his absence and state in their award the circumstances of the other arbitrator's failure to participate in the making of the award.

26.3 Where there are three arbitrators and the Arbitral Tribunal fails to agree on any issue, the arbitrators shall decide that issue by a majority. Failing a majority decision on any issue, the chairman of the Arbitral Tribunal shall decide that issue.

26.4 If any arbitrator refuses or fails to sign the award, the signatures of the majority or (failing a majority) of the chairman shall be sufficient, provided that the reason for the omitted signature is stated in the award by the majority or chairman.

26.5 The sole arbitrator or chairman shall be responsible for delivering the award to the LCIA Court, which shall transmit certified copies to the parties provided that the costs of arbitration have been paid to the LCIA in accordance with Article 28.

26.6 An award may be expressed in any currency. The Arbitral Tribunal may order that simple or compound interest shall be paid by any party on any sum awarded at such rates as the Arbitral Tribunal determines to be appropriate, without being bound by legal rates of interest imposed by any state court, in respect of any period which the Arbitral Tribunal determines to be appropriate ending not later than the date upon which the award is complied with.

26.7 The Arbitral Tribunal may make separate awards on different issues at different times. Such awards shall have the same status and effect as any other award made by the Arbitral Tribunal.

26.8 In the event of a settlement of the parties' dispute, the Arbitral Tribunal may render an award recording the settlement if the parties so request in writing (a "Consent Award"), provided always that such award contains an express statement that it is an award made by the parties' consent. A Consent Award need not contain reasons. If the parties do not require a consent award, then on written confirmation by the parties to the LCIA Court that a settlement has been reached, the Arbitral Tribunal shall be discharged and the arbitration proceedings concluded, subject to payment by the parties of any outstanding costs of the arbitration under Article 28.

26.9 All awards shall be final and binding on the parties. By agreeing to arbitration under these Rules, the parties undertake to carry out any award immediately and without any delay (subject only to Article 27); and the parties also waive irrevocably their right to any form of appeal, review or recourse to any state court or other judicial authority, insofar as such waiver may be validly made.

Article 27   Correction of Awards and Additional Awards

27.1 Within 30 days of receipt of any award, or such lesser period as may be agreed in writing by the parties, a party may by written notice to the Registrar (copied to all other parties) request the Arbitral Tribunal to correct in the award any errors in computation, clerical or typographical errors or any errors of a similar nature. If the Arbitral Tribunal considers the request to be justified, it shall make the corrections within 30 days of receipt of the request. Any correction shall take the form of separate memorandum dated and signed by the Arbitral Tribunal or (if three arbitrators) those of its members assenting to it; and such memorandum shall become part of the award for all purposes.

27.2 The Arbitral Tribunal may likewise correct any error of the nature described in Article 27.1 on its own initiative within 30 days of the date of the award, to the same effect.

27.3 Within 30 days of receipt of the final award, a party may by written notice to the Registrar (copied to all other parties), request the Arbitral Tribunal to make an additional award as to claims or counterclaims presented in the arbitration but not determined in any award. If the Arbitral Tribunal considers the request to be justified, it shall make the additional award within 60 days of receipt of the request. The provisions of Article 26 shall apply to any additional award.

Article 28   Arbitration and Legal Costs

28.1 The costs of the arbitration (other than the legal or other costs incurred by the parties themselves) shall be determined by the LCIA Court in accordance with the Schedule of Costs. The parties shall be jointly and severally liable to the Arbitral Tribunal and the LCIA for such arbitration costs.

28.2 The Arbitral Tribunal shall specify in the award the total amount of the costs of the arbitration as determined by the LCIA Court. Unless the parties agree otherwise in writing, the Arbitral Tribunal shall determine the proportions in which the parties shall bear all or part of such arbitration costs. If the Arbitral Tribunal has determined that all or any part of the arbitration costs shall be borne by a party other than a party which has already paid them to the LCIA, the latter party shall have the right to recover the appropriate amount from the former party.

28.3 The Arbitral Tribunal shall also have the power to order in its award that all or part of the legal or other costs incurred by a party be paid by another party, unless the parties agree otherwise in writing. The Arbitral Tribunal shall determine and fix the amount of each item comprising such costs on such reasonable basis as it thinks fit.

28.4 Unless the parties otherwise agree in writing, the Arbitral Tribunal shall make its orders on both arbitration and legal costs on the general principle that costs should reflect the parties' relative success and failure in the award or arbitration, except where it appears to the Arbitral Tribunal that in the particular circumstances this general approach is inappropriate. Any order for costs shall be made with reasons in the award containing such order.

28.5 If the arbitration is abandoned, suspended or concluded, by agreement or otherwise, before the final award is made, the parties shall remain jointly and severally liable to pay to the LCIA and the Arbitral Tribunal the costs of the arbitration as determined by the LCIA Court in accordance with the Schedule of Costs. In the event that such arbitration costs are less than the deposits made by the parties, there shall be a refund by the LCIA in such proportion as the parties may agree in writing, or failing such agreement, in the same proportions as the deposits were made by the parties to the LCIA.

Article 29   Decisions by the LCIA Court

29.1 The decisions of the LCIA Court with respect to all matters relating to the arbitration shall be conclusive and binding upon the parties and the Arbitral Tribunal. Such decisions are to be treated as administrative in nature and the LCIA Court shall not be required to give any reasons.

29.2 To the extent permitted by the law of the seat of the arbitration, the parties shall be taken to have waived any right of appeal or review in respect of any such decisions of the LCIA Court to any state court or other judicial authority. If such appeals or review remain possible due to mandatory provisions of any applicable law, the LCIA Court shall, subject to the provisions of that applicable law, decide whether the arbitral proceedings are to continue, notwithstanding an appeal or review.

Article 30   Confidentiality

30.1 Unless the parties expressly agree in writing to the contrary, the parties undertake as a general principle to keep confidential all awards in their arbitration, together with all materials in the proceedings created for the purpose of the arbitration and all other documents produced by another party in the proceedings not otherwise in the public domain — save and to the extent that disclosure may be required of a party by legal duty, to protect or pursue a legal right or to enforce or challenge an award in bona fide legal proceedings before a state court or other judicial authority. 30.2 The deliberations of the Arbitral Tribunal are likewise confidential to its members, save and to the extent that disclosure of an arbitrator's refusal to participate in the arbitration is required of the other members of the Arbitral Tribunal under Articles 10, 12 and 26. 30.3 The LCIA Court does not publish any award or any part of an award without the prior written consent of all parties and the Arbitral Tribunal.

Article 31   Exclusion of Liability

31.1 None of the LCIA, the LCIA Court (including its President, Vice- Presidents and individual members), the Registrar, any deputy Registrar, any arbitrator and any expert to the Arbitral Tribunal shall be liable to any party howsoever for any act or omission in connection with any arbitration conducted by reference to these Rules, save where the act or omission is shown by that party to constitute conscious and deliberate wrongdoing committed by the body or person alleged to be liable to that party.

31.2 After the award has been made and the possibilities of correction and additional awards referred to in Article 27 have lapsed or been exhausted, neither the LCIA, the LCIA Court (including its President, Vice-Presidents and individual members), the Registrar, any deputy Registrar, any arbitrator or expert to the Arbitral Tribunal shall be under any legal obligation to make any statement to any person about any matter concerning the arbitration, nor shall any party seek to make any of these persons a witness in any legal or other proceedings arising out of the arbitration.

Article 32   General Rules

32.1 A party who knows that any provision of the Arbitration Agreement (including these Rules) has not been complied with and yet proceeds with the arbitration without promptly stating its objection to such non-compliance, shall be treated as having irrevocably waived its right to object.

32.2 In all matters not expressly provided for in these Rules, the LCIA Court, the Arbitral Tribunal and the parties shall act in the spirit of these Rules and shall make every reasonable effort to ensure that an award is legally enforceable.

Schedule of Arbitration Costs
(effective 1 July 2012)

For all arbitrations in which the LCIA provides services, whether as administrator, or as appointing authority only, and whether under the LCIA Rules, UNCITRAL Rules or other, ad hoc, rules or procedures agreed by the parties to the arbitration.

1. **Administrative charges under LCIA Rules, UNCITRAL Rules, or other, ad hoc, rules or procedures***

1(a) Registration Fee (payable in advance with Request for Arbitration non-refundable).

£1,750

1(b) Time spent** by the Secretariat of the LCIA in the administration of the

---

* Charges may be subject to Value Added Tax at the prevailing rate.

** Minimum unit of time in all cases: 15 minutes.

arbitration.***

Registrar / Deputy Registrar / Counsel   £225 per hour
Other Secretariat personnel depending   £100 or £150 per hour
on activity

1(c) Time spent by members of the LCIA Court in carrying out their functions in deciding any challenge brought under the applicable rules.***

At hourly rates advised by members of the LCIA Court

1(d) A sum equivalent to 5% of the fees of the Tribunal (excluding expenses) in respect of the LCIA's general overhead.***

1(e) Expenses incurred by the Secretariat and by members of the LCIA Court, in connection with the arbitration (such as postage, telephone, facsimile, travel etc.), and additional arbitration support services, whether provided by the Secretariat or the members of the LCIA Court from their own resources or otherwise.***

At applicable hourly rates or at cost

1(f) The LCIA's fees and expenses will be invoiced in sterling, but may be paid in other convertible currencies, at rates prevailing at the time of payment, provided that any transfer and/or currency exchange charges shall be borne by the payer.

2. Request to act as Appointing Authority only*

2(a) Appointment Fee (payable in advance with request – non-refundable).

£1,250

2(b) As for 1(b) and 1(e), above.

3. Request to act in deciding challenges to arbitrators in non-LCIA arbitrations*

3(a) As for 2(a) and 2(b), above; plus

3(b) Time spent by members of the LCIA Court in carrying out their functions in deciding the challenges.

At hourly rates advised by members of the LCIA Court

*** Items 1(b), 1(c), 1(d) and 1(e) above, are payable on interim invoice; with the award, or as directed by the LCIA Court under Article 24.1 of the Rules.

*** Items 1(b), 1(c), 1(d) and 1(e) above, are payable on interim invoice; with the award, or as directed by the LCIA Court under Article 24.1 of the Rules.

*** Items 1(b), 1(c), 1(d) and 1(e) above, are payable on interim invoice; with the award, or as directed by the LCIA Court under Article 24.1 of the Rules.

*** Items 1(b), 1(c), 1(d) and 1(e) above, are payable on interim invoice; with the award, or as directed by the LCIA Court under Article 24.1 of the Rules.

* Charges may be subject to Value Added Tax at the prevailing rate.

* Charges may be subject to Value Added Tax at the prevailing rate.

4.   Fees and expenses of the Tribunal*

4(a) The Tribunal's fees will be calculated by reference to work done by its members in connection with the arbitration and will be charged at rates appropriate to the particular circumstances of the case, including its complexity and the special qualifications of the arbitrators. The Tribunal shall agree in writing upon fee rates conforming to this Schedule of Arbitration Costs prior to its appointment by the LCIA Court. The rates will be advised by the Registrar to the parties at the time of the appointment of the Tribunal, but may be reviewed annually if the duration of the arbitration requires.

Fees shall be at hourly rates not exceeding £450

However, in exceptional cases, the rate may be higher provided that, in such cases, (a) the fees of the Tribunal shall be fixed by the LCIA Court on the recommendation of the Registrar, following consultations with the arbitrator(s), and (b) the fees shall be agreed expressly by all parties.

4(b) The Tribunal's fees may include a charge for time spent travelling.

4(c) The Tribunal's fees may also include a charge for time reserved but not used as a result of late postponement or cancellation of hearings, provided that the basis for such charge shall be advised in writing to, and approved by, the LCIA Court.

4(d) The Tribunal may also recover such expenses as are reasonably incurred in connection with the arbitration, and as are in a reasonable amount, provided that claims for expenses should be supported by invoices or receipts.

4(e) The Tribunal's fees may be invoiced either in the currency of account between the Tribunal and the parties, or in sterling. The Tribunal's expenses may be invoiced in the currency in which they were incurred, or in sterling.

4(f) In the event of the revocation of the appointment of any arbitrator, pursuant to the provisions of Article 10 of the LCIA Rules, the LCIA Court shall decide upon the amount of fees and expenses to be paid for the former arbitrator's services (if any) as it may consider appropriate in all the circumstances.

5.   Deposits

5(a) The LCIA Court may direct the parties, in such proportions as it thinks appropriate, to make one or several interim or final payments on account of the costs of the arbitration. The LCIA Court may limit such payments to a sum sufficient to cover fees, expenses and costs for the next stage of the arbitration.

5(b) The Tribunal shall not proceed with the arbitration without ascertaining at all times from the Registrar or any deputy Registrar that the LCIA is in requisite funds.

5(c) In the event that a party fails or refuses to provide any deposit as directed by the LCIA Court, the LCIA Court may direct the other party or parties to effect a substitute payment to allow the arbitration to proceed (subject to any award on costs). In such circumstances, the party paying the substitute payment shall be

---

*   Charges may be subject to Value Added Tax at the prevailing rate.

entitled to recover that amount as a debt immediately due from the defaulting party.

5(d) Failure by a claimant or counterclaiming party to provide promptly and in full the required deposit may be treated by the LCIA Court and the Arbitral Tribunal as a withdrawal of the claim or counterclaim, respectively.

5(e) Funds lodged by the parties on account of the fees and expenses of the Tribunal and of the LCIA are held on trust in client bank accounts which are controlled by reference to each individual case and are disbursed by the LCIA, in accordance with the LCIA Rules and with this Schedule of Arbitration Fees and Costs. In the event that funds lodged by the parties exceed the costs of the arbitration at the conclusion of the arbitration, surplus monies will be returned to the parties as the ultimate default beneficiaries under the trust.

6. Interest on deposits

Interest on sums deposited shall be credited to the account of each party depositing them, at the rate applicable to an amount equal to the amount so credited.

7. Interim payments

When interim payments are required to cover the LCIA's administrative costs, or the fees or expenses of members of the LCIA Court, or the Tribunal's fees or expenses, including the fees or expenses of any expert appointed by the Tribunal, such payments may be made against the invoices of any of the above from funds held on deposit. If no or insufficient funds are held at the time the interim payment is required, the invoices of any of the above may be submitted for payment direct by the parties.

8. Registrar's authority

8(a) For the purposes of sections 5(a) and 5(c) above, and of Articles 24.1 and 24.3 of the LCIA Rules, the Registrar has the authority of the LCIA Court to make the directions referred to, under the supervision of the Court.

8(b) For the purposes of section 7(a) above, and of Article 24.1 of the LCIA Rules, the Registrar has the authority of the LCIA Court to approve the payments referred to.

8(c) Any request by an arbitrator for payment on account of his fees shall be supported by a fee note, which shall include, or be accompanied by, details of the time spent at the rates that have been advised to the parties by the LCIA.

8(d) Any dispute regarding administration costs or the fees and expenses of the Tribunal shall be determined by the LCIA Court.

9. Arbitration costs

9(a) The parties shall be jointly and severally liable to the Arbitral Tribunal and the LCIA for the arbitration costs (other than the legal or other costs incurred by the parties themselves).

9(b) The Tribunal's Award(s) shall be transmitted to the parties by the LCIA

Court provided that the costs of the arbitration have been paid in accordance with Article 28 of the LCIA Rules.

RESTATEMENT (THIRD) OF THE U.S. LAW OF INTERNATIONAL COMMERCIAL ARBITRATION*

Tentative Draft No. 2 (April 2012)

§ 1-1. Definitions

(a) An "arbitral award" is a decision in writing by an arbitral tribunal that sets forth the final and binding determination on the merits of a claim, defense, or issue, regardless of whether that decision resolves the entire controversy before the tribunal. Such a decision may consist of a grant of interim relief.

(b) An "arbitral tribunal" is a body consisting of one or more persons designated directly or indirectly by the parties to an arbitration agreement and empowered by them to adjudicate a dispute that has arisen between or among them.

(c) "Arbitration" is a dispute resolution method in which the disputing parties empower an arbitral tribunal to decide a dispute in a final and binding manner.

(d) An "arbitration agreement" is an agreement by which parties consent to submit one or more existing or future disputes to resolution by an arbitral tribunal.

(e) "Commercial" matters or relationships are those matters or relationships, whether contractual or not, that arise out of or in connection with commerce.

(f) A "competent authority" is a court or other body that is empowered to entertain set-aside proceedings with respect to a particular arbitral award and that is either part of the legal system of the arbitral seat or of a legal system whose arbitration law was designated unambiguously by the parties to govern the arbitral proceedings that produced the award.

(g) "Confirmation" is a determination that reduces to judgment a Convention award made in the United States.

(h) A "Convention award" is an arbitral award that is either a New York Convention award or a Panama Convention award. A "Convention award" does not include an award rendered in an arbitration governed by the Convention on the Settlement of Investment Disputes between States and Nationals of Other States ("ICSID Convention").

(i) A "Convention award made in the United States" (or "U.S. Convention award") is an international arbitral award rendered in the United States that arises out of a legal relationship involving property located abroad, envisaging performance or enforcement abroad, or having some other reasonable relation with one or more foreign States.

(j) A "court" is any court within the United States.

(k) A "domestic award" is an arbitral award that has no reasonable relation with

---

one or more foreign States.

(l) "Enforcement" is the reduction to a judgment of an international arbitral award, other than a Convention award made in the United States.

(m) "Execution" is the granting of relief provided in a judgment through measures ordered by or under the auspices of a court.

(n) The "final award" means the last award that the tribunal makes with respect to the particular dispute before it.

(o) A "foreign award" is an international arbitral award made in an arbitration seated outside the United States.

(p) A "foreign State" is an entity other than the United States that is recognized as a State under international law.

(q) An "interim measure" is a grant of temporary relief by an arbitral tribunal to preserve the status quo, help ensure the satisfaction of a subsequent award, or otherwise protect the rights of one or more parties and promote the efficacy of an arbitration and the resulting award. An interim measure is presumptively treated as a partial award.

A competent court may also order interim relief in aid of arbitration, which is distinguishable from interim measures granted by an arbitral tribunal and which is referred to as "provisional relief."

(r) An "international arbitral award" is an arbitral award that, by virtue of its reasonable relation with one or more foreign States, is not a domestic award. The term includes Convention awards (both foreign awards and Convention awards made in the United States) and non-Convention awards. An "international arbitral award" does not include an award rendered in an arbitration governed by the ICSID Convention.

(s) An arbitral award is "made" when under the arbitration law governing the proceedings that gave rise to the award it is deemed to come into existence.

(t) A "New York Convention award" is an arbitral award that is subject to the provisions of the Convention on the Recognition and Enforcement of Foreign Arbitral Awards ("New York Convention").

(u) A "non-Convention award" is a foreign award that is not a New York Convention award or Panama Convention award.

(v) A "Panama Convention award" is an arbitral award that is subject to the provisions of the Inter-American Convention on International Commercial Arbitration ("Panama Convention").

(w) A "partial award" is an arbitral award that disposes of some, but not all, of the claims, defenses, or issues before the arbitral tribunal. A partial award does not include an order addressing scheduling, procedural, or evidentiary matters.

(x) A "post-award action" is a summary court proceeding brought to vacate, confirm, or enforce an international award.

(y) "Post-award relief" is a ruling by a court that vacates, confirms, recognizes, or enforces an international arbitral award.

(z) "Recognition" is a determination by a court or other tribunal that an international arbitral award is presumptively entitled to preclusive effect with respect to one or more matters determined therein.

(aa) The "seat" (or "arbitral seat") is the jurisdiction designated by the parties or by an entity empowered to do so on their behalf to be the juridical home of the arbitration. An arbitral proceeding is ordinarily governed by the arbitration law of the jurisdiction in which it is seated, and the resulting award is deemed made in that jurisdiction.

(bb) A "set-aside proceeding" is a legal action by which a party seeks to have an arbitral award annulled by a competent authority.

(cc) A "state" is a commonwealth, district, state, or territory of the United States.

(dd) The "United States" is all territory and waters subject to the jurisdiction of the United States.

§ 4-1. Post-Award Actions — Generally

(a) A party may seek confirmation of a U.S. Convention award in a competent court of the United States. A court confirms such an award unless a ground for vacatur set out in §§ 4-12 through 4-18 is established. If confirmed, the award becomes a judgment of the confirming court.

(b) A party may seek vacatur of a U.S. Convention award in a competent court of the United States. A court vacates such an award only on the grounds set out in §§ 4-12 through 4-18. If vacated, the award becomes a nullity within the jurisdiction of the court.

(c) The defendant in a proceeding to confirm or vacate a U.S. Convention award may, in addition to defending against that action and in accordance with applicable procedural rules, make a cross-motion to confirm or vacate the award. The law of the forum on compulsory counterclaims governs whether such relief must be sought by cross-motion or may be sought through an independent proceeding.

(d) A party may seek enforcement of a foreign award in a competent court of the United States. A court enforces a foreign Convention award unless a ground for denying enforcement set out in §§ 4-12 through 4-18 is established. A court enforces a foreign non-Convention award unless a ground for denying enforcement set out in §§ 4-19 through 4-22 is established. If enforced, the award becomes a judgment of the enforcing court.

(e) A court may grant partial post-award relief regarding an international arbitral award. A grant of partial post-award relief is appropriate only if the portion of the award as to which relief is granted is reasonably separable from the remainder of the award and is otherwise eligible for the relief requested.

§ 4-2. No Authority to Vacate Foreign Awards

A court may not vacate a foreign award, unless the parties expressly agreed that the arbitration proceeding was to be governed by federal arbitration law or state arbitration law.

§ 4-3. Law Applicable to Post-Award Relief

(a) The law applicable to confirmation or vacatur of a U.S. Convention award and to recognition or enforcement of a foreign Convention award is:

   (1) the relevant Convention as implemented by the Federal Arbitration Act; or

   (2) state law, to the extent it is not preempted by applicable federal law.

(b) The law applicable to recognition or enforcement of a non-Convention award is:

   (1) Chapter One of the Federal Arbitration Act; or

   (2) state law, to the extent it is not preempted by applicable federal law.

(c) In giving effect to the grounds set forth in §§ 4-12 through 4-18 and §§ 4-19 through 4-22, a court may be required to interpret and apply the law of a foreign jurisdiction.

(d) If a foreign award has been reduced to judgment by a court in the arbitral seat, a party may seek either:

   (1) recognition or enforcement of the award in accordance with the provisions of this Chapter; or

   (2) recognition or enforcement of the judgment in accordance with the foreign judgment recognition and enforcement standards of the forum in which such relief is sought.

§ 4-4. Formal Requirements for Post-Award Relief

(a) A party seeking confirmation of a U.S. Convention award or recognition or enforcement of a foreign award must:

   (1) if in federal court, submit the original or an authenticated copy of the arbitration agreement and arbitral award; or

   (2) if in state court, comply with the formal filing requirements of the law of the forum to the extent that those requirements are not preempted by federal law.

(b) The arbitration agreement referred to in paragraph (a)(1) must be an "agreement in writing" as defined in § 2-___.

(c) A party seeking vacatur of a U.S. Convention award must:

   (1) if in federal court, submit the original or an authenticated copy of the arbitral award; or

   (2) if in state court, comply with the formal filing requirements of the law of the forum to the extent that those requirements are not preempted by federal law.

(d) Whether vacatur or confirmation of a U.S. Convention award or recognition or enforcement of a foreign award is sought in federal or state court, the materials referred to in subsections (a) and (c) must be in a language that the court accepts for filings, or, if the original is not in such a language, must be accompanied by an accurate and certified translation into such language.

§ 4-5. Reciprocity

(a) Recognition or enforcement of a Convention award is subject to a requirement of reciprocity. The requirement is satisfied if the seat of the arbitration that produced the award is a Contracting State to the applicable Convention. Recognition or enforcement of a Convention award is not subject to any other reciprocity requirement.

(b) Recognition or enforcement of a non-Convention award is not subject to any reciprocity requirement unless recognition or enforcement is sought under a treaty or state arbitration law that imposes such a requirement.

§ 4-6. Burden of Proof for Post-Award Relief

(a) A party seeking confirmation of a U.S. Convention award or recognition or enforcement of a foreign award bears the burden of satisfying the requirements of § 4-4(a) and (b).

(b) A party seeking vacatur or opposing confirmation of a U.S. Convention award or opposing recognition or enforcement of a foreign Convention award bears the burden of establishing the existence of one or more of the grounds set forth in §§ 4-12 through 4-18.

(c) A party opposing recognition or enforcement of a non-Convention award bears the burden of establishing the existence of one or more of the grounds set forth in §§ 4-19 through 4-22.

§ 4-7. Standard of Review for Granting Post-Award Relief

(a) Except as provided in §§ 4-12 through 4-18, a court determines de novo whether a ground exists to vacate or deny confirmation of a U.S. Convention award or to deny recognition or enforcement of a foreign Convention award.

(b) Except as provided in §§ 4-19 through 4-22, a court determines de novo whether a ground exists to deny recognition or enforcement of a non-Convention award.

§ 4-8. Effect of Prior Judicial Determinations on the Grant of Post-Award Relief

In deciding whether to grant post-award relief, a court may reexamine a matter decided at an earlier stage of the proceedings by a court within the United States or by a foreign court, to the extent consistent with the forum's applicable principles governing the law of the case, claim and issue preclusion, and recognition of foreign judgments.

§ 4-9. Claim Preclusion

A court precludes relitigation of a claim that was previously adjudicated in an international arbitral award to the extent that the party seeking preclusive effect demonstrates that the award:

(a) is entitled to recognition under this Chapter;

(b) involves the same parties and the same claim as required by the law of the court in which claim preclusion is sought; and

(c) barring relitigation of the claim is consistent with the arbitration agreement and the reasonable expectations of the parties.

§ 4-10. Issue Preclusion

A court precludes relitigation of a specific issue of fact or law made by an international arbitral award if:

(a) the award is entitled to recognition under this Chapter;

(b) the award satisfies the requirements for issue preclusion prescribed for an arbitral award by the law of the forum in which such recognition is sought, and

(c) barring relitigation of the issue is consistent with the arbitration agreement and the reasonable expectations of the parties.

§ 4-11. Grounds for Post-Award Relief — Generally

(a) A court may vacate or deny confirmation, recognition, or enforcement of a Convention award only on the grounds set forth in §§ 4-12 through 4-18.

(b) A court may deny recognition or enforcement of a non-Convention award only on the grounds set forth in §§ 4-19 through 4-22.

(c) A court may, in exceptional circumstances:

(1) confirm or decline to vacate a U.S. Convention award notwithstanding the existence of a ground for vacatur; or

(2) recognize or enforce a foreign award notwithstanding the existence of a ground for denying recognition or enforcement.

§ 4-12. Arbitration Agreement Does Not Exist or Is Invalid

(a) A court may vacate or deny confirmation of a U.S. Convention award or deny recognition or enforcement of a foreign Convention award to the extent that no arbitration agreement exists or the arbitration agreement is invalid.

(b) Whether the arbitration agreement referred to in paragraph (a) does not exist, or whether a party lacked capacity to enter into the arbitration agreement, is determined by the law applicable to that issue under the choice-of-law rules of the forum where post-award relief is sought.

(c) Whether the arbitration agreement referred to in paragraph (a) is invalid is determined by the law to which the parties have subjected the arbitration agreement or, if no such law has been selected, by the law identified in the general choice-of-law clause in the underlying contract or, in the absence of such a clause, by the law of the seat of arbitration.

(d) Under this Section, a court does not review the arbitral tribunal's determination of the validity of a contract that includes the arbitration agreement. However, a court determines de novo (1) the existence of the arbitration agreement, (2) the validity of the arbitration agreement, unless the parties clearly and unmistakably submitted the validity issue to arbitration, and (3) the existence of the contract that includes the arbitration agreement.

§ 4-13. Denial of Notice or Opportunity to Present Case

(a) A court may vacate or deny confirmation of a U.S. Convention award or deny recognition or enforcement of a foreign Convention award to the extent that the party opposing such grant of relief did not receive adequate notice of the appointment of the arbitral tribunal or of other important phases of the arbitration proceedings.

(b) A court may vacate or deny confirmation of a U.S. Convention award or deny recognition or enforcement of a foreign Convention award to the extent that a serious procedural defect in the arbitral process resulted in a material denial of the party's opportunity to present its case or to rebut its opponent's case.

(c) A party is denied an opportunity to present its case or rebut its opponent's case under this Section to the extent that the court finds evident partiality by an arbitrator. Evident partiality exists when there is proof that would cause an objective, disinterested observer who is fully informed of the relevant facts related to the arbitrator's conduct or alleged conflicts to develop a serious doubt regarding the fundamental fairness of the arbitral proceedings.

(d) The adequacy of notice and of a party's opportunity to present its case under this Section is determined by reference to federal law and, to the extent not in conflict with federal law, state law.

§ 4-14. Award on Matters Beyond the Terms of the Submission to Arbitration

(a) A court may vacate or deny confirmation of a U.S. Convention award or deny recognition or enforcement of a foreign Convention award to the extent that it deals with matters that were not submitted to arbitration. An award deals with matters that were not submitted to arbitration if (i) it resolves claims or issues not encompassed by the arbitration agreement or (ii) it is based on the exercise by the arbitral tribunal of authority expressly denied to it by the parties' agreement.

(b) Whether a Convention award deals with matters that were not submitted to arbitration is determined by the law to which the parties have subjected the arbitration agreement or, if no such law has been selected, by the law identified in the general choice-of-law clause in the underlying contract or, in the absence of such a clause, by the law of the seat of arbitration.

(c) A court determines de novo whether a Convention award deals with matters that were not submitted to arbitration. If, however, the parties clearly and unmistakably agreed that the arbitral tribunal would determine the claims or issues encompassed by the arbitration agreement or the effect or validity of the restriction on the arbitral tribunal's authority, the court will not review the tribunal's determination.

§ 4-15. Arbitral Procedure or Composition of Arbitral Tribunal Violates Party Agreement or Law of the Arbitral Seat

(a) A court may vacate or deny confirmation, recognition, or enforcement of a

Convention award to the extent that the composition of the arbitral tribunal or the arbitral procedure is contrary in a material respect to the agreement of the parties or, in the absence of such agreement, to the law of the seat of the arbitration.

(b) In resolving challenges based on alleged violations under this Section, a court affords substantial deference to the procedural decisions of the arbitral tribunal.

§ 4-16. Award Set Aside or Subject to Set-Aside Proceedings

(a) A court may deny confirmation, recognition, or enforcement of a Convention award to the extent that the award has been set aside by a competent authority of the country in which or under the arbitration law of which the award was made.

(b) Even if a Convention award has been set aside by a competent authority, a court of the United States may confirm, recognize, or enforce the award if the judgment setting it aside is not entitled to recognition under the principles governing the recognition of judgments in the court where such relief is sought, or in other extraordinary circumstances.

(c) If a Convention award is the subject of a set-aside proceeding before a competent authority, a court of the United States may defer the decision whether to grant confirmation, recognition, or enforcement pending the outcome of that proceeding.

(d) For purposes of this Section, a Convention award is deemed made under a particular arbitration law if that law is unambiguously designated by the parties to govern the arbitration.

§ 4-17. Award Decides Matters Not Capable of Resolution by Arbitration

(a) A court may vacate or deny confirmation of a U.S. Convention award or deny recognition or enforcement of a foreign Convention award to the extent that the award purports to decide matters that are not capable of resolution by arbitration.

(b) Whether a Convention award decides matters that are not capable of resolution by arbitration is determined by federal law.

(c) A court may examine whether a Convention award decides matters that are not capable of resolution by arbitration even if a party does not raise the issue.

(d) A limitation on arbitrability may be categorical or conditional. An objection that a matter is categorically non-arbitrable cannot be waived. However, if a matter may be arbitrated only if a particular condition is satisfied, an objection that the condition was not satisfied can be waived through a post-dispute agreement or by failure to raise the objection in a clear and timely manner.

§ 4-18. Post-Award Relief Violates Public Policy

(a) A court may vacate or deny confirmation of a U.S. Convention award or deny recognition or enforcement of a foreign Convention award to the extent that the grant of post-award relief would be repugnant to the public policy of the United States.

(b) A court may examine whether the grant of post-award relief referred to in paragraph (a) would be repugnant to public policy even if a party does not raise the issue.

(c) A court generally determines whether a grant of post-award relief referred to in paragraph (a) violates public policy in accordance with federal law. However, in exceptional circumstances, a court may vacate or deny confirmation of a U.S. Convention award or deny recognition or enforcement of a foreign Convention award based on repugnance to the public policy of a state if that state has a sufficiently compelling and predominant interest in the matter, and provided that the state policy is not inconsistent with federal policy.

§ 4-19. Award Procured by Corruption, Fraud, or Undue Means

A court may deny recognition or enforcement of a non-Convention award to the extent that the court finds that the award was procured through corruption, fraud, or undue means.

§ 4-20. Evident Partiality by the Arbitrators

A court may deny recognition or enforcement of a non-Convention award to the extent that the court finds evident partiality on the part of an arbitrator. Evident partiality exists when there is proof that would cause an objective, disinterested observer who is fully informed of the relevant facts relating to the arbitrator's conduct or alleged conflicts to have a serious doubt regarding the fundamental fairness of the arbitral proceedings.

§ 4-21. Arbitrator Misconduct

A court may refuse recognition or enforcement of a non-Convention award to the extent that:

(1) there was misconduct by an arbitrator in unjustifiably refusing to postpone a hearing, improperly refusing to hear pertinent and material evidence, or engaging in other misconduct; and

(2) such misconduct affected the fundamental fairness of the arbitral proceedings or resulted in significant prejudice to the basic procedural rights of a party.

§ 4-22. Arbitral Tribunal Exceeded Its Powers

(a) A court may deny recognition or enforcement of a non-Convention award to the extent that the arbitral tribunal exceeded its powers in making the award.

(b) An arbitral tribunal exceeds its powers in making an award if:

(1) the arbitration agreement does not exist or is invalid under § 4-12;

(2) the arbitral award decides a matter beyond the terms of the submission to arbitration under § 4-14;

(3) the arbitral procedure is contrary in a material respect to the agreement of the parties under § 4-15;

(4) the arbitral award decides a matter not capable of arbitral adjudication under § 4-17; or

(5) recognizing or enforcing the arbitral award would be repugnant to public

policy under § 4-18.

§ 4-23. Agreements to Expand Grounds for Post-Award Relief

(a) Parties may not by agreement expand or supplement the grounds for vacating or denying confirmation of a U.S. Convention award or for denying recognition or enforcement of a foreign Convention award, including by agreeing to subject their dispute to the arbitration law of a state within the United States that allows expanded review or provides grounds for such relief other than those provided in the applicable Convention.

(b) Parties may not by agreement expand or supplement the grounds for denying recognition or enforcement of a non-Convention award, including by agreeing to subject their dispute to the arbitration law of a state within the United States that allows expanded review or provides grounds for such relief other than those provided in Chapter One of the Federal Arbitration Act.

§ 4-24. Agreements to Reduce or Eliminate Grounds for Post-Award Relief

(a) Parties may not by agreement reduce or eliminate the grounds for vacating or denying confirmation of a U.S. Convention award or for denying recognition or enforcement of a foreign Convention award, including by agreeing to subject their dispute to the arbitration law of a state within the United States that allows reduced review or provides fewer grounds for such relief than those provided in the applicable Convention.

(b) Parties may not by agreement reduce or eliminate the grounds for denying recognition or enforcement of a non-Convention award, including by agreeing to subject their dispute to the arbitration law of a state within the United States that allows reduced review or provides fewer grounds for such relief than those provided in the applicable Convention.

§ 4-25. Waiver of Objections

(a) Except as provided in §§ 4-17 and 4-18, a party may at any time waive its right to invoke an objection that would justify a court vacating or denying confirmation, recognition, or enforcement of a Convention award after that party knew or should have known the basis for such objection.

(b) Except as provided in § 4-22(b)(4) and (b)(5), a party may at any time waive its right to invoke an objection that would justify a court in denying recognition and enforcement of a non-Convention award after that party knew or should have known the basis for such objection.

(c) Waiver under paragraphs (a) and (b) may be the result of either express consent or a failure to raise an objection in a clear and timely manner.

(d) A court may vacate or deny confirmation, recognition, or enforcement of a Convention award based on an objection that was not raised by a party only to the extent that such an objection would constitute a ground under §§ 4-17 and 4-18.

(e) A court may deny recognition or enforcement of a non-Convention award based on an objection that was not raised by a party only to the extent that such an objection would constitute a ground under § 4-22(b)(4) and (b)(5).

(f) A party ordinarily does not waive a particular objection merely by failing to bring a timely action to stay the arbitration or by failing to seek to have the award set aside. However, a party waives an objection to the extent that it:

(1) participated in judicial proceedings to enforce the arbitration agreement, to stay the arbitration, or to set aside the award;

(2) knew or should have known at that time the relevant facts underlying an objection; and

(3) failed to raise the objection in any such proceedings.

§ 4-26. Subject Matter Jurisdiction in Post-Award Actions

(a) Federal courts have subject matter jurisdiction over actions to confirm or to vacate a U.S. Convention award and actions to enforce a foreign Convention award.

(b) Federal courts have subject matter jurisdiction over an action to enforce a non-Convention award to the extent that an independent basis of federal subject matter jurisdiction exists.

(c) Unless the parties have designated an exclusive forum for a post-award action:

(1) an action to confirm or vacate a U.S. Convention award may be brought in the federal court in the district within which the award was made or in any other federal court that has jurisdiction over the defendant; and

(2) an action to enforce a foreign award may be brought in any federal court that has jurisdiction over the defendant.

(d) A post-award action may also be brought in a competent state court.

(e) A state court action to confirm or vacate a U.S. Convention award or to enforce a foreign Convention award may be removed to federal court. A state court action to enforce a non-Convention award may be removed to federal court to the extent that an independent basis of federal subject matter jurisdiction exists. A party may seek removal to federal court of a post-award action in state court pursuant either to the specific removal provisions of the Federal Arbitration Act or to other provisions of law applicable to removal.

§ 4-27. Personal Jurisdiction in Post-Award Actions

(a) The adequacy of jurisdiction over the defendant in a post-award action is subject to the generally applicable statutory and constitutional standards governing the exercise of such jurisdiction.

(b) Unless forum law provides otherwise, jurisdiction over the defendant in a post-award action may be based on the presence of the defendant's property within the court's jurisdiction, whether or not the property bears any relationship to the underlying dispute. Whether this exercise of jurisdiction requires the attachment of such property is determined by the forum's rules governing quasi-in-rem jurisdiction. If jurisdiction over the defendant is based solely on the presence of property within the court's jurisdiction, the resulting judgment may be entered only up to the value of that property, or any bond posted in substitution thereof.

§ 4-28.   Sovereign Immunity and Act of State in Post-Award Actions

(a) A post-award action against a foreign State or an agency or instrumentality of a foreign State is not subject, either in state or federal court, to a defense of sovereign immunity as to any claim to which an exception to immunity under the Foreign Sovereign Immunities Act applies.

(b) Execution against property of a foreign State or an agency or instrumentality of a foreign State in an action to confirm a U.S. Convention award or enforce a foreign award is proper to the extent that the property against which execution is sought is not protected from execution under the Foreign Sovereign Immunities Act.

(c) The relief sought in a post-award action may not be refused on the basis of the Act of State doctrine.

§ 4-29.   Forum Non Conveniens in Post-Award Actions

(a) An action to confirm a U.S. Convention award or enforce a foreign Convention award is not subject to a stay or dismissal in favor of a foreign court on forum non conveniens grounds.

(b) An action to vacate a U.S. Convention award may, in exceptional circumstances, be subject to stay or dismissal on forum non conveniens grounds in favor of a foreign court that also has authority to vacate the award, in accordance with the standards generally applicable to forum non conveniens motions in the court where confirmation is sought.

(c) An action to enforce a non-Convention award may, in exceptional circumstances, be subject to stay or dismissal on forum non conveniens grounds in favor of a foreign court, in accordance with the standards generally applicable to forum non conveniens motions in the court where enforcement is sought.

§ 4-30.   Proper Plaintiff

(a) Any person that participates in an arbitral proceeding as a party by asserting or defending against a claim is a proper plaintiff in a post-award action. In addition, any person that the arbitral tribunal determines to be a party to an arbitral proceeding is a proper plaintiff in a post-award action, even if the person did not participate in the arbitral proceeding.

(b) A court may, in exceptional circumstances, determine that a person not a party to an arbitral proceeding is a proper plaintiff in a post-award action if it satisfies one of the grounds on which a non-party is permitted to enforce the arbitration agreement under § 2-___, unless the court, in its discretion, declines to recognize the person as a proper plaintiff because:

(1) determining the status of the non-party in the post-award action would unduly complicate that action, or

(2) the non-party could and reasonably should have participated in the arbitration but failed to do so.

§ 4-31. Proper Defendant

(a) Any person that participates in an arbitral proceeding as a party by asserting or defending against a claim is a proper defendant in a post-award action. In addition, any person that the arbitral tribunal determines to be a party to an arbitral proceeding is a proper defendant in a post-award action, even if the person did not participate in the arbitral proceeding.

(b) A court may, in exceptional circumstances, determine that a person not a party to an arbitral proceeding is a proper defendant in a post-award action if it satisfies one of the grounds on which a non-party would be bound to the arbitration agreement under § 2-___, unless the court, in its discretion, declines to recognize the person as a proper defendant because:

(1) determining the status of the non-party in the post-award action would unduly complicate that action, or

(2) the non-party was improperly excluded from participating in the arbitration.

§ 4-32. Statute of Limitations

(a) The limitations period applicable to a post-award action under federal law and the rules pertaining to its application are governed by federal law, irrespective of whether the action is brought in federal or state court.

(b) The limitations period applicable to a post-award action under state law and the rules pertaining to its application are governed by state law to the extent that they are not preempted by federal law.

(c) The limitations period applicable to a post-award action on an award begins to run on the date the award is issued. A party bringing a post-award action in connection with a partial award may do so within the prescribed limitations period following issuance of either the partial or the final award.

(d) A cross-motion to confirm or to vacate a U.S. Convention award is subject to the same statute of limitations as would apply if the motion were brought independently.

(e) A party opposing confirmation of an award may raise defenses to confirmation, even if the limitations period for seeking vacatur of the award on those grounds has passed.

(f) The applicable limitations period may be tolled by agreement of the parties, except to the extent that the applicable law provides otherwise. It may also be tolled on any other ground recognized under the law designated in paragraphs (a) and (b).

(g) A defense based on an applicable limitations period may be waived, except to the extent that the applicable law provides otherwise.

§ 4-33. Procedural Issues in Post-Award Actions

(a) A post-award action is ordinarily a summary proceeding, whether brought by motion or otherwise.

(b) Notwithstanding paragraph (a), in exceptional circumstances a court may order discovery or receive evidence to the extent necessary to determine relevant issues of fact.

§ 4-34. Appeal in Post-Award Action

(a) A party to a post-award action in federal court has a right of appeal from the final disposition of the action.

(b) A party to a post-award action in state court has a right of appeal from the final disposition of the action to the extent that it is permitted by the law of the forum and not preempted by federal law.

(c) An appeal from the final disposition of a post-award action, whether in federal or state court, is subject to the forum's general rules of appellate procedure.

§ 4-35. Correction and Modification of Convention Awards Made in the United States

A court may correct or modify a U.S. Convention award to the extent that:

(a) the award contains an evident and material miscalculation of figures;

(b) the award contains an evident and material mistake in the description of any person, thing, or property;

(c) the form of the award is imperfect in a way that does not affect the substantive outcome of the proceeding; or

(d) the award determines a matter not submitted to the arbitral tribunal, unless the determination does not affect the substantive outcome of the proceeding.

§ 4-36. Remand to the Arbitral Tribunal of Convention Awards Made in the United States

A court may in exceptional circumstances remand a U.S. Convention award to the arbitral tribunal with instructions to complete the award or to clarify its meaning.

A DUE PROCESS PROTOCOL FOR MEDIATION AND ARBITRATION OF STATUTORY DISPUTES ARISING OUT OF THE EMPLOYMENT RELATIONSHIP*

The following protocol is offered by the undersigned individuals, members of the Task Force on Alternative Dispute Resolution in Employment, as a means of providing due process in the resolution by mediation and binding arbitration of employment disputes involving statutory rights. The signatories were designated by their respective organizations, but the protocol reflects their personal views and should not be construed as representing the policy of the designating organizations.

Genesis

This Task Force was created by individuals from diverse organizations involved in labor and employment law to examine questions of due process arising out of the use of mediation and arbitration for resolving employment disputes. In this protocol we confine ourselves to statutory disputes.

The members of the Task Force felt that mediation and arbitration of statutory disputes conducted under proper due process safeguards should be encouraged in order to provide expeditious, accessible, inexpensive and fair private enforcement of statutory employment disputes for the 100,000,000 members of the workforce who might not otherwise have ready, effective access to administrative or judicial relief. They also hope that such a system will serve to reduce the delays which now arise out of the huge backlog of cases pending before administrative agencies and courts and that it will help forestall an even greater number of such cases.

A. Pre or Post Dispute Arbitration

The Task Force recognizes the dilemma inherent in the timing of an agreement to mediate and/or arbitrate statutory disputes. It did not achieve consensus on this difficult issue. The views in this spectrum are set forth randomly, as follows:

- Employers should be able to create mediation and/or arbitration systems to resolve statutory claims, but any agreement to mediate and/or arbitrate disputes should be informed, voluntary, and not a condition of initial or continued employment.

- Employers should have the right to insist on an agreement to mediate and/or arbitrate statutory disputes as a condition of initial or continued employment.

- Postponing such an agreement until a dispute actually arises, when there will likely exist a stronger re-disposition to litigate, will result in very few agreements to mediate and/or arbitrate, thus negating the likelihood of effectively utilizing alternative dispute resolution and overcoming the problems of administrative and judicial delays which now plague the system.

- Employees should not be permitted to waive their right to judicial relief of statutory claims arising out of the employment relationship for any reason.

- Employers should be able to create mediation and/or arbitration systems to resolve statutory claims, but the decision to mediate and/or arbitrate individual cases should not be made until after the dispute arises.

- The Task Force takes no position on the timing of agreements to mediate and/or arbitrate statutory employment disputes, though it agrees that such agreements be knowingly made. The focus of this protocol is on standards of exemplary due process.

B. Right of Representation

1. Choice of Representative

Employees considering the use of or, in fact, utilizing mediation and/or arbitration procedures should have the right to be represented by a spokesperson of their own choosing. The mediation and arbitration procedure should so specify and should include reference to institutions which might offer assistance, such as bar associations, legal service associations, civil rights organizations, trade unions, etc.

2. Fees for Representation

The amount and method of payment for representation should be determined between the claimant and the representative. We recommend, however, a number of existing systems which provide employer reimbursement of at least a portion of the employee's attorney fees, especially for lower paid employees. The arbitrator should have the authority to provide for fee reimbursement, in whole or in part, as part of the remedy in accordance with applicable law or in the interests of justice.

3. Access to Information

One of the advantages of arbitration is that there is usually less time and money spent in pre-trial discovery. Adequate but limited pre-trial discovery is to be encouraged and employees should have access to all information reasonably relevant to mediation and/or arbitration of their claims. The employees' representative should also have reasonable pre-hearing and hearing access to all such information and documentation.

Necessary pre-hearing depositions consistent with the expedited nature of arbitration should be available. We also recommend that prior to selection of an arbitrator, each side should be provided with the names, addresses and phone numbers of the representatives of the parties in that arbitrator's six most recent cases to aid them in selection.

C. Mediator and Arbitrator Qualification

1. Roster Membership

Mediators and arbitrators selected for such cases should have skill in the conduct of hearings, knowledge of the statutory issues at stake in the dispute, and familiarity with the workplace and employment environment. The roster of available mediators and arbitrators should be established on a non-discriminatory basis, diverse by gender, ethnicity, background, experience, etc. to satisfy the parties that their interest and objectives will be respected and fully considered.

Our recommendation is for selection of impartial arbitrators and mediators. We recognize the right of employers and employees to jointly select as mediator and/or arbitrator one in whom both parties have requisite trust, even though not possessing the qualifications here recommended, as most promising to bring finality and to withstand judicial scrutiny. The existing cadre of labor and employment mediators and arbitrators, some lawyers, some not, although skilled in conducting hearings and familiar with the employment milieu is unlikely, without special training, to consistently possess knowledge of the statutory environment in which these disputes arise and of the characteristics of the non-union workplace. There is a manifest need for mediators and arbitrators with expertise in statutory require-ments in the employment field who may, without special training, lack experience in the employment area and in the conduct of arbitration hearings and mediation sessions. Reexamination of rostering eligibility by designating agencies, such as the American Arbitration Association, may permit the expedited inclusion in the pool of this most valuable source of expertise.

The roster of arbitrators and mediators should contain representatives with all such skills in order to meet the diverse needs of this caseload.

Regardless of their prior experience, mediators and arbitrators on the roster must be independent of bias toward either party. They should reject cases if they believe the procedure lacks requisite due process.

2. Training

The creation of a roster containing the foregoing qualifications dictates the development of a training program to educate existing and potential labor and employment mediators and arbitrators as to the statutes, including substantive, procedural and remedial issues to be confronted and to train experts in the statutes as to employer procedures governing the employment relationship as well as due process and fairness in the conduct and control of arbitration hearings and mediation sessions.

Training in the statutory issues should be provided by the government agencies, bar associations, academic institutions, etc., administered perhaps by the designat-ing agency, such as the AAA, at various locations throughout the country. Such training should be updated periodically and be required of all mediators and arbitrators. Training in the conduct of mediation and arbitration could be provided by a mentoring program with experienced panelists.

Successful completion of such training would be reflected in the resume or panel cards of the arbitrators supplied to the parties for their selection process.

3. Panel Selection

Upon request of the parties, the designating agency should utilize a list procedure such as that of the AAA or select a panel composed of an odd number of mediators and arbitrators from its roster or pool. The panel cards for such individuals should be submitted to the parties for their perusal prior to alternate striking of the names on the list, resulting in the designation of the remaining mediator and/or arbitrator.

The selection process could empower the designating agency to appoint a mediator and/or arbitrator if the striking procedure is unacceptable or unsuccessful. As noted above, subject to the consent of the parties, the designating agency should provide the names of the parties and their representatives in recent cases decided by the listed arbitrators.

4. Conflicts of Interest

The mediator and arbitrator for a case has a duty to disclose any relationship which might reasonably constitute or be perceived as a conflict of interest. The designated mediator and/or arbitrator should be required to sign an oath provided by the designating agency, if any, affirming the absence of such present or preexisting ties.

5. Authority of the Arbitrator

The arbitrator should be bound by applicable agreements, statutes, regulations and rules of procedure of the designating agency, including the authority to determine the time and place of the hearing, permit reasonable discovery, issue subpoenas, decide arbitrability issues, preserve order and privacy in the hearings, rule on evidentiary matters, determine the close of the hearing and procedures for post-hearing submissions, and issue an award resolving the submitted dispute.

The arbitrator should be empowered to award whatever relief would be available in court under the law. The arbitrator should issue an opinion and award setting forth a summary of the issues, including the type(s) of dispute(s), the damages and/or other relief requested and awarded, a statement of any other issues resolved, and a statement regarding the disposition of any statutory claim(s).

6. Compensation of the Mediator and Arbitrator

Impartiality is best assured by the parties sharing the fees and expenses of the mediator and arbitrator. In cases where the economic condition of a party does not permit equal sharing, the parties should make mutually acceptable arrangements to achieve that goal if at all possible. In the absence of such agreement, the arbitrator should determine allocation of fees. The designating agency, by negotiating the parties share of costs and collecting such fees, might be able to reduce the bias potential of disparate contributions by forwarding payment to the mediator and/or arbitrator without disclosing the parties share therein.

D. Scope of Review

The arbitrator's award should be final and binding and the scope of review should be limited.

Dated: May 9, 1995

CONSUMER DUE PROCESS PROTOCOL*

Statement of Principles of the National Consumer Disputes Advisory Committee

INTRODUCTION: GENESIS OF THE ADVISORY COMMITTEE

Recent years have seen a pronounced trend toward incorporation of out-of-court conflict resolution processes in standardized agreements presented to consumers of goods and services. Some of these processes (such as mediation and non-binding evaluation) involve third party intervention in settlement negotiations; others involve adjudication (binding arbitration). Such processes have the potential to be of significant value in making dispute resolution quicker, less costly, and more satisfying.

Yet because consumer contracts often do not involve arm's length negotiation of terms, and frequently consist of boilerplate language presented on a take-it-or-leave it basis by suppliers of goods or services, there are legitimate concerns regarding the fairness of consumer conflict resolution mechanisms required by suppliers. This is particularly true in the realm of binding arbitration, where the courts are displaced by private adjudication systems. In such cases, consumers are often unaware of their procedural rights and obligations until the realities of out-of-court arbitration are revealed to them after disputes have arisen. While the results may be entirely satisfactory, they may also fall short of consumers' reasonable expectations of fairness and have a significant impact on consumers' substantive rights and remedies.

The use of mediation and other forms of alternative dispute resolution (ADR) by various state and federal courts has also raised concerns regarding quality, effectiveness and fairness. The response has been a number of national, state and local initiatives to establish standards for the guidance and information of courts. Until now, however, there has been no comparable national effort in the private consumer sphere.

In the spring of 1997, the American Arbitration Association (AAA) announced the establishment of a National Consumer Disputes Advisory Committee. The stated mission of the Advisory Committee is:

To bring together a broad, diverse, representative national advisory committee to advise the American Arbitration Association in the development of standards and procedures for the equitable resolution of consumer disputes

In light of its stated mission, the Advisory Committee's recommendations are likely to have a direct impact on the development of rules, procedures and policies for the resolution of consumer disputes under the auspices of the AAA.

The Advisory Committee's recommendations may also have a significant impact in the broader realm of consumer ADR. A Statement of Principles which is perceived as a broadly-based consensus regarding minimum requirements for mediation and arbitration programs for consumers of goods and services may influence the evolution of consumer rules generally and the development of state

---

and federal laws governing consumer arbitration agreements. The standards may affect the drafting of statutes and influence judicial opinions addressing the enforceability of arbitration agreements pursuant to existing state or federal law.

SCOPE OF THE CONSUMER DUE PROCESS PROTOCOL

The Consumer Due Process Protocol (Protocol) was developed to address the wide range of consumer transactions — those involving the purchase or lease of goods or services for personal, family or household use. These include, among other things, transactions involving: banking, credit cards, home loans and other financial services; health care services; brokerage services; home construction and improvements; insurance; communications; and the purchase and lease of motor vehicles and other personal property.

Across this broad spectrum of consumer transactions, the Protocol applies to all possible conflicts — from small claims to complex disputes. In light of these realities, the Advisory Committee sought to develop principles which would establish clear benchmarks for conflict resolution processes involving consumers, while recognizing that a process appropriate in one context may be inappropriate in another. Therefore, the Protocol embodies flexible standards which permit consideration of specific circumstances.

. . .

PRINCIPLE 1. FUNDAMENTALLY-FAIR PROCESS

All parties are entitled to a fundamentally-fair ADR process. As embodiments of fundamental fairness, these Principles should be observed in structuring ADR Programs.

PRINCIPLE 2. ACCESS TO INFORMATION REGARDING ADR PROGRAM

Providers of goods or services should undertake reasonable measures to provide Consumers with full and accurate information regarding Consumer ADR Programs. At the time the Consumer contracts for goods or services, such measures should include (1) clear and adequate notice regarding the ADR provisions, including a statement indicating whether participation in the ADR Program is mandatory or optional, and (2) reasonable means by which Consumers may obtain additional information regarding the ADR Program. After a dispute arises, Consumers should have access to all information necessary for effective participation in ADR.

PRINCIPLE 3. INDEPENDENT AND IMPARTIAL NEUTRAL; INDEPENDENT ADMINISTRATION

1. Independent and Impartial Neutral. All parties are entitled to a Neutral who is independent and impartial.

2. Independent Administration. If participation in mediation or arbitration is mandatory, the procedure should be administered by an Independent ADR Institution. Administrative services should include the maintenance of a panel of prospective Neutrals, facilitation of Neutral selection, collection and distribution of Neutral's fees and expenses, oversight and implementation of ADR rules and procedures, and monitoring of Neutral qualifications, performance, and adherence to pertinent rules, procedures and ethical standards.

3. Standards for Neutrals. The Independent ADR Institution should make reasonable efforts to ensure that Neutrals understand and conform to pertinent ADR rules, procedures and ethical standards.

4. Selection of Neutrals. The Consumer and Provider should have an equal voice in the selection of Neutrals in connection with a specific dispute.

5. Disclosure and Disqualification. Beginning at the time of appointment, Neutrals should be required to disclose to the Independent ADR Institution any circumstance likely to affect impartiality, including any bias or financial or personal interest which might affect the result of the ADR proceeding, or any past or present relationship or experience with the parties or their representatives, including past ADR experiences. The Independent ADR Institution should communicate any such information to the parties and other Neutrals, if any. Upon objection of a party to continued service of the Neutral, the Independent ADR Institution should determine whether the Neutral should be disqualified and should inform the parties of its decision. The disclosure obligation of the Neutral and procedure for disqualification should continue throughout the period of appointment.

PRINCIPLE 4. QUALITY AND COMPETENCE OF NEUTRALS

All parties are entitled to competent, qualified Neutrals. Independent ADR Institutions are responsible for establishing and maintaining standards for Neutrals in ADR Programs they administer.

PRINCIPLE 5. SMALL CLAIMS

Consumer ADR Agreements should make it clear that all parties retain the right to seek relief in a small claims court for disputes or claims within the scope of its jurisdiction.

PRINCIPLE 6. REASONABLE COST

1. Reasonable Cost. Providers of goods and services should develop ADR programs which entail reasonable cost to Consumers based on the circumstances of the dispute, including, among other things, the size and nature of the claim, the nature of goods or services provided, and the ability of the Consumer to pay. In some cases, this may require the Provider to subsidize the process.

2. Handling of Payment. In the interest of ensuring fair and independent Neutrals, the making of fee arrangements and the payment of fees should be administered on a rational, equitable and consistent basis by the Independent ADR Institution.

PRINCIPLE 7. REASONABLY CONVENIENT LOCATION

In the case of face-to-face proceedings, the proceedings should be conducted at a location which is reasonably convenient to both parties with due consideration of their ability to travel and other pertinent circumstances. If the parties are unable to agree on a location, the determination should be made by the Independent ADR Institution or by the Neutral.

PRINCIPLE 8. REASONABLE TIME LIMITS

ADR proceedings should occur within a reasonable time, without undue delay. The rules governing ADR should establish specific reasonable time periods for each step in the ADR process and, where necessary, set forth default procedures in the event a party fails to participate in the process after reasonable notice.

PRINCIPLE 9. RIGHT TO REPRESENTATION

All parties participating in processes in ADR Programs have the right, at their own expense, to be represented by a spokesperson of their own choosing. The ADR rules and procedures should so specify.

PRINCIPLE 10. MEDIATION

The use of mediation is strongly encouraged as an informal means of assisting parties in resolving their own disputes.

SPECIAL PROVISIONS RELATING TO BINDING ARBITRATION

PRINCIPLE 11. AGREEMENTS TO ARBITRATE

Consumers should be given:

a.   clear and adequate notice of the arbitration provision and its conse-quences, including a statement of its mandatory or optional character;

b.   reasonable access to information regarding the arbitration process, includ-ing basic distinctions between arbitration and court proceedings, related costs, and advice as to where they may obtain more complete information regarding arbitration procedures and arbitrator rosters;

c.   notice of the option to make use of applicable small claims court procedures as an alternative to binding arbitration in appropriate cases; and,

d.   a clear statement of the means by which the Consumer may exercise the option (if any) to submit disputes to arbitration or to court process.

PRINCIPLE 12. ARBITRATION HEARINGS

1. Fundamentally-Fair Hearing. All parties are entitled to a fundamentally fair arbitration hearing. This requires adequate notice of hearings and an opportunity to be heard and to present relevant evidence to impartial decision-makers. In some cases, such as some small claims, the requirement of fundamental fairness may be met by hearings conducted by electronic or telephonic means or by a submission of documents. However, the Neutral should have discretionary authority to require a face-to-face hearing upon the request of a party.

2. Confidentiality in Arbitration. Consistent with general expectations of privacy in arbitration hearings, the arbitrator should make reasonable efforts to maintain the privacy of the hearing to the extent permitted by applicable law. The arbitrator

should also carefully consider claims of privilege and confidentiality when addressing evidentiary issues.

PRINCIPLE 13. ACCESS TO INFORMATION

No party should ever be denied the right to a fundamentally-fair process due to an inability to obtain information material to a dispute. Consumer ADR agreements which provide for binding arbitration should establish procedures for arbitrator-supervised exchange of information prior to arbitration, bearing in mind the expedited nature of arbitration.

PRINCIPLE 14. ARBITRAL REMEDIES

The arbitrator should be empowered to grant whatever relief would be available in court under law or in equity.

PRINCIPLE 15. ARBITRATION AWARDS

1. Final and Binding Award; Limited Scope of Review. If provided in the agreement to arbitrate, the arbitrator's award should be final and binding, but subject to review in accordance with applicable statutes governing arbitration awards.

2. Standards to Guide Arbitrator Decision-Making. In making the award, the arbitrator should apply any identified, pertinent contract terms, statutes and legal precedents.

3. Explanation of Award. At the timely request of either party, the arbitrator should provide a brief written explanation of the basis for the award. To facilitate such requests, the arbitrator should discuss the matter with the parties prior to the arbitration hearing.

UNCITRAL NOTES ON ORGANIZING ARBITRAL PROCEEDINGS

Preface

The United Nations Commission on International Trade Law (UNCITRAL) finalized the Notes at its twenty-ninth session (New York, 28 May -14 June 1996). In addition to the 36 member States of the Commission, representatives of many other States and of a number of international organizations had participated in the deliberations. In preparing the draft materials, the Secretariat consulted with experts from various legal systems, national arbitration bodies, as well as international professional associations.

The Commission, after an initial discussion on the project in 1993, considered in 1994 a draft entitled "Draft Guidelines for Preparatory Conferences in Arbitral Proceedings." That draft was also discussed at several meetings of arbitration practitioners, including the XIIth International Arbitration Congress, held by the International Council for Commercial Arbitration (ICCA) at Vienna from 3 to 6 November 1994. On the basis of those discussions in the Commission and elsewhere, the Secretariat prepared "draft Notes on Organizing Arbitral Proceedings." The Commission considered the draft Notes in 1995, and a revised draft in 1996, when the Notes were finalized.

Purpose of the Notes

1. The purpose of the Notes is to assist arbitration practitioners by listing and briefly describing questions on which appropriately timed decisions on organizing arbitral proceedings may be useful. The text, prepared with a particular view to international arbitrations, may be used whether or not the arbitration is administered by an arbitral institution.

Non-binding character of the Notes

2. No legal requirement binding on the arbitrators or the parties is imposed by the Notes. The arbitral tribunal remains free to use the Notes as it sees fit and is not required to give reasons for disregarding them.

3. The Notes are not suitable to be used as arbitration rules, since they do not establish any obligation of the arbitral tribunal or the parties to act in a particular way. Accordingly, the use of the Notes cannot imply any modification of the arbitration rules that the parties may have agreed upon.

Discretion in conduct of proceedings and usefulness of timely decisions on organizing proceedings

4. Laws governing the arbitral procedure and arbitration rules that parties may agree upon typically allow the arbitral tribunal broad discretion and flexibility in the conduct of arbitral proceedings. This is useful in that it enables the arbitral tribunal to take decisions on the organization of proceedings that take into account the circumstances of the case, the expectations of the parties and of the members of the arbitral tribunal, and the need for a just and cost-efficient resolution of the dispute.

5. Such discretion may make it desirable for the arbitral tribunal to give the

parties a timely indication as to the organization of the proceedings and the manner in which the tribunal intends to proceed. This is particularly desirable in international arbitrations, where the participants may be accustomed to differing styles of conducting arbitrations. Without such guidance, a party may find aspects of the proceedings unpredictable and difficult to prepare for. That may lead to misunderstandings, delays and increased costs.

Multi-party arbitration

6. These Notes are intended for use not only in arbitrations with two parties but also in arbitrations with three or more parties. Use of the Notes in multi-party arbitration is referred to below in paragraphs 86-88 (item 18).

Process of making decisions on organizing arbitral proceedings

7. Decisions by the arbitral tribunal on organizing arbitral proceedings may be taken with or without previous consultations with the parties. The method chosen depends on whether, in view of the type of the question to be decided, the arbitral tribunal considers that consultations are not necessary or that hearing the views of the parties would be beneficial for increasing the predictability of the proceedings or improving the procedural atmosphere.

8. The consultations, whether they involve only the arbitrators or also the parties, can be held in one or more meetings, or can be carried out by correspondence or telecommunications such as telefax or conference telephone calls or other electronic means. Meetings may be held at the venue of arbitration or at some other appropriate location.

9. In some arbitrations a special meeting may be devoted exclusively to such procedural consultations; alternatively, the consultations may be held in conjunction with a hearing on the substance of the dispute. Practices differ as to whether such special meetings should be held and how they should be organized. Special procedural meetings of the arbitrators and the parties separate from hearings are in practice referred to by expressions such as "preliminary meeting", "pre-hearing conference", "preparatory conference", "pre-hearing review", or terms of similar meaning. The terms used partly depend on the stage of the proceedings at which the meeting is taking place.

List of matters for possible consideration in organizing arbitral proceedings

10. The Notes provide a list, followed by annotations, of matters on which the arbitral tribunal may wish to formulate decisions on organizing arbitral proceedings.

11. Given that procedural styles and practices in arbitration vary widely, that the purpose of the Notes is not to promote any practice as best practice, and that the Notes are designed for universal use, it is not attempted in the Notes to describe in detail different arbitral practices or express a preference for any of them.

12. The list, while not exhaustive, covers a broad range of situations that may arise in an arbitration. In many arbitrations, however, only a limited number of the matters mentioned in the list need to be considered. It also depends on the circumstances of the case at which stage or stages of the proceedings it would be

useful to consider matters concerning the organization of the proceedings. Generally, in order not to create opportunities for unnecessary discussions and delay, it is advisable not to raise a matter prematurely, i.e. before it is clear that a decision is needed.

13. When the Notes are used, it should be borne in mind that the discretion of the arbitral tribunal in organizing the proceedings may be limited by arbitration rules, by other provisions agreed to by the parties and by the law applicable to the arbitral procedure. When an arbitration is administered by an arbitral institution, various matters discussed in the Notes may be covered by the rules and practices of that institution.

LIST OF MATTERS FOR POSSIBLE CONSIDERATION IN ORGANIZING ARBITRAL PROCEEDINGS

Paragraphs

ANNOTATIONS

1. Set of arbitration rules

If the parties have not agreed on a set of arbitration rules, would they wish to do so

14. Sometimes parties who have not included in their arbitration agreement a stipulation that a set of arbitration rules will govern their arbitral proceedings might wish to do so after the arbitration has begun. If that occurs, the UNCITRAL Arbitration Rules may be used either without modification or with such modifications as the parties might wish to agree upon. In the alternative, the parties might wish to adopt the rules of an arbitral institution; in that case, it may be necessary

to secure the agreement of that institution and to stipulate the terms under which the arbitration could be carried out in accordance with the rules of that institution.

15. However, caution is advised as consideration of a set of arbitration rules might delay the proceedings or give rise to unnecessary controversy.

16. It should be noted that agreement on arbitration rules is not a necessity and that, if the parties do not agree on a set of arbitration rules, the arbitral tribunal has the power to continue the proceedings and determine how the case will be conducted.

2. Language of proceedings

17. Many rules and laws on arbitral procedure empower the arbitral tribunal to determine the language or languages to be used in the proceedings, if the parties have not reached an agreement thereon.

(a) Possible need for translation of documents, in full or in part

18. Some documents annexed to the statements of claim and defence or submitted later may not be in the language of the proceedings. Bearing in mind the needs of the proceedings and economy, it may be considered whether the arbitral tribunal should order that any of those documents or parts thereof should be accompanied by a translation into the language of the proceedings.

(b) Possible need for interpretation of oral presentations

19. If interpretation will be necessary during oral hearings, it is advisable to consider whether the interpretation will be simultaneous or consecutive and whether the arrangements should be the responsibility of a party or the arbitral tribunal. In an arbitration administered by an institution, interpretation as well as translation services are often arranged by the arbitral institution.

(c) Cost of translation and interpretation

20. In taking decisions about translation or interpretation, it is advisable to decide whether any or all of the costs are to be paid directly by a party or whether they will be paid out of the deposits and apportioned between the parties along with the other arbitration costs.

3. Place of arbitration

(a) Determination of the place of arbitration, if not already agreed upon by the parties

21. Arbitration rules usually allow the parties to agree on the place of arbitration, subject to the requirement of some arbitral institutions that arbitrations under their rules be conducted at a particular place, usually the location of the institution. If the place has not been so agreed upon, the rules governing the arbitration typically provide that it is in the power of the arbitral tribunal or the institution administering the arbitration to determine the place. If the arbitral tribunal is to make that determination, it may wish to hear the views of the parties before doing so.

22. Various factual and legal factors influence the choice of the place of arbitration, and their relative importance varies from case to case. Among the more prominent factors are: *(a)* suitability of the law on arbitral procedure of the place of arbitration; *(b)* whether there is a multilateral or bilateral treaty on enforcement of arbitral awards between the State where the arbitration takes place and the State or States where the award may have to be enforced; *(c)* convenience of the parties and the arbitrators, including the travel distances; *(d)* availability and cost of support services needed; and *(e)* location of the subject-matter in dispute and proximity of evidence.

(b) Possibility of meetings outside the place of arbitration

23. Many sets of arbitration rules and laws on arbitral procedure expressly allow the arbitral tribunal to hold meetings elsewhere than at the place of arbitration. For example, under the UNCITRAL Model Law on International Commercial Arbitration "the arbitral tribunal may, unless otherwise agreed by the parties, meet at any place it considers appropriate for consultation among its members, for hearing witnesses, experts or the parties, or for inspection of goods, other property or documents" (article 20(2)). The purpose of this discretion is to permit arbitral proceedings to be carried out in a manner that is most efficient and economical.

4. Administrative services that may be needed for the arbitral tribunal to carry out its functions

24. Various administrative services (e.g. hearing rooms or secretarial services) may need to be procured for the arbitral tribunal to be able to carry out its functions. When the arbitration is administered by an arbitral institution, the institution will usually provide all or a good part of the required administrative support to the arbitral tribunal. When an arbitration administered by an arbitral institution takes place away from the seat of the institution, the institution may be able to arrange for administrative services to be obtained from another source, often an arbitral institution; some arbitral institutions have entered into cooperation agreements with a view to providing mutual assistance in servicing arbitral proceedings.

25. When the case is not administered by an institution, or the involvement of the institution does not include providing administrative support, usually the administrative arrangements for the proceedings will be made by the arbitral tribunal or the presiding arbitrator; it may also be acceptable to leave some of the arrangements to the parties, or to one of the parties subject to agreement of the other party or parties. Even in such cases, a convenient source of administrative support might be found in arbitral institutions, which often offer their facilities to arbitrations not governed by the rules of the institution. Otherwise, some services could be procured from entities such as chambers of commerce, hotels or specialized firms providing secretarial or other support services.

26. Administrative services might be secured by engaging a secretary of the arbitral tribunal (also referred to as registrar, clerk, administrator or rapporteur), who carries out the tasks under the direction of the arbitral tribunal. Some arbitral institutions routinely assign such persons to the cases administered by them. In arbitrations not administered by an institution or where the arbitral institution does

not appoint a secretary, some arbitrators frequently engage such persons, at least in certain types of cases, whereas many others normally conduct the proceedings without them.

27. To the extent the tasks of the secretary are purely organizational (e.g. obtaining meeting rooms and providing or coordinating secretarial services), this is usually not controversial. Differences in views, however, may arise if the tasks include legal research and other professional assistance to the arbitral tribunal (e.g. collecting case law or published commentaries on legal issues defined by the arbitral tribunal, preparing summaries from case law and publications, and sometimes also preparing drafts of procedural decisions or drafts of certain parts of the award, in particular those concerning the facts of the case). Views or expectations may differ especially where a task of the secretary is similar to professional functions of the arbitrators. Such a role of the secretary is in the view of some commentators inappropriate or is appropriate only under certain conditions, such as that the parties agree thereto. However, it is typically recognized that it is important to ensure that the secretary does not perform any decision-making function of the arbitral tribunal.

5. Deposits in respect of costs

(a) Amount to be deposited

28. In an arbitration administered by an institution, the institution often sets, on the basis of an estimate of the costs of the proceedings, the amount to be deposited as an advance for the costs of the arbitration. In other cases it is customary for the arbitral tribunal to make such an estimate and request a deposit. The estimate typically includes travel and other expenses by the arbitrators, expenditures for administrative assistance required by the arbitral tribunal, costs of any expert advice required by the arbitral tribunal, and the fees for the arbitrators. Many arbitration rules have provisions on this matter, including on whether the deposit should be made by the two parties (or all parties in a multi-party case) or only by the claimant.

(b) Management of deposits

29. When the arbitration is administered by an institution, the institution's services may include managing and accounting for the deposited money. Where that is not the case, it might be useful to clarify matters such as the type and location of the account in which the money will be kept and how the deposits will be managed.

(c) Supplementary deposits

30. If during the course of proceedings it emerges that the costs will be higher than anticipated, supplementary deposits may be required (e.g. because the arbitral tribunal decides pursuant to the arbitration rules to appoint an expert).

6. Confidentiality of information relating to the arbitration; possible agreement thereon

31. It is widely viewed that confidentiality is one of the advantageous and helpful features of arbitration. Nevertheless, there is no uniform answer in national laws as

to the extent to which the participants in an arbitration are under the duty to observe the confidentiality of information relating to the case. Moreover, parties that have agreed on arbitration rules or other provisions that do not expressly address the issue of confidentiality cannot assume that all jurisdictions would recognize an implied commitment to confidentiality. Furthermore, the participants in an arbitration might not have the same understanding as regards the extent of confidentiality that is expected. Therefore, the arbitral tribunal might wish to discuss that with the parties and, if considered appropriate, record any agreed principles on the duty of confidentiality.

32. An agreement on confidentiality might cover, for example, one or more of the following matters: the material or information that is to be kept confidential (e.g. pieces of evidence, written and oral arguments, the fact that the arbitration is taking place, identity of the arbitrators, content of the award); measures for maintaining confidentiality of such information and hearings; whether any special procedures should be employed for maintaining the confidentiality of information transmitted by electronic means (e.g. because communication equipment is shared by several users, or because electronic mail over public networks is considered not sufficiently protected against unauthorized access); circumstances in which confidential information may be disclosed in part or in whole (e.g. in the context of disclosures of information in the public domain, or if required by law or a regulatory body).

7. Routing of written communications among the parties and the arbitrators

33. To the extent the question how documents and other written communications should be routed among the parties and the arbitrators is not settled by the agreed rules, or, if an institution administers the case, by the practices of the institution, it is useful for the arbitral tribunal to clarify the question suitably early so as to avoid misunderstandings and delays.

34. Among various possible patterns of routing, one example is that a party transmits the appropriate number of copies to the arbitral tribunal, or to the arbitral institution, if one is involved, which then forwards them as appropriate. Another example is that a party is to send copies simultaneously to the arbitrators and the other party or parties. Documents and other written communications directed by the arbitral tribunal or the presiding arbitrator to one or more parties may also follow a determined pattern, such as through the arbitral institution or by direct transmission. For some communications, in particular those on organizational matters (e.g. dates for hearings), more direct routes of communication may be agreed, even if, for example, the arbitral institution acts as an intermediary for documents such as the statements of claim and defence, evidence or written arguments.

8. Telefax and other electronic means of sending documents

(a) Telefax

35. Telefax, which offers many advantages over traditional means of communication, is widely used in arbitral proceedings. Nevertheless, should it be thought that, because of the characteristics of the equipment used, it would be preferable not to

rely only on a telefacsimile of a document, special arrangements may be considered, such as that a particular piece of written evidence should be mailed or otherwise physically delivered, or that certain telefax messages should be confirmed by mailing or otherwise delivering documents whose facsimile were transmitted by electronic means. When a document should not be sent by telefax, it may, however, be appropriate, in order to avoid an unnecessarily rigid procedure, for the arbitral tribunal to retain discretion to accept an advance copy of a document by telefax for the purposes of meeting a deadline, provided that the document itself is received within a reasonable time thereafter.

(b) Other electronic means (e.g. electronic mail and magnetic or optical disk)

36. It might be agreed that documents, or some of them, will be exchanged not only in paper-based form, but in addition also in an electronic form other than telefax (e.g. as electronic mail, or on a magnetic or optical disk), or only in electronic form. Since the use of electronic means depends on the aptitude of the persons involved and the availability of equipment and computer programs, agreement is necessary for such means to be used. If both paper-based and electronic means are to be used, it is advisable to decide which one is controlling and, if there is a time-limit for submitting a document, which act constitutes submission.

37. When the exchange of documents in electronic form is planned, it is useful, in order to avoid technical difficulties, to agree on matters such as: data carriers (e.g. electronic mail or computer disks) and their technical characteristics; computer programs to be used in preparing the electronic records; instructions for transforming the electronic records into human-readable form; keeping of logs and back-up records of communications sent and received; information in human-readable form that should accompany the disks (e.g. the names of the originator and recipient, computer program, titles of the electronic files and the back-up methods used); procedures when a message is lost or the communication system otherwise fails; and identification of persons who can be contacted if a problem occurs.

9. Arrangements for the exchange of written submissions

38. After the parties have initially stated their claims and defences, they may wish, or the arbitral tribunal might request them, to present further written submissions so as to prepare for the hearings or to provide the basis for a decision without hearings. In such submissions, the parties, for example, present or comment on allegations and evidence, cite or explain law, or make or react to proposals. In practice such submissions are referred to variously as, for example, statement, memorial, counter-memorial, brief, counter-brief, reply, replique, duplique, rebuttal or rejoinder; the terminology is a matter of linguistic usage and the scope or sequence of the submission.

(a) Scheduling of written submissions

39. It is advisable that the arbitral tribunal set time-limits for written submissions. In enforcing the time-limits, the arbitral tribunal may wish, on the one hand, to make sure that the case is not unduly protracted and, on the other hand, to reserve a degree of discretion and allow late submissions if appropriate under the circumstances. In some cases the arbitral tribunal might prefer not to plan the

written submissions in advance, thus leaving such matters, including time-limits, to be decided in light of the developments in the proceedings. In other cases, the arbitral tribunal may wish to determine, when scheduling the first written submissions, the number of subsequent submissions.

40. Practices differ as to whether, after the hearings have been held, written submissions are still acceptable. While some arbitral tribunals consider post-hearing submissions unacceptable, others might request or allow them on a particular issue. Some arbitral tribunals follow the procedure according to which the parties are not requested to present written evidence and legal arguments to the arbitral tribunal before the hearings; in such a case, the arbitral tribunal may regard it as appropriate that written submissions be made after the hearings.

(b) Consecutive or simultaneous submissions

41. Written submissions on an issue may be made consecutively, i.e. the party who receives a submission is given a period of time to react with its counter submission. Another possibility is to request each party to make the submission within the same time period to the arbitral tribunal or the institution administering the case; the received submissions are then forwarded simultaneously to the respective other party or parties. The approach used may depend on the type of issues to be commented upon and the time in which the views should be clarified. With consecutive submissions, it may take longer than with simultaneous ones to obtain views of the parties on a given issue. Consecutive submissions, however, allow the reacting party to comment on all points raised by the other party or parties, which simultaneous submissions do not; thus, simultaneous submissions might possibly necessitate further submissions.

10. Practical details concerning written submissions and evidence (e.g. method of submission, copies, numbering, references)

42. Depending on the volume and kind of documents to be handled, it might be considered whether practical arrangements on details such as the following would be helpful:

- Whether the submissions will be made as paper documents or by electronic means, or both (see paragraphs 35-37);

- The number of copies in which each document is to be submitted;

- A system for numbering documents and items of evidence, and a method for marking them, including by tabs;

- The form of references to documents (e.g. by the heading and the number assigned to the document or its date);

- Paragraph numbering in written submissions, in order to facilitate precise references to parts of a text;

- When translations are to be submitted as paper documents, whether the translations are to be contained in the same volume as the original texts or included in separate volumes.

11. Defining points at issue; order of deciding issues; defining relief or remedy sought

(a) Should a list of points at issue be prepared

43. In considering the parties' allegations and arguments, the arbitral tribunal may come to the conclusion that it would be useful for it or for the parties to prepare, for analytical purposes and for ease of discussion, a list of the points at issue, as opposed to those that are undisputed. If the arbitral tribunal determines that the advantages of working on the basis of such a list outweigh the disadvantages, it chooses the appropriate stage of the proceedings for preparing a list, bearing in mind also that subsequent developments in the proceedings may require a revision of the points at issue. Such an identification of points at issue might help to concentrate on the essential matters, to reduce the number of points at issue by agreement of the parties, and to select the best and most economical process for resolving the dispute. However, possible disadvantages of preparing such a list include delay, adverse effect on the flexibility of the proceedings, or unnecessary disagreements about whether the arbitral tribunal has decided all issues submitted to it or whether the award contains decisions on matters beyond the scope of the submission to arbitration. The terms of reference required under some arbitration rules, or in agreements of parties, may serve the same purpose as the above-described list of points at issue.

(b) In which order should the points at issue be decided

44. While it is often appropriate to deal with all the points at issue collectively, the arbitral tribunal might decide to take them up during the proceedings in a particular order. The order may be due to a point being preliminary relative to another (e.g. a decision on the jurisdiction of the arbitral tribunal is preliminary to consideration of substantive issues, or the issue of responsibility for a breach of contract is preliminary to the issue of the resulting damages). A particular order may be decided also when the breach of various contracts is in dispute or when damages arising from various events are claimed.

45. If the arbitral tribunal has adopted a particular order of deciding points at issue, it might consider it appropriate to issue a decision on one of the points earlier than on the other ones. This might be done, for example, when a discrete part of a claim is ready for decision while the other parts still require extensive consideration, or when it is expected that after deciding certain issues the parties might be more inclined to settle the remaining ones. Such earlier decisions are referred to by expressions such as "partial", "interlocutory" or "interim" awards or decisions, depending on the type of issue dealt with and on whether the decision is final with respect to the issue it resolves. Questions that might be the subject of such decisions are, for example, jurisdiction of the arbitral tribunal, interim measures of protection, or the liability of a party.

(c) Is there a need to define more precisely the relief or remedy sought

46. If the arbitral tribunal considers that the relief or remedy sought is insufficiently definite, it may wish to explain to the parties the degree of definiteness with which their claims should be formulated. Such an explanation may be useful

since criteria are not uniform as to how specific the claimant must be in formulating a relief or remedy.

12. Possible settlement negotiations and their effect on scheduling proceedings

47. Attitudes differ as to whether it is appropriate for the arbitral tribunal to bring up the possibility of settlement. Given the divergence of practices in this regard, the arbitral tribunal should only suggest settlement negotiations with caution. However, it may be opportune for the arbitral tribunal to schedule the proceedings in a way that might facilitate the continuation or initiation of settlement negotiations.

13. Documentary evidence

(a) Time-limits for submission of documentary evidence intended to be submitted by the parties; consequences of late submission

48. Often the written submissions of the parties contain sufficient information for the arbitral tribunal to fix the time-limit for submitting evidence. Otherwise, in order to set realistic time periods, the arbitral tribunal may wish to consult with the parties about the time that they would reasonably need.

49. The arbitral tribunal may wish to clarify that evidence submitted late will as a rule not be accepted. It may wish not to preclude itself from accepting a late submission of evidence if the party shows sufficient cause for the delay.

(b) Whether the arbitral tribunal intends to require a party to produce documentary evidence

50. Procedures and practices differ widely as to the conditions under which the arbitral tribunal may require a party to produce documents. Therefore, the arbitral tribunal might consider it useful, when the agreed arbitration rules do not provide specific conditions, to clarify to the parties the manner in which it intends to proceed.

51. The arbitral tribunal may wish to establish time-limits for the production of documents. The parties might be reminded that, if the requested party duly invited to produce documentary evidence fails to do so within the established period of time, without showing sufficient cause for such failure, the arbitral tribunal is free to draw its conclusions from the failure and may make the award on the evidence before it.

(c) Should assertions about the origin and receipt of documents and about the correctness of photocopies be assumed as accurate

52. It may be helpful for the arbitral tribunal to inform the parties that it intends to conduct the proceedings on the basis that, unless a party raises an objection to any of the following conclusions within a specified period of time: *(a)* a document is accepted as having originated from the source indicated in the document; *(b)* a copy of a dispatched communication (e.g. letter, telex, telefax or other electronic message) is accepted without further proof as having been received by the

addressee; and *(c)* a copy is accepted as correct. A statement by the arbitral tribunal to that effect can simplify the introduction of documentary evidence and discourage unfounded and dilatory objections, at a late stage of the proceedings, to the probative value of documents. It is advisable to provide that the time-limit for objections will not be enforced if the arbitral tribunal considers the delay justified.

(d) Are the parties willing to submit jointly a single set of documentary evidence

53. The parties may consider submitting jointly a single set of documentary evidence whose authenticity is not disputed. The purpose would be to avoid duplicate submissions and unnecessary discussions concerning the authenticity of documents, without prejudicing the position of the parties concerning the content of the documents. Additional documents may be inserted later if the parties agree. When a single set of documents would be too voluminous to be easily manageable, it might be practical to select a number of frequently used documents and establish a set of "working" documents. A convenient arrangement of documents in the set may be according to chronological order or subject matter. It is useful to keep a table of contents of the documents, for example, by their short headings and dates, and to provide that the parties will refer to documents by those headings and dates.

(e) Should voluminous and complicated documentary evidence be presented through summaries, tabulations, charts, extracts or samples

54. When documentary evidence is voluminous and complicated, it may save time and costs if such evidence is presented by a report of a person competent in the relevant field (e.g. public accountant or consulting engineer). The report may present the information in the form of summaries, tabulations, charts, extracts or samples. Such presentation of evidence should be combined with arrangements that give the interested party the opportunity to review the underlying data and the methodology of preparing the report.

14. Physical evidence other than documents

55. In some arbitrations the arbitral tribunal is called upon to assess physical evidence other than documents, for example, by inspecting samples of goods, viewing a video recording or observing the functioning of a machine.

(a) What arrangements should be made if physical evidence will be submitted

56. If physical evidence will be submitted, the arbitral tribunal may wish to fix the time schedule for presenting the evidence, make arrangements for the other party or parties to have a suitable opportunity to prepare itself for the presentation of the evidence, and possibly take measures for safekeeping the items of evidence.

(b) What arrangements should be made if an on-site inspection is necessary

57. If an on-site inspection of property or goods will take place, the arbitral tribunal may consider matters such as timing, meeting places, other arrangements to provide the opportunity for all parties to be present, and the need to avoid communications between arbitrators and a party about points at issue without the presence of the other party or parties.

58. The site to be inspected is often under the control of one of the parties, which typically means that employees or representatives of that party will be present to give guidance and explanations. It should be borne in mind that statements of those representatives or employees made during an on-site inspection, as contrasted with statements those persons might make as witnesses in a hearing, should not be treated as evidence in the proceedings.

15. Witnesses

59. While laws and rules on arbitral procedure typically leave broad freedom concerning the manner of taking evidence of witnesses, practices on procedural points are varied. In order to facilitate the preparations of the parties for the hearings, the arbitral tribunal may consider it appropriate to clarify, in advance of the hearings, some or all of the following issues.

(a) Advance notice about a witness whom a party intends to present; written witnesses' statements

60. To the extent the applicable arbitration rules do not deal with the matter, the arbitral tribunal may wish to require that each party give advance notice to the arbitral tribunal and the other party or parties of any witness it intends to present. As to the content of the notice, the following is an example of what might be required, in addition to the names and addresses of the witnesses: *(a)* the subject upon which the witnesses will testify; *(b)* the language in which the witnesses will testify; and *(c)* the nature of the relationship with any of the parties, qualifications and experience of the witnesses if and to the extent these are relevant to the dispute or the testimony, and how the witnesses learned about the facts on which they will testify. However, it may not be necessary to require such a notice, in particular if the thrust of the testimony can be clearly ascertained from the party's allegations.

61. Some practitioners favour the procedure according to which the party presenting witness evidence submits a signed witness's statement containing testimony itself. It should be noted, however, that such practice, which implies interviewing the witness by the party presenting the testimony, is not known in all parts of the world and, moreover, that some practitioners disapprove of it on the ground that such contacts between the party and the witness may compromise the credibility of the testimony and are therefore improper (see paragraph 67). Notwithstanding these reservations, signed witness's testimony has advantages in that it may expedite the proceedings by making it easier for the other party or parties to prepare for the hearings or for the parties to identify uncontested matters. However, those advantages might be outweighed by the time and expense involved in obtaining the written testimony.

62. If a signed witness's statement should be made under oath or similar affirmation of truthfulness, it may be necessary to clarify by whom the oath or affirmation should be administered and whether any formal authentication will be required by the arbitral tribunal.

(b) Manner of taking oral evidence of witnesses

(i) Order in which questions will be asked and the manner in which the hearing of witnesses will be conducted

63. To the extent that the applicable rules do not provide an answer, it may be useful for the arbitral tribunal to clarify how witnesses will be heard. One of the various possibilities is that a witness is first questioned by the arbitral tribunal, whereupon questions are asked by the parties, first by the party who called the witness. Another possibility is for the witness to be questioned by the party presenting the witness and then by the other party or parties, while the arbitral tribunal might pose questions during the questioning or after the parties on points that in the tribunal's view have not been sufficiently clarified. Differences exist also as to the degree of control the arbitral tribunal exercises over the hearing of witnesses. For example, some arbitrators prefer to permit the parties to pose questions freely and directly to the witness, but may disallow a question if a party objects; other arbitrators tend to exercise more control and may disallow a question on their initiative or even require that questions from the parties be asked through the arbitral tribunal.

(ii) Whether oral testimony will be given under oath or affirmation and, if so, in what form an oath or affirmation should be made

64. Practices and laws differ as to whether or not oral testimony is to be given under oath or affirmation. In some legal systems, the arbitrators are empowered to put witnesses on oath, but it is usually in their discretion whether they want to do so. In other systems, oral testimony under oath is either unknown or may even be considered improper as only an official such as a judge or notary may have the authority to administer oaths.

(iii) May witnesses be in the hearing room when they are not testifying

65. Some arbitrators favour the procedure that, except if the circumstances suggest otherwise, the presence of a witness in the hearing room is limited to the time the witness is testifying; the purpose is to prevent the witness from being influenced by what is said in the hearing room, or to prevent that the presence of the witness would influence another witness. Other arbitrators consider that the presence of a witness during the testimony of other witnesses may be beneficial in that possible contradictions may be readily clarified or that their presence may act as a deterrent against untrue statements. Other possible approaches may be that witnesses are not present in the hearing room before their testimony, but stay in the room after they have testified, or that the arbitral tribunal decides the question for each witness individually depending on what the arbitral tribunal considers most appropriate. The arbitral tribunal may leave the procedure to be decided during the hearings, or may give guidance on the question in advance of the hearings.

(c) The order in which the witnesses will be called

66. When several witnesses are to be heard and longer testimony is expected, it is likely to reduce costs if the order in which they will be called is known in advance and their presence can be scheduled accordingly. Each party might be invited to

suggest the order in which it intends to present the witnesses, while it would be up to the arbitral tribunal to approve the scheduling and to make departures from it.

(d) Interviewing witnesses prior to their appearance at a hearing

67. In some legal systems, parties or their representatives are permitted to interview witnesses, prior to their appearance at the hearing, as to such matters as their recollection of the relevant events, their experience, qualifications or relation with a participant in the proceedings. In those legal systems such contacts are usually not permitted once the witness's oral testimony has begun. In other systems such contacts with witnesses are considered improper. In order to avoid misunderstandings, the arbitral tribunal may consider it useful to clarify what kind of contacts a party is permitted to have with a witness in the preparations for the hearings.

(e) Hearing representatives of a party

68. According to some legal systems, certain persons affiliated with a party may only be heard as representatives of the party but not as witnesses. In such a case, it may be necessary to consider ground rules for determining which persons may not testify as witnesses (e.g. certain executives, employees or agents) and for hearing statements of those persons and for questioning them.

16. Experts and expert witnesses

69. Many arbitration rules and laws on arbitral procedure address the participation of experts in arbitral proceedings. A frequent solution is that the arbitral tribunal has the power to appoint an expert to report on issues determined by the tribunal; in addition, the parties may be permitted to present expert witnesses on points at issue. In other cases, it is for the parties to present expert testimony, and it is not expected that the arbitral tribunal will appoint an expert.

(a) Expert appointed by the arbitral tribunal

70. If the arbitral tribunal is empowered to appoint an expert, one possible approach is for the tribunal to proceed directly to selecting the expert. Another possibility is to consult the parties as to who should be the expert; this may be done, for example, without mentioning a candidate, by presenting to the parties a list of candidates, soliciting proposals from the parties, or by discussing with the parties the "profile" of the expert the arbitral tribunal intends to appoint, i.e. the qualifications, experience and abilities of the expert.

(i) The expert's terms of reference

71. The purpose of the expert's terms of reference is to indicate the questions on which the expert is to provide clarification, to avoid opinions on points that are not for the expert to assess and to commit the expert to a time schedule. While the discretion to appoint an expert normally includes the determination of the expert's terms of reference, the arbitral tribunal may decide to consult the parties before finalizing the terms. It might also be useful to determine details about how the expert will receive from the parties any relevant information or have access to any relevant documents, goods or other property, so as to enable the expert to prepare

the report. In order to facilitate the evaluation of the expert's report, it is advisable to require the expert to include in the report information on the method used in arriving at the conclusions and the evidence and information used in preparing the report.

(ii) The opportunity of the parties to comment on the expert's report, including by presenting expert testimony

72. Arbitration rules that contain provisions on experts usually also have provisions on the right of a party to comment on the report of the expert appointed by the arbitral tribunal. If no such provisions apply or more specific procedures than those prescribed are deemed necessary, the arbitral tribunal may, in light of those provisions, consider it opportune to determine, for example, the time period for presenting written comments of the parties, or, if hearings are to be held for the purpose of hearing the expert, the procedures for interrogating the expert by the parties or for the participation of any expert witnesses presented by the parties.

(b) Expert opinion presented by a party (expert witness)

73. If a party presents an expert opinion, the arbitral tribunal might consider requiring, for example, that the opinion be in writing, that the expert should be available to answer questions at hearings, and that, if a party will present an expert witness at a hearing, advance notice must be given or that the written opinion must be presented in advance, as in the case of other witnesses (see paragraphs 60-62).

17. Hearings

(a) Decision whether to hold hearings

74. Laws on arbitral procedure and arbitration rules often have provisions as to the cases in which oral hearings must be held and as to when the arbitral tribunal has discretion to decide whether to hold hearings.

75. If it is up to the arbitral tribunal to decide whether to hold hearings, the decision is likely to be influenced by factors such as, on the one hand, that it is usually quicker and easier to clarify points at issue pursuant to a direct confrontation of arguments than on the basis of correspondence and, on the other hand, the travel and other cost of holding hearings, and that the need of finding acceptable dates for the hearings might delay the proceedings. The arbitral tribunal may wish to consult the parties on this matter.

(b) Whether one period of hearings should be held or separate periods of hearings

76. Attitudes vary as to whether hearings should be held in a single period of hearings or in separate periods, especially when more than a few days are needed to complete the hearings. According to some arbitrators, the entire hearings should normally be held in a single period, even if the hearings are to last for more than a week. Other arbitrators in such cases tend to schedule separate periods of hearings. In some cases issues to be decided are separated, and separate hearings set for those issues, with the aim that oral presentation on those issues will be completed within the allotted time. Among the advantages of one period of hearings

are that it involves less travel costs, memory will not fade, and it is unlikely that people representing a party will change. On the other hand, the longer the hearings, the more difficult it may be to find early dates acceptable to all participants. Furthermore, separate periods of hearings may be easier to schedule, the subsequent hearings may be tailored to the development of the case, and the period between the hearings leaves time for analysing the records and negotiations between the parties aimed at narrowing the points at issue by agreement.

(c) Setting dates for hearings

77. Typically, firm dates will be fixed for hearings. Exceptionally, the arbitral tribunal may initially wish to set only "target dates" as opposed to definitive dates. This may be done at a stage of the proceedings when not all information necessary to schedule hearings is yet available, with the understanding that the target dates will either be confirmed or rescheduled within a reasonably short period. Such provisional planning can be useful to participants who are generally not available on short notice.

(d) Whether there should be a limit on the aggregate amount of time each party will have for oral arguments and questioning witnesses

78. Some arbitrators consider it useful to limit the aggregate amount of time each party has for any of the following: *(a)* making oral statements; *(b)* questioning its witnesses; and *(c)* questioning the witnesses of the other party or parties. In general, the same aggregate amount of time is considered appropriate for each party, unless the arbitral tribunal considers that a different allocation is justified. Before deciding, the arbitral tribunal may wish to consult the parties as to how much time they think they will need.

79. Such planning of time, provided it is realistic, fair and subject to judiciously firm control by the arbitral tribunal, will make it easier for the parties to plan the presentation of the various items of evidence and arguments, reduce the likelihood of running out of time towards the end of the hearings and avoid that one party would unfairly use up a disproportionate amount of time.

(e) The order in which the parties will present their arguments and evidence

80. Arbitration rules typically give broad latitude to the arbitral tribunal to determine the order of presentations at the hearings. Within that latitude, practices differ, for example, as to whether opening or closing statements are heard and their level of detail; the sequence in which the claimant and the respondent present their opening statements, arguments, witnesses and other evidence; and whether the respondent or the claimant has the last word. In view of such differences, or when no arbitration rules apply, it may foster efficiency of the proceedings if the arbitral tribunal clarifies to the parties, in advance of the hearings, the manner in which it will conduct the hearings, at least in broad lines.

(f) Length of hearings

81. The length of a hearing primarily depends on the complexity of the issues to be argued and the amount of witness evidence to be presented. The length also depends on the procedural style used in the arbitration. Some practitioners prefer

to have written evidence and written arguments presented before the hearings, which thus can focus on the issues that have not been sufficiently clarified. Those practitioners generally tend to plan shorter hearings than those practitioners who prefer that most if not all evidence and arguments are presented to the arbitral tribunal orally and in full detail. In order to facilitate the parties' preparations and avoid misunderstandings, the arbitral tribunal may wish to clarify to the parties, in advance of the hearings, the intended use of time and style of work at the hearings.

(g) Arrangements for a record of the hearings

82. The arbitral tribunal should decide, possibly after consulting with the parties, on the method of preparing a record of oral statements and testimony during hearings. Among different possibilities, one method is that the members of the arbitral tribunal take personal notes. Another is that the presiding arbitrator during the hearing dictates to a typist a summary of oral statements and testimony. A further method, possible when a secretary of the arbitral tribunal has been appointed, may be to leave to that person the preparation of a summary record. A useful, though costly, method is for professional stenographers to prepare verbatim transcripts, often within the next day or a similarly short time period. A written record may be combined with tape-recording, so as to enable reference to the tape in case of a disagreement over the written record.

83. If transcripts are to be produced, it may be considered how the persons who made the statements will be given an opportunity to check the transcripts. For example, it may be determined that the changes to the record would be approved by the parties or, failing their agreement, would be referred for decision to the arbitral tribunal.

(h) Whether and when the parties are permitted to submit notes summarizing their oral arguments

84. Some legal counsel are accustomed to giving notes summarizing their oral arguments to the arbitral tribunal and to the other party or parties. If such notes are presented, this is usually done during the hearings or shortly thereafter; in some cases, the notes are sent before the hearing. In order to avoid surprise, foster equal treatment of the parties and facilitate preparations for the hearings, advance clarification is advisable as to whether submitting such notes is acceptable and the time for doing so.

85. In closing the hearings, the arbitral tribunal will normally assume that no further proof is to be offered or submission to be made. Therefore, if notes are to be presented to be read after the closure of the hearings, the arbitral tribunal may find it worthwhile to stress that the notes should be limited to summarizing what was said orally and in particular should not refer to new evidence or new argument.

18. Multi-party arbitration

86. When a single arbitration involves more than two parties (multi-party arbitration), considerations regarding the need to organize arbitral proceedings, and matters that may be considered in that connection, are generally not different from two-party arbitrations. A possible difference may be that, because of the need to deal with more than two parties, multi-party proceedings can be more compli-

cated to manage than bilateral proceedings. The Notes, notwithstanding a possible greater complexity of multi-party arbitration, can be used in multi-party as well as in two-party proceedings.

87. The areas of possibly increased complexity in multi-party arbitration are, for example, the flow of communications among the parties and the arbitral tribunal (see paragraphs 33, 34 and 38-41); if points at issue are to be decided at different points in time, the order of deciding them (paragraphs 44-45); the manner in which the parties will participate in hearing witnesses (paragraph 63); the appointment of experts and the participation of the parties in considering their reports (paragraphs 70-72); the scheduling of hearings (paragraph 76); the order in which the parties will present their arguments and evidence at hearings (paragraph 80).

88. The Notes, which are limited to pointing out matters that may be considered in organizing arbitral proceedings in general, do not cover the drafting of the arbitration agreement or the constitution of the arbitral tribunal, both issues that give rise to special questions in multi-party arbitration as compared to two-party arbitration.

19. Possible requirements concerning filing or delivering the award

89. Some national laws require that arbitral awards be filed or registered with a court or similar authority, or that they be delivered in a particular manner or through a particular authority. Those laws differ with respect to, for example, the type of award to which the requirement applies (e.g. to all awards or only to awards not rendered under the auspices of an arbitral institution); time periods for filing, registering or delivering the award (in some cases those time periods may be rather short); or consequences for failing to comply with the requirement (which might be, for example, invalidity of the award or inability to enforce it in a particular manner).

Who should take steps to fulfil any requirement

90. If such a requirement exists, it is useful, some time before the award is to be issued, to plan who should take the necessary steps to meet the requirement and how the costs are to be borne.

INTERNATIONAL BAR ASSOCIATION, RULES ON THE TAKING OF EVIDENCE IN INTERNATIONAL ARBITRATION*

Adopted by a resolution of the IBA Council 29 May 2010

Preamble

1. These IBA Rules on the Taking of Evidence in International Arbitration are intended to provide an efficient, economical and fair process for the taking of evidence in international arbitrations, particularly those between Parties from different legal traditions. They are designed to supplement the legal provisions and the institutional, ad hoc or other rules that apply to the conduct of the arbitration.

2. Parties and Arbitral Tribunals may adopt the IBA Rules of Evidence, in whole or in part, to govern arbitration proceedings, or they may vary them or use them as guidelines in developing their own procedures. The Rules are not intended to limit the flexibility that is inherent in, and an advantage of, international arbitration, and Parties and Arbitral Tribunals are free to adapt them to the particular circumstances of each arbitration.

3. The taking of evidence shall be conducted on the principles that each Party shall act in good faith and be entitled to know, reasonably in advance of any Evidentiary Hearing or any fact or merits determination, the evidence on which the other Parties rely.

Definitions

In the IBA Rules of Evidence:

'Arbitral Tribunal' means a sole arbitrator or a panel of arbitrators;

'Claimant' means the Party or Parties who commenced the arbitration and any Party who, through joinder or otherwise, becomes aligned with such Party or Parties;

'Document' means a writing, communication, picture, drawing, program or data of any kind, whether recorded or maintained on paper or by electronic, audio, visual or any other means;

"Evidentiary Hearing' means any hearing, whether or not held on consecutive days, at which the Arbitral Tribunal, whether in person, by teleconference, videoconference or other method, receives oral or other evidence;

'Expert Report' means a written statement by a Tribunal- Appointed Expert or a Party-Appointed Expert;

'General Rules' mean the institutional, ad hoc or other rules that apply to the conduct of the arbitration;

'IBA Rules of Evidence' or *'Rules'* means these IBA Rules on the Taking of

---

* The IBA Rules on the Taking of Evidence in International Arbitration are reproduced by kind permission of the International Bar Association, London, UK. Copyright © International Bar Association.

Evidence in International Arbitration, as they may be revised or amended from time to time;

'Party' means a party to the arbitration;

'Party-Appointed Expert' means a person or organisation appointed by a Party in order to report on specific issues determined by the Party;

'Request to Produce' means a written request by a Party that another Party produce Documents;

'Respondent' means the Party or Parties against whom the Claimant made its claim, and any Party who, through joinder or otherwise, becomes aligned with such Party or Parties, and includes a Respondent making a counterclaim;

'Tribunal-Appointed Expert' means a person or organisation appointed by the Arbitral Tribunal in order to report to it on specific issues determined by the Arbitral Tribunal; and

'Witness Statement' means a written statement of testimony by a witness of fact.

Article 1   Scope of Application

1. Whenever the Parties have agreed or the Arbitral Tribunal has determined to apply the IBA Rules of Evidence, the Rules shall govern the taking of evidence, except to the extent that any specific provision of them may be found to be in conflict with any mandatory provision of law determined to be applicable to the case by the Parties or by the Arbitral Tribunal.

2. Where the Parties have agreed to apply the IBA Rules of Evidence, they shall be deemed to have agreed, in the absence of a contrary indication, to the version as current on the date of such agreement.

3. In case of conflict between any provisions of the IBA Rules of Evidence and the General Rules, the Arbitral Tribunal shall apply the IBA Rules of Evidence in the manner that it determines best in order to accomplish the purposes of both the General Rules and the IBA Rules of Evidence, unless the Parties agree to the contrary.

4. In the event of any dispute regarding the meaning of the IBA Rules of Evidence, the Arbitral Tribunal shall interpret them according to their purpose and in the manner most appropriate for the particular arbitration.

5. Insofar as the IBA Rules of Evidence and the General Rules are silent on any matter concerning the taking of evidence and the Parties have not agreed otherwise, the Arbitral Tribunal shall conduct the taking of evidence as it deems appropriate, in accordance with the general principles of the IBA Rules of Evidence.

Article 2   Consultation on Evidentiary Issues

1. The Arbitral Tribunal shall consult the Parties at the earliest appropriate time in the proceedings and invite them to consult each other with a view to agreeing on an efficient, economical and fair process for the taking of evidence.

2. The consultation on evidentiary issues may address the scope, timing and

manner of the taking of evidence, including:

(a) the preparation and submission of Witness Statements and Expert Reports;

(b) the taking of oral testimony at any Evidentiary Hearing;

(c) the requirements, procedure and format applicable to the production of Documents;

(d) the level of confidentiality protection to be afforded to evidence in the arbitration; and

(e) the promotion of efficiency, economy and conservation of resources in connection with the taking of evidence.

3. The Arbitral Tribunal is encouraged to identify to the Parties, as soon as it considers it to be appropriate, any issues:

(a) that the Arbitral Tribunal may regard as relevant to the case and material to its outcome; and/or

(b) for which a preliminary determination may be appropriate.

Article 3   Documents

1. Within the time ordered by the Arbitral Tribunal, each party shall submit to the Arbitral Tribunal and to the other Parties all Documents available to it on which it relies, including public Documents and those in the public domain, except for any Documents that have already been submitted by another Party.

2. Within the time ordered by the Arbitral Tribunal, any party may submit to the Arbitral Tribunal and to the other Parties a Request to Produce.

3. A Request to Produce shall contain:

(a) *(i)* a description of each requested Document sufficient to identify it, or *(ii)* a description in sufficient detail (including subject matter) of a narrow and specific requested category of Documents that are reasonably believed to exist; in the case of Documents maintained in electronic form, the requesting Party may, or the Arbitral Tribunal may order that it shall be required to, identify specific files, search terms, individuals or other means of searching for such Documents in an efficient and economical manner;

(b) a statement as to how the Documents requested are relevant to the case and material to its outcome; and

(c) *(i)* a statement that the Documents requested are not in the possession, custody or control of the requesting Party or a statement of the reasons why it would be unreasonably burdensome for the requesting Party to produce such Documents, and *(ii)* a statement of the reasons why the requesting Party assumes the Documents requested are in the possession, custody or control of another Party.

4. Within the time ordered by the Arbitral Tribunal, the Party to whom the Request to Produce is addressed shall produce to the other Parties and, if the

Arbitral Tribunal so orders, to it, all the Documents requested in its possession, custody or control as to which it makes no objection.

5. If the Party to whom the Request to Produce is addressed has an objection to some or all of the Documents requested, it shall state the objection in writing to the Arbitral Tribunal and the other Parties within the time ordered by the Arbitral Tribunal. The reasons for such objection shall be any of those set forth in Article 9.2 or a failure to satisfy any of the requirements of Article 3.3.

6. Upon receipt of any such objection, the Arbitral Tribunal may invite the relevant Parties to consult with each other with a view to resolving the objection.

7. Either Party may, within the time ordered by the Arbitral Tribunal, request the Arbitral Tribunal to rule on the objection. The Arbitral Tribunal shall then, in consultation with the Parties and in timely fashion, consider the Request to Produce and the objection. The Arbitral Tribunal may order the Party to whom such Request is addressed to produce any requested Document in its possession, custody or control as to which the Arbitral Tribunal determines that *(i)* the issues that the requesting Party wishes to prove are relevant to the case and material to its outcome; *(ii)* none of the reasons for objection set forth in Article 9.2 applies; and *(iii)* the requirements of Article 3.3 have been satisfied. Any such Document shall be produced to the other Parties and, if the Arbitral Tribunal so orders, to it.

8. In exceptional circumstances, if the propriety of an objection can be determined only by review of the Document, the Arbitral Tribunal may determine that it should not review the Document. In that event, the Arbitral Tribunal may, after consultation with the Parties, appoint an independent and impartial expert, bound to confidentiality, to review any such Document and to report on the objection. To the extent that the objection is upheld by the Arbitral Tribunal, the expert shall not disclose to the Arbitral Tribunal and to the other Parties the contents of the Document reviewed.

9. If a Party wishes to obtain the production of Documents from a person or organisation who is not a Party to the arbitration and from whom the Party cannot obtain the Documents on its own, the Party may, within the time ordered by the Arbitral Tribunal, ask it to take whatever steps are legally available to obtain the requested Documents, or seek leave from the Arbitral Tribunal to take such steps itself. The Party shall submit such request to the Arbitral Tribunal and to the other Parties in writing, and the request shall contain the particulars set forth in Article 3.3, as applicable. The Arbitral Tribunal shall decide on this request and shall take, authorize the requesting Party to take, or order any other Party to take, such steps as the Arbitral Tribunal considers appropriate if, in its discretion, it determines that *(i)* the Documents would be relevant to the case and material to its outcome, *(ii)* the requirements of Article 3.3, as applicable, have been satisfied and *(iii)* none of the reasons for objection set forth in Article 9.2 applies

10. At any time before the arbitration is concluded, the Arbitral Tribunal may *(i)* request any Party to produce Documents, *(ii)* request any Party to use its best efforts to take or *(iii)* itself take, any step that it considers appropriate to obtain Documents from any person or organisation. A Party to whom such a request for Documents is addressed may object to the request for any of the reasons set forth

in Article 9.2. In such cases, Article 3.4 to Article 3.8 shall apply correspondingly.

11. Within the time ordered by the Arbitral Tribunal, the Parties may submit to the Arbitral Tribunal and to the other Parties any additional Documents on which they intend to rely or which they believe have become relevant to the case and material to its outcome as a consequence of the issues raised in Documents, Witness Statements or Expert Reports submitted or produced, or in other submissions of the Parties.

12. With respect to the form of submission or production of Documents:

(a) copies of Documents shall conform to the originals and, at the request of the Arbitral Tribunal, any original shall be presented for inspection;

(b) Documents that a Party maintains in electronic form shall be submitted or produced in the form most convenient or economical to it that is reasonably usable by the recipients, unless the Parties agree otherwise or, in the absence of such agreement, the Arbitral Tribunal decides otherwise;

(c) a Party is not obligated to produce multiple copies of Documents which are essentially identical unless the Arbitral Tribunal decides otherwise; and

(d) translations of Documents shall be submitted together with the originals and marked as translations with the original language identified.

13. Any Document submitted or produced by a Party or non-Party in the arbitration and not otherwise in the public domain shall be kept confidential by the Arbitral Tribunal and the other Parties, and shall be used only in connection with the arbitration. This requirement shall apply except and to the extent that disclosure may be required of a Party to fulfil a legal duty, protect or pursue a legal right, or enforce or challenge an award in bona fide legal proceedings before a state court or other judicial authority. The Arbitral Tribunal may issue orders to set forth the terms of this confidentiality. This requirement shall be without prejudice to all other obligations of confidentiality in the arbitration.

14. If the arbitration is organised into separate issues or phases (such as jurisdiction, preliminary determinations, liability or damages), the Arbitral Tribunal may, after consultation with the Parties, schedule the submission of Documents and Requests to Produce separately for each issue or phase.

Article 4   Witnesses of Fact

1. Within the time ordered by the Arbitral Tribunal, each Party shall identify the witnesses on whose testimony it intends to rely and the subject matter of that testimony.

2. Any person may present evidence as a witness, including a Party or a Party's officer, employee or other representative.

3. It shall not be improper for a Party, its officers, employees, legal advisors or other representatives to interview its witnesses or potential witnesses and to discuss their prospective testimony with them.

4. The Arbitral Tribunal may order each Party to submit within a specified time to the Arbitral Tribunal and to the other Parties Witness Statements by each

witness on whose testimony it intends to rely, except for those witnesses whose testimony is sought pursuant to Articles 4.9 or 4.10. If Evidentiary Hearings are organised into separate issues or phases (such as jurisdiction, preliminary determinations, liability or damages), the Arbitral Tribunal or the Parties by agreement may schedule the submission of Witness Statements separately for each issue or phase.

5. Each Witness Statement shall contain:

(a) the full name and address of the witness, a statement regarding his or her present and past relationship (if any) with any of the Parties, and a description of his or her background, qualifications, training and experience, if such a description may be relevant to the dispute or to the contents of the statement;

(b) a full and detailed description of the facts, and the source of the witness's information as to those facts, sufficient to serve as that witness's evidence in the matter in dispute. Documents on which the witness relies that have not already been submitted shall be provided;

(c) a statement as to the language in which the Witness Statement was originally prepared and the language in which the witness anticipates giving testimony at the Evidentiary Hearing;

(d) an affirmation of the truth of the Witness Statement; and

(e) the signature of the witness and its date and place.

6. If Witness Statements are submitted, any Party may, within the time ordered by the Arbitral Tribunal, submit to the Arbitral Tribunal and to the other Parties revised or additional Witness Statements, including statements from persons not previously named as witnesses, so long as any such revisions or additions respond only to matters contained in another Party's Witness Statements, Expert Reports or other submissions that have not been previously presented in the arbitration.

7. If a witness whose appearance has been requested pursuant to Article 8.1 fails without a valid reason to appear for testimony at an Evidentiary Hearing, the Arbitral Tribunal shall disregard any Witness Statement related to that Evidentiary Hearing by that witness unless, in exceptional circumstances, the Arbitral Tribunal decides otherwise.

8. If the appearance of a witness has not been requested pursuant to Article 8.1, none of the other Parties shall be deemed to have agreed to the correctness of the content of the Witness Statement.

9. If a Party wishes to present evidence from a person who will not appear voluntarily at its request, the Party may, within the time ordered by the Arbitral Tribunal, ask it to take whatever steps are legally available to obtain the testimony of that person, or seek leave from the Arbitral Tribunal to take such steps itself. In the case of a request to the Arbitral Tribunal, the Party shall identify the intended witness, shall describe the subjects on which the witness's testimony is sought and shall state why such subjects are relevant to the case and material to its outcome. The Arbitral Tribunal shall decide on this request and shall take, authorize the requesting Party to take or order any other Party to take, such steps as the Arbitral

Tribunal considers appropriate if, in its discretion, it determines that the testimony of that witness would be relevant to the case and material to its outcome.

10. At any time before the arbitration is concluded, the Arbitral Tribunal may order any Party to provide for, or to use its best efforts to provide for, the appearance for testimony at an Evidentiary Hearing of any person, including one whose testimony has not yet been offered. A Party to whom such a request is addressed may object for any of the reasons set forth in Article 9.2.

Article 5   Party-Appointed Experts

1. A Party may rely on a Party-Appointed Expert as a means of evidence on specific issues. Within the time ordered by the Arbitral Tribunal, (i) each Party shall identify any Party-Appointed Expert on whose testimony it intends to rely and the subject-matter of such testimony; and (ii) the Party-Appointed Expert shall submit an Expert Report.

2. The Expert Report shall contain:

(a) the full name and address of the Party- Appointed Expert, a statement regarding his or her present and past relationship (if any) with any of the Parties, their legal advisors and the Arbitral Tribunal, and a description of his or her background, qualifications, training and experience;

(b) a description of the instructions pursuant to which he or she is providing his or her opinions and conclusions;

(c) a statement of his or her independence from the Parties, their legal advisors and the Arbitral Tribunal;

(d) a statement of the facts on which he or she is basing his or her expert opinions and conclusions;

(e) his or her expert opinions and conclusions, including a description of the methods, evidence and information used in arriving at the conclusions. Documents on which the Party-Appointed Expert relies that have not already been submitted shall be provided;

(f) if the Expert Report has been translated, a statement as to the language in which it was originally prepared, and the language in which the Party-Appointed Expert anticipates giving testimony at the Evidentiary Hearing;

(g) an affirmation of his or her genuine belief in the opinions expressed in the Expert Report;

(h) the signature of the Party-Appointed Expert and its date and place; and

(i) if the Expert Report has been signed by more than one person, an attribution of the entirety or specific parts of the Expert Report to each author.

3. If Expert Reports are submitted, any Party may, within the time ordered by the Arbitral Tribunal, submit to the Arbitral Tribunal and to the other Parties revised or additional Expert Reports, including reports or statements from persons not previously identified as Party-Appointed Experts, so long as any such revisions or additions respond only to matters contained in another Party's Witness

Statements, Expert Reports or other submissions that have not been previously presented in the arbitration.

4. The Arbitral Tribunal in its discretion may order that any Party-Appointed Experts who will submit or who have submitted Expert Reports on the same or related issues meet and confer on such issues. At such meeting, the Party-Appointed Experts shall attempt to reach agreement on the issues within the scope of their Expert Reports, and they shall record in writing any such issues on which they reach agreement, any remaining areas of disagreement and the reasons therefore.

5. If a Party-Appointed Expert whose appearance has been requested pursuant to Article 8.1 fails without a valid reason to appear for testimony at an Evidentiary Hearing, the Arbitral Tribunal shall disregard any Expert Report by that Party-Appointed Expert related to that Evidentiary Hearing unless, in exceptional circumstances, the Arbitral Tribunal decides otherwise.

6. If the appearance of a Party-Appointed Expert has not been requested pursuant to Article 8.1, none of the other Parties shall be deemed to have agreed to the correctness of the content of the Expert Report.

Article 6 Tribunal-Appointed Experts

1. The Arbitral Tribunal, after consulting with the Parties, may appoint one or more independent Tribunal-Appointed Experts to report to it on specific issues designated by the Arbitral Tribunal. The Arbitral Tribunal shall establish the terms of reference for any Tribunal-Appointed Expert Report after consulting with the Parties. A copy of the final terms of reference shall be sent by the Arbitral Tribunal to the Parties.

2. The Tribunal-Appointed Expert shall, before accepting appointment, submit to the Arbitral Tribunal and to the Parties a description of his or her qualifications and a statement of his or her independence from the Parties, their legal advisors and the Arbitral Tribunal. Within the time ordered by the Arbitral Tribunal, the Parties shall inform the Arbitral Tribunal whether they have any objections as to the Tribunal-Appointed Expert's qualifications and independence. The Arbitral Tribunal shall decide promptly whether to accept any such objection. After the appointment of a Tribunal- Appointed Expert, a Party may object to the expert's qualifications or independence only if the objection is for reasons of which the Party becomes aware after the appointment has been made. The Arbitral Tribunal shall decide promptly what, if any, action to take.

3. Subject to the provisions of Article 9.2, the Tribunal- Appointed Expert may request a Party to provide any information or to provide access to any Documents, goods, samples, property, machinery, systems, processes or site for inspection, to the extent relevant to the case and material to its outcome. The authority of a Tribunal-Appointed Expert to request such information or access shall be the same as the authority of the Arbitral Tribunal. The Parties and their representatives shall have the right to receive any such information and to attend any such inspection. Any disagreement between a Tribunal- Appointed Expert and a Party as to the relevance, materiality or appropriateness of such a request shall be decided by the Arbitral Tribunal, in the manner provided in Articles 3.5 through 3.8. The Tribunal-

Appointed Expert shall record in the Expert Report any non-compliance by a Party with an appropriate request or decision by the Arbitral Tribunal and shall describe its effects on the determination of the specific issue.

4. The Tribunal-Appointed Expert shall report in writing to the Arbitral Tribunal in an Expert Report. The Expert Report shall contain:

(a) the full name and address of the Tribunal- Appointed Expert, and a description of his or her background, qualifications, training and experience;

(b) a statement of the facts on which he or she is basing his or her expert opinions and conclusions;

(c) his or her expert opinions and conclusions, including a description of the methods, evidence and information used in arriving at the conclusions. Documents on which the Tribunal-Appointed Expert relies that have not already been submitted shall be provided;

(d) if the Expert Report has been translated, a statement as to the language in which it was originally prepared, and the language in which the Tribunal-Appointed Expert anticipates giving testimony at the Evidentiary Hearing;

(e) an affirmation of his or her genuine belief in the opinions expressed in the Expert Report;

(f) the signature of the Tribunal-Appointed Expert and its date and place; and

(g) if the Expert Report has been signed by more than one person, an attribution of the entirety or specific parts of the Expert Report to each author.

5. The Arbitral Tribunal shall send a copy of such Expert Report to the Parties. The Parties may examine any information, Documents, goods, samples, property, machinery, systems, processes or site for inspection that the Tribunal-Appointed Expert has examined and any correspondence between the Arbitral Tribunal and the Tribunal-Appointed Expert. Within the time ordered by the Arbitral Tribunal, any Party shall have the opportunity to respond to the Expert Report in a submission by the Party or through a Witness Statement or an Expert Report by a Party-Appointed Expert. The Arbitral Tribunal shall send the submission, Witness Statement or Expert Report to the Tribunal-Appointed Expert and to the other Parties.

6. At the request of a Party or of the Arbitral Tribunal, the Tribunal-Appointed Expert shall be present at an Evidentiary Hearing. The Arbitral Tribunal may question the Tribunal-Appointed Expert, and he or she may be questioned by the Parties or by any Party-Appointed Expert on issues raised in his or her Expert Report, the Parties' submissions or Witness Statement or the Expert Reports made by the Party- Appointed Experts pursuant to Article 6.5.

7. Any Expert Report made by a Tribunal-Appointed Expert and its conclusions shall be assessed by the Arbitral Tribunal with due regard to all circumstances of the case.

8. The fees and expenses of a Tribunal-Appointed Expert, to be funded in a manner determined by the Arbitral Tribunal, shall form part of the costs of the

arbitration.

Article 7   Inspection

Subject to the provisions of Article 9.2, the Arbitral Tribunal may, at the request of a Party or on its own motion, inspect or require the inspection by a Tribunal-Appointed Expert or a Party-Appointed Expert of any site, property, machinery or any other goods, samples, systems, processes or Documents, as it deems appropriate. The Arbitral Tribunal shall, in consultation with the Parties, determine the timing and arrangement for the inspection. The Parties and their representatives shall have the right to attend any such inspection.

Article 8   Evidentiary Hearing

1. Within the time ordered by the Arbitral Tribunal, each Party shall inform the Arbitral Tribunal and the other Parties of the witnesses whose appearance it requests. Each witness (which term includes, for the purposes of this Article, witnesses of fact and any experts) shall, subject to Article 8.2, appear for testimony at the Evidentiary Hearing if such person's appearance has been requested by any Party or by the Arbitral Tribunal. Each witness shall appear in person unless the Arbitral Tribunal allows the use of videoconference or similar technology with respect to a particular witness.

2. The Arbitral Tribunal shall at all times have complete control over the Evidentiary Hearing. The Arbitral Tribunal may limit or exclude any question to, answer by or appearance of a witness, if it considers such question, answer or appearance to be irrelevant, immaterial, unreasonably burdensome, duplicative or otherwise covered by a reason for objection set forth in Article 9.2. Questions to a witness during direct and re-direct testimony may not be unreasonably leading.

3. With respect to oral testimony at an Evidentiary Hearing:

(a) the Claimant shall ordinarily first present the testimony of its witnesses, followed by the Respondent presenting the testimony of its witnesses;

(b) following direct testimony, any other Party may question such witness, in an order to be determined by the Arbitral Tribunal. The Party who initially presented the witness shall subsequently have the opportunity to ask additional questions on the matters raised in the other Parties' questioning;

(c) thereafter, the Claimant shall ordinarily first present the testimony of its Party-Appointed Experts, followed by the Respondent presenting the testimony of its Party-Appointed Experts. The Party who initially presented the Party-Appointed Expert shall subsequently have the opportunity to ask additional questions on the matters raised in the other Parties' questioning;

(d) the Arbitral Tribunal may question a Tribunal-Appointed Expert, and he or she may be questioned by the Parties or by any Party-Appointed Expert, on issues raised in the Tribunal-Appointed Expert Report, in the Parties' submissions or in the Expert Reports made by the Party-Appointed Experts;

(e) if the arbitration is organised into separate issues or phases (such as jurisdiction, preliminary determinations, liability and damages), the Parties may agree or the Arbitral Tribunal may order the scheduling of testimony separately for each issue or phase;

(f) the Arbitral Tribunal, upon request of a Party or on its own motion, may vary this order of proceeding, including the arrangement of testimony by particular issues or in such a manner that witnesses be questioned at the same time and in confrontation with each other (witness conferencing);

(g) the Arbitral Tribunal may ask questions to a witness at any time.

4. A witness of fact providing testimony shall first affirm, in a manner determined appropriate by the Arbitral Tribunal, that he or she commits to tell the truth or, in the case of an expert witness, his or her genuine belief in the opinions to be expressed at the Evidentiary Hearing. If the witness has submitted a Witness Statement or an Expert Report, the witness shall confirm it. The Parties may agree or the Arbitral Tribunal may order that the Witness Statement or Expert Report shall serve as that witness's direct testimony.

5. Subject to the provisions of Article 9.2, the Arbitral Tribunal may request any person to give oral or written evidence on any issue that the Arbitral Tribunal considers to be relevant to the case and material to its outcome. Any witness called and questioned by the Arbitral Tribunal may also be questioned by the Parties.

Article 9   Admissibility and Assessment of Evidence

1. The Arbitral Tribunal shall determine the admissibility, relevance, materiality and weight of evidence.

2. The Arbitral Tribunal shall, at the request of a Party or on its own motion, exclude from evidence or production any Document, statement, oral testimony or inspection for any of the following reasons:

(a) lack of sufficient relevance to the case or materiality to its outcome;

(b) legal impediment or privilege under the legal or ethical rules determined by the Arbitral Tribunal to be applicable;

(c) unreasonable burden to produce the requested evidence;

(d) loss or destruction of the Document that has been shown with reasonable likelihood to have occurred;

(e) grounds of commercial or technical confidentiality that the Arbitral Tribunal determines to be compelling;

(f) grounds of special political or institutional sensitivity (including evidence that has been classified as secret by a government or a public international institution) that the Arbitral Tribunal determines to be compelling; or

(g) considerations of procedural economy, proportionality, fairness or equality of the Parties that the Arbitral Tribunal determines to be compelling.

3. In considering issues of legal impediment or privilege under Article 9.2(b), and insofar as permitted by any mandatory legal or ethical rules that are determined by it to be applicable, the Arbitral Tribunal may take into account:

(a) any need to protect the confidentiality of a Document created or statement or oral communication made in connection with and for the purpose of providing or obtaining legal advice;

(b) any need to protect the confidentiality of a Document created or statement or oral communication made in connection with and for the purpose of settlement negotiations;

(c) the expectations of the Parties and their advisors at the time the legal impediment or privilege is said to have arisen;

(d) any possible waiver of any applicable legal impediment or privilege by virtue of consent, earlier disclosure, affirmative use of the Document, statement, oral communication or advice contained therein, or otherwise; and

(e) the need to maintain fairness and equality as between the Parties, particularly if they are subject to different legal or ethical rules.

4. The Arbitral Tribunal may, where appropriate, make necessary arrangements to permit evidence to be presented or considered subject to suitable confidentiality protection.

5. If a Party fails without satisfactory explanation to produce any Document requested in a Request to Produce to which it has not objected in due time or fails to produce any Document ordered to be produced by the Arbitral Tribunal, the Arbitral Tribunal may infer that such document would be adverse to the interests of that Party.

6. If a Party fails without satisfactory explanation to make available any other relevant evidence, including testimony, sought by one Party to which the Party to whom the request was addressed has not objected in due time or fails to make available any evidence, including testimony, ordered by the Arbitral Tribunal to be produced, the Arbitral Tribunal may infer that such evidence would be adverse to the interests of that Party.

7. If the Arbitral Tribunal determines that a Party has failed to conduct itself in good faith in the taking of evidence, the Arbitral Tribunal may, in addition to any other measures available under these Rules, take such failure into account in its assignment of the costs of the arbitration, including costs arising out of or in connection with the taking of evidence.

AMERICAN ARBITRATION ASSOCIATION & AMERICAN BAR ASSOCIATION, CODE OF ETHICS FOR ARBITRATORS IN COMMERCIAL DISPUTES (2004)*

The Code of Ethics for Arbitrators in Commercial Disputes was originally prepared in 1977 by a joint committee consisting of a special committee of the American Arbitration Association and a special committee of the American Bar Association. The Code was revised in 2003 by an ABA Task Force and special committee of the AAA.

Preamble

The use of arbitration to resolve a wide variety of disputes has grown extensively and forms a significant part of the system of justice on which our society relies for a fair determination of legal rights. Persons who act as arbitrators therefore undertake serious responsibilities to the public, as well as to the parties. Those responsibilities include important ethical obligations.

Few cases of unethical behavior by commercial arbitrators have arisen. Nevertheless, this Code sets forth generally accepted standards of ethical conduct for the guidance of arbitrators and parties in commercial disputes, in the hope of contributing to the maintenance of high standards and continued confidence in the process of arbitration.

This Code provides ethical guidelines for many types of arbitration but does not apply to labor arbitration, which is generally conducted under the Code of Professional Responsibility for Arbitrators of Labor-Management Disputes.

There are many different types of commercial arbitration. Some proceedings are conducted under arbitration rules established by various organizations and trade associations, while others are conducted without such rules. Although most proceedings are arbitrated pursuant to voluntary agreement of the parties, certain types of disputes are submitted to arbitration by reason of particular laws. This Code is intended to apply to all such proceedings in which disputes or claims are submitted for decision to one or more arbitrators appointed in a manner provided by an agreement of the parties, by applicable arbitration rules, or by law. In all such cases, the persons who have the power to decide should observe fundamental standards of ethical conduct. In this Code, all such persons are called "arbitrators," although in some types of proceeding they might be called "umpires," "referees," "neutrals," or have some other title.

Arbitrators, like judges, have the power to decide cases. However, unlike full-time judges, arbitrators are usually engaged in other occupations before, during, and after the time that they serve as arbitrators. Often, arbitrators are purposely chosen from the same trade or industry as the parties in order to bring special knowledge to the task of deciding. This Code recognizes these fundamental differences between arbitrators and judges.

In those instances where this Code has been approved and recommended by organizations that provide, coordinate, or administer services of arbitrators, it provides ethical standards for the members of their respective panels of arbitrators. However, this Code does not form a part of the arbitration rules of any such organization unless its rules so provide.

Note on Neutrality

In some types of commercial arbitration, the parties or the administering institution provide for three or more arbitrators. In some such proceedings, it is the practice for each party, acting alone, to appoint one arbitrator (a "party-appointed arbitrator") and for one additional arbitrator to be designated by the party-appointed arbitrators, or by the parties, or by an independent institution or individual. The sponsors of this Code believe that it is preferable for all arbitrators including any party-appointed arbitrators to be neutral, that is, independent and impartial, and to comply with the same ethical standards. This expectation generally is essential in arbitrations where the parties, the nature of the dispute, or the enforcement of any resulting award may have international aspects. However, parties in certain domestic arbitrations in the United States may prefer that party-appointed arbitrators be non-neutral and governed by special ethical considerations. These special ethical considerations appear in Canon X of this Code.

This Code establishes a presumption of neutrality for all arbitrators, including party-appointed arbitrators, which applies unless the parties' agreement, the arbitration rules agreed to by the parties or applicable laws provide otherwise. This Code requires all party-appointed arbitrators, whether neutral or not, to make pre-appointment disclosures of any facts which might affect their neutrality, independence, or impartiality. This Code also requires all party-appointed arbitrators to ascertain and disclose as soon as practicable whether the parties intended for them to serve as neutral or not. If any doubt or uncertainty exists, the party-appointed arbitrators should serve as neutrals unless and until such doubt or uncertainty is resolved in accordance with Canon IX. This Code expects all arbitrators, including those serving under Canon X, to preserve the integrity and fairness of the process.

Note on Construction

Various aspects of the conduct of arbitrators, including some matters covered by this Code, may also be governed by agreements of the parties, arbitration rules to which the parties have agreed, applicable law, or other applicable ethics rules, all of which should be consulted by the arbitrators. This Code does not take the place of or supersede such laws, agreements, or arbitration rules to which the parties have agreed and should be read in conjunction with other rules of ethics. It does not establish new or additional grounds for judicial review of arbitration awards.

All provisions of this Code should therefore be read as subject to contrary provisions of applicable law and arbitration rules. They should also be read as subject to contrary agreements of the parties. Nevertheless, this Code imposes no obligation on any arbitrator to act in a manner inconsistent with the arbitrator's fundamental duty to preserve the integrity and fairness of the arbitral process.

Canons I through VIII of this Code apply to all arbitrators. Canon IX applies to all party-appointed arbitrators, except that certain party-appointed arbitrators are exempted by Canon X from compliance with certain provisions of Canons I-IX related to impartiality and independence, as specified in Canon X.

CANON I.　AN ARBITRATOR SHOULD UPHOLD THE INTEGRITY AND FAIRNESS OF THE ARBITRATION PROCESS.

A. An arbitrator has a responsibility not only to the parties but also to the process of arbitration itself, and must observe high standards of conduct so that the integrity and fairness of the process will be preserved. Accordingly, an arbitrator should recognize a responsibility to the public, to the parties whose rights will be decided, and to all other participants in the proceeding. This responsibility may include pro bono service as an arbitrator where appropriate.

B. One should accept appointment as an arbitrator only if fully satisfied:

(1) that he or she can serve impartially;

(2) that he or she can serve independently from the parties, potential witnesses, and the other arbitrators;

(3) that he or she is competent to serve; and

(4) that he or she can be available to commence the arbitration in accordance with the requirements of the proceeding and thereafter to devote the time and attention to its completion that the parties are reasonably entitled to expect.

C. After accepting appointment and while serving as an arbitrator, a person should avoid entering into any business, professional, or personal relationship, or acquiring any financial or personal interest, which is likely to affect impartiality or which might reasonably create the appearance of partiality. For a reasonable period of time after the decision of a case, persons who have served as arbitrators should avoid entering into any such relationship, or acquiring any such interest, in circumstances which might reasonably create the appearance that they had been influenced in the arbitration by the anticipation or expectation of the relationship or interest. Existence of any of the matters or circumstances described in this paragraph C does not render it unethical for one to serve as an arbitrator where the parties have consented to the arbitrator's appointment or continued services following full disclosure of the relevant facts in accordance with Canon II.

D. Arbitrators should conduct themselves in a way that is fair to all parties and should not be swayed by outside pressure, public clamor, and fear of criticism or self-interest. They should avoid conduct and statements that give the appearance of partiality toward or against any party.

E. When an arbitrator's authority is derived from the agreement of the parties, an arbitrator should neither exceed that authority nor do less than is required to exercise that authority completely. Where the agreement of the parties sets forth procedures to be followed in conducting the arbitration or refers to rules to be followed, it is the obligation of the arbitrator to comply with such procedures or rules. An arbitrator has no ethical obligation to comply with any agreement, procedures or rules that are unlawful or that, in the arbitrator's judgment, would be inconsistent with this Code.

F. An arbitrator should conduct the arbitration process so as to advance the fair and efficient resolution of the matters submitted for decision. An arbitrator should make all reasonable efforts to prevent delaying tactics, harassment of parties or other participants, or other abuse or disruption of the arbitration process.

G. The ethical obligations of an arbitrator begin upon acceptance of the appointment and continue throughout all stages of the proceeding. In addition, as set forth in this Code, certain ethical obligations begin as soon as a person is requested to serve as an arbitrator and certain ethical obligations continue after the decision in the proceeding has been given to the parties.

H. Once an arbitrator has accepted an appointment, the arbitrator should not withdraw or abandon the appointment unless compelled to do so by unanticipated circumstances that would render it impossible or impracticable to continue. When an arbitrator is to be compensated for his or her services, the arbitrator may withdraw if the parties fail or refuse to provide for payment of the compensation as agreed.

I. An arbitrator who withdraws prior to the completion of the arbitration, whether upon the arbitrator's initiative or upon the request of one or more of the parties, should take reasonable steps to protect the interests of the parties in the arbitration, including return of evidentiary materials and protection of confidentiality.

Comment to Canon I

A prospective arbitrator is not necessarily partial or prejudiced by having acquired knowledge of the parties, the applicable law or the customs and practices of the business involved. Arbitrators may also have special experience or expertise in the areas of business, commerce, or technology which are involved in the arbitration. Arbitrators do not contravene this Canon if, by virtue of such experience or expertise, they have views on certain general issues likely to arise in the arbitration, but an arbitrator may not have prejudged any of the specific factual or legal determinations to be addressed during the arbitration.

During an arbitration, the arbitrator may engage in discourse with the parties or their counsel, draw out arguments or contentions, comment on the law or evidence, make interim rulings, and otherwise control or direct the arbitration. These activities are integral parts of an arbitration. Paragraph D of Canon I is not intended to preclude or limit either full discussion of the issues during the course of the arbitration or the arbitrator's management of the proceeding.

CANON II. AN ARBITRATOR SHOULD DISCLOSE ANY INTEREST OR RELATIONSHIP LIKELY TO AFFECT IMPARTIALITY OR WHICH MIGHT CREATE AN APPEARANCE OF PARTIALITY.

A. Persons who are requested to serve as arbitrators should, before accepting, disclose:

(1) any known direct or indirect financial or personal interest in the outcome of the arbitration;

(2) any known existing or past financial, business, professional or personal relationships which might reasonably affect impartiality or lack of independence in the eyes of any of the parties. For example, prospective arbitrators should disclose any such relationships which they personally have with any party or its lawyer, with any co-arbitrator, or with any individual whom they have been told will be a witness. They should also disclose any such relationships involving their families or household members or their current employers, partners, or professional or business associates that can be ascertained by reasonable efforts;

(3) the nature and extent of any prior knowledge they may have of the dispute; and

(4) any other matters, relationships, or interests which they are obligated to disclose by the agreement of the parties, the rules or practices of an institution, or applicable law regulating arbitrator disclosure.

B. Persons who are requested to accept appointment as arbitrators should make a reasonable effort to inform themselves of any interests or relationships described in paragraph A.

C. The obligation to disclose interests or relationships described in paragraph A is a continuing duty which requires a person who accepts appointment as an arbitrator to disclose, as soon as practicable, at any stage of the arbitration, any such interests or relationships which may arise, or which are recalled or discovered.

D. Any doubt as to whether or not disclosure is to be made should be resolved in favor of disclosure.

E. Disclosure should be made to all parties unless other procedures for disclosure are provided in the agreement of the parties, applicable rules or practices of an institution, or by law. Where more than one arbitrator has been appointed, each should inform the others of all matters disclosed.

F. When parties, with knowledge of a person's interests and relationships, nevertheless desire that person to serve as an arbitrator, that person may properly serve.

G. If an arbitrator is requested by all parties to withdraw, the arbitrator must do so. If an arbitrator is requested to withdraw by less than all of the parties because of alleged partiality, the arbitrator should withdraw unless either of the following circumstances exists:

(1) An agreement of the parties, or arbitration rules agreed to by the parties, or applicable law establishes procedures for determining challenges to arbitrators, in which case those procedures should be followed; or

(2) In the absence of applicable procedures, if the arbitrator, after carefully considering the matter, determines that the reason for the challenge is not substantial, and that he or she can nevertheless act and decide the case impartially and fairly.

H. If compliance by a prospective arbitrator with any provision of this Code would require disclosure of confidential or privileged information, the prospective arbitrator should either:

(1) Secure the consent to the disclosure from the person who furnished the information or the holder of the privilege; or

(2) Withdraw.

CANON III.   AN ARBITRATOR SHOULD AVOID IMPROPRIETY OR THE APPEARANCE OF IMPROPRIETY IN COMMUNICATING WITH PARTIES.

A. If an agreement of the parties or applicable arbitration rules establishes the manner or content of communications between the arbitrator and the parties, the arbitrator should follow those procedures notwithstanding any contrary provision of paragraphs B and C.

B. An arbitrator or prospective arbitrator should not discuss a proceeding with any party in the absence of any other party, except in any of the following circumstances:

(1) When the appointment of a prospective arbitrator is being considered, the prospective arbitrator:

(a) may ask about the identities of the parties, counsel, or witnesses and the general nature of the case; and

(b) may respond to inquiries from a party or its counsel designed to determine his or her suitability and availability for the appointment. In any such dialogue, the prospective arbitrator may receive information from a party or its counsel disclosing the general nature of the dispute but should not permit them to discuss the merits of the case.

(2) In an arbitration in which the two party-appointed arbitrators are expected to appoint the third arbitrator, each party-appointed arbitrator may consult with the party who appointed the arbitrator concerning the choice of the third arbitrator;

(3) In an arbitration involving party-appointed arbitrators, each party-appointed arbitrator may consult with the party who appointed the arbitrator concerning arrangements for any compensation to be paid to the party-appointed arbitrator. Submission of routine written requests for payment of compensation and expenses in accordance with such arrangements and written communications pertaining solely to such requests need not be sent to the other party;

(4) In an arbitration involving party-appointed arbitrators, each party-appointed arbitrator may consult with the party who appointed the arbitrator concerning the status of the arbitrator (*i.e.*, neutral or non-neutral), as contemplated by paragraph C of Canon IX;

(5) Discussions may be had with a party concerning such logistical matters as setting the time and place of hearings or making other arrangements for the conduct of the proceedings. However, the arbitrator should promptly inform each other party of the discussion and should not make any final determination concerning the matter discussed before giving each absent party an opportunity to express the party's views; or

(6) If a party fails to be present at a hearing after having been given due notice, or if all parties expressly consent, the arbitrator may discuss the case with any party who is present.

C. Unless otherwise provided in this Canon, in applicable arbitration rules or in an agreement of the parties, whenever an arbitrator communicates in writing with one party, the arbitrator should at the same time send a copy of the communication to every other party, and whenever the arbitrator receives any written communication concerning the case from one party which has not already been sent to every other party, the arbitrator should send or cause it to be sent to the other parties.

CANON IV.   AN ARBITRATOR SHOULD CONDUCT THE PROCEEDINGS FAIRLY AND DILIGENTLY.

A. An arbitrator should conduct the proceedings in an even-handed manner. The arbitrator should be patient and courteous to the parties, their representatives, and the witnesses and should encourage similar conduct by all participants.

B. The arbitrator should afford to all parties the right to be heard and due notice of the time and place of any hearing. The arbitrator should allow each party a fair opportunity to present its evidence and arguments.

C. The arbitrator should not deny any party the opportunity to be represented by counsel or by any other person chosen by the party.

D. If a party fails to appear after due notice, the arbitrator should proceed with the arbitration when authorized to do so, but only after receiving assurance that appropriate notice has been given to the absent party.

E. When the arbitrator determines that more information than has been presented by the parties is required to decide the case, it is not improper for the arbitrator to ask questions, call witnesses, and request documents or other evidence, including expert testimony.

F. Although it is not improper for an arbitrator to suggest to the parties that they discuss the possibility of settlement or the use of mediation, or other dispute resolution processes, an arbitrator should not exert pressure on any party to settle or to utilize other dispute resolution processes. An arbitrator should not be present or otherwise participate in settlement discussions or act as a mediator unless requested to do so by all parties.

G. Co-arbitrators should afford each other full opportunity to participate in all aspects of the proceedings.

Comment to paragraph G

Paragraph G of Canon IV is not intended to preclude one arbitrator from acting in limited circumstances (e.g., ruling on discovery issues) where authorized by the agreement of the parties, applicable rules or law, nor does it preclude a majority of the arbitrators from proceeding with any aspect of the arbitration if an arbitrator is unable or unwilling to participate and such action is authorized by the agreement of the parties or applicable rules or law. It also does not preclude ex parte requests for interim relief.

CANON V.   AN ARBITRATOR SHOULD MAKE DECISIONS IN A JUST, INDEPENDENT AND DELIBERATE MANNER.

A. The arbitrator should, after careful deliberation, decide all issues submitted for determination. An arbitrator should decide no other issues.

B. An arbitrator should decide all matters justly, exercising independent judgment, and should not permit outside pressure to affect the decision.

C. An arbitrator should not delegate the duty to decide to any other person.

D. In the event that all parties agree upon a settlement of issues in dispute and request the arbitrator to embody that agreement in an award, the arbitrator may do so, but is not required to do so unless satisfied with the propriety of the terms of settlement. Whenever an arbitrator embodies a settlement by the parties in an award, the arbitrator should state in the award that it is based on an agreement of the parties.

CANON VI.   AN ARBITRATOR SHOULD BE FAITHFUL TO THE RELATIONSHIP OF TRUST AND CONFIDENTIALITY INHERENT IN THAT OFFICE.

A. An arbitrator is in a relationship of trust to the parties and should not, at any time, use confidential information acquired during the arbitration proceeding to gain personal advantage or advantage for others, or to affect adversely the interest of another.

B. The arbitrator should keep confidential all matters relating to the arbitration proceedings and decision. An arbitrator may obtain help from an associate, a research assistant or other persons in connection with reaching his or her decision if the arbitrator informs the parties of the use of such assistance and such persons agree to be bound by the provisions of this Canon.

C. It is not proper at any time for an arbitrator to inform anyone of any decision in advance of the time it is given to all parties. In a proceeding in which there is more than one arbitrator, it is not proper at any time for an arbitrator to inform anyone about the substance of the deliberations of the arbitrators. After an arbitration award has been made, it is not proper for an arbitrator to assist in proceedings to enforce or challenge the award.

D. Unless the parties so request, an arbitrator should not appoint himself or herself to a separate office related to the subject matter of the dispute, such as receiver or trustee, nor should a panel of arbitrators appoint one of their number to such an office.

CANON VII.   AN ARBITRATOR SHOULD ADHERE TO STANDARDS OF INTEGRITY AND FAIRNESS WHEN MAKING ARRANGEMENTS FOR COMPENSATION AND REIMBURSEMENT OF EXPENSES.

A. Arbitrators who are to be compensated for their services or reimbursed for their expenses shall adhere to standards of integrity and fairness in making arrangements for such payments.

B. Certain practices relating to payments are generally recognized as tending to preserve the integrity and fairness of the arbitration process. These practices include:

(1) Before the arbitrator finally accepts appointment, the basis of payment, including any cancellation fee, compensation in the event of withdrawal and compensation for study and preparation time, and all other charges, should be established. Except for arrangements for the compensation of party-appointed arbitrators, all parties should be informed in writing of the terms established;

(2) In proceedings conducted under the rules or administration of an institution that is available to assist in making arrangements for payments, communication related to compensation should be made through the institution. In proceedings where no institution has been engaged by the parties to administer the arbitration, any communication with arbitrators (other than party-appointed arbitrators) concerning payments should be in the presence of all parties; and

(3) Arbitrators should not, absent extraordinary circumstances, request increases in the basis of their compensation during the course of a proceeding.

CANON VIII. AN ARBITRATOR MAY ENGAGE IN ADVERTISING OR PROMOTION OF ARBITRAL SERVICES WHICH IS TRUTHFUL AND ACCURATE.

A. Advertising or promotion of an individual's willingness or availability to serve as an arbitrator must be accurate and unlikely to mislead. Any statements about the quality of the arbitrator's work or the success of the arbitrator's practice must be truthful.

B. Advertising and promotion must not imply any willingness to accept an appointment otherwise than in accordance with this Code.

Comment to Canon VIII

This Canon does not preclude an arbitrator from printing, publishing, or disseminating advertisements conforming to these standards in any electronic or print medium, from making personal presentations to prospective users of arbitral services conforming to such standards or from responding to inquiries concerning the arbitrator's availability, qualifications, experience, or fee arrangements.

CANON IX. ARBITRATORS APPOINTED BY ONE PARTY HAVE A DUTY TO DETERMINE AND DISCLOSE THEIR STATUS AND TO COMPLY WITH THIS CODE, EXCEPT AS EXEMPTED BY CANON X.

A. In some types of arbitration in which there are three arbitrators, it is customary for each party, acting alone, to appoint one arbitrator. The third arbitrator is then appointed by agreement either of the parties or of the two arbitrators, or failing such agreement, by an independent institution or individual. In tripartite arbitrations to which this Code applies, all three arbitrators are presumed to be neutral and are expected to observe the same standards as the third arbitrator.

B. Notwithstanding this presumption, there are certain types of tripartite arbitration in which it is expected by all parties that the two arbitrators appointed by the parties may be predisposed toward the party appointing them. Those arbitrators, referred to in this Code as "Canon X arbitrators," are not to be held to the standards of neutrality and independence applicable to other arbitrators. Canon X describes the special ethical obligations of party-appointed arbitrators who are not expected to meet the standard of neutrality.

C. A party-appointed arbitrator has an obligation to ascertain, as early as possible but not later than the first meeting of the arbitrators and parties, whether the parties have agreed that the party-appointed arbitrators will serve as neutrals or whether they shall be subject to Canon X, and to provide a timely report of their conclusions to the parties and other arbitrators:

(1) Party-appointed arbitrators should review the agreement of the parties, the applicable rules and any applicable law bearing upon arbitrator neutrality. In reviewing the agreement of the parties, party-appointed arbitrators should consult any relevant express terms of the written or oral arbitration agreement. It may also be appropriate for them to inquire into agreements that have not been expressly set forth, but which may be implied from an established course of dealings of the parties or well-recognized custom and usage in their trade or profession;

(2) Where party-appointed arbitrators conclude that the parties intended for the party-appointed arbitrators not to serve as neutrals, they should so inform the parties and the other arbitrators. The arbitrators may then act as provided in Canon X unless or until a different determination of their status is made by the parties, any administering institution or the arbitral panel; and

(3) Until party-appointed arbitrators conclude that the party-appointed arbitrators were not intended by the parties to serve as neutrals, or if the party-appointed arbitrators are unable to form a reasonable belief of their status from the foregoing sources and no decision in this regard has yet been made by the parties, any administering institution, or the arbitral panel, they should observe all of the obligations of neutral arbitrators set forth in this Code.

D. Party-appointed arbitrators not governed by Canon X shall observe all of the obligations of Canons I through VIII unless otherwise required by agreement of the parties, any applicable rules, or applicable law.

CANON X. EXEMPTIONS FOR ARBITRATORS APPOINTED BY ONE PARTY WHO ARE NOT SUBJECT TO RULES OF NEUTRALITY.

Canon X arbitrators are expected to observe all of the ethical obligations prescribed by this Code except those from which they are specifically excused by Canon X.

A. *Obligations under Canon I*

Canon X arbitrators should observe all of the obligations of Canon I subject only to the following provisions:

(1) Canon X arbitrators may be predisposed toward the party who appointed them but in all other respects are obligated to act in good faith and with integrity and fairness. For example, Canon X arbitrators should not engage in delaying tactics or harassment of any party or witness and should not knowingly make untrue or misleading statements to the other arbitrators; and

(2) The provisions of subparagraphs B(1), B(2), and paragraphs C and D of Canon I, insofar as they relate to partiality, relationships, and interests are not applicable to Canon X arbitrators.

B.   *Obligations under Canon II*

(1) Canon X arbitrators should disclose to all parties, and to the other arbitrators, all interests and relationships which Canon II requires be disclosed. Disclosure as required by Canon II is for the benefit not only of the party who appointed the arbitrator, but also for the benefit of the other parties and arbitrators so that they may know of any partiality which may exist or appear to exist; and

(2) Canon X arbitrators are not obliged to withdraw under paragraph G of Canon II if requested to do so only by the party who did not appoint them.

C.   *Obligations under Canon III*

Canon X arbitrators should observe all of the obligations of Canon III subject only to the following provisions:

(1) Like neutral party-appointed arbitrators, Canon X arbitrators may consult with the party who appointed them to the extent permitted in paragraph B of Canon III;

(2) Canon X arbitrators shall, at the earliest practicable time, disclose to the other arbitrators and to the parties whether or not they intend to communicate with their appointing parties. If they have disclosed the intention to engage in such communications, they may thereafter communicate with their appointing parties concerning any other aspect of the case, except as provided in paragraph (3);

(3) If such communication occurred prior to the time they were appointed as arbitrators, or prior to the first hearing or other meeting of the parties with the arbitrators, the Canon X arbitrator should, at or before the first hearing or meeting of the arbitrators with the parties, disclose the fact that such communication has taken place. In complying with the provisions of this subparagraph, it is sufficient that there be disclosure of the fact that such communication has occurred without disclosing the content of the communication. A single timely disclosure of the Canon X arbitrator's intention to participate in such communications in the future is sufficient;

(4) Canon X arbitrators may not at any time during the arbitration:

(a) disclose any deliberations by the arbitrators on any matter or issue submitted to them for decision;

(b) communicate with the parties that appointed them concerning any matter or issue taken under consideration by the panel after the record is closed or such matter or issue has been submitted for decision; or

(c) disclose any final decision or interim decision in advance of the time that it is disclosed to all parties.

(5) Unless otherwise agreed by the arbitrators and the parties, a Canon X arbitrator may not communicate orally with the neutral arbitrator concerning any matter or issue arising or expected to arise in the arbitration in the absence of the other Canon X arbitrator. If a Canon X arbitrator communicates in writing with the neutral arbitrator, he or she shall simultaneously provide a copy of the written communication to the other Canon X arbitrator;

(6) When Canon X arbitrators communicate orally with the parties that appointed them concerning any matter on which communication is permitted under this Code, they are not obligated to disclose the contents of such oral communications to any other party or arbitrator; and

(7) When Canon X arbitrators communicate in writing with the party who appointed them concerning any matter on which communication is permitted under this Code, they are not required to send copies of any such written communication to any other party or arbitrator.

D. *Obligations under Canon IV*

Canon X arbitrators should observe all of the obligations of Canon IV.

E. *Obligations under Canon V*

Canon X arbitrators should observe all of the obligations of Canon V, except that they may be predisposed toward deciding in favor of the party who appointed them.

F. *Obligations under Canon VI*

Canon X arbitrators should observe all of the obligations of Canon VI.

G. *Obligations Under Canon VII*

Canon X arbitrators should observe all of the obligations of Canon VII.

H. *Obligations Under Canon VIII*

Canon X arbitrators should observe all of the obligations of Canon VIII.

I. *Obligations Under Canon IX*

The provisions of paragraph D of Canon IX are inapplicable to Canon X arbitrators, except insofar as the obligations are also set forth in this Canon.

INTERNATIONAL BAR ASSOCIATION, ETHICS FOR INTERNATIONAL ARBITRATORS*

Introductory Note

International arbitrators should be impartial, independent, competent, diligent and discreet. These rules seek to establish the manner in which these abstract qualities may be assessed in practice. Rather than rigid rules, they reflect internationally acceptable guidelines developed by practising lawyers from all continents. They will attain their objectives only if they are applied in good faith.

The rules cannot be directly binding either on arbitrators, or on the parties themselves, unless they are adopted by agreement. Whilst the International Bar Association hopes that they will be taken into account in the context of challenges to arbitrators, it is emphasised that these guidelines are not intended to create grounds for the setting aside of awards by national courts.

If parties wish to adopt the rules they may add the following to their arbitration clause or arbitration agreement: "The parties agree that the rules of Ethics for International Arbitrators established by the International Bar Association, in force at the date of the commencement of any arbitration under this clause, shall be applicable to the arbitrators appointed in respect of such arbitration."

The International Bar Association takes the position that (whatever may be the case in domestic arbitration) international arbitrators should in principle be granted immunity from suit under national laws, except in extreme cases of wilful or reckless disregard of their legal obligations. Accordingly, the International Bar Association wishes to make it clear that it is not the intention of these rules to create opportunities for aggrieved parties to sue international arbitrators in national courts. The normal sanction for breach of an ethical duty is removal from office, with consequent loss of entitlement to remuneration. The International Bar Association also emphasises that these rules do not affect, and are intended to be consistent with, the International Code of Ethics for lawyers, adopted at Oslo on 25th July 1956, and amended by the General Meeting of the International Bar Association at Mexico City on 24th July 1964.

1. Fundamental Rule

Arbitrators shall proceed diligently and efficiently to provide the parties with a just and effective resolution of their disputes, and shall be and shall remain free from bias.

2. Acceptance of Appointment

2.1 A prospective arbitrator shall accept an appointment only if he is fully satisfied that he is able to discharge his duties without bias.

2.2 A prospective arbitrator shall accept an appointment only if he is fully satisfied that he is competent to determine the issues in dispute, and has an adequate knowledge of the language of the arbitration.

2.3 A prospective arbitrator should accept an appointment only if he is able to give to the arbitration the time and attention which the parties are reasonably entitled to expect.

2.4 It is inappropriate to contact parties in order to solicit appointment as arbitrator.

3. Elements of Bias

3.1 The criteria for assessing questions relating to bias are impartiality and independence. Partiality arises where an arbitrator favours one of the parties, or where he is prejudiced in relation to the subject-matter of the dispute. Dependence arises from relationships between an arbitrator and one of the parties, or with someone closely connected with one of the parties.

3.2 Facts which might lead a reasonable person, not knowing the arbitrator's true state of mind, to consider that he is dependent on a party create an appearance of bias. The same is true if an arbitrator has a material interest in the outcome of the dispute, or if he has already taken a position in relation to it. The appearance of bias is best overcome by full disclosure as described in Article 4 below.

3.3 Any current direct or indirect business relationship between an arbitrator and a party, or with a person who is known to be a potentially important witness, will normally give rise to justifiable doubts as to a prospective arbitrator's impartiality or independence. He should decline to accept an appointment in such circumstances unless the parties agree in writing that he may proceed. Examples of indirect relationships are where a member of the prospective arbitrator's family, his firm, or any business partner has a business relationship with one of the parties.

3.4 Past business relationships will not operate as an absolute bar to acceptance of appointment, unless they are of such magnitude or nature as to be likely to affect a prospective arbitrator's judgment.

3.5 Continuous and substantial social or professional relationships between a prospective arbitrator and a party, or with a person who is known to be a potentially important witness in the arbitration, will normally give rise to justifiable doubts as to the impartiality or independence of a prospective arbitrator.

4. Duty of Disclosure

4.1 A prospective arbitrator should disclose all facts or circumstances that may give rise to justifiable doubts as to his impartiality or independence. Failure to make such disclosure creates an appearance of bias, and may of itself be a ground for disqualification even though the non-disclosed facts or circumstances would not of themselves justify disqualification.

4.2 A prospective arbitrator should disclose: (a) any past or present business relationship, whether direct or indirect as illustrated in Article 3.3, including prior appointment as arbitrator, with any party to the dispute, or any representative of a party, or any person known to be a potentially important witness in the arbitration. With regard to present relationships, the duty of disclosure applies irrespective of their magnitude, but with regard to past relationships only if they were of more than a trivial nature in relation to the arbitrator's professional or business affairs. Nondisclosure of an indirect relationship unknown to a prospective arbitrator will not be a ground for disqualification unless it could have been ascertained by making reasonable enquiries; (b) the nature and duration of any substantial social relationships with any party or any person known to be likely to be an important witness in the arbitration; (c) the nature of any previous relationship with any fellow arbitrator (including prior joint service as an arbitrator); (d) the extent of any prior knowledge he may have of the dispute; (e) the extent of any commitments which may affect his availability to perform his duties as arbitrator as may be reasonably anticipated.

4.3 The duty of disclosure continues throughout the arbitral proceedings as regards new facts or circumstances.

4.4 Disclosure should be made in writing and communicated to all parties and arbitrators. When an arbitrator has been appointed, any previous disclosure made to the parties should be communicated to the other arbitrators.

5. Communications with Parties

5.1 When approached with a view to appointment, a prospective arbitrator should make sufficient enquiries in order to inform himself whether there may be any justifiable doubts regarding his impartiality or independence; whether he is competent to determine the issues in dispute; and whether he is able to give the arbitration the time and attention required. He may also respond to enquiries from those approaching him, provided that such enquiries are designed to determine his suitability and availability for the appointment and provided that the merits of the case are not discussed. In the event that a prospective sole arbitrator or presiding arbitrator is approached by one party alone, or by one arbitrator chosen unilaterally by a party (a "party-nominated" arbitrator), he should ascertain that the other party or parties, or the other arbitrator, has consented to the manner in which he has been approached. In such circumstances he should, in writing or orally, inform the other party or parties, or the other arbitrator, of the substance of the initial conversation.

5.2 If a party-nominated arbitrator is required to participate in the selection of a third or presiding arbitrator, it is acceptable for him (although he is not so required) to obtain the views of the party who nominated him as to the acceptability of candidates being considered.

5.3 Throughout the arbitral proceedings, an arbitrator should avoid any unilateral communications regarding the case with any party, or its representatives. If such communication should occur, the arbitrator should inform the other party or parties and arbitrators of its substance.

5.4 If an arbitrator becomes aware that a fellow arbitrator has been in improper communication with a party, he may inform the remaining arbitrators and they should together determine what action should be taken. Normally, the appropriate initial course of action is for the offending arbitrator to be requested to refrain from making any further improper communications with the party. Where the offending arbitrator fails or refuses to refrain from improper communications, the remaining arbitrators may inform the innocent party in order that he may consider what action he should take. An arbitrator may act unilaterally to inform a party of the conduct of another arbitrator in order to allow the said party to consider a challenge of the offending arbitrator only in extreme circumstances, and after communicating his intention to his fellow arbitrators in writing.

5.5 No arbitrator should accept any gift or substantial hospitality, directly or indirectly, from any party to the arbitration. Sole arbitrators and presiding arbitrators should be particularly meticulous in avoiding significant social or professional contacts with any party to the arbitration other than in the presence of the other parties.

6. Fees

Unless the parties agree otherwise or a party defaults, an arbitrator shall make no unilateral arrangements for fees or expenses.

7. Duty of Diligence

All arbitrators should devote such time and attention as the parties may reasonably require having regard to all the circumstances of the case, and shall do their best to conduct the arbitration in such a manner that costs do not rise to an unreasonable proportion of the interests at stake.

8. Involvement in Settlement Proposals

Where the parties have so requested, or consented to a suggestion to this effect by the arbitral tribunal, the tribunal as a whole (or the presiding arbitrator where appropriate), may make proposals for settlement to both parties simultaneously, and preferably in the presence of each other. Although any procedure is possible with the agreement of the parties, the arbitral tribunal should point out to the parties that it is undesirable that any arbitrator should discuss settlement terms with a party in the absence of the other parties since this will normally have the result that any arbitrator involved in such discussions will become disqualified from any future participation in the arbitration.

9. Confidentiality of the Deliberations

The deliberations of the arbitral tribunal, and the contents of the award itself, remain confidential in perpetuity unless the parties release the arbitrators from this obligation. An arbitrator should not participate in, or give any information for the purpose of assistance in, any proceedings to consider the award unless, exceptionally, he considers it his duty to disclose any material misconduct or fraud on the part of his fellow arbitrators.

INTERNATIONAL BAR ASSOCIATION, GUIDELINES ON CONFLICTS OF INTEREST IN INTERNATIONAL ARBITRATION*

Approved on 22 May 2004

Introduction

1. Problems of conflicts of interest increasingly challenge international arbitration. Arbitrators are often unsure about what facts need to be disclosed, and they may make different choices about disclosures than other arbitrators in the same situation. The growth of international business and the manner in which it is conducted, including interlocking corporate relationships and larger international law firms, have caused more disclosures and have created more difficult conflict of interest issues to determine. Reluctant parties have more opportunities to use challenges of arbitrators to delay arbitrations or to deny the opposing party the arbitrator of its choice. Disclosure of any relationship, no matter how minor or serious, has too often led to objections, challenge and withdrawal or removal of the arbitrator.

2. Thus, parties, arbitrators, institutions and courts face complex decisions about what to disclose and what standards to apply. In addition, institutions and courts face difficult decisions if an objection or a challenge is made after a disclosure. There is a tension between, on the one hand, the parties' right to disclosure of situations that may reasonably call into question an arbitrator's impartiality or independence and their right to a fair hearing and, on the other hand, the parties' right to select arbitrators of their choosing. Even though laws and arbitration rules provide some standards, there is a lack of detail in their guidance and of uniformity in their application. As a result, quite often members of the international arbitration community apply different standards in making decisions concerning disclosure, objections and challenges.

3. It is in the interest of everyone in the international arbitration community that international arbitration proceedings not be hindered by these growing conflicts of interest issues. The Committee on Arbitration and ADR of the International Bar Association appointed a Working Group of 19 experts . . . in international arbitration from 14 countries to study, with the intent of helping this decision-making process, national laws, judicial decisions, arbitration rules and practical considerations and applications regarding impartiality and independence and disclosure in international arbitration. The Working Group has determined that existing standards lack sufficient clarity and uniformity in their application. It has therefore prepared these Guidelines, which set forth some General Standards and Explanatory Notes on the Standards. Moreover, the Working Group believes that greater consistency and fewer unnecessary challenges and arbitrator withdrawals and removals could be achieved by providing lists of specific situations that, in the view of the Working Group, do or do not warrant disclosure or disqualification of an arbitrator. Such lists — designated Red, Orange and Green (the 'Application Lists')

— appear at the end of these Guidelines. . . .

4. The Guidelines reflect the Working Group's understanding of the best current international practice firmly rooted in the principles expressed in the General Standards. The Working Group has based the General Standards and the Application Lists upon statutes and case law in jurisdictions and upon the judgment and experience of members of the Working Group and others involved in international commercial arbitration. The Working Group has attempted to balance the various interests of parties, representatives, arbitrators and arbitration institutions, all of whom have a responsibility for ensuring the integrity, reputation and efficiency of international commercial arbitration. In particular, the Working Group has sought and considered the views of many leading arbitration institutions, as well as corporate counsel and other persons involved in international arbitration. The Working Group also published drafts of the Guidelines and sought comments at two annual meetings of the International Bar Association and other meetings of arbitrators. While the comments received by the Working Group varied, and included some points of criticisms, the arbitration community generally supported and encouraged these efforts to help reduce the growing problems of conflicts of interests. The Working Group has studied all the comments received and has adopted many of the proposals that it has received. The Working Group is very grateful indeed for the serious considerations given to its proposals by so many institutions and individuals all over the globe and for the comments and proposals received.

5. Originally, the Working Group developed the Guidelines for international commercial arbitration. However, in the light of comments received, it realized that the Guidelines should equally apply to other types of arbitration, such as investment arbitrations (insofar as these may not be considered as commercial arbitrations). . . .

6. These Guidelines are not legal provisions and do not override any applicable national law or arbitral rules chosen by the parties. However, the Working Group hopes that these Guidelines will find general acceptance within the international arbitration community (as was the case with the IBA Rules on the Taking of Evidence in International Commercial Arbitration) and that they thus will help parties, practitioners, arbitrators, institutions and the courts in their decision-making process on these very important questions of impartiality, independence, disclosure, objections and challenges made in that connection. The Working Group trusts that the Guidelines will be applied with robust common sense and without pedantic and unduly formalistic interpretation.

The Working Group is also publishing a Background and History, which describes the studies made by the Working Group and may be helpful in interpreting the Guidelines.

7. The IBA and the Working Group view these Guidelines as a beginning, rather than an end, of the process. The Application Lists cover many of the varied situations that commonly arise in practice, but they do not purport to be comprehensive, nor could they be. Nevertheless, the Working Group is confident that the Application Lists provide better concrete guidance than the General Standards (and certainly more than existing standards).

The IBA and the Working Group seek comments on the actual use of the Guidelines, and they plan to supplement, revise and refine the Guidelines based on that practical experience.

8. In 1987, the IBA published Rules of Ethics for International Arbitrators. Those Rules cover more topics than these Guidelines, and they remain in effect as to subjects that are not discussed in the Guidelines. The Guidelines supersede the Rules of Ethics as to the matters treated here.

Part I: General Standards Regarding Impartiality, Independence And Disclosure

(1)   General Principle

Every arbitrator shall be impartial and independent of the parties at the time of accepting an appointment to serve and shall remain so during the entire arbitration proceeding until the final award has been rendered or the proceeding has otherwise finally terminated.

Explanation to General Standard 1:

The Working Group is guided by the fundamental principle in international arbitration that each arbitrator must be impartial and independent of the parties at the time he or she accepts an appointment to act as arbitrator and must remain so during the entire course of the arbitration proceedings. The Working Group considered whether this obligation should extend even during the period that the award may be challenged but has decided against this. The Working Group takes the view that the arbitrator's duty ends when the Arbitral Tribunal has rendered the final award or the proceedings have otherwise been finally terminated (e.g., because of a settlement). If, after setting aside or other proceedings, the dispute is referred back to the same arbitrator, a fresh round of disclosure may be necessary.

(2)   Conflicts of Interest

(a) *An arbitrator shall decline to accept an appointment or, if the arbitration has already been commenced, refuse to continue to act as an arbitrator if he or she has any doubts as to his or her ability to be impartial or independent.*

(b) *The same principle applies if facts or circumstances exist, or have arisen since the appointment, that, from a reasonable third person's point of view having knowledge of the relevant facts, give rise to justifiable doubts as to the arbitrator's impartiality or independence, unless the parties have accepted the arbitrator in accordance with the requirements set out in General Standard (4).*

(c) *Doubts are justifiable if a reasonable and informed third party would reach the conclusion that there was a likelihood that the arbitrator may be influenced by factors other than the merits of the case as presented by the parties in reaching his or her decision.*

(d) *Justifiable doubts necessarily exist as to the arbitrator's impartiality or independence if there is an identity between a party and the arbitrator, if the arbitrator is a legal representative of a legal entity that is a party in the arbitration, or if the arbitrator has a significant financial or personal interest in the matter at stake.*

Explanation to General Standard 2:

(a) It is the main ethical guiding principle of every arbitrator that actual bias from the arbitrator's own point of view must lead to that arbitrator declining his or her appointment. This standard should apply regardless of the stage of the proceedings. This principle is so self evident that many national laws do not explicitly say so. See e.g., Article 12, UNCITRAL Model Law. The Working Group, however, has included it in the General Standards because explicit expression in these Guidelines helps to avoid confusion and to create confidence in procedures before arbitral tribunals. In addition, the Working Group believes that the broad standard of 'any doubts as to an ability to be impartial and independent' should lead to the arbitrator declining the appointment.

(b) In order for standards to be applied as consistently as possible, the Working Group believes that the test for disqualification should be an objective one. The Working Group uses the wording 'impartiality or independence' derived from the broadly adopted Article 12 of the UNCITRAL Model Law, and the use of an appearance test, based on justifiable doubts as to the impartiality or independence of the arbitrator, as provided in Article 12(2) of the UNCITRAL Model Law, to be applied objectively (a 'reasonable third person test'). As described in the Explanation to General Standard 3(d), this standard should apply regardless of the stage of the proceedings.

(c) Most laws and rules that apply the standard of justifiable doubts do not further define that standard. The Working Group believes that this General Standard provides some context for making this determination.

(d) The Working Group supports the view that no one is allowed to be his or her own judge; i.e., there cannot be identity between an arbitrator and a party. The Working Group believes that this situation cannot be waived by the parties. The same principle should apply to persons who are legal representatives of a legal entity that is a party in the arbitration, like board members, or who have a significant economic interest in the matter at stake. Because of the importance of this principle, this non-waivable situation is made a General Standard, and examples are provided in the non-waivable Red List. The General Standard purposely uses the terms 'identity' and 'legal representatives.' In the light of comments received, the Working Group considered whether these terms should be extended or further defined, but decided against doing so. It realizes that there are situations in which an employee of a party or a civil servant can be in a position similar, if not identical, to the position of an official legal representative. The Working Group decided that it should suffice to state the principle.

(3) Disclosure by the Arbitrator

(a) *If facts or circumstances exist that may, in the eyes of the parties, give rise to doubts as to the arbitrator's impartiality or independence, the arbitrator shall disclose such facts or circumstances to the parties, the arbitration institution or other appointing authority (if any, and if so required by the applicable institutional rules) and to the co-arbitrators, if any, prior to accepting his or her appointment or, if thereafter, as soon as he or she learns about them.*

(b) *It follows from General Standards 1 and 2(a) that an arbitrator who has made a disclosure considers himself or herself to be impartial and independent of the parties despite the disclosed facts and therefore capable of performing his or her duties as arbitrator. Otherwise, he or she would have declined the nomination or appointment at the outset or resigned.*

(c) *Any doubt as to whether an arbitrator should disclose certain facts or circumstances should be resolved in favour of disclosure.*

(d) *When considering whether or not facts or circumstances exist that should be disclosed, the arbitrator shall not take into account whether the arbitration proceeding is at the beginning or at a later stage.*

Explanation to General Standard 3:

(a) General Standard 2(b) above sets out an objective test for disqualification of an arbitrator. However, because of varying considerations with respect to disclosure, the proper standard for disclosure may be different. A purely objective test for disclosure exists in the majority of the jurisdictions analyzed and in the UNCITRAL Model Law. Nevertheless, the Working Group recognizes that the parties have an interest in being fully informed about any circumstances that may be relevant in their view. Because of the strongly held views of many arbitration institutions (as reflected in their rules and as stated to the Working Group) that the disclosure test should reflect the perspectives of the parties, the Working Group in principle accepted, after much debate, a subjective approach for disclosure. The Working Group has adapted the language of Article 7(2) of the ICC Rules for this standard. However, the Working Group believes that this principle should not be applied without limitations. Because some situations should never lead to disqualification under the objective test, such situations need not be disclosed, regardless of the parties' perspective. These limitations to the subjective test are reflected in the Green List, which lists some situations in which disclosure is not required. Similarly, the Working Group emphasizes that the two tests (objective test for disqualification and subjective test for disclosure) are clearly distinct from each other, and that a disclosure shall not automatically lead to disqualification, as reflected in General Standard 3(b). In determining what facts should be disclosed, an arbitrator should take into account all circumstances known to him or her, including to the extent known the culture and the customs of the country of which the parties are domiciled or nationals.

(b) Disclosure is not an admission of a conflict of interest. An arbitrator who has made a disclosure to the parties considers himself or herself to be impartial and independent of the parties, despite the disclosed facts, or else he or she would have declined the nomination or resigned. An arbitrator making disclosure thus feels capable of performing his or her duties. It is the purpose of disclosure to allow the parties to judge whether or not they agree with the evaluation of the arbitrator and, if they so wish, to explore the situation further. The Working Group hopes that the promulgation of this General Standard will eliminate the misunderstanding that disclosure demonstrates doubts sufficient to disqualify the arbitrator. Instead, any challenge should be successful only if an objective test, as set forth above, is met.

(c) Unnecessary disclosure sometimes raises an incorrect implication in the minds of the parties that the disclosed circumstances would affect his or her impartiality or independence. Excessive disclosures thus unnecessarily undermine the parties' confidence in the process. Nevertheless, after some debate, the Working Group believes it important to provide expressly in the General Standards that in case of doubt the arbitrator should disclose. If the arbitrator feels that he or she should disclose but that professional secrecy rules or other rules of practice prevent such disclosure, he or she should not accept the appointment or should resign.

(d) The Working Group has concluded that disclosure or disqualification (as set out in General Standard 2) should not depend on the particular stage of the arbitration. In order to determine whether the arbitrator should disclose, decline the appointment or refuse to continue to act or whether a challenge by a party should be successful, the facts and circumstances alone are relevant and not the current stage of the procedure or the consequences of the withdrawal. As a practical matter, institutions make a distinction between the commencement of an arbitration proceeding and a later stage. Also, courts tend to apply different standards. Nevertheless, the Working Group believes it important to clarify that no distinction should be made regarding the stage of the arbitral procedure. While there are practical concerns if an arbitrator must withdraw after an arbitration has commenced, a distinction based on the stage of arbitration would be inconsistent with the General Standards.

(4) Waiver by the Parties

(a) *If, within 30 days after the receipt of any disclosure by the arbitrator or after a party learns of facts or circumstances that could constitute a potential conflict of interest for an arbitrator, a party does not raise an express objection with regard to that arbitrator, subject to paragraphs (b) and (c) of this General Standard, the party is deemed to have waived any potential conflict of interest by the arbitrator based on such facts or circumstances and may not raise any objection to such facts or circumstances at a later stage.*

(b) *However, if facts or circumstances exist as described in General Standard 2(d), any waiver by a party or any agreement by the parties to have such a person serve as arbitrator shall be regarded as invalid.*

(c) *A person should not serve as an arbitrator when a conflict of interest, such as those exemplified in the waivable Red List, exists. Nevertheless, such a person may accept appointment as arbitrator or continue to act as an arbitrator, if the following conditions are met:*

(i) *All parties, all arbitrators and the arbitration institution or other appointing authority (if any) must have full knowledge of the conflict of interest; and*

(ii) *All parties must expressly agree that such person may serve as arbitrator despite the conflict of interest.*

(d) *An arbitrator may assist the parties in reaching a settlement of the dispute at any stage of the proceedings. However, before doing so, the arbitrator should receive an express agreement by the parties that acting in such a manner shall not disqualify the arbitrator from continuing to serve as arbitrator. Such express agreement shall be considered to be an effective waiver of any potential conflict of interest that may arise from the arbitrator's participation in such process or from information that the arbitrator may learn in the process. If the assistance by the arbitrator does not lead to final settlement of the case, the parties remain bound by their waiver. However, consistent with General Standard 2(a) and notwithstanding such agreement, the arbitrator shall resign if, as a consequence of his or her involvement in the settlement process, the arbitrator develops doubts as to his or her ability to remain impartial or independent in the future course of the arbitration proceedings.*

Explanation to General Standard 4:

(a) The Working Group suggests a requirement of an explicit objection by the parties within a certain time limit. In the view of the Working Group, this time limit should also apply to a party who refuses to be involved.

(b) This General Standard is included to make General Standard 4(a) consistent with the non-waivable provisions of General Standard 2(d). Examples of such circumstances are described in the non-waivable Red List.

(c) In a serious conflict of interest, such as those that are described by way of example in the waivable Red List, the parties may nevertheless wish to use such a person as an arbitrator. Here, party autonomy and the desire to have only impartial and independent arbitrators must be balanced. The Working Group believes persons with such a serious conflict of interests may serve as arbitrators only if the parties make fully informed, explicit waivers.

(d) The concept of the Arbitral Tribunal assisting the parties in reaching a settlement of their dispute in the course of the arbitration proceedings is well established in some jurisdictions but not in others. Informed consent by the parties to such a process prior to its beginning should be regarded as effective waiver of a potential conflict of interest. Express consent is generally sufficient, as opposed to a consent made in writing which in certain jurisdictions requires signature. In practice, the requirement of an express waiver allows such consent to be made in the minutes or transcript of a hearing. In addition, in order to avoid parties using an arbitrator as mediator as a means of disqualifying the arbitrator, the General Standard makes clear that the waiver should remain effective if the mediation is unsuccessful. Thus, parties assume the risk of what the arbitrator may learn in the settlement process. In giving their express consent, the parties should realize the consequences of the arbitrator assisting the parties in a settlement process and agree on regulating this special position further where appropriate.

(5) Scope

These Guidelines apply equally to tribunal chairs, sole arbitrators and party-appointed arbitrators. These Guidelines do not apply to non-neutral arbitrators, who do not have an obligation to be independent and impartial, as may be permitted by some arbitration rules or national laws.

Explanation to General Standard 5:

Because each member of an Arbitral Tribunal has an obligation to be impartial and independent, the General Standards should not distinguish among sole arbitrators, party-appointed arbitrators and tribunal chairs. With regard to secretaries of Arbitral Tribunals, the Working Group takes the view that it is the responsibility of the arbitrator to ensure that the secretary is and remains impartial and independent. Some arbitration rules and domestic laws permit party-appointed arbitrators to be non-neutral. When an arbitrator is serving in such a role, these Guidelines should not apply to him or her, since their purpose is to protect impartiality and independence.

(6) Relationships

(a) *When considering the relevance of facts or circumstances to determine whether a potential conflict of interest exists or whether disclosure should be made, the activities of an arbitrator's law firm, if any, should be reasonably considered in each individual case. Therefore, the fact that the activities of the arbitrator's firm involve one of the parties shall not automatically constitute a source of such conflict or a reason for disclosure.*

(b) *Similarly, if one of the parties is a legal entity which is a member of a group with which the arbitrator's firm has an involvement, such facts or circumstances should be reasonably considered in each individual case. Therefore, this fact alone shall not automatically constitute a source of a conflict of interest or a reason for disclosure.*

(c) *If one of the parties is a legal entity, the managers, directors and members of a supervisory board of such legal entity and any person having a similar controlling influence on the legal entity shall be considered to be the equivalent of the legal entity.*

Explanation to General Standard 6:

(a) The growing size of law firms should be taken into account as part of today's reality in international arbitration. There is a need to balance the interests of a party to use the arbitrator of its choice and the importance of maintaining confidence in the impartiality and independence of international arbitration. In the opinion of the Working Group, the arbitrator must in principle be considered as identical to his or her law firm, but nevertheless the activities of the arbitrator's firm should not automatically constitute a conflict of interest. The relevance of such activities, such as the nature, timing and scope of the work by the law firm, should be reasonably considered in each individual case. The Working Group uses the term 'involvement' rather than 'acting for' because a law firm's relevant connections with a party may include activities other than representation on a legal matter.

(b) When a party to an arbitration is a member of a group of companies, special questions regarding conflict of interest arise. As in the prior paragraph, the Working Group believes that because individual corporate structure arrangements vary so widely an automatic rule is not appropriate. Instead, the particular circumstances of an affiliation with another entity within the same group of companies should be reasonably considered in each individual case.

(c) The party in international arbitration is usually a legal entity. Therefore, this General Standard clarifies which individuals should be considered effectively to be that party.

(7)   Duty of Arbitrator and Parties

(a) *A party shall inform an arbitrator, the Arbitral Tribunal, the other parties and the arbitration institution or other appointing authority (if any) about any direct or indirect relationship between it (or another company of the same group of companies) and the arbitrator. The party shall do so on its own initiative before the beginning of the proceeding or as soon as it becomes aware of such relationship.*

(b) *In order to comply with General Standard 7(a), a party shall provide any information already available to it and shall perform a reasonable search of publicly available information.*

(c) *An arbitrator is under a duty to make reasonable enquiries to investigate any potential conflict of interest, as well as any facts or circumstances that may cause his or her impartiality or independence to be questioned. Failure to disclose a potential conflict is not excused by lack of knowledge if the arbitrator makes no reasonable attempt to investigate.*

Explanation to General Standard 7:

To reduce the risk of abuse by unmeritorious challenge of an arbitrator's impartiality or independence, it is necessary that the parties disclose any relevant relationship with the arbitrator. In addition, any party or potential party to an arbitration is, at the outset, required to make a reasonable effort to ascertain and to disclose publicly available information that, applying the general standard, might affect the arbitrator's impartiality and independence. It is the arbitrator or putative arbitrator's obligation to make similar enquiries and to disclose any information that may cause his or her impartiality or independence to be called into question.

Part II: Practical Application of the General Standards

1. The Working Group believes that if the Guidelines are to have an important practical influence, they should reflect situations that are likely to occur in today's arbitration practice. The Guidelines should provide specific guidance to arbitrators, parties, institutions and courts as to what situations do or do not constitute conflicts of interest or should be disclosed. For this purpose, the members of the Working Group analyzed their respective case law and categorized situations that can occur in the following Application Lists. These lists obviously cannot contain every situation, but they provide guidance in many circumstances, and the Working Group has sought to make them as comprehensive as possible. In all cases, the General Standards should control.

2. The Red List consists of two parts: 'a non-waivable Red List' (see General Standards 2(c) and 4(b)) and 'a waivable Red List' (see General Standard 4(c)).

These lists are a non-exhaustive enumeration of specific situations which, depending on the facts of a given case, give rise to justifiable doubts as to the arbitrator's impartiality and independence; i.e., in these circumstances an objective conflict of interest exists from the point of view of a reasonable third person having knowledge of the relevant facts (see General Standard 2(b)). The non-waivable Red List includes situations deriving from the overriding principle that no person can be his or her own judge. Therefore, disclosure of such a situation cannot cure the conflict. The waivable Red List encompasses situations that are serious but not as severe. Because of their seriousness, unlike circumstances described in the Orange List, these situations should be considered waivable only if and when the parties, being aware of the conflict of interest situation, nevertheless expressly state their willingness to have such a person act as arbitrator, as set forth in General Standard 4(c).

3. The Orange List is a non-exhaustive enumeration of specific situations which (depending on the facts of a given case) in the eyes of the parties may give rise to justifiable doubts as to the arbitrator's impartiality or independence. The Orange List thus reflects situations that would fall under General Standard 3(a), so that the arbitrator has a duty to disclose such situations. In all these situations, the parties are deemed to have accepted the arbitrator if, after disclosure, no timely objection is made. (General Standard 4(a)).

4. It should be stressed that, as stated above, such disclosure should not automatically result in a disqualification of the arbitrator; no presumption regarding disqualification should arise from a disclosure. The purpose of the disclosure is to inform the parties of a situation that they may wish to explore further in order to determine whether objectively – i.e., from a reasonable third person's point of view having knowledge of the relevant facts – there is a justifiable doubt as to the arbitrator's impartiality or independence. If the conclusion is that there is no justifiable doubt, the arbitrator can act. He or she can also act if there is no timely objection by the parties or, in situations covered by the waivable Red List, a specific acceptance by the parties in accordance with General Standard 4(c). Of course, if a party challenges the appointment of the arbitrator, he or she can nevertheless act if the authority that has to rule on the challenge decides that the challenge does not meet the objective test for disqualification.

5. In addition, a later challenge based on the fact that an arbitrator did not disclose such facts or circumstances should not result automatically in either nonappointment, later disqualification or a successful challenge to any award. In the view of the Working Group, non-disclosure cannot make an arbitrator partial or lacking independence; only the facts or circumstances that he or she did not disclose can do so.

6. The Green List contains a non-exhaustive enumeration of specific situations where no appearance of, and no actual, conflict of interest exists from the relevant objective point of view. Thus, the arbitrator has no duty to disclose situations falling within the Green List. In the opinion of the Working Group, as already expressed in the Explanation to General Standard 3(a), there should be a limit to disclosure, based on reasonableness; in some situations, an objective test should prevail over the purely subjective test of 'the eyes of the parties.'

7. Situations falling outside the time limit used in some of the Orange List situations should generally be considered as falling in the Green List, even though they are not specifically stated. An arbitrator may nevertheless wish to make disclosure if, under the General Standards, he or she believes it to be appropriate. While there has been much debate with respect to the time limits used in the Lists, the Working Group has concluded that the limits indicated are appropriate and provide guidance where none exists now. For example, the three-year period in Orange List 3.1 may be too long in certain circumstances and too short in others, but the Working Group believes that the period is an appropriate general criterion, subject to the special circumstances of any case.

8. The borderline between the situations indicated is often thin. It can be debated whether a certain situation should be on one List of instead of another. Also, the Lists contain, for various situations, open norms like 'significant'. The Working Group has extensively and repeatedly discussed both of these issues, in the light of comments received. It believes that the decisions reflected in the Lists reflect international principles to the best extent possible and that further definition of the norms, which should be interpreted reasonably in light of the facts and circumstances in each case, would be counter-productive.

9. There has been much debate as to whether there should be a Green List at all and also, with respect to the Red List, whether the situations on the Non-Waivable Red List should be waivable in light of party autonomy. With respect to the first question, the Working Group has maintained its decision that the subjective test for disclosure should not be the absolute criterion but that some objective thresholds should be added. With respect to the second question, the conclusion of the Working Group was that party autonomy, in this respect, has its limits.

1.   Non-Waivable Red List

1.1. There is an identity between a party and the arbitrator, or the arbitrator is a legal representative of an entity that is a party in the arbitration.

1.2. The arbitrator is a manager, director or member of the supervisory board, or has a similar controlling influence in one of the parties.

1.3. The arbitrator has a significant financial interest in one of the parties or the outcome of the case.

1.4. The arbitrator regularly advises the appointing party or an affiliate of the appointing party, and the arbitrator or his or her firm derives a significant financial income therefrom.

2.   Waivable Red List

2.1. Relationship of the arbitrator to the dispute

2.1.1 The arbitrator has given legal advice or provided an expert opinion on the dispute to a party or an affiliate of one of the parties.

2.1.2 The arbitrator has previous involvement in the case.

2.2. Arbitrator's direct or indirect interest in the dispute.

2.2.1 The arbitrator holds shares, either directly or indirectly, in one of the parties or an affiliate of one of the parties that is privately held.

2.2.2 A close family member[4] of the arbitrator has a significant financial interest in the outcome of the dispute.

2.2.3 The arbitrator or a close family member of the arbitrator has a close relationship with a third party who may be liable to recourse on the part of the unsuccessful party in the dispute.

2.3. Arbitrator's relationship with the parties or counsel

2.3.1 The arbitrator currently represents or advises one of the parties or an affiliate of one of the parties.

2.3.2 The arbitrator currently represents the lawyer or law firm acting as counsel for one of the parties.

2.3.3 The arbitrator is a lawyer in the same law firm as the counsel to one of the parties.

2.3.4 The arbitrator is a manager, director or member of the supervisory board, or has a similar controlling influence, in an affiliate[5] of one of the parties if the affiliate is directly involved in the matters in dispute in the arbitration.

2.3.5 The arbitrator's law firm had a previous but terminated involvement in the case without the arbitrator being involved himself or herself.

2.3.6 The arbitrator's law firm currently has a significant commercial relationship with one of the parties or an affiliate of one of the parties.

2.3.7 The arbitrator regularly advises the appointing party or an affiliate of the appointing party, but neither the arbitrator nor his or her firm derives a significant financial income therefrom.

2.3.8 The arbitrator has a close family relationship with one of the parties or with a manager, director or member of the supervisory board or any person having a similar controlling influence in one of the parties or an affiliate of one of the parties or with a counsel representing a party.

2.3.9 A close family member of the arbitrator has a significant financial interest in one of the parties or an affiliate of one of the parties.

3.   Orange List

3.1. Previous services for one of the parties or other involvement in the case

3.1.1 The arbitrator has within the past three years served as counsel for one of the parties or an affiliate of one of the parties or has previously advised or been consulted by the party or an affiliate of the party making the appointment in an unrelated matter, but the arbitrator and the party or the affiliate of the party

---

[4] Throughout the Application Lists, the term 'close family member' refers to a spouse, sibling, child, parent or life partner.

[5] Throughout the Application Lists, the term 'affiliate' encompasses all companies in one group of companies including the parent company.

have no ongoing relationship.

3.1.2 The arbitrator has within the past three years served as counsel against one of the parties or an affiliate of one of the parties in an unrelated matter.

3.1.3 The arbitrator has within the past three years been appointed as arbitrator on two or more occasions by one of the parties or an affiliate of one of the parties.[6]

3.1.4 The arbitrator's law firm has within the past three years acted for one of the parties or an affiliate of one of the parties in an unrelated matter without the involvement of the arbitrator.

3.1.5 The arbitrator currently serves, or has served within the past three years, as arbitrator in another arbitration on a related issue involving one of the parties or an affiliate of one of the parties.

3.2. Current services for one of the parties

3.2.1 The arbitrator's law firm is currently rendering services to one of the parties or to an affiliate of one of the parties without creating a significant commercial relationship and without the involvement of the arbitrator.

3.2.2 A law firm that shares revenues or fees with the arbitrator's law firm renders services to one of the parties or an affiliate of one of the parties before the arbitral tribunal.

3.2.3 The arbitrator or his or her firm represents a party or an affiliate to the arbitration on a regular basis but is not involved in the current dispute.

3.3. Relationship between an arbitrator and another arbitrator or counsel.

3.3.1 The arbitrator and another arbitrator are lawyers in the same law firm.

3.3.2 The arbitrator and another arbitrator or the counsel for one of the parties are members of the same barristers' chambers. . . . .

3.3.3 The arbitrator was within the past three years a partner of, or otherwise affiliated with, another arbitrator or any of the counsel in the same arbitration.

3.3.4 A lawyer in the arbitrator's law firm is an arbitrator in another dispute involving the same party or parties or an affiliate of one of the parties.

3.3.5 A close family member of the arbitrator is a partner or employee of the law firm representing one of the parties, but is not assisting with the dispute.

3.3.6 A close personal friendship exists between an arbitrator and a counsel of one party, as demonstrated by the fact that the arbitrator and the counsel regularly spend considerable time together unrelated to professional work commitments or the activities of professional associations or social organizations.

3.3.7 The arbitrator has within the past three years received more than three

---

[6] It may be the practice in certain specific kinds of arbitration, such as maritime or commodities arbitration, to draw arbitrators from a small, specialized pool. If in such fields it is the custom and practice for parties frequently to appoint the same arbitrator in different cases, no disclosure of this fact is required where all parties in the arbitration should be familiar with such custom and practice.

appointments by the same counsel or the same law firm.

3.4. Relationship between arbitrator and party and others involved in the arbitration

3.4.1 The arbitrator's law firm is currently acting adverse to one of the parties or an affiliate of one of the parties.

3.4.2 The arbitrator had been associated within the past three years with a party or an affiliate of one of the parties in a professional capacity, such as a former employee or partner.

3.4.3 A close personal friendship exists between an arbitrator and a manager or director or a member of the supervisory board or any person having a similar controlling influence in one of the parties or an affiliate of one of the parties or a witness or expert, as demonstrated by the fact that the arbitrator and such director, manager, other person, witness or expert regularly spend considerable time together unrelated to professional work commitments or the activities of professional associations or social organizations.

3.4.4 If the arbitrator is a former judge, he or she has within the past three years heard a significant case involving one of the parties.

3.5. Other circumstances

3.5.1 The arbitrator holds shares, either directly or indirectly, which by reason of number or denomination constitute a material holding in one of the parties or an affiliate of one of the parties that is publicly listed.

3.5.2 The arbitrator has publicly advocated a specific position regarding the case that is being arbitrated, whether in a published paper or speech or otherwise.

3.5.3 The arbitrator holds one position in an arbitration institution with appointing authority over the dispute.

3.5.4 The arbitrator is a manager, director or member of the supervisory board, or has a similar controlling influence, in an affiliate of one of the parties, where the affiliate is not directly involved in the matters in dispute in the arbitration.

4. Green List

4.1. Previously expressed legal opinions

4.1.1 The arbitrator has previously published a general opinion (such as in a law review article or public lecture) concerning an issue which also arises in the arbitration (but this opinion is not focused on the case that is being arbitrated).

4.2. Previous services against one party

4.2.1 The arbitrator's law firm has acted against one of the parties or an affiliate of one of the parties in an unrelated matter without the involvement of the arbitrator.

4.3. Current services for one of the parties

4.3.1 A firm in association or in alliance with the arbitrator's law firm, but which does not share fees or other revenues with the arbitrator's law firm, renders services to one of the parties or an affiliate of one of the parties in an unrelated matter.

4.4. Contacts with another arbitrator or with counsel for one of the parties

4.4.1 The arbitrator has a relationship with another arbitrator or with the counsel for one of the parties through membership in the same professional association or social organization.

4.4.2 The arbitrator and counsel for one of the parties or another arbitrator have previously served together as arbitrators or as co-counsel.

4.5. Contacts between the arbitrator and one of the parties

4.5.1 The arbitrator has had an initial contact with the appointing party or an affiliate of the appointing party (or the respective counsels) prior to appointment, if this contact is limited to the arbitrator's availability and qualifications to serve or to the names of possible candidates for a chairperson and did not address the merits or procedural aspects of the dispute.

4.5.2 The arbitrator holds an insignificant amount of shares in one of the parties or an affiliate of one of the parties, which is publicly listed.

4.5.3 The arbitrator and a manager, director or member of the supervisory board, or any person having a similar controlling influence, in one of the parties or an affiliate of one of the parties, have worked together as joint experts or in another professional capacity, including as arbitrators in the same case.

. . .

AMERICAN ARBITRATION ASSOCIATION, DRAFTING DISPUTE RESOLUTION CLAUSES — A PRACTICAL GUIDE*

Amended and Effective September 1, 2007

I. A Checklist for the Drafter

It is not enough to state that "disputes arising under the agreement shall be settled by arbitration." While that language indicates the parties' intention to arbitrate and may authorize a court to enforce the clause, it leaves many issues unresolved. Issues such as when, where, how and before whom a dispute will be arbitrated are subject to disagreement once a controversy has arisen, with no way to resolve them except to go to court.

Some of the more important elements a practitioner should keep in mind when drafting, adopting or recommending a dispute resolution clause follow.

- The clause might cover all disputes that may arise, or only certain types.

- It could specify only arbitration — which yields a binding decision — or also provide an opportunity for non-binding negotiation or mediation.

- The arbitration clause should be signed by as many potential parties to a future dispute as possible.

- To be fully effective, "entry of judgment" language in domestic cases is important.

- It is normally a good idea to state whether a panel of one or three arbitrator(s) is to be selected, and to include the place where the arbitration will occur.

- If the contract includes a general choice of law clause, it may govern the arbitration proceeding. The consequences should be considered.

- Consideration should be given to incorporating the AAA's Procedures for Large, Complex Commercial Disputes for potentially substantial or complicated cases.

- The drafter should keep in mind that the AAA has specialized rules for arbitration in the construction, patent, securities and certain other fields. If anticipated disputes fall into any of these areas, the specialized rules should be considered for incorporation in the arbitration clause. An experienced AAA administrative staff manages the processing of cases under AAA rules.

- The parties are free to customize and refine the basic arbitration procedures to meet their particular needs. If the parties agree on a procedure that conflicts with otherwise applicable AAA rules, the AAA will almost always respect the wishes of the parties.

. . .

III. Clauses Approved by the AAA for General Commercial Use

The standard arbitration clause suggested by the American Arbitration Association addresses many basic drafting questions by incorporating AAA Rules. This simple approach has proven highly effective in hundreds of thousands of disputes. Additional language, which parties may wish to add in specific contexts, is discussed in Section IV. . . .

The standard arbitration clause also may include reference to the AAA's Optional Rules for Emergency Measures of Protection (before an arbitrator is selected) and for expedited arbitration. If the parties wish, standard clauses also may be used for negotiation and mediation. There are also standard clauses for use in large, complex cases.

. . .

Arbitration

The parties can provide for arbitration of future disputes by inserting the following clause into their contracts (the language in the brackets suggests possible alternatives or additions).

STD 1

Any controversy or claim arising out of or relating to this contract, or the breach thereof, shall be settled by arbitration administered by the American Arbitration Association in accordance with its Commercial [or other] Arbitration Rules [including the Optional Rules for Emergency Measures of Protection], and judgment on the award rendered by the arbitrator(s) may be entered in any court having jurisdiction thereof.

Arbitration of existing disputes may be accomplished by use of the following.

STD 2

We, the undersigned parties, hereby agree to submit to arbitration administered by the American Arbitration Association under its Commercial [or other] Arbitration Rules the following controversy: [describe briefly]. We further agree that a judgment of any court having jurisdiction may be entered upon the award.

The preceding clauses, which refer to the time-tested rules of the AAA, have consistently received judicial support. The standard clause is often the best to include in a contract.

. . .

Negotiation

The parties may wish to attempt to resolve their disputes through negotiation prior to arbitration. A sample of a clause which provides for negotiation follows.

NEG 1

In the event of any dispute, claim, question, or disagreement arising from or relating to this agreement or the breach thereof, the parties hereto shall use their best efforts to settle the dispute, claim, question, or disagreement. To this effect, they shall consult and negotiate with each other in good faith and, recognizing their mutual interests, attempt to reach a just and equitable solution satisfactory to both parties. If they do not reach such solution within a period of 60 days, then, upon notice by either party to the other, all disputes, claims, questions, or differences shall be finally settled by arbitration administered by the American Arbitration Association in accordance with the provisions of its Commercial Arbitration Rules.

Mediation

The parties may wish to attempt mediation before submitting their dispute to arbitration. This can be accomplished by making reference to mediation (which may be terminated at any time by either party) in the arbitration clause.

MED 1

If a dispute arises out of or relates to this contract, or the breach thereof, and if the dispute cannot be settled through negotiation, the parties agree first to try in good faith to settle the dispute by mediation administered by the American Arbitration Association under its Commercial Mediation Procedures before resorting to arbitration, litigation, or some other dispute resolution procedure.

MED 2

The parties hereby submit the following dispute to mediation administered by the American Arbitration Association under its Commercial Mediation Procedures [the clause may also provide for the qualifications of the mediator(s), the method for allocating fees and expenses, the locale of meetings, time limits, or any other item of concern to the parties].

Large, Complex Cases

The large, complex case framework offered by the AAA is designed primarily for business disputes involving claims of at least $500,000, although parties are free to provide for use of the LCC Rules in other disputes. The key elements of the program are (1) selection of arbitrators who satisfy rigorous criteria to insure that the panel is an extremely select one; (2) training, orientation, and coordination of those arbitrators in a manner designed to facilitate the program; (3) establishment of procedures for administration of those cases that elect to be included in the program; (4) flexibility of those procedures so that parties can more speedily and efficiently resolve their disputes; and (5) administration of large, complex cases by specially trained, experienced AAA staff.

The procedures provide for an early administrative conference with the AAA, and a preliminary hearing with the arbitrators. Documentary exchanges and other essential exchanges of information are facilitated. The procedures also provide that a statement of reasons may accompany the award, if requested by the parties. The procedures are meant to supplement the applicable rules that the parties have agreed to use. They include the possibility of the use of mediation to resolve some or all issues at an early stage.

The parties can provide for future application of the procedures by including the following arbitration clause in their contract.

LCCP 1

Any controversy or claim arising from or relating to this contract or the breach thereof shall be settled by arbitration administered by the American Arbitration Association under its [applicable] Procedures for Large, Complex Commercial Disputes, and judgment on the award rendered by the arbitrator(s) may be entered in any court having jurisdiction thereof. A pending dispute can be referred to the program by the completion of a Submission to Dispute Resolution form if the underlying contract documents do not provide for AAA administration.

LCCP 2

We, the undersigned parties, hereby agree to submit to arbitration administered by the American Arbitration Association under its [applicable] Procedures for Large, Complex Commercial Disputes the following controversy [describe briefly]. Judgment of any court having jurisdiction may be entered on the award.

IV. Clauses for Use in Specific Contexts

The following clauses, which also can provide for periods of negotiation and/or mediation prior to arbitration, may be considered for use in specific contexts. The checklist of considerations in Section I above also should be consulted.

A. Clauses for Use in International Disputes

The International Centre for Dispute Resolution (ICDR), the international division of the American Arbitration Association, administers international commercial cases under various arbitration rules worldwide. The ICDR administers cases under its own International Dispute Resolution Procedures, various AAA rules, the Commercial Arbitration and Mediation Center for the Americas (CAMCA) Rules, the Rules of the Inter-American Commercial Arbitration Commission (IACAC) and the UNCITRAL Arbitration Rules. Under Article 1 of the International Arbitration Rules, parties may designate either the ICDR or the AAA in the arbitration clause for the purposes of naming an administrative agency and conferring proper jurisdiction to the ICDR or the AAA. Following are samples of arbitration clauses pertinent to international disputes.

INTL 1

Any controversy or claim arising out of or relating to this contract shall be determined by arbitration in accordance with the International Arbitration Rules of the International Centre for Dispute Resolution.

INTL 2

Any dispute, controversy, or claim arising out of or relating to this contract, or the breach thereof, shall be finally settled by arbitration administered by the Commercial Arbitration and Mediation Center for the Americas in accordance with its rules, and judgment on the award rendered by the arbitrator(s) may be entered in any court having jurisdiction thereof.

INTL 3

Any dispute, controversy, or claim arising from or relating to this contract, or the breach, termination, or invalidity thereof, shall be settled by arbitration in accordance with the Rules of Procedure of the Inter-American Commercial Arbitration Commission in effect on the date of this agreement.

INTL 4

Any dispute, controversy, or claim arising out of or relating to this contract, or the breach, termination, or invalidity thereof, shall be settled by arbitration under the UNCITRAL Arbitration Rules in effect on the date of this contract. The appointing authority shall be the International Centre for Dispute Resolution. The case shall be administered by the International Centre for Dispute Resolution under its Procedures for Cases under the UNCITRAL Arbitration Rules. The parties should consider adding a requirement regarding the number of arbitrators appointed to the dispute and designating the place and language of the arbitration. The parties may also submit an international dispute under the AAA's commercial and other specialized arbitration rules. Those procedures do not supersede any provision of the applicable rules but merely codify various procedures customarily used in international arbitration. Included among them are provisions specifying the neutrality of arbitrators, consecutive hearing days, the language of hearings, and opinions. The thrust of the procedures is to expedite international proceedings and keep them as economical as possible. For strategic or long term commercial contracts, the parties may wish to provide a "step" dispute resolution process encouraging negotiated solutions, or mediation in advance of arbitration or litigation. A model step clause and mediation clause follow.

INTL 5

In the event of any controversy or claim arising out of or relating to this contract, the parties hereto shall consult and negotiate with each other and, recognizing their mutual interests, attempt to reach a solution satisfactory to both parties. If they do not reach settlement within a period of 60 days, then either party may, by notice to the other party and the International Centre for Dispute Resolution, demand mediation under the International Mediation Procedures of the International Centre for Dispute Resolution. If settlement is not reached within 60 days after service of a written demand for mediation, any unresolved controversy or claim arising out of or relating to this contract shall be settled by arbitration in accordance with the International Arbitration Rules of the International Centre for Dispute Resolution.

INTL 6

In the event of any controversy or claim arising out of or relating to this contract, the parties hereto agree first to try and settle the dispute by mediation administered by the International Centre for Dispute Resolution under its rules before resorting to arbitration, litigation, or some other dispute resolution technique.

Usually, the effective management of time and expense in arbitration is best left in the hands of experienced case managers and arbitrators. Occasionally, however, parties wish to ensure that matters are resolved in a minimum of time and without recourse to the expense and time necessitated by common law methods of pre-hearing information exchange. The clauses that follow limit the time frame of arbitration (clauses presented in the alternative) and the amount of pre-hearing information exchange available to the parties. One word of caution: once entered into, these clauses will limit the arbitrator's authority to mold the process to the specific dictates of the case.

INTL 7

The award shall be rendered within nine months of the commencement of the arbitration, unless such time limit is extended by the arbitrator.

Alternative

It is the intent of the Parties that, barring extraordinary circumstances, arbitration proceedings will be concluded within 60 days from the date the arbitrator(s) are appointed. The arbitral tribunal may extend this time limit in the interests of justice. Failure to adhere to this time limit shall not constitute a basis for challenging the award.

INTL 8

Consistent with the expedited nature of arbitration, pre-hearing information exchange shall be limited to the reasonable production of relevant, non-privileged documents, carried out expeditiously. Enforcement of international awards is facilitated by the 1958 UN Convention on the Recognition and Enforcement of Foreign Arbitral Awards (the "New York Convention"), which has been ratified by more than 110 nations, and facilitated in this hemisphere by the Inter-American Convention on International Commercial Arbitration (the "Panama Convention").

B. Clauses for Use in Construction Disputes

The AAA Construction Industry Arbitration Rules and Mediation Procedures are designed to expedite the dispute resolution process and help the AAA be more responsive to the needs of the construction industry. The rules contain a "fast track" arbitration system for cases involving claims of less than $75,000; enhancements to the "regular track" rules; and a Large, Complex Construction case track for use in cases involving claims of at least $500,000.

The parties can provide for arbitration of future disputes by inserting the following clause into their contracts.

CONST 1

Any controversy or claim arising out of or relating to this contract, or the breach thereof, shall be settled by arbitration administered by the American Arbitration Association under its Construction Industry Arbitration Rules, and judgment on the award rendered by the arbitrator(s) may be entered in any court having jurisdiction thereof.

CONST 2

We, the undersigned parties, hereby agree to submit to arbitration administered by the American Arbitration Association under its Construction Industry Arbitration Rules the following controversy: (cite briefly). We further agree that the controversy be submitted to (one) (three) arbitrator(s). We further agree that we will faithfully observe this agreement and the rules, and that a judgment of any court having jurisdiction may be entered on the award.

If parties wish to adopt mediation as part of their contractual dispute settlement procedure, they can insert the following mediation clause in conjunction with a standard arbitration provision, and may also provide that the requirement of filing a notice of claim with respect to the dispute submitted to mediation shall be suspended until the conclusion of the mediation process.

CONST 3

If a dispute arises out of or relates to this contract, or the breach thereof, and if the dispute cannot be settled through negotiation, the parties agree first to try in good faith to settle the dispute by mediation administered by the American Arbitration Association under its Construction Industry Mediation Procedures before resorting to arbitration, litigation, or some other dispute resolution technique.

Parties also have the option of inserting a "step" mediation-arbitration clause into their contracts. A dispute resolution hybrid, the clause provides first for mediation and then, if the dispute is not resolved within a specified time frame, arbitration.

CONST 4

Any controversy or claim arising out of or relating to this contract or breach thereof, shall be settled by mediation under the Construction Industry Mediation Procedures of the American Arbitration Association. If within 30 days after service of a written demand for mediation, the mediation does not result in settlement of the dispute, then any unresolved controversy or claim arising from or relating to this contract or breach thereof shall be settled by arbitration administered by the American Arbitration Association in accordance with its Construction Industry Arbitration Rules and judgment on the award rendered by the arbitrator(s) may be entered in any court having jurisdiction thereof.

If the parties want to use a mediator to resolve an existing dispute, they can enter into the following submission.

CONST 5

The parties hereby submit the following dispute to mediation administered by the American Arbitration Association under its Construction
Industry Mediation Procedures (the clause may also provide for the
qualifications of the mediator(s), method of payment, locale of meetings, the
tolling of the statute of limitations, pre-arbitration step clause with time
frames and any other item of concern to the parties).

C. Clauses for Use in Employment Disputes

Conflicts which arise during the course of employment, such as wrongful
termination, sexual harassment and discrimination based on race, color, religion,
sex, national origin, age and disability, have redefined responsible corporate
practice and employee relations. The AAA therefore has developed special rules
called the National Rules for the Resolution of Employment Disputes. The AAA's
policy on employment ADR is guided by the state of existing law, as well as its
obligation to act in an impartial manner. In following the law, and in the interest of
providing an appropriate forum for the resolution of employment disputes, the
Association administers dispute resolution programs which meet the due process
standards as outlined in its National Rules for the Resolution of Employment
Disputes and the Due Process Protocol for Mediation and Arbitration of Statutory
Disputes Arising out of the Employment Relationship. If the Association determines that a dispute resolution program on its face substantially and materially
deviates from the minimum due process standards of the National Rules for the
Resolution of Employment Disputes and the protocol, the Association will decline to
administer cases under that program. Other issues will be presented to the
arbitrator for determination.

An employer intending to incorporate these rules or to refer to the dispute
resolution services of the AAA in an employment ADR plan, shall, at least 30 days
prior to the planned effective date of the program, (1) notify and (2) provide the
Association with a copy of the employment dispute resolution plan. If an employer
does not comply with this requirement, the Association reserves the right to decline
its administrative services.

Parties can provide for arbitration of future disputes by inserting the following
clause into their employment contracts, personnel manuals or policy statements,
employment applications, or other agreements.

EMPL 1

Any controversy or claim arising out of or relating to this [employment
application; employment ADR program; employment contract] shall be
settled by arbitration administered by the American Arbitration Association under its National Rules for the Resolution of Employment Disputes
and judgment upon the award rendered by the arbitrator(s) may be
entered in any court having jurisdiction thereof.

Arbitration of existing disputes can be accomplished by use of the
following clause.

EMPL 2

We, the undersigned parties, hereby agree to submit to arbitration, administered by the American Arbitration Association under its National Rules for the Resolution of Employment Disputes, the following controversy: (describe briefly). We further agree that the above controversy be submitted to (one) (three) arbitrator(s) selected from the roster of arbitrators of the American Arbitration Association, and that a judgment of any court having jurisdiction may be entered on the award.

Parties may agree to use mediation on an informal basis for selected disputes, or mediation may be designated in a personnel manual as a step prior to arbitration, litigation or some other dispute resolution technique. If the parties want to adopt mediation as a part of their contractual dispute-settlement procedure, they can add the following mediation clause to their contract.

EMPL 3

If a dispute arises out of or relates to this [employment application; employment ADR program; employment contract] or the breach thereof, and if the dispute cannot be settled through negotiation, the parties agree first to try in good faith to settle the dispute by mediation administered by the American Arbitration Association under its National Rules for the Resolution of Employment Disputes, before resorting to arbitration, litigation or some other dispute resolution procedure.

If the parties want to use a mediator to resolve an existing dispute, they can enter into the following submission.

EMPL 4

The parties hereby submit the following dispute to mediation administered by the American Arbitration Association under its National Rules for the Resolution of Employment Disputes (the clause may also provide for the qualifications of the mediator(s), method of payment, locale of meetings, and any other item of concern to the parties).

D. Clauses for Use in Patent Disputes

The suitability of arbitration as a prompt and effective means of resolving intellectual property disputes has been well recognized in recent years. Those who use and support arbitration as a way of resolving intellectual property and licensing disputes have acknowledged the following advantages of arbitration over litigation in this technical field: relative speed and economy, privacy, convenience, informality, reduced likelihood of damage to ongoing business relationships, greater suitability to international problems, and, especially important, the ability of the parties to select arbitrators who are experts and familiar with the subject matter of the dispute.

The award is binding only on the parties to the arbitration, and the parties may agree that the award will be modified if the patent that is the subject of the arbitration is subsequently determined to be invalid or unenforceable. If parties foresee the possibility of needing emergency relief akin to a temporary restraining order, they might specify an arbitrator by name for that purpose in their arbitration clause or authorize the AAA to name a preliminary relief arbitrator; for sample clauses, consult Section V, discussion of Preliminary Relief. Parties can provide for arbitration of future disputes by inserting the following clause into their contracts.

PATENT 1

Any controversy or claim arising out of or relating to this contract, or the breach thereof, shall be settled by arbitration administered by the American Arbitration Association under its Patent Arbitration Rules, and judgment on the award rendered by the arbitrator(s) may be entered by any court having jurisdiction thereof.

Arbitration of existing disputes may be accomplished by use of the following clause.

PATENT 2

We, the undersigned parties, hereby agree to submit to arbitration administered by the American Arbitration Association under its Patent Arbitration Rules the following controversy: (describe briefly). We further agree that the above controversy be submitted to (one) (three) arbitrator(s), and that a judgment of any court having jurisdiction may be entered on the award.

If parties want to adopt mediation as a part of their contractual dispute settlement procedure, they can insert the following mediation clause in conjunction with a standard arbitration provision.

PATENT 3

If a dispute arises out of or relates to this contract, or the breach thereof, and if the dispute cannot be settled through negotiation, the parties agree first to try in good faith to settle the dispute by mediation administered by the American Arbitration Association under its Commercial Mediation Procedures before resorting to arbitration, litigation, or some other dispute resolution procedure.

If the parties want to use a mediator to resolve an existing dispute, they can enter into the following submission.

PATENT 4

The parties hereby submit the following dispute to mediation administered by the American Arbitration Association under its Commercial Mediation Procedures (the clause may also provide for the qualifications of the mediator(s), method of payment, locale of meetings, and any other item of concern to the parties).

V. Other Provisions That Might Be Considered

This section contains various provisions which expand upon and are supplemental to the basic dispute resolution clauses set forth in Sections III and IV. The listing of such provisions is not intended to be all-inclusive and does not necessarily indicate that the AAA endorses the use of such additional language. The AAA recognizes, however, that some drafters choose to expand their dispute resolution clauses to reflect at least some of these ideas. Since it is important that practitioners be well informed when making choices in drafting, the section also sets forth, where appropriate, certain of the pros and cons of adopting the various supplemental provisions.

A. Specifying a Method of Selection and the Number of Arbitrators

Under the AAA's arbitration rules, arbitrators are generally selected using a listing process. The AAA case manager provides each party with a list of proposed arbitrators who are generally familiar with the subject matter involved in the dispute. Each side is provided a number of days to strike any unacceptable names, number the remaining names in order of preference, and return the list to the AAA. The case manager then invites persons to serve from the names remaining on the list, in the designated order of mutual preference. The parties may agree to have one arbitrator or three (which increases the cost). If parties do not agree on the number of arbitrator(s), it will be left to the discretion of the case manager.

The parties may use other arbitrator appointment systems, such as the party-appointed method in which each side designates one arbitrator and the two thus selected appoint the chair of the panel.

The Commercial Arbitration Rules and the Construction Industry Arbitration Rules provide that unless the parties specifically agree in writing that the party-appointed arbitrators are to be non-neutral, arbitrators appointed by the parties must meet the impartiality and independence standards set forth within the rules. If parties intend that their party appointed arbitrators serve in a non-neutral capacity, this should be clearly stated within their clause.

The arbitration clause can also specify by name the individual whom the parties want as their arbitrator. However, the potential unavailability of the named individual in the future may pose a risk.

All of these issues and others can be dealt with in the arbitration clause.

Some illustrative provisions follow.

ARBSEL 1

The arbitrator selected by the claimant and the arbitrator selected by respondent shall, within ten days of their appointment, select a third neutral arbitrator. In the event that they are unable to do so, the parties or their attorneys may request the American Arbitration Association to appoint the third neutral arbitrator. Prior to the commencement of hearings, each of the arbitrators appointed shall provide an oath or undertaking of impartiality.

ARBSEL 2

Within 15 days after the commencement of arbitration, each party shall select one person to act as arbitrator and the two selected shall select a third arbitrator within ten days of their appointment. [The party selected arbitrators will serve in a non-neutral capacity.] If the arbitrators selected by the parties are unable or fail to agree upon the third arbitrator, the third arbitrator shall be selected by the American Arbitration Association.

ARBSEL 3

In the event that arbitration is necessary, [name of specific arbitrator] shall act as the arbitrator. When providing for direct appointment of the arbitrator(s) by the parties, it is best to specify a time frame within which it must be accomplished. Also, in many jurisdictions, the law permits the court to appoint arbitrators where privately-agreed means fail. Such a result may be time consuming, costly, and unpredictable. Parties who seek to establish an ad-hoc method of arbitrator appointment might be well advised to provide a fallback, such as, should the particular procedure fail for any reason, "arbitrators shall be appointed as provided in the AAA Commercial Arbitration Rules."

B. Arbitrator Qualifications

The parties may wish that one or more of the arbitrators be a lawyer or an accountant or an expert in computer technology, etc. In some instances, it makes more sense to specify that one of three arbitrators be an accountant, for example, than to turn the entire proceeding over to three accountants. Sample clauses providing for specific qualifications of arbitrators are set forth below.

QUAL 1

The arbitrator shall be a certified public accountant.

QUAL 2

The arbitrator shall be a practicing attorney [or a retired judge] [of the [specify] Court].

QUAL 3

The arbitration proceedings shall be conducted before a panel of three neutral arbitrators, all of whom shall be members of the bar of the state of [specify], actively engaged in the practice of law for at least ten years.

QUAL 4

The panel of three arbitrators shall consist of one contractor, one architect, and one construction attorney.

QUAL 5

The arbitrators will be selected from a panel of persons having experience with and knowledge of electronic computers and the computer business, and at least one of the arbitrators selected will be an attorney.

QUAL 6

In the event that any party's claim exceeds $1 million, exclusive of interest and attorneys' fees, the dispute shall be heard and determined by three arbitrators.

Parties might wish to specify that the arbitrator should or should not be a national or citizen of a particular country. The following examples can be added to the arbitration clause to deal with this concern.

NATLY 1

The arbitrator shall be a national of [country].

NATLY 2

The arbitrator shall not be a national of either [country A] or [country B].

NATLY 3

The arbitrator shall not be of the nationality of either of the parties.

C. Locale Provisions

Parties might want to add language specifying the place of the arbitration. The choice of the proper place to arbitrate is most important because the place of arbitration implies generally a choice of the applicable procedural law, which in turn affects questions of arbitrability, procedure, court intervention and enforcement.

In specifying a locale, parties should consider (1) the convenience of the location (e.g., availability of witnesses, local counsel, transportation, hotels, meeting facilities, court reporters, etc.); (2) the available pool of qualified arbitrators within the geographical area; and (3) the applicable procedural and substantive law. Of particular importance in international cases is the applicability of a convention providing for recognition and enforcement of arbitral agreements and awards and the arbitration regime at the chosen site.

An example of locale provisions that might appear in an arbitration clause follows.

LOC 1

The place of arbitration shall be [city], [state], or [country].

D. Language

In matters involving multilingual parties, the arbitration agreement often specifies the language in which the arbitration will be conducted.

Examples of such language follow.

LANG 1

The language(s) of the arbitration shall be [specify].

LANG 2

The arbitration shall be conducted in the language in which the contract was written.

Such arbitration clauses could also deal with selection and cost allocation of an interpreter.

E. Governing Law

It is common for parties to specify the law that will govern the contract and/or the arbitration proceedings. Some examples follow.

GOV 1

This agreement shall be governed by and interpreted in accordance with the laws of the State of [specify]. The parties acknowledge that this agreement evidences a transaction involving interstate commerce. The United States Arbitration Act shall govern the interpretation, enforcement, and proceedings pursuant to the arbitration clause in this agreement.

GOV 2

Disputes under this clause shall be resolved by arbitration in accordance with Title 9 of the US Code (United States Arbitration Act) and the Commercial Arbitration Rules of the American Arbitration Association.

GOV 3

This contract shall be governed by the laws of the State of [specify].

In international cases, where the parties have not provided for the law applicable to the substance of the dispute, the AAA's International Arbitration Rules contain specific guidelines for arbitrators regarding applicable law. See the discussion concerning International Disputes.

F. Conditions Precedent to Arbitration

Under an agreement of the parties, satisfaction of specified conditions may be required before a dispute is ready for arbitration. Examples of such conditions precedent include written notification of claims within a fixed period of time and exhaustion of other contractually established procedures, such as submission of claims to an architect or engineer. These kinds of provisions may, however, be a source of delay and may require linkage with a statute of limitations waiver (see below). An example of a "condition precedent" clause follows.

CONPRE 1

If a dispute arises from or relates to this contract, the parties agree that upon request of either party they will seek the advice of [a mutually selected engineer] and try in good faith to settle the dispute within 30 days of that request, following which either party may submit the matter to mediation under the Commercial Mediation

Procedures of the American Arbitration Association. If the matter is not resolved within 60 days after initiation of mediation, either party may demand arbitration administered by the American Arbitration Association under its [applicable] rules.

G. Preliminary Relief

While preliminary relief is permitted under the AAA's commercial rules, it is appropriate to provide specifically for it if a need for an interim remedy is anticipated. One way to do so is to incorporate the Optional Rules for Emergency Measures of Protection of the AAA Commercial Arbitration Rules and Mediation Procedures, discussed above. Alternatively, if the parties foresee the possibility of needing emergency relief akin to a temporary restraining order, they might specify an arbitrator by name for that purpose in their arbitration clause or authorize the

AAA to name a preliminary relief arbitrator to ensure an arbitrator is in place in sufficient time to address appropriate issues.

Specific clauses providing for preliminary relief are set forth below.

PRELIM 1

Either party may apply to the arbitrator seeking injunctive relief until the arbitration award is rendered or the controversy is otherwise resolved. Either party also may, without waiving any remedy under this agreement, seek from any court having jurisdiction any interim or provisional relief that is necessary to protect the rights or property of that party, pending the establishment of the arbitral tribunal (or pending the arbitral tribunal's determination of the merits of the controversy).

Note that the AAA's rules provide for interim relief by the arbitrator upon application of a party.

Pending the outcome of the arbitration, parties may agree to hold in escrow money, a letter of credit, goods, or the subject matter of the arbitration. A sample of a clause providing for such escrow follows.

ESCROW 1

Pending the outcome of the arbitration [name of party] shall place in escrow with [law firm, institution, or AAA] as the escrow agent, [the sum of _____, a letter of credit, goods, or the subject matter in dispute]. The escrow agent shall be entitled to release the [funds, letter of credit, goods, or subject matter in dispute] as directed by the arbitrator(s) in the award, unless the parties agree otherwise in writing.

H. Consolidation

Where there are multiple parties with disputes arising from the same transaction, complications can often be reduced by the consolidation of all disputes. Since arbitration is a process based on voluntary contractual participation, parties may not be required to arbitrate a dispute without their consent. However, parties can provide for the consolidation of two or more separate arbitrations into a single proceeding or permit the joinder of a third party into an arbitration. In a construction dispute, consolidated proceedings may eliminate the need for duplicative presentations of claims and avoid the possibility of conflicting rulings from different panels of arbitrators. However, consolidating claims might be a source of delay and expense. An example of language that can be included in an arbitration clause follows.

CONSOL 1

The owner, the contractor, and all subcontractors, specialty contractors, material suppliers, engineers, designers, architects, construction lenders, bonding companies, and other parties concerned with the construction of the structure are bound, each to each other, by this arbitration clause, provided that they have signed this contract or a contract that incorporates this contract by reference or signed any other agreement to be bound by this arbitration clause. Each such party agrees that it may be joined as an additional party to an arbitration involving other parties under any such agreement. If more than one arbitration is begun under any such agreement and any party contends that two or more arbitrations are substantially related and that the issues should be heard in one proceeding, the arbitrator(s) selected in the first-filed of such proceedings shall determine whether, in the interests of justice and efficiency, the proceedings should be consolidated before that (those) arbitrator(s).

I. Document Discovery

Under the AAA rules, arbitrators are authorized to direct a prehearing exchange of documents. The parties typically discuss such an exchange and seek to agree on its scope. In most (but not all) instances, arbitrators will order prompt production of limited numbers of documents which are directly relevant to the issues involved. In some instances, parties might want to ensure that such production will in fact occur and thus provide for it in their arbitration clause. In doing so, however, they should be mindful of what scope of document production they desire. This may be difficult to decide at the outset. If the parties address discovery in the clause, they might include time limitations as to when all discovery should be completed and might specify that the arbitrator shall resolve outstanding discovery issues. Sample language is set forth below.

> DOC 1
>
> Consistent with the expedited nature of arbitration, each party will, upon the written request of the other party, promptly provide the other with copies of documents [relevant to the issues raised by any claim or counterclaim] [on which the producing party may rely in support of or in opposition to any claim or defense]. Any dispute regarding discovery, or the relevance or scope thereof, shall be determined by the [arbitrator(s)] [chair of the arbitration panel], which determination shall be conclusive. All discovery shall be completed within [45] [60] days following the appointment of the arbitrator(s).

The AAA's various commercial arbitration rules provide an opportunity for an administrative conference with the AAA staff and/or a preliminary hearing with the arbitrator. The purposes of such meetings include establishing the extent of and a schedule for production of relevant documents and other information.

J. Depositions

Generally arbitrators prefer to hear and be able to question witnesses at a hearing rather than rely on deposition testimony. However, parties are free to provide in their arbitration clause for a tailored discovery program, preferably to be managed by the arbitrator. This might occur, for example, if the parties anticipate the need for distant witnesses who would not be able to testify except through depositions or, in the alternative, by the arbitrator holding a hearing where the witness is located and subject to subpoena. In most cases where parties provide for depositions, they do so in very limited fashion, i.e., they might specify a 30-day deposition period, with each side permitted three depositions, none of which would last more than three hours. All objections would be reserved for the arbitration hearing and would not even be noted at the deposition except for objections based on privilege or extreme confidentiality. Sample language providing for such depositions is set forth below.

DEP 1

At the request of a party, the arbitrator(s) shall have the discretion to order examination by deposition of witnesses to the extent the arbitrator deems such additional discovery relevant and appropriate. Depositions shall be limited to a maximum of [three] [insert number] per party and shall be held within 30 days of the making of a request. Additional depositions may be scheduled only with the permission of the [arbitrator(s)] [chair of the arbitration panel], and for good cause shown. Each deposition shall be limited to a maximum of [three hours] [six hours] [one day's] duration. All objections are reserved for the arbitration hearing except for objections based on privilege and proprietary or confidential information.

K. Duration of Arbitration Proceeding

While AAA Commercial Arbitration Rules normally provide for an award within 30 days of the closing of the hearing, parties sometimes underscore their wish for an expedited result by providing in the arbitration clause, for example, that there will be an award within a specified number of months of the notice of intention to arbitrate and that the arbitrator(s) must agree to the time constraints before accepting appointment. Before adopting such language, however, the parties should consider whether the deadline is realistic and what would happen if the deadline were not met under circumstances where the parties had not mutually agreed to extend it (e.g., whether the award would be enforceable). It thus may be helpful to allow the arbitrator to extend time limits in appropriate circumstances. Sample language is set forth below.

TIME 1

The award shall be made within nine months of the filing of the notice of intention to arbitrate (demand), and the arbitrator(s) shall agree to comply with this schedule before accepting appointment. However, this time limit may be extended by agreement of the parties or by the arbitrator(s) if necessary.

L. Remedies

Under a broad arbitration clause and most AAA rules, the arbitrator may grant "any remedy or relief that the arbitrator deems just and equitable" within the scope of the parties' agreement. Sometimes parties want to include or exclude certain specific remedies. Examples of clauses dealing with remedies follow.

REM 1

The arbitrators will have no authority to award punitive or other damages not measured by the prevailing party's actual damages, except as may be required by statute.

REM 2

In no event shall an award in an arbitration initiated under this clause exceed $_____.

REM 3

In no event shall an award in an arbitration initiated under this clause exceed $_____ for any claimant.

REM 4

The arbitrator(s) shall not award consequential damages in any arbitration initiated under this section.

REM 5

Any award in an arbitration initiated under this clause shall be limited to monetary damages and shall include no injunction or direction to any party other than the direction to pay a monetary amount.

REM 6

If the arbitrator(s) find liability in any arbitration initiated under this clause, they shall award liquidated damages in the amount of $_____.

REM 7

Any monetary award in an arbitration initiated under this clause shall include pre-award interest at the rate of ____% from the time of the act or acts giving rise to the award.

M. "Baseball" Arbitration

"Baseball" arbitration is a methodology used in many different contexts in addition to baseball players' salary disputes, and is particularly effective when parties have a long-term relationship. The procedure involves each party submitting a number to the arbitrator(s) and serving the number on his or her adversary on the understanding that, following a hearing, the arbitrator(s) will pick one of the submitted numbers, nothing else. A key aspect of this approach is that there is incentive for a party to submit a highly reasonable number, since this increases the likelihood that the arbitrator(s) will select that number. In some instances, the process of submitting the numbers moves the parties so close together that the dispute is settled without a hearing. Sample language providing for "baseball" arbitration is set forth below.

BASEBALL 1

Each party shall submit to the arbitrator and exchange with each other in advance of the hearing their last, best offers. The arbitrator shall be limited to awarding only one or the other of the two figures submitted.

N. Arbitration Within Monetary Limits

Parties are often able to negotiate to a point but are then unable to close the remaining gap between their respective positions. By setting up an arbitration that must result in an award within the gap that remains between the parties, the parties are able to eliminate extreme risk, while gaining the benefit of the extent to which their negotiations were successful.

There are two commonly-used approaches. The first involves informing the arbitrator(s) that the award should be somewhere within a specified monetary range. Sample contract language providing for this methodology is set forth below.

LIMITS 1

Any award of the arbitrator in favor of [specify party] and against [specify party] shall be at least [specify a dollar amount] but shall not exceed [specify a dollar amount]. [Specify a party] expressly waives any claim in excess of [specify a dollar amount] and agrees that its recovery shall not exceed that amount. Any such award shall be in satisfaction of all claims by [specify a party] against [specify a party].

A second approach is for the parties to agree but not tell the arbitrator(s) that the amount of recovery will, for example, be somewhere between $5 and $10. If the award is less than $5, then it is raised to $5 pursuant to the agreement; if the award is more than $10, then it is lowered to $10 pursuant to the agreement; if the award is within the $5-10 range, then the amount awarded by the arbitrator(s) is unchanged. Sample contract language providing for this methodology is set forth below.

LIMITS 2

In the event that the arbitrator denies the claim or awards an amount less than the minimum amount of [specify], then this minimum amount shall be paid to the claimant. Should the arbitrator's award exceed the maximum amount of [specify], then only this maximum amount shall be paid to the claimant. It is further understood between the parties that, if the arbitrator awards an amount between the minimum and the maximum stipulated range, then the exact awarded amount will be paid to the claimant. The parties further agree that this agreement is private between them and will not be disclosed to the arbitrator.

O. Assessment of Attorneys' Fees

The AAA rules generally provide that the administrative fees be borne as incurred and that the arbitrators' compensation be allocated equally between the parties and, except for international rules, are silent concerning attorneys' fees; but this can be modified by agreement of the parties. Fees and expenses of the arbitration, including attorneys' fees, can be dealt with in the arbitration clause. Some typical language dealing with fees and expenses follow.

FEE 1

The prevailing party shall be entitled to an award of reasonable attorney fees.

FEE 2

The arbitrators shall award to the prevailing party, if any, as determined by the arbitrators, all of its costs and fees. "Costs and fees" mean all reasonable pre-award expenses of the arbitration, including the arbitrators' fees, administrative fees, travel expenses, out-of-pocket expenses such as copying and telephone, court costs, witness fees, and attorneys' fees.

FEE 3

Each party shall bear its own costs and expenses and an equal share of the arbitrators' and administrative fees of arbitration.

FEE 4

The arbitrators may determine how the costs and expenses of the arbitration shall be allocated between the parties, but they shall not award attorneys' fees.

P. Reasoned Opinion Accompanying the Award

In domestic commercial cases, arbitrators usually will not write a reasoned opinion explaining their award unless such an opinion is requested by all parties. While some take the position that reasoned opinions detract from finality if they facilitate post-arbitration resort to the courts, parties sometimes desire such opinions, particularly in large, complex cases or as already provided by most applicable rules in international disputes. If the parties want such an opinion, they can include language such as the following in their arbitration clause.

OPIN 1

The award of the arbitrators shall be accompanied by a reasoned opinion.

OPIN 2

The award shall be in writing, shall be signed by a majority of the arbitrators, and shall include a statement setting forth the reasons for the disposition of any claim.

OPIN 3

The award shall include findings of fact [and conclusions of law].

OPIN 4

The award shall include a breakdown as to specific claims.

Q. Confidentiality

While the AAA and arbitrators adhere to certain standards concerning the privacy or confidentiality of the hearings (see the AAA-ABA Code of Ethics for Arbitrators in Commercial Disputes, Canon VI), parties might also wish to impose limits on themselves as to how much information regarding the dispute may be disclosed outside the hearing. The following language might help serve this purpose.

CONF 1

Except as may be required by law, neither a party nor an arbitrator may disclose the existence, content, or results of any arbitration hereunder without the prior written consent of both parties.

The preceding language could also be modified to restrict only disclosure of certain information (e.g., trade secrets).

R. Appeal

The basic objective of arbitration is a fair, fast and expert result, achieved economically. Consistent with this goal, an arbitration award traditionally will be set aside only in egregious circumstances such as demonstrable bias of an arbitrator. Sometimes, however, the parties desire a more comprehensive appeal, most often in the setting of legally complex cases. Providing a mechanism for such an appeal assures that the losing party will use it. While parties can attempt to provide for an appeal in the court system pursuant to traditional standards of court review, the authority is mixed as to whether courts will accept appeals from arbitration on such a basis. Another approach is to provide for an appeal to another panel of arbitrators who would apply whatever standard of review the parties might specify. Set forth below is an example of arbitration clause language providing for this latter type of appeal.

APP 1

Within 30 days of receipt of any award (which shall not be binding if an appeal is taken), any party may notify the AAA of an intention to appeal to a second arbitral tribunal, constituted in the same manner as the initial tribunal. The appeal tribunal shall be entitled to adopt the initial award as its own, modify the initial award or substitute its own award for the initial award. The appeal tribunal shall not modify or replace the initial award except [for manifest disregard of law or facts] [for clear errors of law or because of clear and convincing factual errors]. The award of the appeal tribunal shall be final and binding, and judgment may be entered by a court having jurisdiction thereof.

S. Mediation-Arbitration

A clause may provide first for mediation under the AAA's mediation procedures. If the mediation is unsuccessful, the mediator could be authorized to resolve the dispute under the AAA's arbitration rules. This process, is sometimes referred to as "Med-Arb." Except in unusual circumstances, a procedure whereby the same individual who has been serving as a mediator becomes an arbitrator when the mediation fails is not recommended, because it could inhibit the candor which should characterize the mediation process and/or it could convey evidence, legal points or settlement positions ex parte, improperly influencing the arbitrator. A sample of a med-arb clause follows.

MEDARB 1

If a dispute arises from or relates to this contract or the breach thereof, and if the dispute cannot be settled through direct discussions, the parties agree to endeavor first to settle the dispute by mediation administered by the American Arbitration Association under its Commercial Mediation Procedures before resorting to arbitration. Any unresolved controversy or claim arising from or relating to this contract or breach thereof shall be settled by arbitration administered by the American Arbitration Association in accordance with its Commercial Arbitration Rules, and judgment on the award rendered by the arbitrator may be entered in any court having jurisdiction thereof. If all parties to the dispute agree, a mediator involved in the parties' mediation may be asked to serve as the arbitrator.

T. Statute of Limitations

Parties may wish to consider whether the applicable statute of limitations will be tolled for the duration of mediation proceedings, and can refer to the following language.

> STATLIM 1
>
> The requirements of filing a notice of claim with respect to the dispute submitted to mediation shall be suspended until the conclusion of the mediation process.

U. Dispute Resolution Boards

A Dispute Resolution Board (DRB) provides a prompt, rational, impartial review of disputes by mutually accepted experts, which frequently results in substantial cost savings and can eliminate years of wasted time and energy in litigation. DRB procedures may be made a part of construction contract documents.

The contract should contain a paragraph reflecting the agreement to establish the DRB. The text of the actual procedures also should be physically incorporated into the general conditions or supplementary conditions of the contract for construction wherever possible and practical, and such documents as the invitation to bidders or the request for proposals should mention that the formation of a DRB is contemplated. The DRB procedures should be coordinated with the other dispute resolution procedures required by the contract documents. Suggested language for incorporation in the contract follows.

> DRB 1
>
> The parties shall impanel a Dispute Resolution Board of one or three members in accordance with the Dispute Resolution Board Guide Specifications of the American Arbitration Association. The DRB, in close consultation with all interested parties, will assist and recommend the resolution of any disputes, claims, and other controversies that might arise among the parties.

V. Mass Torts

ADR techniques can be employed privately by parties facing the prospect of mass tort litigation to explore in a nonbinding fashion the options for management, evaluation, and/or resolution of the dispute. A wide range of binding and nonbinding techniques, including neutral evaluation, mediation, and arbitration can be used to explore the potential for resolution of a dispute and/or to develop a basic framework for discussions. Although these options have limitations and may not be a substitute for litigation with possible full evidentiary trials, they can provide a useful framework for early discussion of the issues. The parties should be able to formulate procedures to assure confidentiality and to protect against the inappropriate use of information.

INTERNATIONAL BAR ASSOCIATION, GUIDELINES FOR DRAFTING INTERNATIONAL ARBITRATION CLAUSES*

Adopted by a resolution of the IBA Council (7 October 2010)

I. Introduction

1. The purpose of these Guidelines is to provide a succinct and accessible approach to the drafting of international arbitration clauses. Poorly drafted arbitration clauses may be unenforceable and often cause unnecessary cost and delay. By considering these Guidelines, contract drafters should be able to ensure that their arbitration clauses are effective and adapted to their needs.

2. The Guidelines are divided into five sections (in addition to this introduction). The first section offers basic guidelines on what to do and not to do. The second section addresses optional elements that should be considered when drafting arbitration clauses. The third section addresses multi-tier dispute resolution clauses providing for negotiation, mediation and arbitration. The fourth section discusses the drafting of arbitration clauses for multiparty contracts, and the fifth section considers the drafting of arbitration clauses in situations involving multiple, but related contracts.

II. Basic Drafting Guidelines

Guideline 1: The parties should decide between institutional and ad hoc arbitration.

Comments:

3. The first choice facing parties drafting an arbitration clause is whether to opt for institutional or ad hoc arbitration.

4. In institutional (or administered) arbitration, an arbitral institution provides assistance in running the arbitral proceedings in exchange for a fee. The institution can assist with practical matters such as organizing hearings and handling communications with and payments to the arbitrators. The institution can also provide services such as appointing an arbitrator if a party defaults, deciding a challenge against an arbitrator and scrutinizing the award. The institution does not decide the merits of the parties' dispute, however. This is left entirely to the arbitrators.

5. Institutional arbitration may be beneficial for parties with little experience in international arbitration. The institution may contribute significant procedural 'know how' that helps the arbitration run effectively, and may even be able to assist when the parties have failed to anticipate something when drafting their arbitration clause. The services provided by an arbitral institution are often worth the relatively low administrative fee charged.

6. If parties choose administered arbitration, they should seek a reputable

---

institution, usually one with an established track record of administering international cases. The major arbitral institutions can administer arbitrations around the world, and the arbitral proceedings do not need to take place in the city where the institution is headquartered.

7. In ad hoc (or non-administered) arbitration, the burden of running the arbitral proceedings falls entirely on the parties and, once they have been appointed, the arbitrators. As explained below (Guideline 2), the parties can facilitate their task by selecting a set of arbitration rules designed for use in ad hoc arbitration. Although no arbitral institution is involved in running the arbitral proceedings, as explained below (Guideline 6), there still is a need to designate a neutral third party (known as an 'appointing authority') to select arbitrators and deal with possible vacancies if the parties cannot agree.

Guideline 2: The parties should select a set of arbitration rules and use the model clause recommended for these arbitration rules as a starting point.

Comments:

8. The second choice facing parties drafting an arbitration clause is selection of a set of arbitration rules. The selected arbitration rules will provide the procedural framework for the arbitral proceedings. If the parties do not incorporate an established set of rules, many procedural issues that may arise during arbitral proceedings should be addressed in the arbitration clause itself, an effort that is rarely desirable and should be undertaken with specialized advice.

9. When the parties have opted for institutional arbitration, the choice of arbitration rules should always coincide with that of the arbitral institution. When the parties have opted for ad hoc arbitration, the parties can select arbitration rules developed for non-administered arbitration, eg, the Arbitration Rules developed by the United Nations Commission on International Trade Law ('UNCITRAL'). Even if they do so, the parties should designate an arbitral institution (or another neutral entity) as the appointing authority for selection of the arbitrators (see paragraphs 31-32 below).

10. Once a set of arbitration rules is selected, the parties should use the model clause recommended by the institution or entity that authored the rules as a starting point for drafting their arbitration clause. The parties can add to the model clause, but should rarely subtract from it. By doing so, the parties will ensure that all the elements required to make an arbitration agreement valid, enforceable and effective are present. They will ensure that arbitration is unambiguously established as the exclusive dispute resolution method under their contract and that the correct names of the arbitral institution and rules are used (thus avoiding confusion or dilatory tactics when a dispute arises). The parties should assure that language added to a model clause is consistent with the selected arbitration rules.

Recommended Clause:

11. For an institutional arbitration clause, the website of the chosen institution should be accessed in order to use the model clause proposed by the institution as a basis for drafting the arbitration clause. Some institutions have also developed clauses that are specific to certain industries (eg, shipping).

12. For an ad hoc arbitration designating a set of rules, the website of the entity

that issues such rules should be accessed in order to use the entity's model clause as a basis for drafting the arbitration clause.

13. In those instances where contracting parties agree to ad hoc arbitration without designating a set of rules, the following clause can be used for two-party contracts:

> All disputes arising out of or in connection with this agreement, including any question regarding its existence, validity or termination, shall be finally resolved by arbitration.

> The place of arbitration shall be [city, country].

> The language of the arbitration shall be [. . .].

> The arbitration shall be commenced by a request for arbitration by the claimant, delivered to the respondent. The request for arbitration shall set out the nature of the claim(s) and the relief requested.

> The arbitral tribunal shall consist of three arbitrators, one selected by the claimant in the request for arbitration, the second selected by the respondent within [30] days of receipt of the request for arbitration, and the third, who shall act as presiding arbitrator, selected by the two parties within [30] days of the selection of the second arbitrator. If any arbitrators are not selected within these time periods, [the designated appointing authority] shall, upon the request of any party, make the selection(s).

> If a vacancy arises, the vacancy shall be filled by the method by which that arbitrator was originally appointed, provided, however, that, if a vacancy arises during or after the hearing on the merits, the remaining two arbitrators may proceed with the arbitration and render an award.

> The arbitrators shall be independent and impartial. Any challenge of an arbitrator shall be decided by [the designated appointing authority].

> The procedure to be followed during the arbitration shall be agreed by the parties or, failing such agreement, determined by the arbitral tribunal after consultation with the parties.

> The arbitral tribunal shall have the power to rule on its own jurisdiction, including any objections with respect to the existence, validity or effectiveness of the arbitration agreement. The arbitral tribunal may make such ruling in a preliminary decision on jurisdiction or in an award on the merits, as it considers appropriate in the circumstances.

> Default by any party shall not prevent the arbitral tribunal from proceeding to render an award.

> The arbitral tribunal may make its decisions by a majority. In the event that no majority is possible, the presiding arbitrator may make the decision(s) as if acting as a sole arbitrator.

> If the arbitrator appointed by a party fails or refuses to participate, the two other arbitrators may proceed with the arbitration and render an

award if they determine that the failure or refusal to participate was unjustified.

Any award of the arbitral tribunal shall be final and binding on the parties. The parties undertake to carry out any award without delay and shall be deemed to have waived their right to any form of recourse insofar as such waiver can validly be made. Enforcement of any award may be sought in any court of competent jurisdiction.

Guideline 3: Absent special circumstances, the parties should not attempt to limit the scope of disputes subject to arbitration and should define this scope broadly.

Comments:

14. The scope of an arbitration clause refers to the type and ambit of disputes that are subject to arbitration. Absent particular circumstances compelling otherwise, the scope of an arbitration clause should be defined broadly to cover not only all disputes 'arising out of' the contract, but also all disputes 'in connection with' (or 'relating to') the contract. Less inclusive language invites arguments about whether a given dispute is subject to arbitration.

15. In certain circumstances, the parties may have good reasons to exclude some disputes from the scope of the arbitration clause. For example, it may be appropriate to refer pricing and technical disputes under certain contracts to expert determination rather than to arbitration. As another example, licensors may justifiably wish to retain the option to seek orders of specific performance and other injunctive relief directly from the courts in case of infringement of their intellectual property rights or to submit decisions on the ownership or validity of these rights to courts.

16. The parties should bear in mind that, even when drafted carefully, exclusions may not avoid preliminary arguments over whether a given dispute is subject to arbitration. A claim may raise some issues that fall within the scope of the arbitration clause and others that do not. To use one of the above examples, a dispute over the ownership or validity of intellectual property rights under a licensing agreement may also involve issues of non-payment, breach and so forth, which could give rise to intractable jurisdictional problems in situations where certain disputes have been excluded from arbitration.

Recommended Clauses:

17. The parties will ensure that the scope of their arbitration clause is broad by using the model clause associated with the selected arbitration rules.

18. If the parties do not use a model clause, the following clause should be used:

All disputes arising out of or in connection with this agreement, including any question regarding its existence, validity or termination, shall be finally resolved by arbitration under [selected arbitration rules].

19. Exceptionally, if there are special circumstances and the parties wish to limit the scope of disputes subject to arbitration, the following clause can be used: Except for matters that are specifically excluded from arbitration hereunder, all disputes arising out of or in connection with this agreement, including any question regarding its existence, validity or termination, shall be finally resolved by

arbitration under [selected arbitration rules]. The following matters are specifically excluded from arbitration hereunder: [. . .].

Guideline 4: The parties should select the place of arbitration. This selection should be based on both practical and juridical considerations.

Comments:

20. The selection of the place (or 'seat') of arbitration involves obvious practical considerations: neutrality, availability of hearing facilities, proximity to the witnesses and evidence, the parties' familiarity with the language and culture, willingness of qualified arbitrators to participate in proceedings in that place. The place of arbitration may also influence the profile of the arbitrators, especially if not appointed by the parties. Convenience should not be the decisive factor, however, as under most rules the tribunal is free to meet and hold hearings in places other than the designated place of arbitration.

21. The place of arbitration is the juridical home of the arbitration. Close attention must be paid to the legal regime of the chosen place of arbitration because this choice has important legal consequences under most national arbitration legislations as well as under some arbitration rules. While the place of arbitration does not determine the law governing the contract and the merits (see paragraphs 42–46 below), it does determine the law (arbitration law or lex arbitri) that governs certain procedural aspects of the arbitration, eg, the powers of arbitrators and the judicial oversight of the arbitral process. Moreover, the courts at the place of arbitration can be called upon to provide assistance (eg, by appointing or replacing arbitrators, by ordering provisional and conservatory measures, or by assisting with the taking of evidence), and may also interfere with the conduct of the arbitration (eg, by ordering a stay of the arbitral proceedings). Further, these courts have jurisdiction to hear challenges against the award at the end of the arbitration; awards set aside at the place of arbitration may not be enforceable elsewhere. Even if the award is not set aside, the place of arbitration may affect the enforceability of the award under applicable international treaties.

22. As a general rule, the parties should set the place of arbitration in a jurisdiction (i) that is a party to the 1958 Convention on the Recognition and Enforcement of Foreign Arbitral Awards (known as the New York Convention), (ii) whose law is supportive of arbitration and permits arbitration of the subject matter of the contract, and (iii) whose courts have a track record of issuing unbiased decisions that are supportive of the arbitral process.

23. An arbitration clause that fails to specify the place of arbitration will be effective, though undesirable. The arbitral institution, if there is one, or the arbitrators, will choose for the parties if they cannot agree on a place of arbitration after a dispute has arisen. (In ad hoc arbitration, however, if difficulties arise with the appointment of the arbitrators and no place of arbitration is selected, the parties may be unable to proceed with the arbitration unless courts in some country are willing to assist.) The parties should not leave such a critical decision to others.

24. The parties should specify in their arbitration clause the 'place of arbitration', rather than the place of the 'hearing'. By designating only the place of the hearing, the parties leave it uncertain whether they have designated the 'place of arbitration' for the purposes of applicable laws and treaties. Moreover, by designating the place

of the hearing in the arbitration clause, the parties deprive the arbitrators of desired flexibility to hold hearings in other places, as may be convenient.

Recommended Clause:

25. The place of arbitration shall be [city, country]

Guideline 5: The parties should specify the number of arbitrators.

Comments:

26. The parties should specify the number of arbitrators (ordinarily one or three and, in any case, an odd number). The number of arbitrators has an impact on the overall cost, the duration and, on occasion, the quality of the arbitral proceedings. Proceedings before a three-member tribunal will almost inevitably be lengthier and more expensive than those before a sole arbitrator. A three-member tribunal may be better equipped, however, to address complex issues of fact and law, and may reduce the risk of irrational or unfair results. The parties may also desire the increased control of the process afforded by each having the opportunity to select an arbitrator.

27. If the parties do not specify the number of arbitrators (and cannot agree on this once a dispute has arisen), the arbitral institution, if there is one, will make the decision for them, generally on the basis of the amount in dispute and the perceived complexity of the case. In ad hoc arbitration, the selected arbitration rules, if any, will ordinarily specify whether one or three arbitrators are to be appointed absent contrary agreement. Where the parties have not selected such a set of arbitration rules, it is especially important to specify the number of arbitrators in the clause itself.

28. Parties may remain deliberately silent as to the number of arbitrators, reasoning that the choice between a one- or three-member tribunal will be better made if and when a dispute arises. While the opportunity to decide this question after a dispute arises is an advantage, the corresponding disadvantage is that the proceedings may be delayed if the parties disagree on the number of arbitrators, particularly in the ad hoc context. On balance, it is recommended to specify the number of arbitrators in advance in the arbitration clause itself.

Recommended Clause:

29. There shall be [one or three] arbitrator[s].

Guideline 6: The parties should specify the method of selection and replacement of arbitrators and, when ad hoc arbitration is chosen, should select an appointing authority.

Comments:

30. Both institutional and ad hoc arbitration rules provide default mechanisms for selecting and replacing arbitrators. When they have incorporated such set of rules, the parties may be content to rely on the default mechanism set forth in the rules. The parties may also agree on an alternative method. For example, many arbitration rules provide for the chairperson of a three-member tribunal to be selected by the two co-arbitrators or by the institution. Parties often prefer to attempt to select the chairperson themselves in the first instance. If the parties decide to depart from the default mechanism, they should use language consistent

with the terminology of the applicable arbitration rules. For example, under certain institutional rules, the parties 'nominate' arbitrators, and only the institution is empowered to 'appoint' them. When the parties have not incorporated a set of arbitration rules, it is crucial that they spell out the method for selecting and replacing arbitrators in the arbitration clause itself.

31. The need to designate an appointing authority in the context of ad hoc arbitration constitutes a significant difference between drafting an institutional arbitration clause and drafting an ad hoc arbitration clause. In institutional arbitration, the institution is available to select or replace arbitrators when the parties fail to do so. There is no such institution in ad hoc arbitration. It is, therefore, critical that the parties designate an 'appointing authority' in the ad hoc context, to select or replace arbitrators in the event the parties fail to do so. Absent such a choice, the courts at the place of arbitration may be willing to make the necessary appointments and replacement. (Under the UNCITRAL Rules, the Secretary General of the Permanent Court of Arbitration designates the appointing authority if the parties have failed to do so in their arbitration clause.)

32. The appointing authority may be an arbitral institution, a court, a trade or professional association, or another neutral entity. The parties should select an office or title (eg, the president of an arbitral institution, the chief judge of a court, or the chair of a trade or professional association) rather than an individual (as such individual may be unable to act when called upon to do so). The parties should also make sure that the selected authority will agree to perform its duties if and when called upon to do so.

33. Significant time may be wasted at the outset of the proceedings if no time limits are specified for the appointment of the arbitrators. Such time limits are ordinarily set in arbitration rules. Parties that have agreed to incorporate such rules thus need not concern themselves with this issue, unless they wish to depart from the appointment mechanism set forth in the rules. When the parties have not agreed to incorporate a set of arbitration rules, it is important to set such time limits in the arbitration clause itself.

34. When a tribunal is comprised of three arbitrators, it sometimes occurs that one arbitrator resigns, refuses to cooperate or otherwise fails to participate in the proceedings at a late and critical juncture (eg, during the deliberations). In those circumstances, replacement may not be an option as it would overly delay and disrupt the proceedings. Absent specific authorization, however, the remaining two arbitrators may not be able to render a valid and enforceable award. Most (but not all) arbitration rules therefore permit the other two arbitrators in such a situation to continue the proceedings as a 'truncated' tribunal and to issue an award. When the parties do not select a set of arbitration rules (or where the selected arbitration rules do not address the issue), the parties can authorize in the arbitration clause a 'truncated' tribunal to proceed to render an award.

Recommended Clauses:

35. When institutional arbitration is chosen, and the institutional rules do not provide for all arbitrator selections and replacements to be made by the parties in the first instance, and the parties wish to make their own selections, the following clause can be used:

There shall be three arbitrators, one selected by the initiating party in the request for arbitration, the second selected by the other party within [30] days of receipt of the request for arbitration, and the third, who shall act as [chairperson or presiding arbitrator], selected by the two parties within [30] days of the selection of the second arbitrator. If any arbitrators are not selected within these time periods, the [institution] shall make the selection(s). If replacement of an arbitrator becomes necessary, replacement shall be done by the same method(s) as above.

36. When non-administered arbitration is chosen, the parties can provide for a method of selection and replacement of arbitrators by choosing a set of ad hoc arbitration rules, eg, the UNCITRAL Arbitration Rules.

37. The clause proposed above for ad hoc arbitration without a set of arbitration rules (see paragraph 13 above) sets forth a comprehensive mechanism to select and replace the members of a three-member tribunal and includes provisions permitting a truncated tribunal to proceed to render an award without the participation of an obstructive or defaulting arbitrator.

38. In similar circumstances, but where the parties wish to submit their dispute to a sole arbitrator, the parties can amend the clause proposed in paragraph 13 above and use the following language:

There shall be one arbitrator, selected jointly by the parties. If the arbitrator is not selected within [30] days of the receipt of the request for arbitration, the [designated appointing authority] shall make the selection.

Guideline 7: The parties should specify the language of arbitration.

Comments:

39. Arbitration clauses in contracts between parties whose languages differ, or whose shared language differs from that of the place of arbitration, should ordinarily specify the language of arbitration. In making this choice, the parties should consider not only the language of the contract and of the related documentation, but also the likely effect of their choice on the pool of qualified arbitrators and counsel. Absent a choice in the arbitration clause, it is for the arbitrators to determine the language of arbitration. It is likely that the arbitrators will choose the language of the contract or, if different, of the correspondence exchanged by the parties. Leaving this decision to the arbitrators could cause unnecessary cost and delay.

40. Contract drafters are often tempted to provide for more than one language of arbitration. The parties should carefully consider whether to do so. Multi-lingual arbitration, while workable (there are numerous examples of proceedings conducted in both English and Spanish, for example), may present challenges depending on the languages chosen. There may be difficulties in finding arbitrators who are able to conduct arbitration proceedings in two languages, and the required translation and interpretation may add to the costs and delays of the proceedings. A solution may be to specify one language of arbitration, but to provide that documents may be submitted in another language (without translation).

Recommended Clause:

41. The language of the arbitration shall be [. . .].

Guideline 8: The parties should ordinarily specify the rules of law governing the contract and any subsequent disputes.

Comments:

42. In international transactions, it is important for the parties to select in their contract the rules of law that govern the contract and any subsequent disputes (the 'substantive law').

43. The choice of substantive law should be set forth in a clause separate from the arbitration clause or should be addressed together with arbitration in a clause which makes clear that the clause serves a dual purpose, eg, captioning the clause 'Governing Law and Arbitration [or Dispute Resolution].' This is so because issues can arise under the substantive law during the performance of the contract independent of any arbitral dispute.

44. By choosing the substantive law, the parties do not choose the procedural or arbitration law. Such law, absent a contrary agreement, is ordinarily that of the place of arbitration (see paragraph 21 above). Although the parties can agree otherwise, it is rarely advisable to do so.

45. Sometimes parties do not choose a national legal system as the substantive law. Instead, they choose lex mercatoria or other a-national rules of law. In other cases, they empower the arbitral tribunal to determine the dispute on the basis of what is fair and reasonable (ex aequo et bono). Care should be taken before selecting these options. While appropriate in certain situations (eg, when the parties cannot agree on a national law), they may create difficulties by virtue of the relative uncertainty as to their content or impact on the outcome. As it is difficult to ascertain in advance the rules that will ultimately be applied by the arbitrators when the parties select these alternatives to national laws, resolving disputes may become more complex, uncertain and costly.

Recommended Clause:

46. The following clause can be used to select the substantive law:

> This agreement is governed by, and all disputes arising under or in connection with this agreement shall be resolved in accordance with, [selected law or rules of law].

III.   Drafting Guidelines for Optional Elements

47. Arbitration being a matter of agreement, contracting parties have the opportunity in their arbitration clause to tailor the process to their specific needs. There are numerous options that contracting parties can consider. This section sets out and comments upon the few that the parties should consider during the negotiation of an arbitration clause. By setting out these options, these Guidelines do not thereby suggest that these optional elements need to be included in an arbitration clause.

Option 1: The authority of the arbitral tribunal and of the courts with respect to provisional and conservatory measures.

Comments:

48. It is rarely necessary to provide in the arbitration clause that the arbitral

tribunal or the courts or both have the authority to order provisional and conservatory measures pending decision on the merits. The arbitral tribunal and the courts ordinarily have the authority to do so, subject to various conditions, even where the arbitration clause is silent in this respect. The authority of the arbitral tribunal rests with the arbitration rules and the relevant arbitration law. That of the courts rests with the relevant arbitration law.

49. When the governing arbitration law restricts the availability of provisional or conservatory relief, however, or when the availability of provisional and conservatory relief is of special concern (eg, because trade secrets or other confidential information are involved), the parties may want to make the authority of the arbitral tribunal and the courts explicit in the arbitration clause.

50. When the availability of provisional and conservatory relief is of special concern, the parties may also want to modify restrictive aspects of the applicable arbitration rules. For example, certain institutional rules restrict the right of the parties to apply to the courts for provisional and conservatory relief once the arbitral tribunal is appointed. Under other arbitration rules, the arbitral tribunal is authorized to order provisional and conservatory measures with respect to 'the subject matter of the dispute', which leaves uncertain whether the arbitral tribunal can order measures to preserve the position of the parties (eg, injunction, security for costs) or the integrity of the arbitral process (eg, freezing orders, anti-suit injunctions).

Recommended Clauses:

51. The following clause can be used to make explicit the authority of the arbitral tribunal with respect to provisional and conservatory relief:

> Except as otherwise specifically limited in this agreement, the arbitral tribunal shall have the power to grant any remedy or relief that it deems appropriate, whether provisional or final, including but not limited to conservatory relief and injunctive relief, and any such measures ordered by the arbitral tribunal shall, to the extent permitted by applicable law, be deemed to be a final award on the subject matter of the measures and shall be enforceable as such.

52. The following clause can be added to the above clause, or used independently, to specify that resort to courts for provisional and conservatory measures is not precluded by the arbitration agreement:

> Each party retains the right to apply to any court of competent jurisdiction for provisional and/or conservatory relief, including prearbitral attachments or injunctions, and any such request shall not be deemed incompatible with the agreement to arbitrate or a waiver of the right to arbitrate.

53. The following clause can be added to the clause recommended at paragraph 51 above, or used independently, to limit the parties' right to resort to the courts for provisional and conservatory relief after the arbitral tribunal is constituted:

> Each party has the right to apply to any court of competent jurisdiction for provisional and/or conservatory relief, including pre-arbitral attachments or injunctions, and any such request shall not be deemed incompat-

ible with the agreement to arbitrate or a waiver of the right to arbitrate, provided however that, after the arbitral tribunal is constituted, the arbitral tribunal shall have sole jurisdiction to consider applications for provisional and/ or conservatory relief, and any such measures ordered by the arbitral tribunal may be specifically enforced by any court of competent jurisdiction.

54. If, in exceptional circumstances, the parties consider that ex parte provisional relief by the arbitral tribunal may be needed, they should so specify and amend the clause recommended at paragraph 51 above by adding '(including ex parte)' after the word 'provisional'. Even with such addition, however, ex parte remedies ordered by the arbitral tribunal may not be enforceable under the relevant arbitration law.

Option 2: Document production.

Comments:

55. While the extent document production and information exchange in international arbitration varies from case to case and from arbitrator to arbitrator, parties are usually required to produce identified documents (including internal documents) that are shown to be relevant and material to the dispute. Other features particular to 'discovery' in some jurisdictions, such as depositions and interrogatories, are ordinarily absent. The IBA has developed a set of rules, the IBA Rules on the Taking of Evidence in International Arbitration (the 'IBA Rules'), designed to reflect this standard practice. These rules, which address production of both paper documents and electronically-stored information, are often used by international arbitral tribunals, expressly or not, as guidance.

56. The parties have three primary options regarding information or document production. They can say nothing about it and be content to rely on the default provisions of the governing arbitration law, which ordinarily leaves the question to the discretion of the arbitrators. They can adopt the IBA Rules. They can devise their own standards (bearing in mind that extensive document production is likely to have a major impact on the length and cost of the proceedings).

57. A difficulty that may arise in the context of document production in international arbitration is the issue of which rules should govern whether certain documents are exempt from production due to privilege. When, in the rare instance, contracting parties can foresee at the contract drafting stage that issues of privilege may arise and be of consequence, the parties may want to specify in their arbitration clause the principles that will govern all such questions. Article 9 of the IBA Rules provides guidance in this respect.

Recommended Clauses:

58. The following clause can be used to incorporate the IBA Rules either as a mandatory standard or, alternatively, for guidance purpose only:

> [In addition to the authority conferred upon the arbitral tribunal by the [arbitration rules]], the arbitral tribunal shall have the authority to order production of documents [in accordance with] [taking guidance from] the IBA Rules on the Taking of Evidence in International Arbitration [as current on the date of this agreement/the commencement of the arbitration].

59. The following clause can be used if the parties wish to specify the principles that will govern issues of privilege with respect to document disclosure:

> All contentions that a document or communication is privileged and, as such, exempt from production in the arbitration, shall be resolved by the arbitral tribunal in accordance with Article 9 of the IBA Rules on the Taking of Evidence in International Arbitration.

Option 3: Confidentiality issues.

Comments:

60. Parties frequently assume that arbitration proceedings are confidential. While arbitration is private, in many jurisdictions parties are under no duty to keep the existence or content of the arbitration proceedings confidential. Few national laws or arbitration rules impose confidentiality obligations on the parties. Where a general duty is recognized, it is often subject to exceptions.

61. Parties concerned about confidentiality should, therefore, address this issue in their arbitration clause. In doing so, the parties should avoid absolute requirements because disclosure may be required by law, to protect or pursue a legal right or to enforce or challenge an award in subsequent judicial proceedings. The parties should also anticipate that the preparation of their claims, defenses and counterclaims may require disclosure of confidential information to non-parties (witnesses and experts).

62. Conversely, given the common assumption that arbitration proceedings are confidential, where the parties do not wish to be bound by any confidentiality duties, the parties should expressly say so in their arbitration clause.

Recommended Clauses:

63. Some arbitration rules set forth confidentiality obligations, and the parties will accordingly impose such obligations upon themselves if they agree to arbitrate under these rules.

64. The following clause imposes confidentiality obligations upon the parties:

> The existence and content of the arbitral proceedings and any rulings or award shall be kept confidential by the parties and members of the arbitral tribunal except (i) to the extent that disclosure may be required of a party to fulfil a legal duty, protect or pursue a legal right, or enforce or challenge an award in bona fide legal proceedings before a state court or other judicial authority, (ii) with the consent of all parties, (iii) where needed for the preparation or presentation of a claim or defense in this arbitration, (iv) where such information is already in the public domain other than as a result of a breach of this clause, or (v) by order of the arbitral tribunal upon application of a party.

65. The following clause may be used where the parties do not wish to be bound by any confidentiality obligation:

> The parties shall be under no confidentiality obligation with respect to arbitration hereunder except as may be imposed by mandatory provisions of law.

Option 4: Allocation of costs and fees.

Comments:

66. Costs (eg, arbitrators' fees and expenses and, if applicable, institutional fees) and lawyers' fees can be substantial in international arbitration. It is rarely possible to predict how the arbitral tribunal will allocate these costs and fees, if at all, at the end of the proceedings. Domestic approaches diverge widely (from no allocation at all to full recovery by the prevailing party), and arbitrators have wide discretion in this respect.

67. Given these uncertainties, the parties may wish to address the issue of costs and fees in their arbitration clause (bearing in mind that such provisions may not be enforceable in certain jurisdictions). The parties have several options. They may merely confirm that the arbitrators can allocate costs and fees as they see fit. They may provide that the arbitrators make no allocation of costs and fees. They may try to ensure that costs and fees are allocated to the 'winner' or the 'prevailing party' on the merits, or that the arbitrators are to allocate costs and fees in proportion to success or failure. The parties should avoid absolute language ('shall') in drafting such a clause, as the identification of the 'winner' or the 'prevailing party' may be difficult and the clause may needlessly constrain the arbitrators in their allocation of costs and fees.

68. The parties may also wish to consider whether to allow compensation for the time spent by management, in-house counsel, experts and witnesses, as this issue is often uncertain in international arbitration.

Recommended Clauses:

69. The following clause can be used to ensure that the arbitrators have discretion to allocate both costs and fees (or to reaffirm such discretion if the designated arbitration rules include a provision to this effect):

> The arbitral tribunal may include in its award an allocation to any party of such costs and expenses, including lawyers' fees [and costs and expenses of management, in-house counsel, experts and witnesses], as the arbitral tribunal shall deem reasonable.

70. The following clause provides for allocation of costs and fees to the 'prevailing' party:

> The arbitral tribunal may award its costs and expenses, including lawyers' fees, to the prevailing party, if any and as determined by the arbitral tribunal in its discretion.

71. The following clause provides for allocation of costs and fees in proportion to success:

> The arbitral tribunal may include in their award an allocation to any party of such costs and expenses, including lawyers' fees [and costs and expenses of management, in-house counsel, experts and witnesses], as the arbitral tribunal shall deem reasonable. In making such allocation, the arbitral tribunal shall consider the relative success of the parties on their claims and counterclaims and defenses.

72. The following clause can be used to ensure that the arbitrators do not allocate costs and fees:

All costs and expenses of the arbitral tribunal [and of the arbitral institution] shall be borne by the parties equally. Each party shall bear all costs and expenses (including of its own counsel, experts and witnesses) involved in preparing and presenting its case.

Option 5: Qualifications required of arbitrators.

Comments:

73. An advantage of arbitration, as compared to national court proceedings, is that the parties select the arbitrators and can, therefore, choose individuals with expertise or knowledge relevant to their dispute.

74. It is usually not advisable, however, to specify in the arbitration clause the qualifications required of arbitrators. The parties are ordinarily in a better position at the time of a dispute to know whether expertise is required, and if so, which, and each remains free at that time to appoint an arbitrator with the desired qualifications. Specifying qualification requirements in the arbitration clause may also drastically reduce the pool of available arbitrators. Further, a party intent on delaying the proceedings may challenge arbitrators on the basis of the qualification requirements.

75. If the parties nonetheless wish to specify such qualifications in the arbitration clause, they should avoid overly specific requirements, as the arbitration agreement may be unenforceable if, when a dispute arises, the parties are unable to identify suitable candidates who both meet the qualification requirements and are available to act as arbitrators.

76. Parties sometimes specify that the sole arbitrator or, in the case of a three-member panel, the presiding arbitrator shall not share a common nationality with any of the parties. In institutional arbitration, such qualification requirement is often superfluous, as arbitral institutions ordinarily apply such practice in making appointments. In ad hoc arbitration, however, the parties may want so to specify in their arbitration clause.

Recommended Clauses:

77. The qualifications of arbitrators can be specified by adding the following to the arbitration clause:

[Each arbitrator][The presiding arbitrator] shall be [a lawyer/an accountant].

Or

[Each arbitrator][The presiding arbitrator] shall have experience in [specific industry].

Or

[The arbitrators][The presiding arbitrator] shall not be of the same nationality as any of the parties.

Option 6: Time limits.

Comments:

78. Parties sometimes try to save costs and time by providing in the arbitration clause that the award be made within a fixed period from the commencement of arbitration (a process known as 'fast-tracking'). Fast-tracking can save costs, but parties can rarely know at the time of drafting the arbitration clause whether every dispute liable to arise under the contract will be appropriate for resolution within the prescribed period. An award that is not rendered within the prescribed period may be unenforceable or may attract unnecessary challenges.

79. If, despite these considerations, the parties wish to set time limits in the arbitration clause, the tribunal should be allowed to extend these time limits to avoid the risk of an unenforceable award.

Recommended Clauses:

80. The following clause can be used to set time limits:

> The award shall be rendered within [. . .] months of the appointment of [the sole arbitrator] [the chairperson], unless the arbitral tribunal determines, in a reasoned decision, that the interest of justice or the complexity of the case requires that such limit be extended.

Option 7: Finality of arbitration.

Comments:

81. An advantage of arbitration is that arbitral awards are final and not subject to appeal. In most jurisdictions, awards can be challenged only for lack of jurisdiction, serious procedural defects or unfairness, and cannot be reviewed on the merits. Most arbitration rules reinforce the finality of arbitration by providing that awards are final and that the parties waive any recourse against them.

82. When the arbitration clause does not incorporate a set of arbitration rules, or where the incorporated rules do not contain finality and waiver of recourse language, it is prudent to specify in the arbitration clause that awards are final and not subject to recourse. Even where the parties incorporate arbitration rules that contain such language, it may still be advisable to repeat this language in the arbitration clause if the parties anticipate that the award may need to be enforced or otherwise scrutinized in jurisdictions that view arbitration with suspicion. When adding a waiver of recourse to the arbitration clause, the parties should review the law of the seat of arbitration to determine the scope of what is being waived, and the language required under the lex arbitri.

83. Parties are sometimes tempted to expand the scope of judicial review by, for example, allowing review of the merits. It is rarely advisable, and often not open to the parties, to do so. If the parties nonetheless wish to expand the scope of judicial review, specialized advice should be sought and the law at the place of arbitration should be reviewed carefully.

Recommended Clauses:

84. When the parties wish to emphasize the finality of arbitration and to waive any recourse against the award, the following language can be added to the arbitration clause, subject to any requirement imposed by the lex arbitri:

> Any award of the arbitral tribunal shall be final and binding on the parties. The parties undertake to comply fully and promptly with any award without delay and shall be deemed to have waived their right to any form of recourse insofar as such waiver can validly be made.

85. When, in the exceptional case, the parties wish to expand the scope of judicial review and allow appeals on the merits, the parties should seek advice as to their power to do so in the relevant jurisdiction. Where enforceable, the following sentence can be considered:

> The parties shall have the right to seek judicial review of the tribunal's award in the courts of [selected jurisdiction] in accordance with the standard of appellate review applicable to decisions of courts of first instance in such jurisdiction(s).

IV. Drafting Guidelines for Multi-Tier Dispute Resolution Clauses

86. It is common for dispute resolution clauses in international contracts to provide for negotiation, mediation or some other form of alternative dispute resolution as preliminary steps before arbitration. Construction contracts, for example, sometimes require disputes to be submitted to a standing dispute board before they can be referred to arbitration. These clauses, known as multi-tier clauses, present specific drafting challenges.

Multi-Tier Guideline 1: The clause should specify a period of time for negotiation or mediation, triggered by a defined and undisputable event (ie, a written request), after which either party can resort to arbitration.

Comments:

87. A multi-tier clause that requires negotiation or mediation before arbitration may be deemed to create a condition precedent to arbitration. To minimize the risk that a party will use negotiation or mediation in order to gain delay or other tactical advantage, the clause should specify a time period beyond which the dispute can be submitted to arbitration, and this time period should generally be short. In specifying such time period, the parties should be aware that commencing negotiation or mediation may not be sufficient to suspend the prescription or limitation periods.

88. The period of time for negotiation or mediation should be triggered by a defined and indisputable event, such as a written request to negotiate or mediate under the clause or the appointment of a mediator. It is not advisable to define the triggering event by reference to a written notice of the dispute because a mere written exchange about the dispute might then be sufficient to trigger the deadline.

Recommended Clauses:

89. See the clauses recommended below at paragraphs 94-96.

Multi-Tier Guideline 2: The clause should avoid the trap of rendering arbitration permissive, not mandatory.

Comments:

90. Parties drafting multi-tier dispute resolution clauses often inadvertently leave ambiguous their intent to arbitrate disputes that cannot be resolved by negotiation

or mediation. This happens when the parties provide that disputes not resolved by negotiation or mediation 'may' be submitted to arbitration.

Recommended Clauses:

91. See the clauses recommended below at paragraphs 94-96.

Multi-Tier Guideline 3: The clause should define the disputes to be submitted to negotiation or mediation and to arbitration in identical terms.

Comments:

92. Multi-tier dispute resolution clauses sometimes do not define in identical terms the disputes that are subject to negotiation or mediation as a first step and those subject to arbitration. Such ambiguities may suggest that some disputes can be submitted to arbitration immediately without going through negotiation or mediation as a first step.

93. The broad reference to 'disputes' in the clauses recommended below should cover counterclaims. Such counterclaims would thus need to go through the several steps and could not be raised for the first time in the arbitration. If the parties wish to preserve the right to raise counterclaims for the first time in the arbitration, they should so specify in their arbitration clause.

Recommended Clauses:

94. The following clause provides for mandatory negotiation as a first step:

The parties shall endeavor to resolve amicably by negotiation all disputes arising out of or in connection with this agreement, including any question regarding its existence, validity or termination. Any such dispute which remains unresolved [30] days after either party requests in writing negotiation under this clause or within such other period as the parties may agree in writing, shall be finally settled under the [designated set of arbitration rules] by [one or three] arbitrator[s] appointed in accordance with the said Rules. The place of arbitration shall be [city, country]. The language of arbitration shall be [. . .].

[All communications during the negotiation are confidential and shall be treated as made in the course of compromise and settlement negotiations for purposes of applicable rules of evidence and any additional confidentiality and professional secrecy protections provided by applicable law.]

95. The following clause provides for mandatory mediation as a first step:

The parties shall endeavor to resolve amicably by mediation under the [designated set of mediation rules] all disputes arising out of or in connection with this agreement, including any question regarding its existence, validity or termination. Any such dispute not settled pursuant to the said Rules within [45] days after appointment of the mediator or within such other period as the parties may agree in writing, shall be finally settled under the [designated set of arbitration rules] by [one or three] arbitrator[s] appointed in accordance with the said Rules. The place of arbitration shall be [city, country]. The language of arbitration shall be [. . .].

[All communications during the mediation are confidential and shall be treated as made in the course of compromise and settlement negotiations for purposes of applicable rules of evidence and any additional confidentiality and professional secrecy protections provided by applicable law.]

96. The following clause provides for both mandatory negotiation and mediation sequentially before arbitration:

All disputes arising out of or in connection with this agreement, including any question regarding its existence, validity or termination ('Dispute'), shall be resolved in accordance with the procedures specified below, which shall be the sole and exclusive procedures for the resolution of any such Dispute.

(A) Negotiation

The parties shall endeavor to resolve any Dispute amicably by negotiation between executives who have authority to settle the Dispute [and who are at a higher level of management than the persons with direct responsibility for administration or performance of this agreement].

(B) Mediation

Any Dispute not resolved by negotiation in accordance with paragraph (A) within [30] days after either party requested in writing negotiation under paragraph (A), or within such other period as the parties may agree in writing, shall be settled amicably by mediation under the [designated set of mediation rules].

(C) Arbitration

Any Dispute not resolved by mediation in accordance with paragraph (B) within [45] days after appointment of the mediator, or within such other period as the parties may agree in writing, shall be finally settled under the [designated set of arbitration rules] by [one or three] arbitrator[s] appointed in accordance with the said Rules. The place of arbitration shall be [. . .]. The language of arbitration shall be [. . .]. [All communications during the negotiation and mediation pursuant to paragraphs (A) and (B) are confidential and shall be treated as made in the course of compromise and settlement negotiations for purposes of applicable rules of evidence and any additional confidentiality and professional secrecy protections provided by applicable law.]

V.   Drafting Guidelines for Multiparty Arbitration Clauses

97. International contracts often involve more than two parties. Parties drafting arbitration clauses for these contracts may fail to realize the specific drafting difficulties that result from the multiplicity of parties. In particular, one cannot always rely on the model clauses of arbitral institutions, as these are ordinarily drafted with two parties in mind and may need to be adapted to be workable in a multiparty context. Specialized advice should generally be sought to draft such

clauses.

Multiparty Guideline 1: The clause should address the consequences of the multiplicity of parties for the appointment of the arbitral tribunal.

Comments:

98. In a multiparty context, it is often not workable to provide that 'each party' appoints an arbitrator. There is an easy solution if the parties are content to provide for a sole arbitrator: in such case, the parties can provide that the sole arbitrator is to be appointed jointly by the parties or, absent agreement, by the institution or appointing authority. Where there are to be three arbitrators, a solution is to provide that the three arbitrators be appointed jointly by the parties or, absent agreement on all, by the institution or appointing authority.

99. Alternatively, the arbitration clause can require that the parties on each 'side' make joint appointments. This option is available when it can be anticipated at the drafting stage that certain contracting parties will have aligned interests. The overriding requirement is, however, that all parties be treated equally in the appointment process. This means in practice that, when two or more parties on one side fail to agree on an arbitrator, the institution or appointing authority will appoint all arbitrators, as the parties on one side would otherwise have had the opportunity to pick their arbitrator while the others not. This is the solution that has been adopted in some institutional arbitration rules.

Recommended Clauses:

100. The clause recommended below at paragraph 105 specifies a mechanism for appointing arbitrators in a multiparty context.

Multiparty Guideline 2: The clause should address the procedural complexities (intervention, joinder) arising from the multiplicity of parties.

Comments:

101. Procedural complexities may abound in the multiparty context. One is that of intervention: a contracting party that is not party to an arbitration commenced under the clause may wish to intervene in the proceedings. Another is that of joinder: a contracting party that is named as respondent may wish to join another contracting party that has not been named as respondent in the proceedings.

102. An arbitration clause would be workable even if it failed to address these complexities. Such clause would, however, leave open the possibility of overlapping proceedings, conflicting decisions and associated delays, costs and uncertainties.

103. There is no easy way to address these complexities. A multiparty arbitration clause should be carefully drafted with regard to the particular circumstances, and specialized advice should usually be sought. As a general rule, the clause should provide that notice of any proceedings commenced under the clause be given to each contracting party regardless of whether that contracting party is named as respondent. There should be a clear time period after that notice for each contracting party to intervene or join other contracting parties in the proceedings, and no arbitrator should be appointed before the expiry of that time period.

104. Alternatively, the parties can opt to arbitrate under institutional rules that provide for intervention and joinder, bearing in mind that these rules may give wide

discretion to the institution in this respect.

Recommended Clauses:

105. The following provision provides for intervention and joinder of other parties to the same agreement:

All disputes arising out of or in connection with this agreement, including any question regarding its existence, validity or termination, shall be finally resolved by arbitration under [selected arbitration rules], except as they may be modified herein or by mutual agreement of the parties.

The place of arbitration shall be [city, country]. The language of arbitration shall be [. . .]. There shall be three arbitrators, selected as follows.

In the event that the request for arbitration names only one claimant and one respondent, and no party has exercised its right to joinder or intervention in accordance with the paragraphs below, the claimant and the respondent shall each appoint one arbitrator within [15] days after the expiry of the period during which parties can exercise their right to joinder or intervention. If either party fails to appoint an arbitrator as provided, then, upon the application of any party, that arbitrator shall be appointed by [the designated arbitral institution]. The two arbitrators shall appoint the third arbitrator, who shall act as presiding arbitrator. If the two arbitrators fail to appoint the presiding arbitrator within [45] days of the appointment of the second arbitrator, the presiding arbitrator shall be appointed by [the designated arbitral institution/appointing authority].

In the event that more than two parties are named in the request for arbitration or at least one contracting party exercises its right to joinder or intervention in accordance with the paragraphs below, the claimant(s) shall jointly appoint one arbitrator and the respondent(s) shall jointly appoint the other arbitrator, both within [15] days after the expiry of the period during which parties can exercise their right to joinder or intervention. If the parties fail to appoint an arbitrator as provided above, [the designated arbitral institution/appointing authority] shall, upon the request of any party, appoint all three arbitrators and designate one of them to act as presiding arbitrator. If the claimant(s) and the respondent(s) appoint the arbitrators as provided above, the two arbitrators shall appoint the third arbitrator, who shall act as presiding arbitrator. If the two arbitrators fail to appoint the third arbitrator within [45] days of the appointment of the second arbitrator, the presiding arbitrator shall be appointed by [the designated arbitral institution/appointing authority].

Any party to this agreement may, either separately or together with any other party to this agreement, initiate arbitration proceedings pursuant to this clause by sending a request for arbitration to all other parties to this agreement [and to the designated arbitral institution, if any]. Any party to this agreement may intervene in any arbitration proceedings hereunder by submitting a written notice of claim, counterclaim or cross-claim against any party to this agreement, provided that such notice is also sent to all other parties to this agreement [and to the designated arbitral institution, if any] within [30] days from the receipt by such intervening party of the relevant request for arbitration or notice of claim, counterclaim or cross-claim.

Any party to this agreement named as respondent in a request for arbitration, or a notice of claim, counterclaim or cross-claim, may join any other party to this agreement in any arbitration proceedings hereunder by submitting a written notice of claim, counterclaim or cross-claim against that party, provided that such notice is also sent to all other parties to this agreement [and to the designated arbitral institution, if any] within [30] days from the receipt by such respondent of the relevant request for arbitration or notice of claim, counterclaim or cross-claim.

Any joined or intervening party shall be bound by any award rendered by the arbitral tribunal even if such party chooses not to participate in the arbitration proceedings.

VI.   Drafting Guidelines for Multi-Contract Arbitration Clauses

106. It is common for a single international transaction to involve several related contracts. Drafting arbitration clauses in a multi-contract setting presents specific challenges.

Multi-Contract Guideline 1: The arbitration clauses in the related contracts should be compatible.

Comments:

107. The parties should avoid specifying different dispute resolution mechanisms in their related contracts (eg, arbitration under different sets of rules or in different places), lest they run the risk of fragmenting future disputes. An arbitral tribunal appointed under the first contract may not have jurisdiction to consider a dispute that raises questions about the second contract, thus inviting parallel proceedings.

108. Assuming the parties want consistent decisions and wish to avoid parallel proceedings, a straightforward solution is to establish a stand-alone dispute resolution protocol, which is signed by all the parties and then incorporated by reference in all related contracts. If it is impractical to conclude such a protocol, the parties should ensure that the arbitration clauses in the related contract are identical or complementary. It is especially important that the arbitration clauses specify the same set of rules, place of arbitration and number of arbitrators. To avoid difficulties when proceedings are consolidated, the same substantive law and language of arbitration should also be specified. The parties should also make clear that a tribunal appointed under one contract has jurisdiction to consider and decide issues related to the other related contracts.

Recommended Clause:

109. If the parties do not wish to, or cannot, establish a stand-alone dispute resolution protocol, the following provision should be added to the arbitration clause in each related contract:

The parties agree that an arbitral tribunal appointed hereunder or under [the related agreement(s)] may exercise jurisdiction with respect to both this agreement and [the related agreement(s)].

Multi-Contract Guideline 2: The parties should consider whether to provide for consolidation of arbitral proceedings commenced under the related contracts.

Comments:

110. A procedural complexity that arises in a multi-contract setting is that of consolidation. Different arbitrations may be commenced under related contracts at different times. It may, or may not, be in the parties' interest to have these arbitrations dealt with in a single consolidated arbitration. In some situations, the parties may reason that one single consolidated arbitration would be more efficient and cost-effective. In other circumstances, the parties may have reasons to keep the arbitrations separated.

111. If the parties wish to permit consolidation of related arbitrations, they should say so in the arbitration clause. Courts in some jurisdiction have discretion to order consolidation of related arbitration proceedings, but ordinarily will not do so absent parties' agreement. Where the courts at the place of arbitration have no such power, or where the parties do not wish to rely on judicial discretion, the parties should also spell out in the clause the procedure for consolidating related proceedings. The applicable arbitration rules, if any, and the law of the place of arbitration should be reviewed carefully, as they may constrain the parties' ability to consolidate arbitral proceedings. Conversely, in some jurisdictions, the parties may want to exclude the possibility of consolidation (or class arbitration).

112. Specialized advice is required when the related contracts also involve more than two parties. Drafting consolidation provisions in a multiparty context is especially intricate. An obvious difficulty is that each party must be treated equally with respect to the appointment of the arbitrators. A workable, but less than ideal, solution is to provide for all appointments to be made by the institution or appointing authority. The parties should also be aware that a consolidation clause may, in some jurisdictions, be read as consent to class-action arbitration.

Recommended Clauses:

113. The following provision provides for consolidation of related arbitrations between the same two parties:

> The parties consent to the consolidation of arbitrations commenced hereunder and/or under [the related agreements] as follows. If two or more arbitrations are commenced hereunder and/or [the related agreements], any party named as claimant or respondent in any of these arbitrations may petition any arbitral tribunal appointed in these arbitrations for an order that the several arbitrations be consolidated in a single arbitration before that arbitral tribunal (a 'Consolidation Order'). In deciding whether to make such a Consolidation Order, that arbitral tribunal shall consider whether the several arbitrations raise common issues of law or facts and whether to consolidate the several arbitrations would serve the interests of justice and efficiency.
>
> If before a Consolidation Order is made by an arbitral tribunal with respect to another arbitration, arbitrators have already been appointed in that other arbitration, their appointment terminates upon the making of

such Consolidation Order and they are deemed to be functus officio. Such termination is without prejudice to: (i) the validity of any acts done or orders made by them prior to the termination, (ii) their entitlement to be paid their proper fees and disbursements, (iii) the date when any claim or defense was raised for the purpose of applying any limitation bar or any like rule or provision, (iv) evidence adduced and admissible before termination, which evidence shall be admissible in arbitral proceedings after the Consolidation Order, and (v) the parties' entitlement to legal and other costs incurred before termination.

In the event of two or more conflicting Consolidation Orders, the Consolidation Order that was made first in time shall prevail.